Analysing Learner Language

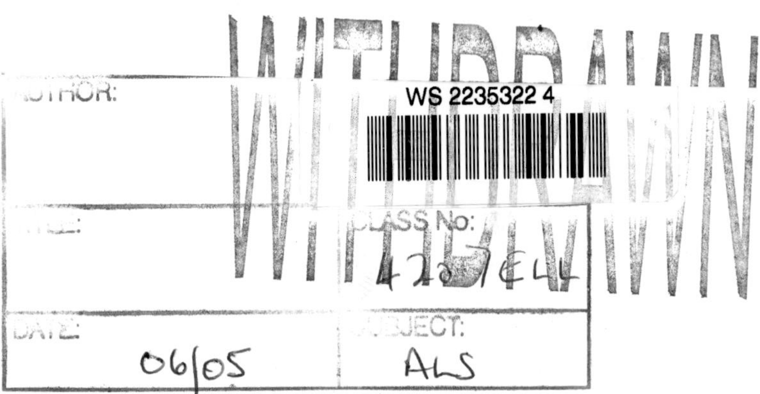

Published in this series:

Bachman: *Fundamental Considerations in Language Testing*
Bachman and Palmer: *Language Testing in Practice*
Brumfit: *Individual Freedom and Language Teaching*
Brumfit and Carter (eds.): *Literature and Language Teaching*
Canagarajah: *Resisting Linguistic Imperialism in Language Teaching*
Cook: *Discourse and Literature*
Cook: *Language Play, Language Learning*
Cook and Seidlhofer (eds.): *Principle and Practice in Applied Linguistics*
Ellis: *SLA Research and Language Teaching*
Ellis: *Task-based Language Learning and Teaching*
Ellis: *The Study of Second Language Acquisition*
Ellis: *Understanding Second Language Acquisition*
Ellis and Barkhuizen: *Analysing Learner Language*
Holliday: *The Struggle to Teach English as an International Language*
Howatt: *A History of English Language Teaching*
Jenkins: *The Phonology of English as an International Language*
Kern: *Literacy and Language Teaching*
Kramsch: *Context and Culture in Language Teaching*
Lantolf (ed.): *Sociocultural Theory and Second Language Learning*
Lantolf and Thorne: *Sociocultural Theory and the Genesis of Second Language Development*
Meinhof: *Language Learning in the Age of Satellite Television*
Nattinger and DeCarrico: *Lexical Phrases and Language Teaching*
Phillipson: *Linguistic Imperialism*
Seidlhofer (ed.): *Controversies in Applied Linguistics*
Seliger and Shohamy: *Second Language Research Methods*
Skehan: *A Cognitive Approach to Language Learning*
Stern: *Fundamental Concepts of Language Teaching*
Stern (eds. P. Allen and B. Harley): *Issues and Options in Language Teaching*
Tarone and Yule: *Focus on the Language Learner*
Widdowson: *Aspects of Language Teaching*
Widdowson: *Defining Issues in English Language Teaching*
Widdowson: *Practical Stylistics*
Widdowson: *Teaching Language as Communication*

Analysing Learner Language

Rod Ellis
Gary Barkhuizen

OXFORD
UNIVERSITY PRESS

Great Clarendon Street, Oxford OX2 6DP

Oxford University Press is a department of the University of Oxford. It furthers the University's objective of excellence in research, scholarship, and education by publishing worldwide in

Oxford New York

Auckland Cape Town Dar es Salaam Hong Kong Karachi Kuala Lumpur Madrid Melbourne Mexico City Nairobi New Delhi Shanghai Taipei Toronto

With offices in

Argentina Austria Brazil Chile Czech Republic France Greece Guatemala Hungary Italy Japan Poland Portugal Singapore South Korea Switzerland Thailand Turkey Ukraine Vietnam

OXFORD and OXFORD ENGLISH are registered trade marks of Oxford University Press in the UK and in certain other countries

First published 2005
2009 2008 2007 2006 2005
10 9 8 7 6 5 4 3 2 1

ISBN-13: 978 0 19 431634 7
ISBN-10: 0 19 431634 3

Typeset by Newgen Imaging Systems (P) Ltd., Chennai, India

Printed in China

Contents

Acknowledgements

The authors would like to thank Ute Knoch for her help in painstakingly checking bibliographical references.

The authors and publisher are grateful to the following for permission to reproduce extracts and figures from copyright material:

Athelstan for a screenshot from Barlow, M.: *MonoConc Pro.*

John Benjamins Publishing Company, Amsterdam/Philadelphia: 'A bird's eye view of computer learner corpus research' by Granger, S.; 'A corpus-based study of the L2 acquisition of the English verb system' by Housen, A. from Granger, S., Hung, J., and Petch Tyson, S.: *Computer Learner Corpora, Second Language Acquisition and Foreign Language Teaching* (p.5).

Blackwell Publishing: 'Negative feedback as regulation and second language learning in the zone of proximal development' by Aljaafreh, A. and Lantolf, J. P.: *Modern Language Journal* 78: 47.

Greenwood Publishing Group, Inc., Westport, CT: 'Discourse Completion Test'; 'Taxonomy of request strategies'; 'Frequency of use of request strategies' from Blum-Kulka, S., House, J., and Kasper, G.: *Cross-cultural Pragmatics: Requests and Apologies*. Copyright © 1989 by S. Blum Kulka, J. House, and G. Kasper.

Hodder Arnold (Arnold Journals): 'Metaphorical conceptualizations of ESL teaching and learning' by de Guerrero, M. C. M. and Villamil, O. S.: *Language Teaching Research* 6/2: 95–121 (2002).

Lawrence Erlbaum Associates, Inc: Table 3.2 from Ohta, A. S.: *Second Language Acquisition Processes in the Classroom: Learning Japanese* (2001, LEA) (p. 89).

Pearson Education (Longman): Fairclough, N.: *Language and Power* (p.110).

Penguin Books Ltd: Table 2a, 'How errors are corrected' from Tsui, A. B. M.: Penguin English Applied Linguistics: *Introducing Classroom Interaction* (Penguin English, 1995) (p.52). Copyright © Amy B. M. Tsui, 1995.

TESOL, Washington, DC: 'Creative construction in second language learning and teaching' from Burt, M. K. & Dulay, H. C. (eds.): On TESOL '75: *New Directions in Second Language Learning, Teaching and Bilingual Education* (pp. 21–32).

Université Catholique de Louvain, Louvain-la-Neuve, Centre for English Corpus Linguistics: Dagneaux, E., Denness, S., Granger, S., and Meunier, F.: *Error Tagging Manual Version 1.1* (1996).

Sources:
Yuan, F.: *The effects of planning on language production in task-based language teaching.*

Although every effort has been made to trace and contact copyright holders before publication, this has not been possible in some cases. We apologize for any apparent infringement of copyright and if notified, the publisher will be pleased to rectify any errors or omissions at the earliest opportunity.

Preface

This book has grown out the authors' experience of teaching SLA to postgraduate students in a wide variety of contexts—the UK, South Africa, Japan, the USA, and New Zealand. It was developed to replace traditional second language acquisition (SLA) courses based on lectures on key topics with a more hands-on, do-it-yourself approach, where students were required to grapple with second language (L2) data in order to address the kinds of research questions that have figured in SLA research. The materials in the book have now been used with a number of postgraduate students at the University of Auckland. We are grateful to these students for the valuable feedback they have provided.

Analysing Learner Language serves as an introduction to SLA research for postgraduate students and teachers wishing to undertake empirical studies of L2 acquisition. It has the following aims:

1 to familiarize readers with different methods for analysing learner language as expression and as content;
2 to examine the theoretical and research bases for the different methods; and
3 to develop readers' ability to undertake the analysis of samples of learner language using different methods.

The book provides full examples of the different methods for analysing learner language and also tasks for readers to practise the methods themselves. The chapters detailing the different methods of analysis (Chapters 3–13) have four main sections. The first provides an account of the historical and theoretical background of the method. This is intended to provide a rationale for the method and to demonstrate the contribution it has made to the study of L2 acquisition. The second offers a step-by-step account of the method together with an illustration of its application to actual data. The third section provides an example of a study that has employed the method; the study is summarized and subjected to critical review. Lastly, the fourth section is a task where readers are provided with a sample of learner language which they are invited to analyse using the method. The purpose of this section is to give hands-on-experience in the actual analysis of learner language. Readers can try out each method for themselves.

However, *Analysing Learner Language* is not a research methodology book in the traditional sense of this term. That is, it does not address issues relating to the choice of a particular research methodology or of research design. Nor is it primarily concerned with methods of data collection. The thrust of the book is an account of the tools that researchers have used to analyse the spoken and written texts produced by L2 learners. The use of these tools in SLA has been motivated by the particular research questions that researchers have addressed. As the nature of these questions has changed over time, so new methods of data analysis have been developed. Thus, an account of the methods of analysis in SLA will necessarily involve consideration of the historical and theoretical contexts of each method. Thus, by learning about the tools for analysing learner language, readers will also be introduced to the key issues that have motivated SLA enquiry.

Because the book provides an overview of key areas in SLA research (by way of contextualizing the different methods of analysis), it can also serve as an introductory SLA text. It may appeal to teachers of SLA who wish to offer a more 'hands-on' approach to teaching SLA in place of the traditional exposition of the main areas of study in SLA. One way of learning about how learners acquire an L2 is by studying the language they produce. Finally, the book may also be used as a reference book for SLA researchers wanting to review the possibilities for data analysis before finalizing a research proposal.

Rod Ellis
Gary Barkhuizen
Department of Applied Language Studies and Linguistics
University of Auckland

1 Introduction

The primary purpose of this book is to provide an account of what is known about how learners acquire a second language (L2) by introducing readers to the methods that have been used to analyse *learner language*. A secondary purpose is to equip readers to carry out analyses of learner language by themselves for research purposes.

There are a number of books that provide overviews of 'second language acquisition' (SLA) as a field of study (for example, Ellis 1985a and 1994; Gass and Selinker 1994; Larsen-Freeman and Long 1991; Mitchell and Myles 1998; Towell and Hawkins 1994). There are also books that review specific areas of SLA—for example, Tarone (1988) on variability in L2 learning, Skehan (1989) on individual differences, Kasper and Kellerman (1997) on second language learners' communication strategies, Gass (1997) on the role of input and interaction and Doughty and Williams (1998) on the role of form-focused instruction. Thus, the field is well-catered for in terms of published works documenting what is known about L2 learning and L2 learners.

As a field with close links to the social sciences, education and applied linguistics, SLA is also well-provided with general accounts of research methodology. In addition to established works such as Ary, Jacobs, and Razavieh (1990), Brown (1988), Cohen and Manion (1994), Neuman (1994) and Seliger and Shohamy (1989), there are a number of more specific books addressing the applications of research methodologies to SLA, such as Brown and Rodgers' (2002) survey of qualitative and quantitative research techniques, Faerch and Kasper's (1987) collection of articles on introspective methods, Brown's (2001) practical guide to the use of surveys in second-language related research and Gass and Mackey's (2000) account of the use of stimulated recall in SLA. Other works (for example, Hatch and Lazaraton 1991) offer explanations of the statistical procedures available to SLA researchers. Together, these books provide detailed accounts of the theoretical underpinnings of different research traditions, the main research approaches and the designs associated with them, methods of data collection and ways of analysing data.

Given the wealth of the published literature on SLA and on research methodology, it seems advisable to us to begin this book by explaining why we have taken the trouble to write this book. In *Analysing Learner*

Language we want to bring together a substantive account of SLA as a field of enquiry through an examination of the methods of data collection and analysis that have informed research in this field. That is, our main goal is to introduce readers to what has been discovered about L2 learning and L2 learners through a consideration of the methods that have produced this knowledge. Indeed, our assumption is that understanding SLA requires an understanding of its established findings (what Long (1990b) calls the 'facts' of SLA) in relation to the ways in which these findings have been established. Thus, we seek to introduce readers to SLA by familiarizing them with the various methods of data collection and analysis SLA researchers have employed.

This approach has been adopted in response to one of the authors' experiences in teaching SLA courses over a period of some fifteen years. The approach he adopted was initially a fairly traditional one, involving lectures on selected topics (error analysis, variability, language transfer, input and interaction, learning strategies, etc.) supported by a range of tasks that required some form of application of the material presented in the lectures. These tasks included a number of data analysis activities. For example, in one such task, students were asked to analyse a set of negative utterances produced by one L2 learner over a nine-month period. In another, they were asked to examine how teachers addressed linguistic form in the context of interactions derived from communicative activities. It was observed that these tasks frequently led to lively discussions of key issues in SLA and, crucially, to problems of interpreting what the data showed. In response to this, a decision was taken to redesign the SLA course around these tasks. This required a new way of structuring the content. Instead, of basing the course on topics in SLA, the new course was organized around the different ways in which learner language has been analysed over the thirty-plus years that SLA has existed as a recognized field of study. The purpose, however, was not so much to train students in how to carry out these methods of analysis (although this was, hopefully, a useful outcome of the course) as to involve the students in 'doing SLA' so that their understanding of its findings were grounded in a hands-on experience of how they were obtained. This book is a direct outcome and extension of this course.

This book, then, is an account of how SLA researchers have set about analysing learner language, of the theoretical positions that underlie their enquiries and of the main empirical findings that have resulted from them. In addition, indeed as an essential part of the whole enterprise, the book provides opportunities, in the form of data-based tasks, for readers to apply the different methods of analysis themselves. It is also important to note what the book does *not* seek to do. The book does not consider culture learning, although it does examine the role of cultural factors in language learning. (See, for example, Chapter 10.) It does not aim to provide advice to teachers about how they should teach. Obviously, though, an understanding of how learners learn an L2 should inform how teachers teach and some chapters include tasks involving data taken from instructional contexts. Also, the book does not examine curricula for teaching an L2.

In this chapter, we briefly explain what we mean by 'SLA', which we will interpret very broadly. We will also consider what is meant by 'learner language', identifying two distinct senses of this term. Finally, we will attempt to demarcate the particular aspect of SLA research methodology we are concerned with (i.e. data analysis) by placing it within a broader framework of the nature of research and the different research paradigms that have been employed in SLA.

SLA

Two different senses of SLA need to be distinguished. The term is frequently used to refer to the learning of another language (second, third, foreign) after acquisition of one's mother tongue is complete. That is, it labels the *object* of enquiry. The term is also used to refer to the *study* of how people learn a second language; that is, it labels the field of enquiry itself. This dual use of the term is unfortunate as it can create confusion. In this book we will use 'L2 acquisition' as the label for the object of enquiry and 'SLA' as the label for the field of study.

SLA is multi-disciplinary. That is, it draws on insights and methods of research from a range of disciplines, including linguistics, sociology, sociolinguistics, psychology, psycholinguistics and education. This multi-disiplinary aspect of SLA is widely accepted and is reflected in all the published surveys of the field referred to above. It has advantages and disadvantages. It affords a rich account of what is a highly complex phenomenon. But, as Gass and Selinker (1994) point out it sometimes results in a failure of communication by scholars committed to different approaches. SLA is characterized by a host of controversies (see Block 2003 for a thoughtful analysis of some of the main ones), many of which are not resolvable as they derive from incommensurable theoretical positions. In this book we will seek an inter-disciplinary perspective. Indeed, such an approach is inevitable, given our intention to present a range of different approaches for analysing learner language, as the different approaches derive from different disciplines and different theoretical orientations. We will acknowledge controversies where they exist, but we will not attempt to resolve them. Nor will we stake out our own 'preferred' position, although, of course, we cannot promise to guard entirely against our own biases.

The study of how people learn a second language involves both an examination of those aspects of learning that are common to all learners—the universals of L2 acquisition—and of those contextual and personal factors that explain the enormous variation in speed and ultimate level of attainment of different L2 learners—the individual differences in L2 learning. Again, the published surveys of SLA acknowledge both aspects. It is probably true to say, however, that they have devoted more attention to the universals of L2 acquisition than to social and individual differences, the latter aspect being generally consigned to one or two chapters after the former has been exhaustively treated. Ideally, these two aspects need to be integrated into a single theory of L2 acquisition. However, we are a long way from achieving this, although a number of recent publications on individual differences (for example, Onwuegbuzie, Bailey, and Daley 2000; Skehan 1998a; Robinson 2002) have attempted to discuss specific variables responsible for variation among learners in terms of a general model of L2 acquisition. In *Analysing Learner Language* we will not attempt an integrated theory but instead present methods of analysis that relate to both the establishment of the universal properties of L2 acquisition and to individual differences in L2 learning. All of these methods are capable of addressing both the universal and differential aspects of L2 acquisition. For example, the analysis of learner language in terms of fluency, complexity and accuracy (see Chapter 7) provides a means of identifying how external factors that shape the learning environment affect the language that learners produce and also a means of researching how individual learners' communicative styles differ. Nevertheless, it is the case that particular methods of analysis have been closely associated with either a nomothetic and universalist orientation or an idiographic and hermeneutic view of L2 learning. Thus, for example, obligatory occasion analysis (Chapter 4) and frequency analysis (Chapter 5) have served to provide evidence of a universal route of acquisition, while critical approaches (Chapter 12) and metaphor analysis (Chapter 13) have led to insights about the different approaches to L2 learning manifested by individual learners.

In this book, then we acknowledge the multidimensionality of SLA, as reflected in the variety of approaches to analysing learner language. We recognize, too, that SLA must include both an examination of the universal properties of L2 acquisition and an account of the social and personal factors responsible for individual differences among learners.

Learner language

Learner language is the oral or written language produced by learners. It serves as the primary data for the study of L2 acquisition, although, as we will see in Chapter 2, it is not the only type of data available to SLA researchers. We will also see that learner language is not a monolithic phenomenon but rather highly variable, raising important issues to do with what kind (or kinds) of learner language constitute the most valid data for the study of how learners learn. These issues are of such theoretical importance, however, that we will briefly examine them here.

For many SLA researchers the goal of SLA is the description and explanation of L2 learners' *competence* and how this develops over time. Definitions of competence vary[1] but all see it as involving underlying systems of linguistic knowledge (Canale and Swain 1980; Taylor 1988). We can ask, then, how the study of learner language can provide information about learners' underlying linguistic knowledge. To address this question we need to consider exactly what we mean by 'linguistic knowledge' and then to examine the relationship between competence and *performance*.

Linguistic knowledge is constituted as shown in Table 1.1. The central distinction is between implicit and explicit linguistic knowledge. Implicit knowledge is the kind of knowledge we possess of our mother tongue. That is, it is unconscious and is proceduralized so that it is available for automatic use in spontaneous production. Implicit knowledge consists of formulaic chunks (for example, 'I don't know' and 'How do you do?') and also unconscious knowledge of abstract patterns or rules relating to both

Type of knowledge	Sub-types	Definitions
Implicit (procedural)	1 formulaic	Sequences of elements that are stored and accessed as ready-made chunks.
	2 rule-based	Unconscious knowledge of major and minor schemas consisting of abstract linguistic categories realizable lexically in an indefinite number of sentences/ utterances.
Explicit (declarative)	1 analysed	Conscious awareness of minor and major schemas.
	2 metalingual	Lexical knowledge of technical and non-technical linguistic terminology.

Table 1.1 Types of linguistic knowledge

minor schemas as in simple collocations (for example, V + verb complement, as in '*suggest* + V*ing*' and '*demand* + Vinfin') and to major schemas (for example, the construction of relative clauses). Explicit knowledge is conscious and declarative (i.e. it takes the form of encyclopaedic facts about a language). It consists of both conscious awareness of the same minor and major schemas that figure in implicit knowledge (but represented in an entirely different mental form) and of the metalanguage that can assist in verbalizing this analysed knowledge. (See Ellis 2004.) As we will see, learner language is capable of providing information about both types of knowledge but it is often difficult to decide which type of knowledge is reflected in learner production. While SLA researchers argue about the role that explicit knowledge plays in both acquisition and language use—compare, for example, Krashen (1994) and N. Ellis (2002)—they broadly agree that the linguistic knowledge comprising competence is essentially of the implicit kind and that the main goal of SLA is to account for learners' implicit knowledge.

A learner's implicit knowledge (competence) is not open to direct inspection. We cannot easily look into someone's mind to see how knowledge of language is represented or what kind of knowledge is being utilized in the performance of a language task. To some extent this is possible through magnetic resonance imaging. (See, for example, Chee, Tan, and Thiel 1999.) This technology enables us to identify those parts of the brain that are activated in performing a language task and, in the long run, may enable us to determine the parts of the brain responsible for different kinds of linguistic processing. However, we are a long way from being able to plot cortical organization with reference to language use in this way. Thus, by and large, researchers are forced to infer competence from some kind of performance. How learners perform some kind of language task serves as the principal source of information about what they know about the language.

This raises the general question about what kind of performance provides the most reliable and valid source of information. Here we find major differences in opinion. On the one hand some SLA researchers choose to rely on learner intuitions (in the form of judgements about the grammaticality of sentences presented to them) to discover what they know. Other researchers, especially those of a more functional orientation, prefer to collect samples of learner language. Not surprisingly analyses based on grammaticality judgements and on learner language frequently produce different results. A learner may succeed in judging a sentence correctly as grammatical and yet be unable to produce the structure exemplified in the sentence in free production. Furthermore, learner language is itself not homogenous but rather highly variable, depending on both social factors (for example, whom a learner is addressing) and psycholinguistic factors (for example, the degree of attention that a learner is paying to correctness of form) and the inter-relationship of the two. Linguistic performance, then, is inherently heterogeneous.

What solutions are there to this problem of variability? There are several:

1 Redefine competence as itself variable. (See, for example, Tarone 1983 and Ellis 1985b.) That is, variability in performance is seen as reflecting a variable competence.
2 Identify one type of performance as the preferred source of information about competence.
3 Recognize the need for multiple sources of performance data and look for points of confluence as evidence of what a learner knows.

It is not our purpose in this book to enter the thorny debates that surround which of these three solutions to choose. The fact that we have elected to address how to analyse *learner language* (rather than data derived from some kind of test), however, reflects our belief about the centrality of this kind of data. In Chapter 2, we examine the different methods for collecting samples of learner language, pointing to what is now widely acknowledged in SLA, namely the need for data that reflects as closely as possible 'natural' language use (i.e. language that is situationally and interactionally authentic) while recognizing that the limitations facing the collection of such data often obligate researchers to resort to clinically elicited data (for example, by using pedagogic tasks). Here, though, we want to emphasize that there is no easy solution to the data problem and that the main requirements that should be placed on researchers are to specify explicitly what kind(s) of data have been collected and to justify the validity of these data in terms of a clearly stated theoretical position regarding the relationship between performance and competence (i.e. to address the validity of the data).

In the foregoing discussion we have implicitly treated learner language as *expression* but it can also be viewed as *content*. That is, we can view learner language in two entirely distinct ways. We can see it as providing evidence of what learners know about an L2 by examining the linguistic forms they produce. We can also view it as a set of propositions relating to whatever topics are being communicated about. These topics can include those relating to the second language itself—that is, learners can inform us about their beliefs and attitudes to the target language and to the target language community and about the behaviours they engage in when learning the language. This distinction between learner language as expression and as content is central to this book. In part, it relates to a distinction we have already mentioned—that between the branches of SLA that have focused on the universal properties of L2 acquisition (the psycholinguistic orientation) and those other branches that have addressed the factors responsible for individual differences in learning (the social or psychological orientation). By and large, learner language treated as expression has served as data for investigating the universal properties of acquisition while learner language viewed as content has provided information about how learners differ in their attitudes and approaches to learning. Of course, as we have already pointed out, it would be possible to examine individual factors in terms of differences in the formal properties of the language produced by different learners and, similarly, it would be possible to build a picture of the universal aspects of L2 learning from learners' reports about learning. In general, though, this has not happened. Learner productions viewed as expression tell us what learners do with the language and thus do not readily shed direct light on such factors as social identity, learning styles, motivation, language aptitude or learning strategies. To investigate these, we need learners to self-report. Conversely, learners are unlikely to be able to tell us in what order/sequence they acquired grammatical structures (for example, whether they acquired unmarked/protypical forms before marked/prototypical ones). Nor will they have much idea why they acquire forms in the order/ sequence they do.

There is, therefore, a strong rational basis for distinguishing learner language as expression and as content. There are also empirical grounds. The methods of analysing learner language we will discuss in the following chapters divide quite clearly into those associated with expression and content. Thus, methods such as error analysis (Chapter 3) and interactional analysis (Chapter 8), borrowed from linguistics, view learner language as expression while other methods, taken from the social sciences, such as critical analytical approaches (Chapter 12) and metaphor analysis (Chapter 13), treat learner language primarily as content. Our claim is that we need to orientate to learner language in both ways to obtain a full account of L2 acquisition.

Research paradigms

The focus of this book is on 'data analysis'. We recognize, however, that data analysis does not occur in a vacuum but is an integral part of the research process. It is shaped by the purpose of the research and the theoretical principles that govern the chosen method of enquiry. In this section, we consider how the analysis of learner language fits into the broader research picture.

Table 1.2 outlines the key differences in the two research paradigms widely recognized in discussions of research methodology in the social sciences. These two paradigms have been variously labelled (for example, quantitative/qualitative; confirmatory/interpretative; positivist/non-positivist; nomothetic/idiographic; analytical-nomological/hermeneutic). The labels we have chosen are those of Cohen and Manion (1994)—-normative/interpretative. However, following Neuman (1994), Table 1.2 also includes a third paradigm, critical research, which differs from the other two in a number of key respects, although it is clearly closer to the interpretative than the normative paradigm.

In Chapters 3 through 13 a number of examples of SLA studies are provided. These are selected to exemplify the various methods of data collection we will consider. They also serve to illustrate the three research paradigms shown in Table 1.2. For example, Chapter 7 provides a summary of Crookes' (1989) study of the effects of planning on learners' performance of communicative tasks. This study was undertaken in the normative paradigm, although, as we will see, it does not conform entirely to the account of this paradigm in Table 1.2. Chapter 13 provides a summary of Rod Ellis's (2002) metaphor analysis of L2 learners' diaries. It is representative of the interpretative paradigm. Chapter 12 considers McKay and Wong's (1996) study of junior high school ESL learners in the United States and is illustrative of the critical paradigm. Readers might like to look at the summaries of these articles as they afford concrete instantiations of the three research paradigms.

It is, however, not always so easy to determine which research paradigm a particular study belongs to. This is because mixed forms of research are possible. Grotjahn (1987), in a thorough presentation of these mixed forms, suggests that they arise because researchers combine type of design, methods of data collection and methods of data analysis by drawing on more than one paradigm. For example, a researcher might adopt a normative design but employ a qualitative method of data collection, and make use of quantitative methods of data analysis. Pica's (1983) study (summarized in Table 4.6) is a good example of this. In terms of theoretical orientation, research purpose, and design, her study belongs to the normative paradigm as she is concerned with discovering the 'ultimate truth' of whether all learners, irrespective of their learning context, manifest a universal order of acquisition and she sets out to investigate this by comparing three groups of learners who vary in terms of a pre-defined variable (type of exposure to the L2). However, the data she collected were qualitative (hour-long conversations where the learners talked about personal topics). The data were subjected to obligatory occasion analysis, which is clearly quantitative in nature, and subsequently analysed statistically. Crookes' (1989) study, referred to above, is similar in that it also utilized a normative design but made use of qualitative methods of data collection.

In fact, much of the research undertaken in SLA is of the mixed kind. This is partly because many SLA researchers (such as ourselves) are not committed to a single theoretical orientation. It also reflects a belief in the validity of learner language as the primary source of evidence for L2 acquisition. As we have already noted, how learners use the L2 in naturally occurring contexts is viewed as affording the best data for examining their underlying knowledge systems (competence). It follows, therefore, that researchers need to obtain samples of such L2 use and this is likely to involve

Dimension	Normative	Interpretative	Critical
Theoretical orientation	L2 acquisition is seen as essentially rule-governed and thus investigatable by the same methods as those used in natural science to identify cause and effect. Researchers in this paradigm see reality in terms of 'ultimate truth', which can be determined objectively.	L2 acquisition is seen as highly individualized as a result of the complex interplay of psychological and social factors. It can only be understood by examining authentic learning contexts and how learners respond to these. Researchers in this paradigm see reality as subjective and relative.	L2 acquisition is seen as rooted in the tensions and historically determined social structures that influence behaviour. But this paradigm views learners as endowed with agency and therefore able to act on as well as be acted on by social context. Researchers in this paradigm adopt a clear value position.
Research purpose	To test a hypothesis drawn from an explicit theory of L2 acquisition objectively. The research tests whether there is a relationship between an independent and dependent variable.	To describe and understand some aspect of L2 acquisition subjectively. The research aims to uncover key variables and their inter-relationships.	To identify and transform the socio-political conditions that unfairly mitigate against learners gaining access to the L2. Unfairness is determined in relation to the researcher's ideological stance.
Design and scope	Typically, an experiment involving a) randomly constituted groups of L2 learners, b) a treatment carefully contrived to control for extraneous variables, constituting the independent variable and	Typically, a case study of one or more L2 learners in an authentic context. The case study can be cross-sectional but is often longitudinal. The scope of the research is thus small-scale.	Typically, a case study of learners learning an L2 in an authentic context where they interact with native speakers. The research is typically cross-sectional and small-scale.

	c) measures of learning outcomes, constituting the dependent variable. An experiment can involve a relatively brief or more extended treatment. The scope of the research is thus medium to large scale.		
Participants	Large groups of L2 learners.	Individual L2 learners.	Individual L2 learners in inequitable power relations with other users of the L2.
Data collection	Typically, quantitative methods (e.g. tests, questionnaires).	Typically, qualitative methods involving a) recordings of naturally occurring uses of the L2, b) observations of L2 learners and c) self-report data from L2 learners. Frequently, more than one method of collecting data is employed.	Typically, qualitative methods involving observation, documentary evidence and self-report data from L2 learners.
Data analysis	Quantitative methods supported by inferential statistics to test the strength of relationships between variables and differences between group scores.	Qualitative methods involving 'thick description' of the aspect of L2 learning under investigation from multiple perspectives (triangulation).	Qualitative methods identifying the 'discourses' learners participate in and how these position them socially.

Table 1.2 Three research paradigms in SLA

qualitative methods of data collection (for example, recording conversations). However, in studies where researchers are testing hypotheses (as in Crookes' and Pica's studies), there is often a need to reduce the qualitative data to some form of numerical measure to allow for statistical analysis. In effect, this is what most of the data analysis methods of the book do (Chapter 9 on conversation analysis and Chapter 10 on sociocultural methods of analysis being exceptions). The methods outlined in Chapters 3 to 8 typically figure in research that can be characterized as normative-qualitative-quantitative. In contrast, the data analysis methods discussed in Chapters 11, 12, and 13 are all qualitative in nature. That is, they are directed at identifying 'themes' in learner language treated as content. However, it should be noted that these methods do not preclude quantification as it is always possible to count the frequency of the themes that have been identified. Indeed, Rod Ellis's (2002) metaphor analysis attempted just this.

What this suggests, then, is that in SLA the ties between research design on the one hand and data collection methods and methods of analysis on the other are relatively loose. Qualitative methods of data collection and of data analysis can accompany a normative research design while, conversely, quantitative methods of data analysis can be found in interpretive designs and (potentially, although we know of no examples) in critical research too. Thus, although, data analysis is clearly to be seen as a step in the research process, it is partially independent of the research design that shapes a study. In the chapters that follow we will see that particular methods of data analysis are linked to particular research questions and thus to particular bodies of findings about SLA but these links are often driven less by the researchers' commitment to a particular research design than by the need to collect and analyse data in ways relevant to their over theoretical orientation and research purpose. One of the main aims of this book is to explore these links.

Conclusion

In this chapter we have endeavoured to explain why we have chosen to focus on methods for analysing learner language and how we have approached our presentation of the different methods. We see the study of learner language and of its methods of analysis as an ideal way to gain an understanding of what the SLA field has discovered about L2 acquisition. We aim to introduce readers to an account of how SLA is done and to provide opportunities for actually doing SLA through data analysis tasks. Also, by examining the historical and theoretical background of research that has employed the different methods we present an overview of SLA itself. The methods divide quite clearly into those that treat learner language as expression (linguistic form) and those that view it as content affording information about learners' attitudes and learning behaviours. The former set has been primarily directed at the universal aspects of L2 acquisition, focusing in particular at identifying the nature of learners' implicit knowledge of the L2 and the processes responsible for its development, while the latter set has been primarily concerned with the social and psychological factors that account for individual differences in rate of learning and ultimate achievement. SLA, as a field, is concerned with both.

This is not a book about research methodology in SLA. (For such a book, see Brown and Rodgers 2002.) However, the analysis of learner language needs to be understood in relation to the theoretical orientations and research purposes that guide how data are analysed. We seek to achieve this by providing a historical and theoretical background to the research that has utilized the different methods.

In the next chapter, we describe the various options available to the SLA researcher for collecting data, especially data consisting of learner language, as a necessary preliminary to investigating how learner language can be analysed.

Notes

1 The main areas of disagreement regarding the definition of competence concern (1) whether the construct should include ability to use one's linguistic knowledge as well as the linguistic knowledge itself and (2) whether it should be broadly defined to include sociolinguistic, discourse and strategic knowledge, or be restricted narrowly to linguistic knowledge (i.e. knowledge of phonological, lexical and grammatical systems).

2 Collecting samples of learner language

Introduction

One way to find out how learners acquire a second language (L2) is to study how they use it in production. Another way is ask them to report on their own learning. In the eyes of many researchers, including the authors of this book, these constitute the main ways of researching L2 acquisition. By collecting and analysing samples of learner language, researchers can achieve the two goals of second language acquisition research (SLA) (Ellis 1994); (1) a description of the linguistic systems (i.e. the interlanguages) that learners construct at different stages of development and (2) an explanation of the processes and factors involved in acquiring an L2.

In this chapter, we will consider the different methods that can be used to obtain samples of language from L2 learners. We will begin by describing the different kinds of L2 data that can be collected as a way of delineating the particular type of data that will be the focus of this book. We will then examine the nature of 'learner language', identifying three basic methods for collecting samples of it. In the sections that follow, each of these types will be considered in detail. Finally, we will tackle the thorny problem of 'validity' (i.e. the extent to which the different sample types permit descriptive and explanatory statements to be made about learners' interlanguages).

Types of data

Many different types of data can be collected from learners. However, it is helpful to identify three broad sets: (1) non-linguistic performance data, (2) samples of learner language, and (3) reports from learners about their own learning. Our concern in this book is with (2) and (3). However, we will begin by considering (1) if only because it has figured strongly in research in SLA.

Non-linguistic performance data

Non-linguistic performance data involve measuring learners' non-verbal responses to linguistic stimuli. They include measures of learners' reaction times to linguistic stimuli, non-verbal measures of learners' comprehension of linguistic input, and measures of learners' intuitions about the grammaticality or acceptability of sentences. These measures enable inferences to be made about learners' linguistic knowledge based on their ability to process language receptively.

Measuring learners' reaction time

This provides evidence of whether the cognitive operations evident in a learner's performance reflect controlled or automatic processing and thus the extent to which specific linguistic features have been mastered. A good example of the use of this measure can be found in sentence-matching tests.

In a sentence-matching test, learners are presented with two sentences, which are either both grammatical or both ungrammatical, and asked to determine whether the two sentences are identical or not. The time it takes learners to make a judgement online is measured. Gass (2001: 423) describes the standard procedure as follows:

> Participants are seated in front of a computer and are presented with one sentence that is either grammatical or ungrammatical. After a short delay, a second sentence appears on a screen, with the first sentence remaining in place. Participants are asked to decide as quickly as possible if the sentences match or do not match, entering their decision by pressing specific keys. The time from the appearance of the second sentence to the participant's pressing the key is recorded and forms the data-base for the analysis.

It is this reaction time that is used to determine the status of learners' L2 knowledge. Following research conducted by native speakers (for example, Freedman and Forster 1985), it is argued that participants take longer to judge the equivalence of ungrammatical than grammatical sentences. Thus, by examining the reaction times, it becomes possible to determine to what extent specific structures are deemed to be grammatical or ungrammatical by a particular learner.[1] The validity of this method of examining learners' intuitive L2 knowledge remains uncertain, however. Gass (2001), for example, found no difference in the response time of L2 learners of French between pairs of grammatical and ungrammatical sentences.

Measuring comprehension

Non-verbal measures of comprehension have been used to establish whether learners are able to process specific linguistic features in the input (for example, VanPatten and Cadierno 1993). In picture matching, for example, learners are presented with a sentence and then asked to select which picture from an array of two or more the sentence matches. For example, they might be shown the following sentence:

The dog was bitten by Thomas.

and then asked to match the sentence with the correct picture from a pair of pictures, which show a dog biting a man and a man biting a dog. There are variations in this procedure. In some studies (for example, Montrul 2001), participants are asked to judge to what extent a particular sentence matches a picture on a Likert scale ('very natural' → 'very unnatural'). In other studies (for example, Bley-Vroman and Joo 2001), participants are given pairs of sentences and pictures and asked to say which sentence matches which picture, with the option of choosing 'neither'.

Obviously, comprehension tests such as picture-matching only work with grammatical structures that have clear, identifiable functions—such as the passive voice in English. They cannot be used for structures that are semantically redundant (for example, 3rd person *-s* in English or noun-adjectival agreement in French). Nevertheless, with this caveat, they constitute a useful tool for investigating a learner's receptive L2 competence.

Measuring learner intuitions about grammaticality

Learners have intuitions about the grammaticality of L2 sentences. These intuitions may differ from those of native speakers. For example, when learners read the sentence

*The policeman explained Thomas the law.

they may think it grammatical even though it is in fact ungrammatical (at least where standard English is concerned). Or when they read the sentence

Hardly had they finished when it started to rain.

they may think it is ungrammatical even though it is in fact grammatical. Of course learners' intuitions are not always incorrect; in many cases their intuitions accord with the norms of the target language. It seems reasonable to suppose that learners' intuitions reflect the current state of their knowledge of the L2, or, to put it more technically, they tell us about their interlanguage.

The main method of eliciting learners' intuitions about the L2 is the grammaticality judgement test (GJT). This comes in a variety of formats, considered below, but in essence entails presenting learners with a set of sentences, some of which are grammatical and some are ungrammatical, and asking them to judge whether each sentence is grammatical or ungrammatical. GJTs have been very widely used in SLA, especially by researchers wishing to test specific hypotheses drawn from some linguistic theory, but they have also been challenged on a number of grounds.

(See Birdsong 1989.) We will first consider the different types of GJT and then the criticisms.

GJTs vary on two dimensions—the design of the GJT and the procedures for implementing the test. Variables in design relate to the way in which learners are asked to make their judgements and in whether they are asked to perform some additional operation. In the 'standard' GJT, learners are simply asked to judge whether the sentences are grammatical or ungrammatical, with (sometimes) the additional option of choosing a 'not sure' option. They can also be offered a wider selection of choices in a multiple choice format (for example, 'clearly grammatical', 'probably grammatical', 'probably ungrammatical' and 'clearly ungrammatical') or given a scale of grammaticality to respond to. Sorace (1996) makes a strong case for the use of 'magnitude estimation'. This involves asking learners to provide a numerical estimation of a series of sentences. They are presented with the first sentence in the test and asked to assign it a numerical value in terms of its acceptability. They are then required to assign a numerical value to each successive sentence relative to their previous judgements. Sorace argues that this type of GJT is superior because it places no constraints on the range of responses available to the participants. Other basic designs are also possible. For example, learners can be given a set of sentences and asked to rank them in terms of grammaticality or they can be given a pair of sentences and asked to choose which sentence in the pair is grammatical. In addition to judging the grammaticality of the sentences in these ways, learners can also be asked to carry out further operations on the sentences they consider ungrammatical: (1) indicate the parts they consider ungrammatical (for example, by underlining) and (2) write out the sentences correctly.

Procedures for administering a GJT also vary considerably. Learners may or may not be given vocabulary support (for example, by being allowed to refer to a dictionary). Each sentence in the test can be presented aurally, graphically or both together. The sentences can be presented in a booklet or on a computer. The sentences can be presented either one at a time or in sets. If the sentences are presented one at a time there is a choice as to whether each sentence is presented just once or more than once. If the sentences are presented in sets in a booklet, the learners can be told not to return to a page in the booklet once they have completed the judgements relating to the set shown on a particular page. But perhaps the most crucial variable is whether the test is administered in a speeded (i.e. pressurized) or unspeeded format. In a speeded test, learners are given a specified amount of time to judge each sentence. The idea is to elicit judgements based on implicit knowledge by preventing them from consulting metalinguistic rules. In an unspeeded test, learners have as much time as they want to judge each sentence. In such a test, learners are more able to utilize their explicit knowledge of learned rules.

GJTs realize three kinds of data. First and foremost they provide information about learners' intuitions as to what is grammatical or ungrammatical.

Second, if the time it takes learners to judge each sentence is recorded, GJTs provide information about reaction times which can be used to evaluate what kind of knowledge (implicit or explicit) the learners used to make their judgements. Third, if learners are asked to correct the ungrammatical sentences, the GJT serves as a device for eliciting samples of learner language. In this respect, a GJT constitutes an example of 'experimental elicitation'. (See below.)

GJTs are controversial. While it is now generally accepted that GJTs do not provide a direct window for viewing learners' interlanguage, there is considerable disagreement as to what exactly they do measure and whether they provide consistent measurements. In other words, both the validity and the reliability of GJTs have been questioned. Sorace (1996) acknowledges a number of factors that result in 'spurious intuitions'. These include parsing strategies (i.e. a participant may judge a sentence ungrammatical because it is difficult to process rather than because it breaks a rule), the context and mode of presentation (i.e. a sentence is more likely to be judged as ungrammatical if it follows a set of clearly grammatical sentences), pragmatic considerations (i.e. decontextualized sentences may be judged in arbitrary ways), and linguistic training (i.e. whether the participants have received explicit grammar instruction). Of crucial importance is what kind of L2 knowledge a GJT measures. Does it provide information about learners' implicit or explicit knowledge? As Sorace comments:

> It can be a complex task to decide about the kind of norm consulted by learners in the process of producing a judgment, particularly in a learning environment that fosters the development of metalinguistic knowledge. It is difficult to tell whether subjects reveal what they think or what they think they should think. (1996: 385)

This problem is exacerbated by the fact that learners' knowledge systems are typically indeterminate—that is, their interlanguages are comprised of vague and fuzzy rather than hard and fast rules. When learners are not sure they may resort to a variety of strategies in order to produce a judgement. (See Ellis 1991; Davies and Kaplan 1998.) There have been two responses to these problems of validity. Some researchers have argued that GJTs are inherently flawed and should not be used in SLA (for example, Goss, Ying-Hua, and Lantolf 1994). Other researchers, such as Sorace, claim that the problems can be overcome through the careful design of GJTs (for example, by using magnitude estimation in tests administered in a speeded format). Ellis (2004) suggests that by manipulating the design features of a GJT it may be possible to obtain relatively separate measures of learners' implicit and explicit knowledge. For example, learners are more likely to draw on their implicit knowledge in judging grammatical sentences in a speeded test and their explicit knowledge in judging ungrammatical sentences in an unspeeded test.

The reliability of GJTs has been examined by asking learners to take the same test a second time after only a short intervening period and then comparing their judgements on the two tests (i.e. test/re-test reliability). Mixed results have been forthcoming. Ellis (1991) found that learners changed up to 45 per cent of their unspeeded judgements, lending support to the point made above about the indeterminancy of L2 knowledge. Han (1996) also reported low levels of test/re-test reliability in a study that examined learners' judgments in a speeded GJT. However, Gass (1994) reported a much higher level of reliability. Interestingly, though, Gass reported that learners were much more likely to keep to the same judgment in the case of sentences where the grammatical structure was relatively simple than where it was more complex.[2] An interpretation of Gass' study is that the reliability of judgements is higher when learners' L2 knowledge is more determinate, as is likely with simple structures that are acquired early, and lower when their knowledge is more indeterminate. This suggests that GJTs may lack reliability when used with learners of low L2 proficiency. If learners have not yet begun to develop grammars in the L2 they are likely to resort to compensatory strategies to find their way through the task, with the result that their responses will become inconsistent.

We have considered three methods of examining learners' knowledge of the L2 using non-verbal performance measures—measuring reaction time to linguistic stimuli as in sentence-matching tests, measuring comprehension by means of non-verbal responses, and measuring learners' intuitions about grammaticality. All three involve learners making a judgement of some kind. However, doubts exist regarding the validity and the reliability of such tests. Given these doubts, which are widely acknowledged even by researchers such as Sorace, who favour the use of such instruments, SLA researchers need to give careful consideration to the validity and reliability of their chosen instrument. As Douglas (2001: 453) points out:

> It is crucial to moving forward with our research that we make explicit the nature of the knowledge and abilities we are attempting to elicit or measure, that we provide empirical evidence for the consistency of the performances we observe, and that we further provide empirical and logical evidence that the interpretations we make of those performances are justified.

In fact, as Douglas notes, this is rarely achieved in SLA. Researchers are generally happy to report results based on judgement tests without bothering to demonstrate that their instrument is reliable and valid.[3]

It is not our purpose, however, to dismiss such instruments. With learners who have developed a degree of proficiency in the L2, they can be used to test hypotheses by investigating specific grammatical structures that often prove difficult, or even impossible, to elicit in learner production. However, we do wish to argue that the elicitation of learners' intuitions should not serve as the primary data for studying L2 acquisition and that where elicitation methods are used they should be carefully evaluated for validity and reliability and, wherever possible, be accompanied by methods that provide samples of actual learner language.

Samples of learner language

From our perspective, then, the primary data for investigating L2 acquisition should be samples of learner language. While we acknowledge the theoretical distinction between 'competence' and 'performance' and that the goal of SLA is to describe and explain L2 competence (either narrowly or broadly defined), we maintain that competence can only be examined by investigating some kind of performance[4] and that the key methodological issue is what kind of performance provides the most valid and reliable information about competence. Ultimately, what learners know is best reflected in their comprehension of input and in the language they produce. Measures of comprehension can provide important evidence of learners' acquisition but, as noted above, there are limitations to the use of such measures. For this reason and also perhaps because production is seen as providing the clearest evidence of what a learner has acquired, SLA researchers have relied extensively on samples of speech and writing. In contrast, to the non-verbal performance measures described above, speaking and writing constitute natural language activities. People do not usually go around matching pairs of sentences, matching sentences to pictures or judging whether isolated sentences are grammatical or ungrammatical as part of their day to day lives. For us, then, the construct validity of a data collection method is best established by demonstrating that the performance it taps reflects, as far as possible, the kind of use for which language is designed and acquired. In fact, though, as we will see, this constitutes a considerable challenge, not least because, as the language that learners produce can vary enormously depending on the type of production that is elicited.

Verbal reports

Samples of learner language provide data that can be used to develop descriptions of learners' interlanguages. These descriptions, in turn, provide the evidence by which theories of L2 acquisition can be developed and tested. However, the process of developing and testing explanations on the basis of descriptions of learner language is necessarily one of inference. For example, we might discover that even advanced learners of L2 English continue to omit 3rd person *-s* (a redundant feature) from their productions from time to time, whereas they more consistently add *-ed* (a meaning-performing feature) to mark regular past tense forms. To explain, this we might propose that learners operate in terms of a general principle, such as:

> Learners prefer processing 'more meaningful' morphology before 'less' or 'non-meaningful' morphology. (VanPatten 1996: 14)

But this is an inference and we cannot be sure. One way of establishing whether such principles have explanatory value is by collecting verbal report data. That is, we can ask learners to comment on their own productions and elicit thereby explanations for why they are and are not making errors.

There are many methods for collecting verbal reports. These can shed light not just on why learners produce what they do, but also such aspects of L2 learning as attitudes to the target language and its speakers, their motivation for learning the L2, the general strategies they use to learn it and the power relationships between themselves and the target language community. Verbal report data, although not unproblematic, can help in explaining L2 acquisition. Also, of course, if the verbal report occurs through the medium of the L2 it serves also as a device for eliciting samples of learner language. Methods for collecting verbal reports together with their problems are considered in detail in a later section.

Three types of samples of learner language

As we noted in Chapter 1, learner production is inherently variable. This variability is evident in a number of different ways. First, as any language teacher is aware, learners sometimes make errors and sometime use the target language form. For example, they may produce a grammatically correct sentence like:

> The big box contained a snake.

and then shortly afterwards commit an error with the same verb:

> * The thieves stole the box that contain the snake.

Second, variability in learner language is evident even when no error has been committed. For example, research (for example, Foster 1996) has shown that learners are more likely to produce complex grammatical constructions when they have time to pre-plan their production than when they have to perform spontaneously. Third, the order of acquisition of different grammatical structures can vary according to the kind of task used to elicit samples of learner language. Ellis (1987) found that the accuracy order of two past tense morphemes (irregular past tense and regular past tense) varied depending on how the data were collected. In the case of careful, written production, the regular past tense was more accurate but in the case of spontaneous production it proved less accurate than the irregular form. Fourth, learners vary in the choice of language, switching from the L2 to their mother tongue according to the situational context and also mixing the two languages in the construction of individual utterances.

There are a number of factors that contribute to this variability. (See Ellis 1994: Chapter 4.) A key factor is the nature of the sample, which depends, crucially, on how the sample is collected. We will distinguish three principal methods for collecting data and, correspondingly, three types of production data. The first method consists of obtaining samples of naturally occurring language use. By 'naturally occurring' we mean that the sample is produced in a real-life situation in order to satisfy some communicative or aesthetic need. Thus, a letter written to a friend, a conversation around the dinner table, or a poem are all examples of naturally occurring language use. Such samples can be oral or written. In the case of oral samples, researchers will need to video or audio record the performance. The other two methods involve elicitation, i.e. the use of specially designed instruments to obtain production samples from the learner. Following Corder (1976; reproduced in 1981), two kinds of elicitation can be distinguished: clinical and experimental elicitation. Corder defines clinical elicitation as 'getting the informant to produce data of any sort' and suggests that it is used 'where the investigator has not yet formed any well-formed hypothesis about the nature of the language he (sic) is investigating' (1976: 69). In contrast, experimental elicitation involves getting the informant 'to produce data incorporating particular features which the linguist is interested in at that moment' and constitutes, therefore, 'a carefully controlled procedure'. The distinction between clinical and experimental elicitation matches the distinction between 'task' and 'exercise'. (See Ellis 2003a.) Clinical elicitation involves the use of tasks where learners are primarily concerned with message conveyance, need to utilize their own linguistic resources to construct utterances, and are focused on achieving some non-linguistic outcome. Experimental elicitation involves the use of some kind of exercise, where learners attend primarily to form, are guided in the form to be produced and thus are focused on displaying usage of a specific linguistic form.

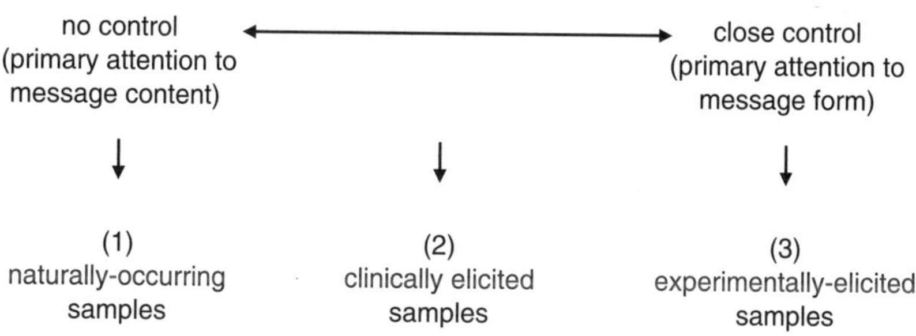

Figure 2.1 Three types of sample of learner language

These three types of data constitute a data continuum as shown in Figure 2.1 on p. 23. At one end of the continuum is language use over which the researcher exercises no control whatsoever, as in (1), naturally occurring samples. At the other end is language use involving very close control of the language produced, as in (3), experimentally elicited samples. Between these two poles lies (2), clinically elicited samples. Here some control is exercised through the choice of task but learners are expected to be primarily engaged in message conveyance for a pragmatic purpose, as in naturally occurring language use. In the eyes of many SLA researchers the ideal data is (1), as they reflect what learners can 'do' with the L2 when engaged in the kind of language use for which language is designed. However, because it is often not possible to obtain naturally occurring samples in sufficient quantity or that contain the specific linguistic features a researcher wishes to investigate, it is often necessary to fall back on (2) or (3). The sections following provide a more detailed account of these three methods of data collection.

Learner variables	Description
Mother tongue	The language(s) the participants learned as a child
Other languages	Any other languages the participants have learned as second/foreign languages.
Age	Stated in years and months (e.g. 8.3 yrs)
Gender	The number of male and female learners in the sample
Education	a Number of years of formal schooling b Number of years studying the target language
Social economic status (SES)	SES assigns participants a score reflecting their social class. Various measures of SES have been used based on one or more of the following: – occupation – level of education – income – area of residence
Opportunity for naturalistic acquisition	Number of years and months spent in a country where the target language serves as the main medium of communication.

Table 2.1 Describing the learner-participants in a study

Naturally occurring samples of learner language

In this section we will describe the principal methods for collecting naturally occurring oral and written samples of learner language. We would like to emphasize the importance of specifying the precise conditions under which data belonging to this type are collected. This can be done by describing who speaks/writes to whom about what, where and when. Situational variables such as these, in particular the addressee's relationship to the learner, can have a profound effect on the language produced by the learner and serve as a major source of variability. As Block (2003) notes, SLA researchers have often been neglectful in providing detailed information about the situational background of the learners they study. Table 2.1 suggests the kinds of variable that need to be considered in producing a full description of the learner-participants in a study. (See also the Publication Manual of the American Psychological Association.) Also, researchers need to specify the actual conditions under which learners are performing, in particular whether and to what extent they have time to plan before producing, as this too influences their spoken and written output (Yuan and Ellis 2003). Thus, in order to explain variation in learners' use of the L2, it is essential to provide a clear specification of the situational and planning conditions under which the samples were produced. Table 2.2, below, based on a study

Situational factor	**Description**
Type of data	Naturally occurring; oral (conversational)
Method of recording	Predominantly video-recorded
Who (learner)	A Chinese boy, called Bob, living in Australia. He is five years old at the beginning of the study and can speak Chinese.
To whom (addressee)	The researcher, who was also a family friend; his relationship with Bob shifted from being a formal teacher–pupil relationship to a more informal adult–friend relationship during the course of the study.
About what (activities)	Activities including drawing pictures together, playing with blocks and talking about school
Where (location)	In Australia in the home of Bob
When (time)	23 sessions stretching over a 26 month period
Planning time	No planning time available—learner production was spontaneous

Table 2.2 Describing situational factors in naturally occurring data collection (information taken from Tarone and Liu 1995)

by Tarone and Liu (1995), provides an example of how these conditions can be described.[5]

Usually, the aim of collecting naturally occurring data is to obtain samples of what sociolinguists call the 'vernacular style' (also referred to as the 'casual style'). Labov (1970) suggests that this arises when speakers are communicating spontaneously and easily with interlocutors familiar to them and thus pay minimum attention to their speech. Thus, it is argued that the vernacular style represents what learners are capable of producing when they are not consciously focused on form; it reflects their implicit rather than explicit knowledge of the L2. The main problem is that the very fact that learners know they are being researched is likely to result in a shift towards a more 'careful style'. This led Labov to formulate the Observer's Paradox. This states that the only way to obtain good data is through systematic observation but that such observation is likely to contaminate the data collected, making it impossible to sample the vernacular style. There are no easy solutions to this problem. One way is to obtain samples that are produced without the participants being aware they are being investigated. However, such an approach is not ethical and is no longer used. Another way is illustrated in Tarone and Liu's study—the researcher endeavours to create a familiar relationship between him/herself and the learner. However, this is usually only possible in longitudinal studies when the researcher has the opportunity to get to know the L2 learner. A third solution is to have learners communicate about a topic that is emotionally significant to them (for example, an event when they felt their lives were in danger). In such cases, language users are likely to be more concerned with message content than message form. However, whereas sociolinguistically oriented research has necessarily paid close attention to the Observer's Paradox, psycholinguistically oriented SLA research generally has not.

Oral samples

Speech is by nature ephemeral. Thus, in order to study it, some record of what is said needs to be made. There are three principal methods of collecting oral samples: (1) pencil-and-paper, (2) audio recording, and (3) video-recording. We will consider the advantages and disadvantages of each method.

The pencil-and-paper method was employed by one of the authors in a study of the naturally occurring language produced by three learners in an ESL classroom context over a two-year period. (See Ellis 1984b.) This method was used because earlier attempts had demonstrated the difficulty of obtaining satisfactory audio or video recordings in classrooms; samples were often characterized by a high level of overlapping, impromptu talk that made it very difficult to identify who was speaking to whom, or indeed what was said when listening to the recording later. The pencil-and-paper method worked well in this context because the researcher was able to sit close to the learner under study and because most of the utterances produced were short and easily noted down. However, a major disadvantage of this method is that it does not allow researchers access to the surrounding discourse in which specific utterances were produced, thus making it impossible to examine the role of input and interaction in learners' use of the L2. Also, of course, there is a danger that what is said will not be accurately recorded and the method will not work well when learners produce longer turns. Given the importance now attached to the role of the interactional context in shaping L2 use and acquisition, the pencil-and-paper method is clearly disadvantaged.

Audio recording is now widely used in sampling naturally occurring language use. The main disadvantage is that the presence of a cassette recorder may induce self-consciousness in learners' speech, thus making it less likely that the resulting samples will reflect their vernacular style. However, participants are likely to forget the presence of the recorder after a while and behave naturally. Another disadvantage is the one referred to in the paragraph above—the difficulty of obtaining clear recordings in 'noisy' environments. This problem can also be overcome through the use of modern clip-on radio microphones. By attaching microphones to all the participants that are the focus of study it is possible to identify both who is speaking and what they say without difficulty. A good example of such a recording method is to be found in Saville-Troike's (1988) study of L2 learners in a kindergarten context. This study was able to obtain clear samples of the learners' private speech (i.e. when they talked to themselves) as well as their social talk. Another possibility is to use mini-disc recorders, which learners carry in their pockets. This provides digital recordings that can be directly entered into a computer program as a sound file for analysis.

Video recording has the obvious advantage of providing detailed visual information relating to the context of an utterance, including important paralinguistic information such as gesture and facial expression (although researchers have not typically made use of such information even when it has been available). However, a video-camera is highly intrusive, especially when it is first introduced. Participants show a high level of awareness of the presence of the camera, often to the point of making it the focus of their attention! Also, video recording suffers from the same problem as traditional audio-recording—it is often difficult to obtain clear samples of speech from all the participants.

Swann (2001) lists the pros and cons of making audio and video recordings. Our own view is that in most situations, audio-recording, especially using radio microphones or mini-disc recorders, is likely to provide the best data. Researchers can also usefully combine a pencil-and-paper record with audio recording. By keeping detailed field notes relating to the situational context of specific speech acts, one of the main disadvantages of audio-recordings can be partially overcome. However, this assumes that the researcher will be physically present when the recording is made and, as we have seen, the researcher's presence can have an effect on the naturalness of the language produced. The researcher, therefore, is faced with a difficult choice: to be present in order to collect detailed background information on what is said or to be absent in order to avoid contaminating the samples recorded. On balance it is probably better to opt for the former.

Recorded data needs to be transcribed before analysis can take place. A first decision concerns whether to describe all the data or just extracts. This will depend on the research question. If this concerns some particular feature of the spoken interaction (for example, episodes where the participants experience a communication problem) then only extracts relevant to this feature need be transcribed. A second decision concerns which method of transcription to employ. Methods vary according to how 'broad' or 'narrow' they are, with the method chosen reflecting the research purpose. The broadest of transcriptions will simply provide a written record in standard orthography, perhaps noting major pauses. A narrower system will indicate such phenomena as pause length, and simultaneous/overlapping speech. Very narrow systems will employ phonetic notation and/or provide means for indicating a variety of characteristics of speech delivery (for example, intonation, extension of a sound, abrupt halts, emphasis, volume, audible aspirations and inhalations). Schiffrin (1994: 422–33) provides several examples of narrow transcription systems. An example of a relatively broad system of transcription is shown in Table 2.3 below. This was designed to transcribe interactions involving L2 learners in a classroom context. (See Ellis 1984b.) Dubois (1991) discusses a number of design principles for transcription systems. Two of these are 'Make the system accessible' by, for example, ensuring that all the notations are 'motivated' in terms of the purpose of the research, and 'Make representations robust' by, for example, avoiding 'fragile contrasts'. A third decision involves the layout of the transcription. Swann (2001) distinguishes between a 'standard layout', where talk is set out like dialogue in a play, and 'column layout', where each speaker's turns are allocated a separate column. Transcribing data, even using a broad system of notation, is a time-consuming business. A rule of thumb is that it takes seven hours to transcribe one hour of speech with broad transcription and much longer with a narrow transcription. It is important, therefore, to ensure that time is not wasted by including details that are not relevant to the research purpose.

Written samples

Written samples are relatively permanent and, for this reason, easier to collect. In recent years there have been large-scale projects of learner language based on written samples and motivated by the availability of

1 The teacher's or researcher's utterances are given on the left-hand side of the page.
2 The pupil's utterances are given on the right-hand side.
3 T = teacher; R = researcher; pupils are designated by their initials.
4 Each utterance is numbered for ease of reference. An 'utterance' consists of a single tone unit except where two tone units are syntactically joined by means of a subordinator or other linking word or contrastive stress has been used to make what would 'normally' be a single tone unit into more than one.
5 Pauses are indicated in brackets;
(.) indicates a pause of a second or shorter
(.3.) indicates the length of a pause beyond one second (e.g. (.3.))
6 XXX is used to indicate speech that could not be deciphered.
7 Phonetic transcription (IPA) is used when the pupil's pronunciation is markedly different from the teacher's pronunciation and also when it was not possible to identify the English word the pupils were using.
8 ... Indicates an incomplete utterance.
9 Words are underlined to show:
–overlapping speech between two speakers
–a very heavily stressed word
10 A limited amount of contextual information is given in brackets.

Table 2.3 Example of a transcription system (Ellis 1984a: 230)

computer-based concordancing tools for analysing the samples.[6] One of the best known of these projects is the International Corpus of Learner English (ICLE) (Granger 1998a). The ICLE is a computerized corpus of argumentative essays on different topics written by advanced learners of English (i.e. university students of English in their second or third years). It is made up of a set of sub-corpora from learners with different L1 backgrounds, including Asian languages (Chinese and Japanese) and European languages (for example, French and Russian). The decisions taken in putting together the sub-corpora (see Chapter 14) are indicative of the issues that need to be considered when collecting written sub-samples of learner language. Another project based on an extensive sample of university-level academic essays can be found in Hinkel (2002).

A key decision concerns the genre to be sampled. In the case of the ICLE only argumentative essays were collected. The choice of genre is likely to influence both the macro- and micro-linguistic characteristics of the samples. Another key decision concerns the conditions under which the written samples are produced. Two conditions are especially important; (1) whether the written sample is timed or untimed and (2) whether the learners have access to reference tools such as dictionaries and grammars while they write. The Swedish component of the ICLE consists of both untimed and timed essays.[7] However, as in the untimed condition learners had access to reference tools while in the timed condition they did not, it is not possible to determine whether any differences in the two types of sample were the product of the pressure to write or of the use of the reference tools. Further, the timed essays were produced in the context of an examination and this may also have had an effect on the written products. However, while ideally samples need to be collected systematically to enable the effects of specific variables to be investigated, it must be acknowledged that this is not always possible when the samples are 'natural' (i.e. being produced for some real-life purpose rather than for purposes of research).

As the ICLE demonstrates, an obvious source of 'natural' written samples is essays produced in an examination.[8] An important issue here is the nature of the prompt used in the examination question. Brown, Hilgers, and Marsella (1991), for example, show that the prompt can have a major impact on learners' essays. They compared the effects of two kinds of prompt. One called for an analytic essay after students had read one and a half pages of prose. The other asked them to write an essay based primarily on their personal experience. This study found a statistically significant and substantial difference in the ratings of the essays produced under these two types of prompt, indicating that the examination tasks were of varying difficulty. Interestingly, this study did not find any effect for topic the learners were asked to write about.

This discussion of the various factors that impact on the linguistic characteristics of written samples points, once again, to the need to provide careful descriptions of the data that have been collected. Such descriptions should minimally provide information about (1) the learners' social and situational background, (2) the situational context in which the writing took place, (3) the genre, (4) the topics, (5) timing and (6) availability of reference tools.

Clinically elicited samples

As described above, clinically elicited samples of learner language differ from naturally occurring samples in that they are collected specifically for the purpose of research. It is important to distinguish two broad types of clinically elicited data depending on whether the researcher's goal is to collect a *general* sample of learner language or a *focused* sample. In the case of a general sample, the elicitation instrument is designed to provide a context for learners to speak or write in the L2 in a purposeful manner. In the case of a focused sample, the elicitation instrument is designed to induce learners to use some specific linguistic feature when speaking or writing. In the case of a general sample, then, there is no attempt to pre-determine what linguistic forms the learners will use whereas in a focused sample there is. A clinically elicited focused sample, however, must still be distinguished from an experimentally elicited sample. While both clinically elicited, focused samples and experimentally elicited ones attempt to elicit specific linguistic features for study, a clinically elicited, focused sample requires learners to be oriented primarily to message conveyance (i.e. fluency), while an experimentally elicited sample involves a primary orientation to form (i.e. accuracy). This is an important distinction as the learner's orientation to the elicitation task can have a profound effect on the language used. (See, for example, Larsen-Freeman 1976; Tarone 1988.)

Eliciting general samples

There are a number of different types of instrument that have been used to elicit general samples of learner language. These all involve some kind of *task*, defined as follows:

> ... an activity in which: meaning is primary; there is some sort of relationship to the real world; task completion has some priority; and the assessment of task performance is in terms of task outcome. (Skehan 1996a)

Thus a task calls for the use of language to achieve some non-linguistic purpose (for example, making a hotel booking, drawing a diagram, completing a timetable, telling a story). A task can be 'authentic' (i.e. correspond to some real-world activity) or 'pedagogic' (i.e. only be found in an instructional setting). Both kinds of tasks, however, can lay claim to 'some sort of relationship with the real world' in that they involve the kinds of communicative processes involved in the real-world (for example, repairing non- or mis-understanding). Tasks can be used to elicit both oral and written samples.

There is no recognized typology of tasks. Below is an account of some of the tasks commonly used in SLA research. These include both tasks that involve social interaction and result in dialogic discourse (for example, role-plays) and tasks that are performed by individual learners, thus providing samples of monologic discourse (for example, text-reconstruction).

1 *Communicative 'gap' tasks*

One of the most popular ways of eliciting data from learners is the use of communicative tasks that involve some kind of 'gap'. A distinction is often made between information-gap tasks (for example, 'Spot-the-difference', where a participant describes a picture in order to identify how it differs from his/her interlocutor's picture), and opinion-gap tasks (for example, a balloon debate, where participants are given information about four applicants for a job and are asked to decide whom to select). These two task types differ from each other in a number of ways. First, as the labels suggest, information-gap tasks involve an exchange of information, while opinion-gap tasks involve learners going beyond the information given by supplying their own ideas. Secondly, in an information-gap task the information provided is split (i.e. the learners do not all have the same information) while in an opinion-gap task it is shared. Thirdly, in information-gap tasks information exchange is *required* (that is, learners cannot complete the task unless they exchange the information) whereas in opinion-gap tasks it is *optional*. Information-gap tasks can also be distinguished according to whether they involve one-way or two-way communication between participants. In one-way tasks only one of the participants speaks, whereas in two-way tasks the information is divided among the participants, so they all must speak. Communicative tasks can also vary according to whether they require a closed solution (i.e. the task has a single 'correct' solution), or open solutions (i.e. ones permitting a number of possible solutions). In the case of tasks with open solutions, there are those where the participants are required to converge on a single solution, and others where they are allowed to diverge. While communicative tasks have figured strongly in SLA as a data collection method for some time, especially in research directed at investigating the role of interaction and input in L2 acquisition (see, for example, Pica, Kanagy, and Falodun 1993), they have more recently become objects of enquiry in their own right (see Skehan 1998b). That is, researchers have become interested in how the kinds of task variables referred to above influence learner production. (See Ellis 2003a.)

2 *Open role plays*

An open role play consists of (1) information about a particular situation, (2) role-play cards which specify in broad terms the participants' relationship and their purpose for communicating with each other. However, in an open role play the participants are not instructed to achieve a specific outcome nor are they told how they are to achieve their communicative purposes. This creates a space for the learners to negotiate and thus helps to foster interaction that is 'real'. Role plays are commonly used by researchers who wish to investigate pragmatic aspects of learner language (for example, how learners perform speech acts such as requests or apologies when speaking to different addressees). The advantage, as Kasper and Dahl (1991: 228–9) point out, is that they enable learner language to be studied in its full discourse context:

> The intriguing potential of open role-plays for the study of IL pragmatics is that they allow us to observe how speech act performance is sequentially organized (i.e. in terms of strategy choice and politeness investment), what kinds of interlocutor responses are elicited by specific strategic choices, and how such responses in turn determine the speaker's next move.

Kasper and Dahl note that in these respects open role-plays provide samples of authentic conversation. However, a word of caution is in order. All clinical-elicitation tasks are likely to induce some degree of consciousness about linguistic choice but, because role-plays place learners in imaginary situations, they may make them especially sensitive to social variables and thus induce a particularly high level of linguistic consciousness.

3 *Text reconstruction tasks*

In a text reconstruction task learners listen to or read a text. This is then removed and the learners are asked to reconstruct the text in their own words. The assumption underlying this task is that in processing a text for meaning learners store the propositional content but not the linguistic forms used to encode the content. Thus, when asked to reconstruct the text, they are forced to draw on their own linguistic resources. Text-reconstruction tasks can be used to elicit different genres. They have been frequently used to elicit oral and written narrative (for example, Dechert 1983). By selecting texts that exemplify different genres it is possible to carry out comparative studies of how learners handle these genres (for example, Lantolf and Appel 1994).

4 *Picture composition tasks*

A popular means of eliciting learner production is to use a picture composition or a short video film. This, like a reproduction task, can be used to investigate oral or written narratives. The basic procedure is to show the learners the picture composition/video and then ask them to retell the story in their own words, either in writing or orally. However, there are a number of options available to the researcher. Skehan and Foster (1999), for example, compared learner production in a watch-and-tell condition (i.e. the subjects had to simultaneously watch a Mr Bean video and speak) and a 'watch-then-tell' condition (i.e. they told the story after they had finished watching the video). Other options include jumbling the pictures and asking learners to describe each picture first before they tell the complete story and, in the watch-then-tell condition, removing the pictures or allowing participants to continue to view them as they speak/write.

5 *Oral interviews*

Interviewing learners provides an obvious means of obtaining samples of learner language. A key issue here is the 'interactional authenticity' of the data so collected. Oral interviews carried out between a distant researcher and a learner are essentially no different in this respect from the Oral Proficiency Interview (OPI) used to measure L2 proficiency. Regarding the discourse that results from the OPI, Van Lier (1989) rightly posed the question 'Is it really a conversation?'. Davies (1978) argued that interactional authenticity in any test situation is a chimera, while He and Young (1998: 8) point out 'LPIs (language proficiency interviews) do not simply sample an ability that exists in the learner prior to the interview; rather they actually produce or fabricate the abilities they supposedly measure'. Thus there are obvious dangers in using interviews to obtain data. However, an interview can become a conversation with a resulting shift in the language produced. Lantolf and Ahmed (1989), for example, found that the learner they investigated redefined an interview as a conversation by engaging the interviewer in an ad hoc discussion of the differences between Islam and

Christianity. Also, this is a problem that arguably applies to all the data elicitation methods described above. Indeed, it is implicit in the very idea of trying to 'elicit' samples of learner language, as Figure 2.1 makes clear. An obvious advantage of an interview is that it can double up as a way of obtaining content information about learners (for example, regarding their language learning history, their beliefs about language learning or their relationships with the target language community) as well as samples of learner language providing, of course, the L2 serves as the medium of communication during the interview.

Eliciting focused samples

The same instruments used to elicit general samples of learner language can be used to elicit focused samples. For example, text reconstruction tasks can be designed to provide learners with opportunities to use specific structures. Wajnryb (1990) describes an activity called 'dictogloss'. This involves the use of a short text that contains several exemplars of the target structure. The text is read aloud twice while the learners take notes. The learners then work collaboratively in small groups to reconstruct the text using the notes.

Dictogloss is an example of a task designed to elicit focused samples; that is, it aims to elicit the specific linguistic feature that is the target of the investigation. Thus, if the target was a specific speech act (say, apologies), we could design a role-play task that required learners to express this speech act. Or, if the target was passive verb constructions, we could design a picture-composition task that depicted the stages in the process of manufacturing some product, such as glass or paper. There is, however, a major problem—learners are adept at avoiding the use of linguistic features they find difficult. For example, Kowal and Swain (1997) report that in completing a dictogloss task learners 'go beyond the assigned grammatical feature' and 'follow their own agenda'. No matter how much care is taken in designing a task, it is difficult to ensure that learners will in fact attempt to use it or, if they do, to do so frequently.

In an attempt to deal with this problem, Loschky and Bley-Vroman (1993) distinguish three degrees of involvement of a targeted feature in a task: task-naturalness, task-utility and task-essentialness. In the case of task-naturalness, the task is such that it affords opportunities for frequent use of the targeted feature. They give the example of an information-gap task involving the exchange of information about a travel itinerary which creates a context for the natural use of the present simple to express planned future actions (for example, 'You leave Honolulu at 7.10 and arrive in Los Angeles at 2.30'). Of course, the use of the present tense is not obligatory in such a task as future actions can also be expressed by mean of the 'will' or going to' forms. A step up from task-naturalness is task-utility. Here it is not only 'natural' to use the target feature but 'useful', in the sense that its use makes the task easier to perform. Loschky and Bley-Vroman give the example of a 'Spot-the-difference' task that was designed to elicit the use of a range of locational prepositions. They point out that the task can be performed by means of a single preposition ('at') but that the likelihood of performing it successfully increases if learners use a full range of locatives (for example, 'on top of' and 'underneath'). They comment 'the challenge ... is to create tasks in which the utility of the targeted structure is so clear that the learners naturally attend to that structure' (1993: 138). Task-essentialness requires that the task is constructed in such a way that it can only be accomplished if learners use the target feature. 'Essentialness' refers both to the idea that the use of the target structure is necessary for performing the task successfully and also to the idea that it is the 'essence' of what learners must attend to. However, the example that Loschky and Bley-Vroman provide involves sentence-comprehension rather than language production and, in fact, involves tapping learner intuitions using a picture-matching task. (See Loshcky and Bley-Vroman 1993: 164.) They admit that in order to achieve task-essentialness it is necessary to exercise more control over the discourse. In effect, task-essentialness can only be achieved by means of experimental elicitation, not through clinical elicitation.

In practice, then, the clinical elicitation of focused samples is dependent on achieving task-naturalness or task-utility. For this reason, researchers run the risk that whatever instrument they use, they will fail to tap the target structure. There are, however, ways of safeguarding against such failure. The most obvious is always to pilot the instrument on native speakers and learners drawn from the same population as the one being investigated. If the native speakers use the target feature but the learners do not, the task is arguably serving a useful purpose as it provides evidence of a gap in the learners' competence. If the learners use the target feature but the native speakers fail to do so, it may be because the learners' orientation is one of display rather than communication. This casts doubt on the validity of the task. Another solution to the problem is to choose a target feature for which obligatory occasions for its use are bound to be created (i.e. they are unavoidable). Examples of such target features are articles in English or *wa/ga* in Japanese. Learners may fail to use these structures when they perform the task but it is very unlikely that they will avoid creating linguistic contexts in which such features are required. This solution, however, is of limited applicability, as without resorting to experimental elicitation, it is only possible to create obligatory linguistic contexts for a relatively small number of features.

The clinical elicitation of learner language is of central importance in SLA research. While it cannot be claimed that data so collected are entirely 'natural', it can be argued that they reflect an essential quality of naturally-occurring data in that they demonstrate how learners use the L2 when they are primarily engaged in message construction. In other words, clinically elicited data can claim to have psycholinguistic validity. Of course, this does not mean that there is no attention to form, as this arises in natural communication, but that attention to form is subservient to the communicative purpose. The obvious advantages of clinical elicitation are that it makes the process of collecting 'good' data practical and less arduous, it affords a ready way of gathering data, and it can, through focused elicitation tasks, provide data relating to specific linguistic features. The choice of instrument will depend on the research purpose. Thus, for example, open role-plays serve as the obvious means for obtaining data to investigate pragmatic aspects of interlanguage, information-gap tasks are ideal for examining the conversational strategies that learners and their interlocutors employ, while picture composition tasks are well-suited to examining fluency in oral language use. Despite the difficulty of collecting samples focused on specific linguistic features by means of clinical elicitation it is important that researchers make the effort, perhaps as a way of judging the validity of samples derived from experimental elicitation.

Experimentally elicited samples

Experimental elicitation involves an attempt to elicit a specific, predetermined linguistic feature in learners' production. It results in a 'constrained constructed response' (Norris and Ortega 2001), i.e. the production of short L2 segments (ranging from a single word up to a full sentence) within highly controlled linguistic contexts. Constrained constructed responses contrast with the 'free constructed responses' obtained through clinical elicitation. In the case of many linguistic features, experimental elicitation may serve as the only way of obtaining sufficient data. However, as we noted previously, experimental elicitation may only tell us what learners can produce under conditions of experimental elicitation and may or may not reflect what they can do under more natural conditions of language use.

The key issue, then, is the validity of experimentally elicited data. On this point there is considerable disagreement. On the one hand there are researchers like Naiman (1974) who argue that such data are valid because they closely match naturally occurring language use. On the other hand, there is ample evidence to suggest that this is not always the case. Schumann (1978) for example found that the learner he investigated (Alberto) produced markedly different types of negative utterances in free speech and elicited data, as shown in Table 2.4. Thus in his spontaneous speech, Alberto typically employed the *no* + verb construction whereas in the data elicited by means of a sentence-transformation test he typically employed '*don't* + verb'. Burmeister and Ufert (1980) carried out careful comparison of data collected from different sources (spontaneous speech and translation tasks) and reported a number of differences. The most worrying of these was that quite a number of non-target like structures that never or rarely occurred in the spontaneous speech were frequent in the elicited data.

Spontaneous utterances	Elicited data
I no understand this question	SHE WANTS SOME DINNER
You after no talk nothing English	She don't want some dinner
	SHE SAW HIM
I no can	She don't saw him
You no like Coca-Cola?	THE BABY IS CRYING
	The baby is don't crying
	THE DOG CAN BARK
	The dog don't can bark

Table 2.4 Samples of spontaneous and elicited language use compared

They suggest that this may reflect the fact that the learners were being pushed to produce structures that were beyond their linguistic resources.

It is helpful to distinguish two broad types of experimental elicitation that differ in the degree to which the learner's response is constrained. The first type consists of 'discrete point tests' where learners are not expected to provide any language of their own or, at most, a single word. The second type consists of 'prompts' where learners are provided with some stimulus, such as the beginning of a sentence, and use it to produce a complete sentence. If, in Figure 2.1, one takes 'spontaneous utterances' and 'elicited data' as being the two end points of a continuum of control, 'discrete point tests' result in language use that lies more or less at the 'close control' end of the continuum, while 'prompts' elicit language closer to the middle of the continuum. Prompts can still be distinguished from focused tasks involved in clinical elicitation, however, in that the learners' responses are still highly constrained (i.e. are no longer than a sentence). It seems reasonable to assume that prompts run less of a risk of eliciting artificial interlanguage forms.

Discrete point tests

Discrete point tests can utilize a number of different formats and procedures:

1 *Traditional language exercise formats*
There are a variety of testing formats that allow for learners to select from choices provided (for example, multiple-choice grammar questions). These measure learners' ability to identify which linguistic form is required in a specific context but do not require them to produce them and, therefore, will not concern us here. Discrete point tests for eliciting production of L2 forms utilize the same formats as traditional language exercises. They include fill-in-the-blanks (where the lexical item to be used may or may not be provided), sentence transformation (as illustrated in Table 2.4 above),

sentence joining, and item replacement (where replacing a given item requires a further grammatical change in the sentence). Rivers and Temperley (1978) provide a comprehensive description of these formats.

2 *Cloze procedure*
Cloze procedure was developed as a technique for measuring reading comprehension. In a standard cloze, words are removed systematically from a passage (for example, each seventh word is blanked) and learners asked to complete the passage by supplying the missing words. When used as a tool for experimental elicitation a 'doctored cloze' is required. That is, only words relating to the linguistic feature to be investigated are deleted. For example, if the target feature is 'plural nouns', then all the plural nouns in the passage are removed. A doctored cloze test has some obvious advantages over a traditional language exercise format—it ensures a full discourse context for the feature under study and it removes the need to contrive test items as passages can be taken from genuine texts. However, it is only effective with those linguistic features that occur frequently in such texts (for example, articles, past tense verbs, subject-verb agreement) and cannot be used to investigate features that typically only occur sporadically (for example, relative clauses, verb complements, participial phrases).

3 *Elicited imitation*
One device that has been widely used in SLA is elicited imitation. Learners listen to a set of sentences one at a time, the sentences having been constructed to contain examples of the target feature. After each sentence they try to imitate it. The idea underlying this procedure is that if the sentences are long enough (Naiman 1974 suggests fifteen syllables but this is likely to depend on the general L2 proficiency of the learners being tested) the learners will not be able to memorize the exact words in the sentence but will have to process it for meaning and thus, when called upon to imitate it, will need to re-encode the meaning using their own linguistic resources. As Larsen-Freeman and Long (1991: 28) note, 'comparable performances between elicited imitation and spontaneous production have been reported'. Ellis (2005) describes an elicited imitation test that incorporated a dual purpose to distract learners from attempting to memorize the sentences prior to production; the sentences to be imitated consisted of belief statements to which learners were asked to respond by agreeing/disagreeing before they attempted to imitate them.

4 *Elicited translation*
Analogous to elicited imitation is elicited translation. (See Swain, Naiman, and Dumas 1974 for a detailed account.) Learners listen (or read) a sentence in the L1 and are asked to translate it into the L2 (orally or in writing). The danger of this device is that it leads to extensive L1 transfer when, in more natural language use, this would not occur. (See, for example, Burmeister and Ufert 1980; Lococo 1976.)

Prompts

1 *Sentence completion*
Sentence completion has been widely used in SLA research. Learners are given the beginning of a sentence (orally or in writing) and asked to complete it. The prompt is constructed in such a way as to elicit the feature that is being targeted. The prompt can also be accompanied by a picture to show the learners what meaning they must encode when they complete the sentence. Han (1996) used prompts with pictures to elicit different kinds of verb complements. For example, to elicit the use of 'stealing', the learners were given a sentence beginning 'I caught him ....' and shown a picture of a hand restraining another hand that was taking some money from a box. It is interesting to compare Han's instrument with that used by Richards (1980) to elicit the same structure. Richards gave learners the beginning of a sentence and the verb they would need to complete it. This is more like a 'discrete point test' than a 'prompt', as the learners did not have to use their own linguistic resources to complete the sentence. Arguably, a test such as Richards' is more likely to encourage learners to pay close attention to the target form in production than the kind of prompt used by Han.

2 *Discourse completion*
Discourse completion has also been widely used in SLA research, to investigate pragmatic aspects of learner language (for example, the performance of illocutionary acts such as requests and apologies). An example is provided in Table 2.5. Learners are asked to read a description of a situation followed by a short dialogue with an empty slot. They then fill in the missing speech act. The advantage of discourse completion is that it allows the researcher to investigate the effects of such factors as social distance and social power in a highly systematic fashion by manipulating factors in the situation, in particular the identity of the speakers. Kasper and Dahl (1991) provide a review of SLA studies that have employed this method of data collection.

Read the description and dialogue that follows. One turn is missing from the dialogue.
Fill in the missing turn.

In the lobby of the university library.
Jim and Charlie have agreed to meet at six o'clock to work on a joint project.
Charlie arrives on time and Jim is half an hour late.
Charlie: I almost gave up on you!
Jim:____________
Charlie: O.K. Let's start working.

Table 2.5 Example of an item from a discourse completion test (Blum-Kulka, House, and Kasper 1989: 274)

Rose and Kasper (2001) offer a collection of reports of empirical studies, several of which made use of it to collect data.

3 *Question-and-answer*
Questions can also be used to elicit specific linguistic forms. In this case, care must be taken not to model the form under study in the question so that learners cannot just 'borrow' it in when producing their answer. As with sentence completion, question-and-answer prompts can also utilize pictures. In the Bilingual Syntax Measure (Burt, Dulay, and Hernandez-Chavez 1973) learners are shown a picture and asked a question about it. This instrument has been used to collect data to investigate the accuracy with which learners perform a number of different grammatical morphemes in English. (See Chapter 3.) Rose (2000) designed a set of cartoon pictures to elicit requests, apologies and compliment responses. In this case, each cartoon had a brief caption describing it. Learners were asked to look at the picture and answer the question 'What do you think Siu Keung [the character shown in the cartoon] would say?' They were also given the chance to opt out (i.e. to say nothing). The data was used to investigate the range of pragmalinguistic devices used by different groups of Chinese learners.

In the case of both discrete point tests and prompts a key procedural issue is whether the learners' responses to the stimulus provided are oral or written and whether they are speeded or unspeeded. In Han's study, for example, the learners were given a fixed time to produce oral responses (6 seconds) while in many studies (for example, Rose 2000) production was unpressured. When given plenty of time to produce a response, learners are able to plan carefully and also pre-monitor their output. This enables them to search their linguistic resources thoroughly and access declarative knowledge of L2 forms. In contrast, when required to respond more immediately learners are forced to rely on proceduralized knowledge (i.e. L2 knowledge that is accessible for automatic processing). There is ample evidence to demonstrate the effect of planning on language production (Ortega 1999). Given that natural language use typically relies on L2 knowledge that has been proceduralized, it can be argued that samples obtained from speeded experimental elicitation are more likely to match those obtained naturally. However, this remains to be demonstrated.

Verbal-report data

In the preceding sections we have examined the different ways in which researchers can obtain samples of learner language in order to investigate different aspects of L2 acquisition. These samples, as we noted earlier, serve principally to provide descriptions of learners' interlanguages. In this section we turn to the last way of collecting data from learners, by means of verbal reports. We note again that the instruments to be discussed can serve a double purpose in providing samples of learner language (as long as the learners' responses are in the L2 and not their L1) and important information about what Grotjahn (1991) calls learners' 'subjective theories',[9] which can assist in providing explanations of L2 acquisition. It should be noted, however, that there is some disagreement over the validity of verbal reports; some researchers such as Seliger (1984) argue that much of language learning is unconscious and thus not reportable by learners.

Grotjahn lists the various methods used to investigate learners' subjective theories. These include interviews, think-aloud tasks, retrospective accounts, diaries, and questionnaires. In essence these all involve some kind of 'verbal report' and, following Cohen (1987) can be divided into 'self-report', 'self-observation' and 'self-revelation'. We will add a fourth type: 'self-assessment'.

Self-report

Cohen defines self-reports as 'learner's descriptions of what they do characterized by generalized statements about learning behaviour... or labels they apply to themselves' (1987: 84). He notes that such statements 'are based on beliefs or concepts that learners have about the way they learn language, and are often not based on the observation of any specific event'. In this book, we will also be concerned with learners' statements about the power relations that hold between themselves and the target language community. Here we will consider briefly three of the most common methods used to obtain self-reports from learners.

1 *Questionnaires*

Questionnaires consist of sets of questions, which can either be 'open' or 'closed' or a mixture of the two. Open questions require learners to write out their answers while closed questions can be answered by selecting from the choices provided. Closed questions often make use of a Likert scale: a statement followed by a set of choices arranged on a scale, as in the example from Oxford (1990) shown in Table 2.6:

---

1 Never or almost never true of me.
2 Usually not true of me.
3 Somewhat true of me.
4 Usually true of me.
5 Always true of me.

Read the item, and choose a response (1 through 5 above), and write it in the space after the item.

I actively seek out opportunities to talk with native speakers of English. ___________

Table 2.6 Example of a Likert scale questionnaire item (Oxford 1990)

An alternative to using a Likert Scale is to ask learners to rank order statements or to make a series of paired comparisons. Open questions typically supply rich information which can, however, be hard to analyse. Closed questions are restrictive but are easier to analyse. Respondents to questionnaires have indicated that they like to have at least some open questions.

Questionnaires are used in survey research to collect verbal reports from large numbers of learners. Questionnaires can be self-administered, as when they are mailed-out, or group-administered, as when they are completed by a ready-formed group of learners at the same time and in the same place. Group-administration is generally to be preferred as it guarantees a high return rate. Furthermore, the researcher administering the questionnaire can provide clarification when needed and the researcher knows the conditions under which the questionnaire was completed.

Designing and administering questionnaires requires considerable expertise. Baker (1997), Brown (2001) and Dornyei (2003) provide useful advice about how to proceed. Table 2.7 below summarizes the main steps involved in questionnaire design and provides a brief description of each step.

2 *Interviews*

Interviews collect data by means of questions that require an oral response from learners. Interviews can be 'structured' (i.e. all the questions are carefully planned and sequenced in advance) or 'unstructured' (i.e. only a few general questions are planned in advance, with additional questions being asked as a reaction to the learner's responses). The extent to which an interview is structured/unstructured is, of course, a matter of degree. A good example of a structured interview can be found in Naiman *et al.'s* (1978) study of 'good language learners'. The interview consisted of two parts. In the first part learners were asked about their own personal language learning experience (for example, 'When did you start and how long did you learn?'). In the second part they were asked more specific questions relating to how they learned a second language (for example, 'Beginning now with the *early* stages of language learning, what would you *mainly* like to do at that level?'). To allow for some flexibility, there are sets of 'subquestions' that could be asked if appropriate. A good example of the use of unstructured interviews can be found in Norton's (2000) study of adult immigrant female learners in Canada.

Interviews are generally conducted individually but they can also be carried out in groups (for example, using focus groups). Individual and group interviews are usually conducted face-to-face but individual interviews can also be carried out over the telephone, through chat-rooms on the internet or via email. Interviewing is a skill. Converse and Schumann (1974) provide a useful account of the strategies a 'good interviewer' needs to use. Brown (2001) also provides helpful information about how to conduct an interview.

Steps	Description
1 Analysing the topic to be investigated.	This involves listing the aspect/ dimensions of the research topic. It serves to determine what is to be measured and contributes to establishing the construct validity of the questionnaire. The aspects/dimensions need to be identified with reference to the following sources of information: – previous research (including previous instruments used to investigate the topic) – exploratory questionnaires and interviews with participants – personal experience
2 Developing the questions	This involves: – deciding what type of questions to include – brainstorming a set of questions – giving the questions to expert judges to determine which questions best address each aspect/dimension of the topic. – selecting the questions
3 Preparing the questionnaire	The questionnaire will generally consist of: – a face-sheet (asking participants to provide general background information about themselves—see Table 2.1) – clear instructions about how to answer the questions – the questions (with spaces for the participants' answers)
4 Piloting the questionnaire	The questionnaire needs to be piloted on a sample of the target population. If possible the questionnaire should be administered twice to the same sample to enable test-retest reliability to be calculated.
5 Analysing the results of the pilot questionnaire	Various statistical procedures are available for investigating the validity of the questionnaire: – item analysis to establish the discriminatory power of the items

Table 2.7 (continued)

	– Cronbach alpha to provide a split-half measure of reliability – Pearson correlation to examine test-retest reliability – Factor analyses to establish construct validity
6 Revising the questionnaire	The results of step 5 are used to make revisions to the questionnaire.

Table 2.7 Designing a questionnaire

3 *Personal learning histories*

A personal learning history is a learner's narrative account of learning an L2 over time. Thus, like diaries (discussed below), they constitute a non-interactive method of collecting verbal reports. However, whereas diaries elicit reports on events that have occurred recently, personal learning histories involve reports on non-proximate events. In this respect they resemble questionnaires and interviews. Personal learning histories can be voluntary, as in the case of Hoffman's (1989) *Lost in Translation*, where the author describes her experiences of moving from Poland to Canada at the age of fourteen and her attempts to master English. Alternatively they can be elicited as in Schumann (1997). As part of a course in SLA, Schumann asked his students to write five-page autobiographical accounts of their language learning. Later in the course, as a final project, he asked them to write a second time about their personal learning experiences but this time to analyse them from a particular theoretical perspective (stimulus-appraisal).

Self-observation

Cohen (1987: 84) describes self-observation as involving 'the inspection of specific behaviour, either while the information is still in short-term memory, i.e. introspectively, or after the event, i.e. retrospectively'. The retrospection can be relatively immediate (i.e. within a day) or delayed. What distinguishes self-observation from self-report is the recency and specificity of the events under consideration. The two main methods of collecting self-observation data are diary studies and stimulated recall.

1 *Diaries*

In a diary study learners are asked to keep journals recording their progress in learning an L2. Diaries differ from questionnaires and interviews in that the data collection does not generally involve learners responding to a researcher's questions.[10] Thus, what learners choose to comment on depends to a much greater extent on them. However, like questionnaires and interviews, diaries can be more or less structured. That is, learners can be given a very general instruction (for example, 'Please write something every day about your experiences in learning English.') or much more specific instructions. Ellis and Rathbone (1987) listed the kinds of topics they were interested in the learners commenting on and also gave examples, taken from other diaries, of the kinds of comment they were looking for. For example, among other topics, students were invited to comment on their feelings about other students and were given this extract as an illustration:

> I am probably the second lowest in the class right now (next to the man who must pass the ETS test). The girl who has been in France seems to think she's too good for the rest of us, but she didn't do all that well today.

Such guidance is helpful in that it can ensure the diary contains data on topics of interest to the researcher but it is also dangerous as it can induce learners to make comments that otherwise would not have occurred to them. Diaries have been widely used in SLA, proving especially useful in investigating affective variables such as anxiety. (See Bailey 1991; Schumann 1997.)

2 *Stimulated recall*

Stimulated recall is an introspective method used to prompt learners to comment on the thoughts and feelings they had while participating in a specific learning event. The aim is to identify the cognitive processes, such as learning strategies, involved in language learning that are not evident through observation. One of the simplest ways of conducting stimulus recall is to stop learners while they are performing a task and ask them to note down what they are thinking about at that moment or what caused them to produce a particular utterance (Cohen 1987). A more common method is to replay a video of learners as they engaged in a learning-teaching event, stopping it at particular points to ask the learners to comment. For example, Mackey, Gass, and McDonough (2000) used video-playbacks to obtain comments from learners on what they noticed about the feedback they had received on utterances produced while performing a communicative task. The instruments used to elicit recall can vary from the completely open (for example, 'What were you thinking here?') to the highly structured (for example, using multiple-choice questions). Gass and Mackey (2000) provide a full and lucid account of the various procedures available for conducting stimulus-recall.

Self-revelation using think-aloud

Self-revelation entails a verbal report made while the learner is still engaged in a teaching-learning event. The report, therefore, is concurrent with the event. As Cohen (1987: 84) points out, it involves 'think-aloud stream-of-consciousness disclosure of thought processes while the information is being attended to'. The theoretical basis of this method is provided by information-processing models, which claim that information recently attended to is kept in short-term memory (STM) and thus is available for reporting. As Ericsson and Simon (1987: 32) point out, a crucial assumption is that 'the information contained in attention and STM remains the same with the verbal report procedure as it would be without the reporting procedure'. In other words, it is assumed that asking learners to comment on their thought processes while performing a task does not affect how they actually perform the task. This assumption has been challenged by some researchers, however. Smagorinsky (1998), for example, argues that verbal reports can change the very process they seek to uncover given that speech activity itself is a powerful way of organizing cognition. More recently Swain and her co-researchers (for example, Swain and Lapkin 2002) have begun to uncover evidence in L2 research that thinking aloud does frequently become a learning process.

Faerch and Kasper (1987), Ericsson and Simon (1987), and Brown and Rodgers (2002: Chapter 3) provide clear accounts of the procedures to be followed for collecting think-aloud reports. The procedure involves providing pre-task training, clear instructions that must emphasize the importance of 'trying to think aloud' rather than offering post-event explanations, a warm-up period where learners can practise thinking aloud before recording starts and the use of reminders to keep speaking when learners lapse into silence.

Clearly, self-revelation using think-aloud is only suited to teaching–learning events where the act of speaking one's thoughts aloud will not unduly interrupt performance of the event itself. In SLA research, it has been primarily used in writing tasks as writing allows for 'dual-tasking'. A good example of the use of think-aloud can be found in Cumming's (1990) study of the writing strategies used by L2 writers with different levels of L2 proficiency and differing L1 writing abilities. Retrospective methods involving self-reports or self-observations are better suited to studying learners' performance of oral tasks.

Self-assessment

This involves asking learners to report on their own knowledge of the L2. A good example is to be found in Paribakht and Wesche's (1999) instrument for eliciting learners' self-assessments of their lexical knowledge. The crucial issue regarding self-assessment is its validity. A number of studies have investigated this. For example, Bachman (1990: 148) refers to two studies showing that the manner in which the self-rating questions are framed affects the test-takers' responses. Questions that refer to the test-takers' language use, needs, and situations as opposed to abstract linguistic abilities and questions, serve as better indicators of language proficiency. So, too, do questions that ask them to judge how difficult they find different aspects of language use as opposed to how well they can use the language. Oscarson (1997: 182), in a review of such studies, concludes that 'although no consensus has been reached on the merits of the self-assessment approach, a clear majority of the studies surveyed report generally favourable results'.

The methods of data collection described in this section are being increasingly used in SLA research. (See Gass and Mackey 2000: Table 5.1.) They have been used to investigate a variety of topics including learners' general learning and communication strategies, how learners cope with specific communication problems, how they handle unknown words in a reading passage, what forms they notice in the input, aspects of the composing process, what they do during pre-task planning, use of the L1, interlanguage pragmatics, learner attitudes to the L2 and the target language community and affective factors such as anxiety and motivation.

In conclusion, two points about the use of self-reports in SLA will be emphasized. First, it is vital that the instruments and procedures used to collect self-report data are chosen or developed with due regard to both their theoretical underpinnings and also the accumulated wisdom of researchers who have utilized this approach. In this respect handbooks such as Brown (2001), Brown and Rodgers (2002) and Gass and Mackey (2000) should be referred to because they provide concrete guidelines about how to proceed. Secondly, because of the doubts that exist about the validity and reliability of self-report methods, it is advisable to combine two or more self-report methods (for example, a combination of questionnaires and in-depth interviews, or of think-aloud and stimulus recall).

Final comment

This chapter has focused on methods of collecting data from L2 learners. It is important to note that for data to be collected it is necessary to obtain the permission of the participants in the research. In this respect most universities now have ethics committees that detail the general principles that researchers should follow. These principles generally include the need to provide an explicit description of what the participants will be required to do, the right of the participants to decline to take part in the research at any time, and the need to ensure confidentiality.

A key theme in the chapter has been the problem of construct validity. In the context of data collection, construct validity refers to the extent to which the data provide information that can shed light on how learners acquire an L2. The validity of a particular data collection method can only be judged with reference to the particular goal a researcher has in mind. Thus, to achieve validity, the researcher must (1) have a clear and explicit goal for the research and (2) ensure that the data collected matches this goal. (1) can be achieved by constructing well-defined research questions. (2), however, is problematic because, as this chapter has been at pains to point out, both learner language and learners' verbal reports are inherently variable—what you see in one data set you do not necessarily see in another, different data set.

Consider again the data shown in Table 2.4. These appear to show that the learner, at the same stage of development, produces negatives in two very different ways depending on whether the data consist of naturally occurring or elicited speech. They constitute a concrete example of what we termed the 'variability problem' in Chapter 1. We are now in a better position to address this problem. One solution rests in the argument that what counts in the study of interlanguage development is learners' procedural knowledge; and this can only be investigated by means of naturally occurring data. As many of the preceding comments in this chapter indicate, we are sympathetic to this position. However, it is probably too extreme and is certainly impractical. Clinically elicited data, we have suggested, can lay claim to psycholinguistic validity in that the conditions of language production (i.e. a primary concern for message conveyance with incidental attention to form) are similar to those found in naturally occurring language use. Also, as we have noted, it is often very difficult to obtain data on specific linguistic features from samples of naturally occurring language. But it follows from this position that experimentally elicited samples are to be treated with circumspection as they involve very different conditions of production—typically, a laboratory-type setting that encourages learners to view language as an object for display rather than as a tool for communication. The second answer, however, adopts a very different position as it treats both sets of data in Table 2.4 as valid. Here, in accordance with Tarone's (1983) idea of 'variable competence', it is argued that naturally occurring data provide information about the learners' vernacular style, while the experimentally elicited data provide information about their careful style. This is a position with which we are also sympathetic. Nor are these positions necessarily in opposition. It is possible to argue that the primary data for studying L2 acquisition are those where learners treat language as a tool for communication but that to study the full extent of learners' L2 knowledge multiple data types are needed.

Clearly, then, what constitutes valid data will depend on one's theoretical position—in this case, how one defines 'competence' and 'acquisition'. The validity of data cannot be evaluated in a theoretical vacuum but only in relation to a clearly articulated theoretical position. Validity is, therefore, largely a relative issue. Nevertheless, two general observations can be made. First, in any study it is necessary to *demonstrate* the validity of the data that have been collected. As Douglas (2001) has pointed out, too many studies simply assume that the data are valid. Where the data consist entirely of experimentally elicited samples this is dangerous and, perhaps, theoretically untenable. For example, does the fact that learners can join two sentences together using relative clauses provide convincing evidence that they have acquired relative clauses? We, and many other researchers, would argue it does not. Second, there is an obvious need to employ multiple data collection methods on the grounds that no one method will provide an entirely valid picture of what a learner knows or thinks. In particular, there is a need to supplement experimentally elicited data with clinically elicited and/or naturally occurring data, or both. It is encouraging to note that many researchers now acknowledge the need for multiple types of data.

These comments have been directed at methods for collecting samples of learner language. However, they apply equally to verbal reports. The validity of a verbal report can only be judged in terms of the particular research question being investigated. Does the data provide an answer to the research question? But it is also necessary to consider the 'trustworthiness' of the data. Can we believe what learners tell us? To address this question, researchers rely on triangulation (i.e. the use of two or more data collection methods in order to search for points of convergence). The aim is to demonstrate convergence in the different data sets. Again, though, the presence of variability in learners' reports need not necessarily constitute evidence that they are untrustworthy as learners' statements about how they learn and what they know are often contradictory and inconsistent. As with samples of learner language, it is for the researcher to demonstrate that any variability in the data is meaningful, not just the product of measurement error. This, of course, is one of the main goals of data analysis, to which we turn in the following chapters.

Notes

1 Whether learners are correct in their judgements in a sentence-matching test is immaterial. The time taken to make a judgement serves as the measure of whether a particular structure is deemed grammatical (and thus part of the learner's interlanguage) or ungrammatical (and thus not part).

2 Gass (1994) reported on the reliability of judgements of English sentences containing relative clauses. She found a much higher level of reliability in the case of sentences where the relative pronoun functioned as subject of its clause than in sentences where it functioned as indirect object. In accordance with the Accessibility Hierarchy, clauses where the subject is relativized can be considered less marked (and therefore easier to acquire and use) than sentences where the indirect object is relativized.

3 In the years 1997 to 2001, *Studies in Second Language Acquisition*, a leading journal in the field of SLA, published eighteen articles that employed some kind of judgement test. Of these only two articles included information about the reliability of the test.

4 Judgement tests elicit a kind of performance. They are not direct measures of competence.

5 Tarone and Liu's (1995) study was actually based on data collected in three different situations: (1) interaction with classroom teachers, (2) interaction with classroom peers, and (3) interaction with the researcher. Table 2.2 specifies the situational variables relating to (3). The study reported qualitative and quantitative differences in the learner's speech in the three situational contexts.

6 Spoken corpora have also been collected (for example, The Louvain International Database of Spoken English Interlanguage (LINDSEI) Project: http://www.fltr.ucl.ac).

7 See http://www.englund.lu.se/research/corpus/corpus/swicle.html.

8 It might be questioned whether samples of written language produced in the context of an examination are 'natural'. We argue they are, on the grounds that an examination constitutes a 'natural' context for learners to use the L2 and that data so obtained have not been designed for purposes of research.

9 Grotjahn (1991: 188) defines 'subjective theories' as follows:
...complex cognitive structures that are highly individual, relatively stable and relatively enduring, and that fulfil the task of explaining and predicting such human phenomena as action, reaction, thinking, emotion, and perception.

10 However, diaries can be 'interactive'. The learner is invited to hand in his/her diary at regular intervals which is then read and reactive comments/questions provided by the researcher/teacher.

3 Error Analysis

Introduction

Error Analysis (EA) consists of a set of procedures for identifying, describing and explaining learner errors. Technically errors can occur in both comprehension and in production but comprehension errors are difficult to detect as it is often impossible to locate the precise linguistic source of an error. Thus, EA is *de facto* the study of the errors that learners make in their speech and writing. *Error evaluation* (EE) is a set of procedures for assessing the relative seriousness of learner errors.

According to Corder (1967), learner errors are significant in three ways: (1) they serve a pedagogic purpose by showing teachers what learners have learned and what they have not yet mastered; (2) they serve a research purpose by providing evidence about how languages are learned; and (3) they serve a learning purpose by acting as devices by which learners can discover the rules of the target language (i.e. by obtaining feedback on their errors). To illuminate (1), it will be necessary to conduct both an EA and an EE. However, (2) and (3) can be achieved by means of EA alone.

Historical background

EA has, perhaps, the longest history of all the methods for analysing learner language to be considered in this book. The study of 'bad language' in the context of native speaker usage can be traced back to the prescriptive grammarians of the 18th century and is reflected in such well-known publications as Fowler's *The King's English* (1906). This early approach to the analysis of errors was essentially proscriptive and prescriptive—it was directed at showing what linguistic forms not to use and which ones to use. It continues today, as illustrated in Howard's *Good English Guide* (1994).

In the context of foreign/second language pedagogy, a number of books detailing 'common errors' have been published. There are dictionaries of general errors (i.e. errors common to learners from different language backgrounds), as for example Fitikides' well-known *Common Mistakes in English* (1936) and Turton and Heaton's *Longman Dictionary of Common Errors* (1996). There are also dictionaries of errors specific to particular groups of learners, as illustrated by Swan and Smith's *Learner English: A Teacher's Guide to Interference and Other Problems* (2001). These books are intended as 'practical reference guides for teachers' (Swan and Smith 2001) and are based on the assumption that teachers can benefit from knowing the likely errors that learners make. It should be noted, however, that whereas few objections are likely to be raised against dictionaries of errors for *foreign* language learners (for example, German learners of L2 English), the compilation of the errors made by *second* language learners (for example, Indian or Nigerian learners of English) is much more controversial if the norms for identifying 'errors' are those of British or American English. This is because 'new Englishes', such as Indian and Nigerian English, have developed their own sets of norms against which, arguably, errors should be identified.

As a research tool for investigating how learners acquire an L2, EA has a much shorter history, dating from the 1960s, when EA was promoted as an alternative (and superior) approach to *contrastive analysis* (CA) for understanding language learning. CA was itself not a method for analysing learner language as it involved contrasting two native-speaker language systems—that of the learner's mother tongue (MT) and that of the target language (TL). It was motivated by the belief that errors were largely the product of negative transfer brought about by linguistic differences between the MT and the TL. CA involved describing comparable features across the two languages, identifying the differences and, then, predicting what errors learners would make. A good example of a CA is Stockwell, Bowen, and Martin's *The Grammatical Structures of English and Spanish* (1965). CA served two major purposes: first it provided an explanation for why learners make errors, and secondly it served as a source of information for identifying which structural areas of the target language teachers needed to teach (i.e. those where negative transfer was likely). In the 1960s, CA came under attack. It was shown, for example, that many of the errors predicted to occur by a CA did not in fact occur and, furthermore, that some errors that were not predicted to occur did occur. On these empirical grounds and also because the theoretical underpinnings of CA in behaviourism were rejected (see Chomsky 1959), researchers began to look for an alternative method for investigating L2 acquisition. The method they initially turned to was EA.

In a series of articles published in the late 1960s and early 1970s (reprinted in Corder 1981), Corder spelt out the theoretical rationale and empirical procedures for carrying out an EA. George's *Common Errors in Language Learning* (1972) offered a model of error production as well as providing an informative account of some of the common types of error made by L2 learners of English (for example, errors in uncountable nouns such as *advice*, in question forms and comparatives). For a while, EA became the primary means of conducting research into L2 acquisition, as reflected in a number of studies of L2 learners such as those published in Richards' *Error Analysis* (1974).

The heyday of EA was short-lived, however, and by the mid-1970s it had begun to give way to other types of analysis of learner language (for example, obligatory occasion analysis—see Chapter 4). Interest in EA in applied linguistics has not faded away entirely, however. Taylor (1988: 162) argued that 'what constitutes significant error is not strictly quantifiable' and proposed a new qualitative approach to examining errors based on 'the interpretative traditions of a humanistic discipline'. Lennon (1991) attempted to show how some of the problems of error identification could be overcome by examining the larger linguistic context in which errors occur (see below). Also, while studies based entirely on EA became less common, EA continued to be used as a tool for measuring accuracy. Bardovi-Harlig and Bofman (1989), for example, used an EA of learners' written compositions to distinguish the kinds of error made by two groups of learners with different levels of overall L2 proficiency. EA is also involved in the calculation of a commonly used measure of accuracy—Error-Free Clauses. (See, for example, Foster and Skehan 1996: 310.) It can be argued, therefore, that EA is still alive and well, even if today it is not perhaps the preferred method of analysis for investigating L2 acquisition. Also, as James (1998) points out, EA figures in other areas of enquiry such as work on mother-tongue literacy and forensic linguistics.

CA also lived on in the form of contrastive rhetoric, defined by Connor (1996: 5) 'as an area of research in second language acquisition that identifies problems in composition encountered by second language writers and, by referring to the rhetorical strategies of the first language, attempts to explain them'. Thus, contrastive rhetoric seeks to describe the typical rhetorical structures in the writing of different languages with a view to showing how they differ and thus how the rhetorical structure of writing in the L1 influences the L2 writer. Contrastive rhetoric, like classical CA, came under considerable attack (see, for example, Mohan and Lo 1985) on the grounds that L2 writing was essentially developmental in the same way as L2 acquisition. It has, however, survived these criticisms better than CA by broadening its frame of reference to include text linguistics, genre analysis and cultural theories of writing.

Theoretical background

As noted above, the theoretical underpinning of CA lay in behaviourist accounts of language learning. These viewed language learning as a largely mechanical process of habit formation. Brooks (1960: 49) for example claimed that 'the single paramount fact about language learning is that it concerns, not problem solving, but the formation and performance of habits'. A behaviour becomes a habit when a specific stimulus elicits an automatic response from the learner. It can be formed either through classical conditioning (i.e. a stimulus in the environment comes to be associated with a particular response through positive reinforcement) or through instrumental learning (i.e. an operant randomly produced as a result of an inner-drive is selectively reinforced). Habits entail 'over-learning', which ensures that learner responses are automatic. Already learned habits interfere with the learning of new habits as a result of proactive inhibition. Thus, the challenge facing the L2 learner (and the language teacher) is to overcome the interference of L1 habits. To this end CA sought to identify the features of the L2 that differed from those of the L1 so learners could be helped to form the 'new habits' of the L2 by practising them intensively.

EA, in contrast, became closely associated with nativist views of language learning and the emergence of interlanguage theory. Whereas behaviourism emphasized the role of environmental stimuli, nativist theories emphasize the mental processes that occur in the 'black box' of the mind when learning takes place. Language learning (both first and second) is explained in terms of a 'computational metaphor' (Lantolf 1996), according to which linguistic data (input) is computed internally by a pre-wired cognitive faculty resulting in a knowledge system that is then utilized in actual performance (output). The cognitive mechanisms dictate both what is attended to in the input (i.e. the intake), and how what is attended to is processed as L2 knowledge (i.e. the learner's interlanguage).

The term 'interlanguage' was coined by Selinker (1972) to refer to the mental grammar that a learner constructs at a specific stage in the learning process. Corder (1971) used the term 'idiosyncratic dialect' to refer to much the same construct. Interlanguage theory has evolved considerably over the years but the central premises have remained largely intact. Building on Ellis (1990a), the following premises can be identified:

1 A learner's interlanguage consists primarily of implicit linguistic knowledge (i.e. there is no awareness of the rules that comprise an interlanguage).
2 A learner's interlanguage knowledge constitutes a system in the same sense that a native speaker's grammar is a system. The system accounts for the regularities that are apparent in the learner's use of the L2.
3 A learner's interlanguage is permeable (i.e. because it is incomplete and unstable, it is easily penetrated by new linguistic forms derived both externally from input and internally through such processes as over-generalization).
4 A learner's interlanguage is transitional. The learner restructures his/her interlanguage grammar over time. Thus development involves the learner passing through a series of stages.
5 A learner's interlanguage is variable. At any one stage of development the learner will employ different forms for the same grammatical structure. This variability may be random in part (i.e. there is 'free variation') but is largely systematic in the sense that it is possible to

identify the probabilities with which the different forms will occur in accordance with such factors as the addressee and the availability of time to plan utterances.

6 A learner's interlanguage is the product of general learning strategies. One such strategy is L1 transfer but other strategies are intralingual (for example, strategies such as over-generalization and simplification).

7 A learner may supplement his/her interlanguage by means of communication strategies (for example, paraphrase or requests for assistance) to compensate for gaps in or difficulty in accessing L2 knowledge while performing.

8 A learner's interlanguage may fossilize (i.e. the learner may stop developing and thus fail to achieve a full native speaker grammar).

It should be noted, however, that some of these premises continue to be disputed. For example, not all researchers agree that interlanguage is variable, preferring to treat the variability inherent in learner language as an aspect of performance rather than of competence. (See Gregg 1990.) Also, the precise nature of the learning strategies responsible for interlanguage development remains a matter of controversy, with some researchers viewing these as specifically linguistic in nature and others as involving processes of a broad, cognitive nature.[1]

Many of the above premises were lent support by the results of error analyses. It was found that the errors produced by learners were highly systematic. For example, L2 learners (like L1 learners) regularly produced forms such as *eated* and regularly double marked verbs in interrogatives (for example, *Does your father lives . . . ?*). Further, the nature of the errors that learners produced changed over time indicating that the learner's interlanguage system was permeable and that the errors themselves were developmental. For example, Shapira (1978) shows that Zoila, the learner she investigated, began by using N *de* N as a possessive structure (for example, *The car de Carlo . . .*) but some 18 months later had added an alternate form NN (for example, *Jody books*). The variability inherent in interlanguage use is also evident in the results of error analyses. Ellis (1984a) shows how J, a Portuguese boy, varied in his use of *no, not* and *don't* in preverbal negative structures (for example, *me no cut, not finished, she don't understand*). Studies such as this showed that variation was not just a matter of using a deviant or a target-language form but also of selecting from a number of different deviant forms. They also showed that the variability was largely systematic. For example, a learner might correctly use 3rd person *-s* in simple sentences (for example, *My brother lives in San Francisco*) but systematically omit it in co-ordinated clauses (for example, *My brother lives in San Francisco but work in Portland*). EA testified to learners' use of both interlingual and intralingual learning strategies and, indeed, became the testing ground for the respective claims of behaviourist and nativist learning theories. Finally, EA provided evidence of fossilization. Shapira (1978), for example, found that many of the errors produced by Zoila persisted throughout the 18 month period in which she studied this learner. She notes that 'as sentence types become more and more complicated with respect to the number of obligatory morphemes and rules they call for, so Zoila's become more ungrammatical' (1978: 252). The closeness of the link between EA and interlanguage theory is demonstrated by the title that Widdowson gave to the posthumous 1981 collection of Corder's articles: *Error Analysis and Interlanguage*.

Conducting an Error Analysis

A starting point for conducting an EA is a clear definition of 'error'. This is not an easy task, as James (1998: Chapter 3) makes clear. In particular, there is the difficulty of deciding whether *grammaticality or acceptability* should serve as the criterion. If grammaticality is chosen, an error can be defined as a 'breach of the rule of the code' (Corder 1971). This is probably the safest definition although, as James points out, it depends on what particular variety of the target language is chosen as the 'code'. This may not be significant where grammar is concerned; what constitutes semantic or phonological well-formedness, though, can vary considerably depending on the variety chosen. Defining errors in terms of grammaticality also necessitates giving consideration to the distinction between *overt* and *covert error*. An error is said to be overt if it can be detected by inspecting the sentence/utterance in which it occurs. An error is covert if it only becomes apparent when a larger stretch of the discourse is considered. Acceptability is more dependent on the subjective evaluation of the researcher and often involves making stylistic rather than grammatical judgements. Determining acceptability also involves attempting to identify a situational context in which the utterance in question might fit. Thus a sentence like *She's doctor* can be considered acceptable despite the missing article if it occurred in the context of children assigning roles in a doctor–patient game. Necessarily, judgements about the acceptability of an utterance are likely to be less reliable in the sense that they will be less consistent across researchers. In the practice of EA, however, the distinction between grammaticality and acceptability becomes blurred, as reflected in the definition Lennon (1991: 182) used in his own research on error:

> A linguistic form or combination of forms which, in the same context and under similar conditions of production, would, in all likelihood, not be produced by the speakers' native speaker counterparts.

Such a definition, while not unproblematic, provides a reasonable basis for performing an EA.

One day an Indian gentleman, a snake charmer, arrived in England by plane. He was coming from Bombay with two pieces of luggage. The big of them contained a snake. A man and a little boy was watching him in the customs area. The man said to the little boy 'Go and speak with this gentleman'. When the little boy was speaking with the traveller, the thief took the big suitcase and went out quickly. When the victim saw that he cried 'Help me! help me! A thief! A thief!' The policeman was in this corner (.4.) whistle but it was too late. The two thieves escape with the big suitcase, took their car and went in the traffic. They passed near a zoo and stop in a forest. There they had a big surprise. The basket contain a big snake.

Table 3.1 Sample of learner language

Following Corder (1974), we can distinguish the following steps in conducting an Error Analysis:

1 Collection of a sample of learner language
2 Identification of errors
3 Description of errors
4 Explanation of errors
5 Error evaluation

The procedures and problems associated with each of these steps are considered below. They are illustrated with reference to the sample of learner language shown in Table 3.1.

Collecting a sample of learner language

Collecting a sample of learner language provides the data for the EA. The researcher needs to be aware that the nature of the sample that is collected may influence the nature and distribution of the errors observed. (See Chapter 2.) The learner, language and production factors shown in Table 3.2 can influence the sample collected. Researchers can take account of these factors in two ways. They can control for them, by narrowly specifying the sample they intend to collect. For example they may define the sample in terms of advanced, instructed Chinese learners of English producing oral narratives with the opportunity to plan before speaking. Such an approach allows for specific research questions to be addressed in the design of the EA. For example, by collecting two such carefully defined samples that vary on a single variable (for example, the learner's L1), it would be possible to investigate the effect of this variable on learner errors. Alternatively, researchers may wish to sample errors more generally by collecting a broad sample reflecting different learners, different types of language and different production conditions. In this case, however, it is advisable to provide full and explicit descriptions of the learner productions that make

Factors	Description
A Learner	
1 Proficiency level	Elementary, intermediate, or advanced
2 Other languages	The learner's L1, other L2s
3 Language learning background	Instructed, naturalistic, mixed
B Language	
1 Medium	Oral or written
2 Genre	e.g. conversation, narrative, essay
3 Content	The topic of the discourse
C Production	
1 Unplanned	The discourse is produced spontaneously.
2 Planned	The discourse is produced after planning or under conditions that allow for careful online planning.

Table 3.2 Factors affecting learner errors in samples of learner language

up the sample so that the effect of different variables on errors can be examined *post hoc*.

The sample of learner language in Table 3.1 was collected from a low intermediate, largely self-instructed learner, whose L1 was French. It takes the form of an oral narrative based on a series of pictures about a robbery at an airport. The learner planned his narrative by first writing it out (i.e. he spoke it after writing it but with no access to his written version). The sample was collected as part of a study designed to investigate how different conditions of production (i.e. planned vs. unplanned) affected learner language. (See Ellis 1987.)

Identification of errors

In accordance with the definition of error given above, the identification of error involves a comparison between what the learner has produced and what a native speaker counterpart would produce in the same context. The basic procedure is as follows:

1 Prepare a reconstruction of the sample as this would have been produced by the learner's native speaker counterpart.
2 Assume that every utterance/sentence produced by the learner is erroneous and systematically eliminate those that an initial comparison with the native speaker sample shows to be well-formed. Those utterances/sentences remaining contain errors.
3 Identify which part(s) of each learner utterance/sentence differs from the reconstructed version.

The key procedure is step (1). It is here that the problems arise. This is because it is not always possible to arrive at an *authoritative reconstruction* of the learner's utterances/sentences. For example, this sentence from the sample in Table 3.1.

The policeman was in this corner whistle but it was too late.

might be reconstructed in several different ways:

1 The policeman who was in this corner whistled but it was too late.
2 The policeman was in this corner and whistled but it was too late.
3 The policeman in this corner whistled but it was too late.

Thus, while all these reconstructions serve to identify the error in 'whistle', they differ in the identification of the error in the syntax of the sentence. Whereas in (1) the error is identified as residing in a missing relative pronoun, in (2) it is located in a missing co-ordinator and in (3) in a superfluous copula verb ('was'). The problem is that we do not know what construction the learner intended. Corder (1974) suggests that one solution to this problem is to seek an *authoritative interpretation* by asking learners what they meant to say. However, this is often impractical and, in any case, as James (1998) emphasizes, errors are often indeterminate, making it impossible for learners to specify which particular construction they were attempting to use. A further problem arises with linguistic forms that are 'possible' but not 'preferred'. An example from Table 3.1 can be found in the sentence:

He was coming from Bombay with two pieces of luggage.

Many native-speakers might reformulate this as:

He had come from Bombay with two pieces of luggage.

but acknowledge that 'was coming' is grammatically possible. Researchers need to decide whether they will restrict their analysis to *absolute errors* or also include *dispreferred forms*. Given that the latter involve subjective judgements of acceptability it may be better to restrict the analysis to the former. The distinction between absolute errors and dispreferred forms is a continuous rather than dichotomous one with the result that deciding what to count as an error is likely to be at least partly subjective.

The problems in identifying errors are traceable in part to two dimensions involved in the process of reconstructing erroneous utterances/sentences. Lennon (1991) defines the *domain* of an error as the breadth of the context (word, phrase, clause, previous sentence, or extended discourse) that needs to be considered in order to identify an error. The *extent* of an error refers to the size of the unit that needs to be reconstructed in order to repair the error. In the following sentence from Table 3.1 the domain of the error is shown by [ ] while the extent is shown by italics.

They [passed near a zoo and *stop*] in a forest.

In this sentence, the domain is fairly narrow (clause) and the extent even narrower (word). Errors such as this are generally easy to identify. In contrast, errors where the domain and/or extent are broad are much more difficult. Lennon suggests that the identification of error might usefully include a specification of the domain and extent of each error.

Description of errors

Corder (1974: 128) writes: 'The description of errors is essentially a comparative process, the data being the original erroneous utterances and the reconstructed utterance'. Thus, description of learner errors involves specifying how the forms produced by the learner differ from those produced by the learner's native-speaker counterparts. It focuses on the surface properties of learner utterances. There are two steps:

1 The development of a set of descriptive categories for coding the errors that have been identified.
2 Recording the frequency of the errors in each category.

Following James (1998), two criteria for the development of descriptive categories can be established. The system of categories (referred to as a taxonomy) must be 'well-developed' and 'elaborated', and thus capable of describing errors with maximum delicacy; it must also be simple and self-explanatory (i.e. 'user-friendly'). Two kinds of taxonomy have been used: (1) a *linguistic taxonomy* and (2) a *surface structure taxonomy*. It is also possible to combine these.

A linguistic taxonomy is usually based on categories drawn from a descriptive grammar of the target language (for example, Quirk *et al.*'s (1985) grammar of English). Such a grammar will include general categories relating to basic sentence structure, the verb phrase, verb complementation, the noun phrase, prepositional phrases, adjuncts, coordinate and subordinate constructions and sentence connection. More delicate categories relating to each of these can then be developed. For example, verb phrase errors can be further classified into categories relating to the different verb tenses (for example, the past simple tense), aspect (for example, perfective and progressive), the subjunctive, auxiliary verbs (primary and modal) and non-finite verbs. Each of these categories can then be further sub-divided (for example, past simple tense might be subdivided into regular and irregular verb forms). However, the categories finally chosen for the analysis need to be data driven. That is, rather than start with a fully-elaborated set of categories derived from a descriptive grammar, the analyst should develop categories (based on a descriptive grammar) to reflect the errors identified in the sample. Errors should be classified in terms of the target language categories that have been violated rather than the linguistic categories used by the learner. For example, the error in this sentence:

Yesterday Martin marry his life-long sweetheart.

would be classified under 'verb phrase—past simple tense—regular verb' and not under 'verb phrase—present simple tense'.

The advantage of a descriptive taxonomy is that it utilizes well-established grammatical categories and thereby maximizes the practical applications (for example, to teaching). The disadvantage is that by taking as its reference point the target language grammar it is guilty of the 'comparative fallacy' (Bley-Vroman 1983). That is, it fails to acknowledge that interlanguages are unique grammars in their own right. James (1998), however, points out that learners are typically targeted on native-speaker norms and as such themselves perform 'cognitive comparisons' in the process of learning an L2. In this respect, then, a descriptive taxonomy can be seen as psycholinguistically valid.

Dulay, Burt, and Krashen's (1982: 150) surface structure taxonomy is based on 'the ways surface structures are altered' in erroneous utterances/sentences. They suggest that there are four principal ways in which learners modify target forms:

1 Omission (for example, omission of copula *be* in the utterance *My sisters very pretty*.)
2 Addition (i.e. the presence of a form that does not appear in a well-formed utterance). This is sub-categorized into:
   a Regularization (for example, *eated* for *ate*)
   b Double-marking (for example, *He didn't came*)
   c Simple additions (i.e. additions not describable as regularizations or as double-markings)
3 Misinformation (i.e. the use of the wrong form of the morpheme or structure)
   a Regularization (for example, *Do they be happy?*)
   b Archi-forms (for example, the learner uses *me* as both a subject and object pronoun).
   c Alternating forms (for example, *Don't* + v and *No* + v).
4 Misordering (i.e. errors characterized by the incorrect placement of a morpheme or group of morphemes in an utterance as in *She fights all the time her brother*).

James (1998) suggests one further category be added:

5 Blends (i.e. errors that reflect the learner's uncertainty as to which of two forms is required). This can result in over-inclusion as in the sentence *The only one thing I want* which is an amalgam of *The only thing I want* and *The one thing I want.*

The surface structure taxonomy is guilty of the comparative fallacy, as learners obviously do not set out to modify target language norms. It is possible, however, that learners carry out their cognitive comparisons by noticing how they have simplified, added, misinformed or misordered elements in their utterances. In this sense, then, such a taxonomy might also lay claim to psycholinguistic validity. Such a taxonomy is, by itself, of less obvious practical use as grammar teaching is organized in terms of traditional descriptive categories. However, it may still be of pedagogic use in helping teachers to show learners how their productions deviate from target language norms.

These two ways of describing errors are not mutually exclusive. A dictionary of errors can usefully combine them. A good example of such a combined taxonomy can be found in Burt and Kiparsky's *The Gooficon: A Repair Manual for English* (1972). This is organized primarily in terms of linguistic categories but distinguishes the different types of error within a linguistic category by means of surface structure categories. For example, the linguistic category 'the skeleton of English clauses' is subdivided into two surface structure categories, 'missing parts' and 'misordered parts'.

Table 3.3 provides an example of a description of errors in the sample shown in Table 3.1. It incorporates both linguistic and a surface structure categories. Table 3.4 illustrates how the second step in the description of errors—the recording of error frequency—can be presented. It shows that the majority of errors produced by this learner involve the verb phrase (failure to mark regular past verbs) and misinformation (regularization).

Explanation of errors

Explaining errors involves determining their sources in order to account for why they were made. From the point of view of SLA research this is the most important stage in an Error Analysis. Our concern here will be with the psycholinguistic sources of error (i.e. those relating to the processing mechanisms involved in L2 use and to the nature of the L2 knowledge system). It should be noted, however, that there are also sociolinguistic sources. Rampton (1987), for example, suggests that learners may sometimes deliberately employ non-standard forms such as *me no like* as a way of managing the impression they wish to have on their interlocutor (for example, to mitigate a refusal by using a form that signals they are just 'little language learners').

One obvious reason why learners make errors is the difficulty they experience in accessing their L2 knowledge when communicating. If L2 forms have not yet been automatized, they require controlled processing, which places a heavy demand on learners' information-processing systems. The result is that they resort to the use of non-standard forms that have been acquired earlier and are automatized. Following Corder (1974), therefore, it is useful, to distinguish *errors* and *mistakes*. The former arise because of gaps in the learner's L2 knowledge; the latter occur because of the difficulty of processing forms that are not yet fully mastered. Corder is of the view that error analysts should focus attention on errors. However, we argue that both are important both practically and theoretically. From a pedagogic

Error	Reconstruction	Linguistic description	Surface structure description
The *big* of them …	The bigger of them	Noun phrase; adjectives; comparative form	Misinformation—regularization
… was watching …	… were watching …	Verb phrase; subject-verb agreement (plural)	Minsinformation—regularization
… was in this corner …	… who was in this corner …	Complex sentence– relative clause– relative pronoun (*who*)	Omission
… whistle …	… whistled …	Verb phrase– simple past tense– regular verb	Misinformation—regularization
… escape …	… escaped …	Verb phrase– simple past tense– regular verb	Misinformation—regularization
… stop …	… stopped …	Verb phrase– simple past tense– regular verb	Misinformation—regularization
… contain …	… contained …	Verb phrase– simple past tense– regular verb	Misinformation—regularization

Table 3.3 An example of error description

Error categories	Frequency	% of total errors
A Descriptive		
1 Noun phrase	1	14.3
2 Verb phrase	1	14.3
a subject-verb agreement	4	57.1
b Simple Past Tense	1	14.3
3 Complex sentence		
B Surface structure		
1 Omission	1	14.3
2 Addition	0	0
3 Misinformation	6	85.7
4 Misordering	0	0
5 Blends	0	0

Table 3.4 Frequency of error types

standpoint, it is useful for teachers to know that their students have not yet mastered certain forms but are capable of self-correcting them. From a theoretical point of view, it can be argued that a form has not been fully acquired until learners can use it with the same degree of accuracy as native speakers. (See Chapter 4.)

The question arises as to how errors and mistakes can be distinguished. One way is to check whether the learner alternates between the erroneous form and the correct target-language form. Using this as a test, the sample of learner language in Table 3.1 suggests that the learner's failure to use the correct form of the simple past tense (for example, *whistle* instead of *whistled*) constitutes a mistake rather than an error because other forms are correctly marked (*arrived*). The problem is, however, what we mean by 'form'. If we take the 'form' to constitute the simple past tense (regular verbs) such a conclusion is justified. However, if we take the 'form' to consist of the past form of a specific verb, it is less clear that an erroneous form like *whistle* is a mistake (as opposed to an error) because there is no occasion in the sample where the correct verb form (*whistled*) is produced. Defining 'form' in this stringent manner, would suggest that the only mistake is in *contain*, which is produced in both erroneous and correct versions. A better way of determining where a particular deviation is an error or a mistake is to consult the learner. If the learner is able to self-correct the deviant form, it can be classified as a mistake. However, as we have already noted, this is often not practicable.

Of course, learners produce some deviant forms consistently (i.e. they do not alternate with use of the correct forms). In such cases, there is a clear gap in the learner's L2 knowledge. Thus errors (with the meaning referred to above) are in a fundamental sense the result of *ignorance*. To explain errors, however, we need to ask what processes learners invoke when they do not know the target-language form. Traditionally, two major processes are identified, distinguishing *interlingual* errors and *intralingual* errors

Interlingual errors are the result of mother tongue influences. Here it is necessary to distinguish the effects of 'transfer' and 'borrowing' (Corder 1983). Transfer relates to the introduction of an L1 form into the interlanguage system; borrowing involves the temporary use of an L1 form as a communication strategy but does not entail incorporation of the form into the interlanguage system.[2] A key question is why learners transfer/borrow some forms but not others. This was the question that CA was ultimately unable to answer and which led to its demise. Various explanations have been advanced by SLA researchers. Kellerman (1979), for example, proposes that two factors are involved; prototypicality (i.e. the extent to which a linguistic form is perceived as 'basic' and 'natural') and language distance (i.e. the extent to which the L2 is linguistically close or distant from the target language). Kellerman produced evidence to show that learners are less likely to transfer forms that are non-prototypical and if their L1 is distant from the target-language.

It should be noted, however, that it is not always easy to determine whether an error is the result of transfer. Spanish learners of English commonly make errors in negative sentences. For example:

Mariana no coming today.

Such errors manifest pre-verbal negation using *no*, the same negative construction as in their L1. However, German learners, whose L1 has post-verbal negation (for example, *Mariana kommt nicht heute*) also produce English utterances using *no* + V in the early stages of acquisition. In order to determine conclusively whether transfer is the cause, it is necessary to compare learners with different L1s and to demonstrate that learners with a particular L1 make an error that those with a different L1 do not.

Intralingual errors reflect the operation of learning strategies that are universal, i.e. evident in all learners irrespective of their L1. James (1998) provides a useful summary of these strategies, the main ones of which are:

1 False analogy (a kind of 'over-generalization'). An example is *boy → boys; child → childs.*
2 Misanalysis (for example, the learner wrongly assumes that the singular possessive pronoun *its* is plural because of the *-s*)
3 Incomplete rule application (a kind of 'under-generalization'). An example, is the failure to utilize indicative word order in *Nobody knew where was Barbie.*

4 Exploiting redundancy (i.e. omitting grammatical features that do not contribute to the meaning of an utterance). A good example is 3rd person *-s* (for example, *Martin like tennis*).
5 Overlooking co-occurrence restrictions (for example, failing to recognize that although *quick* and *fast* are synonyms, *quick food* is not a possible collocation).
6 System-simplification (i.e. simplifying the burden of learning by substituting a single form where the target language uses two or more). An example is the use of *that* as a ubiquitous relative pronoun.

One problem with such a list is that it is not always clear which strategy is responsible for a particular error. For example, the use of the simple form of the verb (for example, *whistle*) for the past tense form (for example, *whistled*), which we have seen is a frequent error in the sample in Table 3.1 can be explained in terms of 'exploiting redundancy', as it is clear the learner is referring to past time, or to 'system-simplification'.

Errors can also be viewed as 'natural' (i.e. reflecting the natural code-breaking strategies of the learner) or as 'induced'. Stenson (1974) coined the term *induced error* to refer to errors that resulted from the way the language was taught. For example, errors may be induced in the classroom through oral practice, as in this example:

TEACHER: Younghee, ask Keiko where she went to school.

SOOK: Keiko, where you went to school?

In this example, as in many others Stenson gives, however, the error can be seen as reflecting the use of a natural learning strategy (for example, misanalysis) as well as induction through instruction.

It should be clear from the foregoing account of error explanation that identifying the source of particular errors is not an easy task. In part this is because the different sources of error have not been defined with sufficient rigour. But even if they were, problems would continue to exist. An error itself can only provide a hint of its source with the result that many errors are ambiguous. For this reason, analysts need to heed the advice of Schachter and Celce-Murcia (1977) to be 'extremely cautious when claiming to have identified the cause of a given error'. In fact, many errors are likely to be explicable in terms of multiple rather than single sources. Thus, it is, perhaps, not surprising that researchers have produced different estimations of the percentage of errors that can be traced to interlingual and intralingual sources. For example, using the same instrument to collect samples of language from Spanish learners of L2 English, Dulay and Burt (1974) and White (1977) reported 5 per cent and 21 per cent errors respectively were interlingual with a corresponding difference in the proportions of intralingual errors.

Error evaluation

Error evaluation is not so much a stage in the analysis of learner errors as a supplementary procedure for applying the results of an EA. It involves determining the gravity of different errors with a view to deciding which ones should receive instruction. Planning for an error evaluation study involves the following steps:

1 Select the errors to be evaluated (these could be all the errors identified in the EA or, more likely, a subset of them). The errors are usually presented either in complete sentences but sometimes in a continuous text.
2 Decide the criterion on which the errors are to be judged. The most commonly chosen criterion is 'gravity' (i.e. 'seriousness') but other criteria are possible (for example, 'intelligibility' or 'irritability').
3 Prepare the error evaluation instrument. This will consist of a set of instructions, the erroneous sentences or text, and a method for evaluating the errors. Common methods used involve ranking the list of erroneous sentences (for example, from the 'most serious' to the 'least serious') or judging each sentence on a Likert scale (for example, from 'very serious' to 'not at all serious').
4 Choose the judges. It is best to have at least two. The more judges, the better, as this increases the reliability and generalizability of the results. If native-speakers and non-native speakers are chosen it is desirable to analyse their judgements separately as research indicates they differ considerably (Hughes and Lascaratou 1982).

Error evaluation studies were popular in the 1970s and 1980s (see Ellis 1994: 66–5 for a survey) but have dried up entirely, in part because of inconclusive results that made it impossible to develop a definite scale for predicting error gravity. Nevertheless, teachers do need to take decisions about which errors to address and thus have a practical need to undertake some kind of error evaluation.

An example of an Error Analysis

In many of the early error analyses, the approach was illustrative with no attempt made to quantify errors. Jain (1974), for example, reports an analysis of the errors produced by Indian students at university in written scripts in the form of tables that simply list examples of errors relating to specific linguistic categories. The study chosen for presentation here, however, serves as a model for a quantitative analysis and also as an example of the problems of this approach.

Dulay and Burt's (1974) study is summarized in Table 3.5. It was designed to address the dominant theoretical issue at the time it was carried out—the relative contributions of L1 transfer and learner-internal mechanisms to L2 acquisition. They used what was then the dominant method of analysing

Research question	Dulay and Burt sought to investigate whether the majority of learners' errors are interlingual or intralingual as a way of addressing whether L2 acquisition was the result of L1 transfer or of 'creative construction'.
Participants	179 Spanish speaking children, 5–8 years old.
Data collection	The data were collected by means of the *Bilingual Syntax Measure* (Burt, Dulay and Hernandez Chavez 1973); this consists of a series of pictures used to elicit a range of basic syntactic structures orally.
Analysis	1 Erroneous utterances in the sample were identified. 2 'Ambiguous utterances' (i.e. those that could not be classified clearly as interference or developmental) were then excluded; 513 unambiguous errors remained in six different grammatical structures. 3 The errors were classified into three categories: – developmental (i.e. similar to L1 acquisition) – interference (i.e. errors that reflected Spanish structure) – unique (i.e. errors that were neither developmental nor interference)
Results	Dulay and Burt present error frequencies for the six grammatical structures. In all six structures developmental errors hugely outnumbered interference errors. The table below provides a summary of the error count for children of different ages. Overall, only 4.7% of the errors reflected L1 interference.

Age	Developmental errors	Interference errors	Unique errors
5 years	98	5	2
6 years	113	6	16
7 years	123	7	16
8 years	113	6	11
TOTAL	447	24	42

Discussion	On the basis of the results, Dulay and Burt argue that child L2 acquisition is primarily a process of 'creative construction' rather than 'habit formation'.
Implications	Dulay and Burt argue that because 'making errors is a necessary condition in the learning process' (p. 135) there is no need for instructional intervention to prevent or correct errors. They recommend making ESL instruction 'more closely related to the natural processes of second language learning'. (p. 135)

Table 3.5 Summary of Dulay and Burt's (1974) EA *study*

learner language—EA—to address this issue, focusing on the explanation of the errors they identified in their sample. The results of the study appear to give a clear-cut answer to their research question, at least where children are concerned—L2 acquisition is primarily a developmental process similar to L1 acquisition (i.e. interlingual errors occur only infrequently).

There are, however, several problems with this study. Probably the most serious is Dulay and Burt's assumption that errors are either interference or developmental, and their failure to entertain the possibility that many errors may be both. By eliminating 'ambiguous errors' they excluded precisely those structures where interference may have played a part. A further problem arises with their operationalization of 'developmental error'. In the case of negation, for example, they classified utterances of the type *He not eat* as developmental (presumably on the grounds that there was no subject deletion as in Spanish and because the negator was English *not* rather than Spanish *no*). However, it can also be argued that utterances like *He not eat* reflect L1 transfer as they entail the same pre-verbal negation found in Spanish. In short, it is often simply not possible to determine whether transfer or developmental processes are responsible for errors in the manner attempted by Dulay and Burt. Finally, their conclusion that, because child L2 acquisition is a process of 'creative construction', instruction should mirror 'natural processes' is unfounded as they have not demonstrated that explicit instruction does not assist by speeding up these processes.

Despite these problems the study is an important one. It served to challenge the prevailing learning theory of the day (behaviourism) and played a part in the development of a theory that sought to explain L2 acquisition in its own right rather than as an appendix to a general theory of learning; it leant empirical support to the ascendancy of interlanguage theory.

Task: Carrying out an Error Analysis

Below is a letter written by a female Japanese junior-college student. The letter was written in response to the following task:

> Think of a problem. It can be a real problem or an imaginary one. Then write a letter to a close friend. In your letter explain the problem and the solutions you have thought of. Ask for your friend's advice.

Carry out an analysis of the *grammatical* errors in this letter. Your analysis should involve the following steps:

1. identification of errors (this will necessitate a reconstruction of the letter)
2. description (including a frequency count)
3. explanation

May 10, Thursday, 1990

Dear Eiko

I want to see you now. How are you?
Maybe, you will be very careful, but I'm very sad and I have trouble on my mind.

You know my boyfriend, Toshiro. He is very nice and we love each other. But he must go to America for his business in this year. He want to go to America with me. I want to go there, too. But we have some problem. One is my school. I'm secound-year college student now and I must go to Tsuda university in this year.

The other one is my parents. I spoke them this story, but they object! They are very angry.

So I am writing a letter for you, and I want your replie soon.

I think some solution. I leave in Japan, and I go to America during my vacation, but this solution's problem is "I must pay big money". I think this cost is very high. I can't pay big money.

A secound choice is to go to America and to get married after graduation. This solution will be glad to my parents, but I'll become an uneasy feeling. Before I go to America, he will fined another girl. So I think the best thing for me to do is "I go to America right now and we get married". This is my solution, but if you have a good solution, please tell me!! I want your advice.

Thank you
Michikox

Table 3.6 Sample of written language

If you were this student's teacher which errors would you choose to try to correct through instruction? Make your criterion for selection explicit.

Final comment

EA suffers from a number of limitations. It offers an incomplete picture of learner language because it examines only what learners do wrongly and ignores what they do correctly. Also, EA cannot account for learners' avoidance of certain L2 forms. Schachter (1974) showed that Japanese and Chinese learners of English made few errors in the use of relative clauses not because they had mastered this structure but because they avoided trying to use them. As we have seen, there are also methodological problems to do with the identification, description and explanation of error. For these reasons EA no longer figures as the preferred method for analysing learner language. Nevertheless, the study of learner error remains of practical significance to language pedagogy. Error correction is discussed in handbooks for language teachers. (See, for example, Hedge 2000: 288–92.) This cannot proceed without a good understanding of the nature of error and deciding which errors to correct.

Notes

1 According to a theory of Universal Grammar, learners possess innate knowledge of linguistic universals which they use to determine the nature of the grammatical rules of the L2 (see White 1989), whereas according to connectionist theories, learners possess a general capacity for identifying and storing information relating to the linguistic sequences (see N. Ellis 2002). Both theories, however, refer to 'interlanguage' and seek to account for its development.

2 Distinguishing 'transfer' and 'borrowing' is problematic, however, as the only evidence for both is the errors that learners make. There are no reliable criteria for deciding whether an L1-based error reflects a communication or learning strategy.

4 Obligatory occasion analysis

Introduction

A limitation of error analysis (EA), which we noted at the end of the preceding chapter, is that it only tells half the story by delimiting the object of study to the errors that learners make. To tell the full story we need to consider what learners get right as well as what they get wrong. This requires an analysis of samples of learner language in their totality and is achieved by means of *performance analysis*, which can be defined broadly as an analysis of learners' L2 productions. In this sense, of course, EA can be considered, one kind of performance analysis. This and the next chapter will focus on two other ways of analysing learners' performance.

Obligatory occasion analysis (Brown 1973) constitutes a method for examining how accurately learners use specific linguistic (usually grammatical) features. Like EA, it involves a comparison between the forms used by learners and target language norms (determined through reference to a standard native speaker variety). It provides a means of specifying how fully learners have acquired a linguistic feature and also of comparing the extent to which different features have been acquired. For example, as a result of obligatory occasion analysis it has been found that English plural *-s* is typically used with greater accuracy than third person *-s*.

Historical and theoretical background

Obligatory occasion analysis was first developed as a tool for investigating first language (L1) acquisition. Brown (1973), in his longitudinal study of three children's acquisition of English, examined the accuracy with which three children performed a number of English grammatical morphemes, such as present progressive *-ing*, plural *-s*, and regular past *-ed* over time. De Villiers and de Villiers (1973) used the same procedure in a cross-sectional study, comparing the accuracy with which different children performed a range of grammatical morphemes at one point in time. The procedure was then adopted by SLA researchers in both longitudinal studies (for example, Hakuta 1974; Rosansky 1976) and cross-sectional studies (for example, Dulay and Burt 1973). These studies, which became known as the *morpheme studies*, were directed at establishing whether there was a universal *order of* *acquisition* (i.e. whether all learners acquired the grammatical morphemes in the same fixed order irrespective of such variables as their L1, their age or the acquisitional setting) and, also, whether this order was the same or different from that found for L1 acquisition.

The morpheme studies were carried out in the context of the debate that took place in the 1960s and 1970s over behaviourist and nativist theories of language acquisition. (See Chapter 2.) The thinking was as follows: if it could be shown that L2 learners followed a universal order of acquisition, then this would suggest that acquisition was not subject to variation as a result of environmental differences but rather was internally driven. Further, if it could be shown that the order of acquisition was the same for L1 and L2 acquisition, this would lend support to the claim that all learners, irrespective of age, possessed a 'Language Acquisition Device' (Chomsky 1965) which directed the course of development. Conversely, if it could be shown that different learners manifested different orders of acquisition, then this would indicate that learning was environmentally controlled as claimed by behaviourist theories of learning. However, any differences between L1 and L2 acquisition orders, if found, would be more difficult to interpret as they could reflect either environmental differences or differences in the cognitive basis of learning.

A series of cross-sectional studies of L2 learners in the 1970s (for example, Dulay and Burt 1973; Bailey, Madden, and Krashen 1974; Larsen-Freeman 1976) indicated that, as in L1 acquisition, there was a remarkably regular order of accuracy for English grammatical morphemes. Krashen (1977a) suggested that it was possible to form an 'acquisition hierarchy' by grouping morphemes according to accuracy, as shown in Figure 4.1. This hierarchy

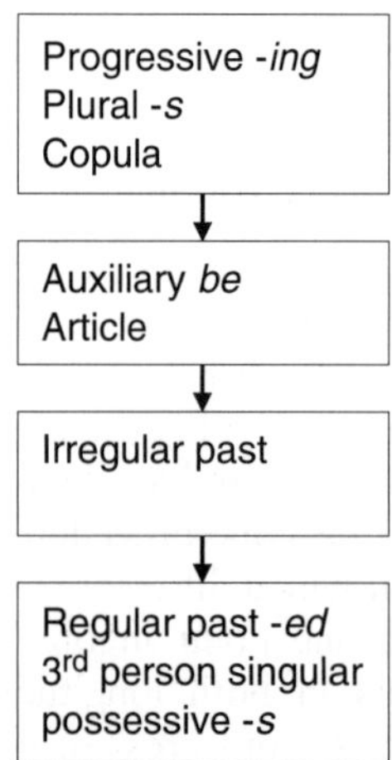

Figure 4.1 Hierarchy of L2 acquisition (Krashen 1977a)

was not influenced by the learners' L1 (there have been studies of Spanish, Chinese, Japanese, and Arabic L2 learners), by age (child and adult L2 learners manifested the same order) or by setting (EFL and ESL learners showed the same order). Only one factor seemed to have an effect on the order—the way in which the data were collected. Larsen-Freeman (1976), for example, found some differences between the order obtained for speaking/imitation and reading/writing tasks. Krashen, Butler, Birnbaum, and Robertson (1978) found that the order they obtained from written tasks did not match that found for oral tasks in other studies. This bears out the observation made in Chapter 2 that the method used to elicit samples of learner language can have a notable effect.

In contrast to these cross-sectional studies, however, a number of longitudinal studies produced more mixed and therefore less conclusive results. Rosansky (1976), for example, carried out a series of analyses of data collected from one L2 learner over a 10-month period. Worryingly, she found that the order of acquisition varied from one data collection point to another and that, overall, the orders did not match that reported for groups of learners in the cross-sectional studies. Hakuta (1974) also found the order of acquisition for Uguisa, a Japanese child learning English, did not match that reported in the cross-sectional studies. Articles, ranked high in the cross-sectional studies, ranked very low in Uguisa, reflecting, perhaps, the absence of articles in Japanese.[1]

The morpheme studies found similarities and differences between L1 and L2 orders. For example, Brown (1973) and Dulay and Burt (1973) both reported that progressive *-ing* was the most accurately used morpheme and that 3rd person *-s* was one of the least accurately used. On the other hand, these studies also reported differences in the use of the articles, the copula and the auxiliary, which were performed more accurately by L2 learners, and in the irregular past tense, which was performed less accurately.

The results of the morpheme studies were interpreted as lending support to a nativist account of L2 acquisition. Dulay, Burt, and Krashen (1982), for example, argued that the results showed that Brown's (1973: 105–6) conclusion for L1 acquisition could be extended to L2 acquisition:

> Children work out rules for the speech they hear, passing from levels of lesser to greater complexity, simply because the human species is programmed at a certain period to operate in this fashion on linguistic input.

and, further, that it applied to adults as well. Addressing the difference in the L1 and L2 orders, they acknowledge that the reasons are not clear but suggest that 'the mental age differences between first and second language learners probably play a major role' (1973: 202). The morpheme studies, therefore, contributed to the demise of behaviourist theories of L2 acquisition, as it was difficult to see how habit-formation could adequately explain why learners, irrespective of age, L1, or acquisition setting, manifested the same accuracy order. The existence of a universal order pointed to a major role for learner-internal mechanisms in language acquisition.

This conclusion was supported by the apparent lack of any relationship between the input frequency of the morphemes and the accuracy of their use. Brown (1973) found no correlation between their frequency in parental speech and the L1 accuracy order. Similarly, Lightbown (1983) failed to find any relationship between input frequency in a teacher's speech and in a textbook on the one hand, and the accuracy of three *-s* morphemes in the language produced by classroom L2 learners in a communication game on the other. However, Lightbown was able to show that a high level of input frequency in the case of progressive *-ing* at one time was reflected in subsequent overuse by the learners. This study suggests that frequency may be related to use but that the relationship is a delayed rather than contiguous one.[2] Ellis (1990a) has argued that it makes little sense to look at input-output relationships in data collected at the same time, as any effect for input will only become apparent later on.

While morpheme studies effectively ceased in the earlier 1980s, interest in the 'natural order' did not. Researchers switched attention from description to explanation by focusing on the factors that accounted for the accuracy order. Two key studies in this respect were Zobl and Liceras (1994) and Goldschneider and DeKeyser (2001). Zobl and Liceras sought a unified theoretical account of the L1 and L2 morpheme orders, drawing on insights provided by Chomsky's Principles and Parameters model of Universal Grammar to explain the differences in the two orders. For example, they propose that whereas L1 acquisition is characterized by nominal categories preceding verbal categories, the L2 order is cross-categorical; they suggest that the explanation for this difference lies in the fact that functional categories maturate gradually in young children but are available from the beginning in L2 learning. Thus, Zobl and Liceras see the morpheme orders as determined by abstract cognitive-linguistic principles.

Goldschneider and DeKeyser (2001) pooled the accuracy results obtained for oral production data in twelve studies involving 924 learners and investigated the predictive power of five variables (one of which was input frequency), as described in Table 4.1. Goldschneider and DeKeyser reported that frequency was significantly related to accuracy of use but that other variables (for example, phonological salience and syntactic category) were even more strongly related. In interpreting their results, they suggest that the five variables reflect one underlying factor—salience—and the effect found for frequency is the result of the contribution it makes to the salience of a morpheme. This study is important because it suggests that no single variable, such as input frequency, can account for the accuracy order, but that a number of variables, all contributing to the differential salience of individual morphemes, are at work.

Variable	Description
Frequency	The frequency with which each morpheme was used in the speech of the parents in Brown's (1973) study.
Phonological salience	The ease of difficulty with which the morpheme can be heard or perceived.
Semantic complexity	Complexity is determined by the number of meanings that are expressed by a morpheme.
Syntactic category	Morphemes can be classified according to whether they are lexical/functional and also according to whether they are free/bound.
Morphophonological regularity	The extent to which a morpheme is affected by its phonological environment. Morphemes with more alternations are considered less regular.

Table 4.1 Variables predicting percentage accuracy in the morpheme studies in Goldschenider and DeKeyser's (2001) study

The results of Goldschneider and DeKeyser's meta-analysis of morpheme studies suggests that L2 acquisition is the product of an interaction between the learner's internal mechanisms and the input. They are more compatible with current cognitive theories of acquisition that posit a general and minimalist cognitive structure tuned to notice and process input features (see, for example, N. Ellis 2002) rather than a specific and elaborated language acquisition device that directs learners merely to seek triggering evidence from the input. Thus, we can see that although the morpheme studies were originally conducted within the theoretical framework provided by Chomsky's nativist views of language and language learning, they have come to be reinterpreted within the theoretical framework provided by connectionist models.

It is pertinent to conclude with a consideration of the methodological problems of the morpheme studies that led to their demise and to review these critically in the light of current theorizing about L2 acquisition.

A central assumption in the morpheme studies is that the accuracy with which learners perform a set of grammatical morphemes indicates the extent to which they have been acquired. In the cross-sectional studies, the *order of accuracy* is equated with the order of acquisition. Thus, it is assumed that if learners perform one grammatical morpheme (for example, English past irregular) more accurately than another (for example, English past regular), they will acquire it earlier. Such an assumption is controversial, however, as at least some morphemes display a U-shaped pattern of development. For example, when learners acquire English past irregular they frequently pass through an early stage of acquisition where they use some irregular forms correctly only to replace these later on with over-generalized *-ed* forms (for example, **goed* supplants *went*). A similar, U-shaped pattern of development occurs with embedded *wh*-questions. Early on learners produce embedded questions with the correct word order (for example, *He ask what my name is*) but when learners have mastered the inversion rule for *wh*-questions (for example, *What is your name?*) they over-generalize this to embedded questions (for example, **He asked what is my name*). Clearly, accuracy in the use of structures where over-generalization is common is not a reliable measure of acquisition. However, this is only a problem of the cross-sectional studies, for, as we will see later, the methodology employed in longitudinal morpheme studies helps to obviate this error. Nor does the existence of U-shaped patterns of development require the abandonment of cross-sectional morpheme studies. Rather it suggests the need to ensure that learner populations are grouped according to general L2 proficiency, and accuracy orders calculated separately for each group.[3] This will enable researchers to investigate proficiency as a co-variate of accuracy order and to identify which morphemes display a lower level of accuracy at higher levels of proficiency.

Another commonly voiced criticism of the morpheme studies is that they have been restricted to a small set of morphemes. Most of the L2 studies have focused on a set of 10–12 English morphemes. It would be possible to extend this set; obvious candidates in the case of L2 English might be pronoun number, the auxiliaries *have* and *do*, and past participle and comparative forms of the adjective. Clearly, though, this would depend on whether the researcher was able to identify instruments that ensured a sufficient number of obligatory contexts for each morpheme. Dulay and Burt (1973, 1974) used the Bilingual Syntax Measure. (See Chapter 2.) The morphemes they investigated by means of this instrument were doubtless chosen, in part at least, according to the feasibility of designing pictures and questions that would elicit them. Nevertheless, with some ingenuity, it ought to be possible to extend the number of morphemes to be studied.

A more serious criticism is that the morphemes constitute a rag-bag of disparate features. They include, for example, case features (for example, subject/object pronouns), features of the verb phrase (for example, progressive *-ing* and 3rd person *-s*) and features of the noun-phrase (for example, plural *-s* and articles). Further, some of the morphemes investigated (for example, articles) do not constitute discrete features but rather clusters of forms (*the, a/an*, and zero article). This is a valid criticism but does not constitute a fatal flaw in the research paradigm itself. It is perfectly possible to adapt the methodology to examine morphemes that have been grouped in a principled manner. J. D. Brown (1983), for example, proposed that morphemes be classified into open and bound classes. Andersen (1978) organized the morphemes he investigated into verb-related and noun-related classes and was able to show a clear implicational ordering of the morphemes within each class. Hawkins (2001) has argued, that such an approach is insightful because it raises interesting questions that require explanation, for example,

'Why does a copular construction become established more accurately than an aspectual one?' Hawkins' preference is to seek an explanation within linguistic theory, as undertaken by Zobl and Liceras (1994), but an alternative might be to adopt Goldschneider and DeKeyser's approach, that is to say, to examine the power of a number of variables to predict the accuracy of use of particular classes or morphemes rather than of a mixed set.

Finally, and perhaps, most seriously, it has been claimed that obligatory occasion analysis fails to tell us anything about whether learners know the functions of the morphemes they have 'acquired' (Long and Sato 1983). Consider for example the learner who uses progressive *-ing* in these contexts:

My father is living with us at the moment.

He was very sick but now he is getting better.

* Every day he is sleeping till midday.

The first two sentences indicate that this learner can use *-ing* correctly to indicate an activity that is in progression but the third sentence shows that this learner also uses *-ing* to refer to habitual activity (a function that requires the use of the present simple tense). A standard obligatory occasion analysis would examine only the first two sentences (the obligatory occasions for the use of *-ing*) and would record this learner's accuracy of use as 100 per cent. Clearly, this is unsatisfactory. However, as we will shortly see, it is possible to address this problem by means of *target-like use analysis* (Pica 1984). While this does not provide information about the specific functions realized by a particular morpheme, it does take account of the functional overuse of a morpheme. As such, it provides an adequate basis for examining why some morphemes come to be used more accurately than others.

This discussion of some of the common criticisms levelled at obligatory occasion analysis and the morpheme studies suggests that the problems may have been overstated and that they can be overcome by:

- expanding the set of morphemes to be investigated;
- undertaking more longitudinal studies;
- grouping learners according to their proficiency so that it is possible to examine the accuracy of morphemes produced by learners at a similar stage of development;
- categorizing the morphemes into classes to ensure that like is compared with like; and
- adopting a method of analysis that takes into account overuse of morphemes as well as correct suppliance.

The study of learners' use of morphemes through obligatory occasion analysis still has much to offer SLA. The descriptive information it provides serves as a basis for testing the validity of different explanations of the order of acquisition.

Conducting an obligatory occasion analysis

We will begin by outlining the basic procedure for conducting an obligatory occasion analysis and its modification to take account of learners' overuse of morphemes (i.e. target-like use analysis). We will then examine how this procedure can be applied in both cross-sectional studies to provide an account of the order of acquisition. This will involve a consideration of three different methods—the group score method, the group means method and implicational scaling. Finally, we will examine how obligatory occasion analysis has been used to determine the order of acquisition in longitudinal studies.

This account of the various methods will be illustrated using the data shown in Table 4.2. These data come from a study by Ellis (1987), who used obligatory occasion analysis to investigate the variable use of three morphemes (past copula, irregular past tense and regular past tense) in the speech of low intermediate learners taking ESL classes in Britain. The data were clinically elicited using a picture composition telling the story of a robbery at an airport. The learners were first asked to write the story in their own time. After their written compositions had been collected in, they were asked to record the same story orally. The data shown in Table 4.2 are transcriptions of three of the learners' oral stories.

Calculating accuracy scores

The basic procedure for calculating accuracy for individual morphemes scores based on suppliance in obligatory occasions is as follows:

1 Determine which morpheme is to be investigated.
2 Go through the data and identify obligatory occasions for the use of the morpheme. Count the total number of occasions.
3 Establish whether the correct morpheme is supplied in each obligatory context. Count the number of times it is supplied.
4 Calculate the percentage of accurate use with this formula:

$$\frac{n \text{ correct suppliance in contexts}}{\text{total obligatory contexts}} \times 100 = \text{per cent accuracy}$$

5 Repeat the procedure for the other morphemes to be investigated.

To take account of overuse of a morpheme (which the above procedure fails to do) Pica (1994) proposed what she called 'target-like use analysis'. This is calculated using the following formula:

$$\frac{n \text{ correct suppliance in contexts}}{n \text{ obligatory contexts} + n \text{ suppliance in non-obligatory contexts}} \times 100 = \text{per cent accuracy}$$

Learner 1

One day a man of (.) a man of the India arrived at the airport//at custom desk the (.) two man watching at the gentleman (.) while (.) while he was wait for someone he had a chat with the child//when he turn over he find that there was no anything behind him//and he was very (.) and he was much surprise and cried 'Where's my basket" Who's steals my basket?'//and he went out and shouted 'Help me. They are stealer'//the policeman saw (.) the thief running over with basket//and he follows them//but they escaped (.) escaped by car//when they reach (.) when they reached at the park and opened the basket and (.) they were very surprised (a) at the (.) at the inside of the basket//and he (.) they shouted 'Where are the important things in the basket?'//

Learner 2

One day (.) one day Ali arrived to (.) airport and he was watching for his friend//a tall man and a little boy standing behind (.) his and watching his//a policemen was standing near the door//a little boy came and asked Ali where is the toilet// and (er) suddenly that man (.) that tall man (.) escape robber his basket//and the little boy escape//Ali saw her (.) his basket there wasn't//he shouted//he shouted an a policeman whistle//the tall man hold (er) his basket and (er) with the little boy escape//they took (er) their (.) they took their car and ride very fast//after the zoo (.) after the zoo they (.) the man and the little boy open the basket and (er) they saw (er) no jewellery and money//a big snake and they were very afraid and shocked//

Learner 3

One day some Indian gentleman arrived (.) at the airport from India and he waited for his friend coming//but his friend (.) friend didn't appear soon//so he waited about one year (.) no one hour//and behind him two mens (.) watched him but he didn't know about this//an one boy told him 'Can I help you?'//and Ali didn't know who was behind him//and then some man (.) stoled his luggage and they escaped//so Ali asked the (.) help him to the policeman//and the policemam blew(.) whistle but it were too late and they escape through the door and (.) went to some place//and they open the luggage and big snake appear//of course they were es (.) scared//

Transcription key:
(.) unfilled pause
(er) filled pause
// utterance boundary

Table 4.2 Oral narratives produced by three L2 learners

Dulay and Burt (1980) propose an alternate method for scoring suppliance that usefully distinguishes between failure to supply any morpheme and suppliance of an incorrect morpheme and awards a 'half-credit' to the latter:

no morpheme supplied (for example, 'Two child') = 0 points

misformed morpheme supplied (for example, 'Two childs') = 1 point

correct morpheme supplied (for example, 'Two children') = 2 points

This is based on the assumption that an attempt to supply a morpheme, even if incorrect, provides evidence of a greater degree of acquisition than failure to use any morpheme. Such an assumption is only justified, however, if it can be shown that suppliance of an incorrect morpheme is characteristic of a later stage of development than omission. There is some evidence that this is the case (see Ellis 1994: Chapter 3).

To illustrate this procedure, we will examine the accuracy of use of three morphemes in the data shown in Table 4.2: past tense copula, irregular past tense and regular past tense. Table 4.3 shows the number of obligatory occasions for each morpheme, the number of times it is correctly supplied and the number of overuses of the morpheme. It also shows the percentage accuracy of use of each morpheme based on the target-like use method of scoring. Table 4.3 shows that for these three learners past copula and past irregular are performed with a similar level of accuracy but that past regular is used much less accurately.

The identification of obligatory occasions is not always as straightforward as it might seem. Let us consider some of the problems. One problem concerns how to deal with repetitions. For example, Learner 1 says

and he *was* very (.) and he *was* much surprise

Learner	**past copula**				**past irregular**				**past regular**			
	OC	S	OU	%	OC	S	OU	%	OC	S	OU	%
1	6	5	0	83	4	3	0	80	9	6	0	67
2	5	4	0	80	6	5	0	83	8	4	0	50
3	3	3	0	100	7	6	0	86	9	6	1	60
Total	14	12	0	86	17	14	0	82	26	16	1	59

Key:
OC = obligatory occasions
S = suppliance
OU = overuse

Table 4.3 Obligatory occasion analysis of three past tense morphemes

Should this count as one or two obligatory occasions for copula? We took the decision to exclude repeated phrases and thus identified only one obligatory occasion here. However, this in turn poses another problem. What should the analyst do with repeated phrases where the learner self-corrects? An example arises when Learner 1 says:

When they *reach* (.) when they *reached* at the park

Should the analyst count this as two obligatory occasions or just one? Again, to be consistent, we decided to count it as one. However, we then had to decide whether the learner had or had not supplied the *-ed* morpheme. We scored this occasion as 'not supplied' on the grounds that *-ed* was omitted when the learner first used the verb *reach*. This might seem arbitrary but given that the purpose of the analysis was to identify accuracy of use in the learners' spontaneous speech it seemed logical to discount occasions where the learners monitored their performance. A further problem concerns whether to identify obligatory occasions for tokens or for types. Learner 2, for example, uses the verb *escape* three times with the learner failing to supply the *-ed* morpheme on each occasion. Here, then, there are three tokens of a single verb. If we scored for type, we would identify a single obligatory occasion; if we scored for tokens, we would identify three obligatory occasions. In this case we decided to score for tokens on the grounds that each use of *escape* provided an opportunity for the learner to supply *-ed*. It should be clear, however, that decisions such as these can have a profound effect on the accuracy scores recorded. For this reason it is important that the analysts (1) are consistent in their decision making, (2) make their coding decisions explicit, and (3) provide a rationale for each decision.

Determining the order of acquisition

The procedure described above serves to identify the accuracy in individual learners' use of a range of grammatical morphemes. How can the results of such an analysis be used to establish the order of acquisition? In the case of cross-sectional studies, one way of establishing the order of acquisition is established by ranking morphemes that have been investigated in terms of their accuracy. Another way is by the use of implicational scaling.

In order to rank morphemes it is necessary for the analyst to first establish a mean accuracy score for each morpheme. Dulay, Burt, and Krashen (1982) propose two ways of computing this. According to the *group method score*, the suppliance scores for a particular morpheme are summed and divided by the total number of obligatory occasions for *all* the learners in the sample. The answer is then expressed as a percentage by multiplying by 100. In this method, then, even learners who produce just one obligatory occasion for a morpheme can be included in the group score. The danger here is that this will lead to error in the accuracy score for a morpheme as one obligatory occasion is not really sufficient to determine to what extent a learner has acquired the morpheme. However, if the size of the sample of learners is large the danger of this measurement error occurring is minimized. In the *group means method*, it is eliminated entirely by excluding from the sample all learners with fewer than three obligatory occasions for a morpheme. For example, if a learner had only two obligatory occasions for 3rd person *-s* and possessive *-s* but had more than three occasions for the other morphemes under study, then this learner would be excluded from the calculation for the first two morphemes but included for the others.

Once group scores have been achieved for individual morphemes, the morphemes can be ranked in decreasing order of accuracy, that is, the morpheme with the highest accuracy score is placed at the top and the morpheme with the lowest score at the bottom. Table 4.4 shows the accuracy order for three past tense morphemes based on the scores shown in Table 4.3. This is then equated with the order of acquisition on the grounds that morphemes that are used more accurately will be acquired earlier. (See discussion above.)

One of the problems with rank ordering should be immediately apparent—it fails to acknowledge differences in the degrees of accuracy among the morphemes. For example, Table 4.3 shows that past copula and past irregular have very similar levels of accuracy, differing by only 4 per cent, whereas past regular has a much lower level of accuracy, differing from the other two morphemes by more than 20 per cent. This problem can be overcome by grouping morphemes with accuracy scores that are close. Thus, a more reasonable interpretation of the scores shown in Table 4.4 might be to propose an acquisition order in which past copula and past irregular are acquired at the same time and past regular some time later. It is this thinking that underlies the acquisition hierarchy shown in Figure 4.1.

In rank-ordering methods such as these, it is not necessary to decide whether a particular morpheme has been 'acquired' or not; the acquisition order is based on accuracy order irrespective of the absolute level of accuracy of individual morphemes. However, an important question—and one that must be answered in order to carry out implicational scaling—concerns the level of accuracy of use a learner must achieve in order to claim that a morpheme has been acquired. Traditionally (see Brown 1973), the level is set at 90 per cent. Thus, if a learner achieves an accuracy score of 90 per cent

Morpheme	Group accuracy score	Rank position
past copula	86%	1
past irregular	82%	2
past regular	59%	3

Table 4.4 Accuracy/acquisition order for three past tense morphemes

or higher, the morpheme is considered 'acquired' but if the score is lower (even 89 per cent), it is deemed 'not acquired'. Implicational scaling requires the analyst to score morphemes, on the basis of their accuracy scores as either 1 ('acquired') or 0 ('not acquired'). The choice of 90 per cent as the acquisition level is based on two assumptions; first, it constitutes a level close to 100 per cent and second, it corresponds to the level achieved by native speakers, who typically fail to perform at 100 per cent accuracy themselves (i.e. they make 'slips').

Implicational scaling is a procedure for establishing the extent to which a proposed acquisition order is statistically valid. It is based on the dichotomous scoring of a given morpheme as 'acquired' or 'not acquired', as described above. The basic steps are as follows:

1 The analyst constructs a matrix where the morphemes are ordered horizontally from 'difficult' to 'easy' according to the number of learners who have acquired each morpheme.
2 The analyst then lists the learners vertically according to the number of morphemes each learner has acquired. The learner who has acquired the greatest number of morphemes is placed at the top and the learner who acquired the fewest at the bottom.
3 The analyst then indicates whether each learner has acquired each morpheme by placing a 1 or a 0 in the rows of the matrix.
4 The analyst then attempts to draw in a 'staircase' showing the acquisition order revealed by the analysis. (See the example in Table 4.5.) This constitutes the proposed scaling.
5 Usually, the analyst will find that the data do not fit into a perfect staircase. That is, there will be instances where an individual learner has failed to acquire an 'easy' morpheme but has acquired a more 'difficult' morpheme. These instances are marked in the table to indicate that they are exceptions to the scaling that is being proposed.
6 It is then possible to calculate the *coefficient of reproducibility* (Crep). This tells us the extent to which we can accurately predict which

Learner	past participle -*en*	3rd person -*s*	long plural -*es*	short plural -*s*	pronoun case
L1	1	1	1	1	1
L2	0	1	1	1	1
L3	0	①	0	1	1
L4	0	0	0	1	1
L5	0	①	0	0	1
L6	0	0	0	0	0

Table 4.5 Implicational scaling matrix for five morphemes

morphemes each learner has acquired on the basis of his/her rank in the matrix. It is calculated by means of this formula:

$$\text{Crep} = \frac{1 - \text{number of errors}}{(\text{number of learners})\ (\text{number of items})}$$

A Crep score of 90 per cent or higher indicates that the proposed scaling is 'valid'.

It is not possible to illustrate this procedure using the accuracy scores shown in Table 4.3 as no learner has reached the 90 per cent accuracy level in any of the three past tense morphemes. A contrived example of a scaling matrix, therefore, is shown in Table 4.5. This shows whether six learners have acquired five morphemes. There are two errors in this scaling (shown in **bold**). The Crep is, therefore, 94 per cent (i.e. $1 - (2/\ 5 \times 6)$). As this is higher than 90 per cent, the proposed acquisition order shown in the implicational scale can be considered valid.

All of these above procedures constitute ways of determining an acquisition order from cross-sectional data. In longitudinal studies, it is obviously much easier to determine the acquisition order. The procedure usually followed is that proposed by Brown (1973) in his study of three children acquiring English as a mother tongue. Brown used the 90 per cent accuracy level to determine whether a particular morpheme had been acquired. However, because he found that the children sometimes reached this level at one data point only to fall below it at the next, he instituted a second requirement: for a morpheme to be acquired a learner had to achieve the 90 per cent criterion level on three consecutive data points.

Summary

Performance analysis based on obligatory occasions has been used to establish an acquisition order for grammatical morphemes. With cross-sectional data this involves two principal steps:

1 Calculating the accuracy of use of each morpheme. This can be achieved by means of an obligatory occasion analysis or a target-like use analysis. Morphemes can be scored as either correct/incorrect or credit can be given for learners' attempts to supply a morpheme even if this is incorrect.
2 Determining the order of acquisition based on accuracy scores. This involves either ranking morphemes to produce an accuracy order, which is then equated with the acquisition order, or carrying out implicational scaling based on the number of learners achieving a criterion level (usually 90 per cent) of accuracy for each morpheme. With longitudinal data, learners are considered to have acquired a morpheme if they achieve the 90 per cent criterion level on three consecutive occasions.

An example of a study using obligatory occasion analysis

As we have seen, the morpheme studies carried out in the 1970s were concerned with whether it was possible to identify a 'natural order' for the acquisition of English grammatical morphemes. The study that we will consider here built on this research to address an important issue for SLA and language pedagogy—what effect instruction has on the acquisition of an L2.

Whereas behaviourist views of language learning (see Chapter 3) lent support to instructional approaches of the direct intervention kind through methods such as audiolingualism, nativist views stressed the 'built-in syllabus' of the learner (Corder 1967). The latter views thus questioned whether instructing learners in specific linguistic features had any effect on interlanguage development. The demonstration of a 'natural order of acquisition' by the morpheme studies lent support to the nativist position and led researchers to investigate whether learners who received instruction manifested the same or a different order. Early studies by Perkins and Larsen-Freeman (1975), Fathman (1978), Turner (1979), and Makino (1980) compared the acquisition orders of groups of naturalistic and instructed learners. The results suggested that the natural order was impervious to instruction. However, Sajaavara (1981) found different acquisitional orders in naturalistic and instructed learners, largely because articles ranked lower in the instructed group. Also, Fathman found differences in the kinds of error committed by the two groups. These studies suggested that by and large learners followed their own syllabus but also that instruction did seem to have some impact on learners' performance of specific grammatical features.

Pica's (1984) study (summarized in Table 4.6) is by far the most insightful of the comparative morpheme studies directed at investigating the effects of instruction on acquisition. She investigated three groups of learners—an instructed group, a naturalistic group, and a mixed group—using performance analysis to compare the accuracy/acquisition orders of the same morphemes reported by Krashen (1977a). Pica's study is methodologically more sophisticated than the earlier studies in that she examined learners' oversuppliance of grammatical morphemes through a target-like use analysis as well as suppliance in obligatory contexts. Also, detailed analyses of specific morphemes ((i.e. progressive *-ing*, 3rd person *-s* and plural *-s*) allowed her to probe how the linguistic nature of specific morphemes affects the way in which they are used in both obligatory and non-obligatory contexts, how linguistic context (for example, the presence of a quantifier before a plural noun) influences their use, and how instruction interacts with these other variables to determine acquisition. Arguably, a performance analysis that examines qualitatively how learners use individual morphemes is more insightful than a quantitative one that simply ranks morphemes according to their general level of accuracy.

Research question	Pica investigated whether learners' production of a number of grammatical morphemes differed according to the conditions of their exposure to linguistic input.
Participants	18 adult native speakers aged 18–50. Six represented an 'instruction only' condition, six a 'naturalistic' condition, and six a 'mixed' condition (i.e. a mixture of the other two conditions).
Data collection	The data consisted of hour-long audio-taped conversations in which the participants were asked to talk about personal topics (e.g. their future plans).
Analysis	Pica carried out the following analyses: 1 Supplied in obligatory context analysis 2 Target-like use analysis 3 Rank orders based on (1) 4 An analysis of morpheme over-generalization and overuse 5 Accuracy of plural -*s* in noun phrases preceded by a quantifier (i.e. where -*s* was redundant).
Results	The main results were: 1 Krashen's 'natural order' held for all three groups, including the instruction group. 2 The accuracy orders for the three groups were highly inter-correlated (i.e. the rank orders were very similar). 3 The instructed group oversupplied morphemes to a greater extent than the other two groups. 4 The naturalistic group was more likely to omit morphemes entirely, including plural -*s* in nouns following a quantifier.
Discussion	Pica notes that the hypothesis that instruction would disturb the natural order of acquisition was not supported. The hypothesis that the instructed learners would make more errors of oversuppliance was partially supported in that the instructed learners oversupplied only certain morphemes (e.g. -*ing* and plural -*s*) more than the other groups. The third hypothesis, that naturalistic learners, would express plurality other than through use of plural -*s* was supported.

Table 4.6 (*continued*)

Implications	Pica suggests that the effects of instruction are twofold; it triggers oversuppliance of some morphemes and inhibits use of ungrammatical but communicative constructions.

Table 4.6 Summary of Pica's (1983) study

Pica's study is limited in a number of ways. As she points out, the small size of the sample (only 18, six in each group) and the fact that it investigated adults with the same L1 background limits the conclusions that can be drawn. Pica is also careful to note that that the study only addresses interlanguage production, not L2 acquisition, although she does refer consistently to 'order of acquisition' throughout the article. The limitations of the study are in part those of obligatory occasion analysis itself (see previous discussion) and in part those of the design of the study. Comparative studies of instructed and naturalistic learners do not constitute a strong test of the effects of instruction on acquisition for the simple reason that the researcher is forced to assume that the learning contexts are different and has no way of determining exactly how they are distinguished. While there is evidence to show that instructed and naturalistic learning contexts are generally different in several respects, these differences are not *necessary* ones. Naturalistic learners can engage in self-instruction; instructed learners can experience opportunities for meaning-focused communication.

Pica's study was the last of the morpheme studies to be published in a major SLA journal. In a sense, through its detailed analysis of specific morphemes, it paved the way for the research that followed. This consisted of descriptive studies addressing the acquisition of specific grammatical features and experimental studies investigating the effects of form-focused instruction directed at specific features.

Task: Carrying out an obligatory occasion analysis

Below are transcriptions of the oral narratives produced by five learners. The learners were shown a picture composition for two minutes and then asked to tell the story into a cassette recorder. The were told to begin their story with *One day* ... The learners were of low-intermediate proficiency and were all enrolled in the same adult ESL class in London.

Carry out a performance analysis of the following grammatical morphemes:

1 pronoun case
2 copula (Your concern here is not whether the correct past form of the copula is used but simply whether a copula form is supplied in a context requiring it.)
3 plural *-s*

Learner 1 (L1 French; 46 years old; studied English for approximately 4 years)

one evening a little boy was going back at home after the classroom (.) after the class//he went out of the bus with three packets//one of them the small xx falled on the ground//he don't saw it//but the man who was passing by this way saw it and he would given this packet to the little boy//also he took the same way (.)//it was dark but the moon was full//when the little boy saw the man who follow him he was afraid//he ran quickly followed by the man//just before that little boy arrive in his house the man join him and gave him his packet//then the little boy was very happy to receive his packet

Learner 2 (L1 Polish; 28 years old; studied English for 5.5 years)

one day Peter went back to home with his shopping//he has two big boxes and one small//when he get out bus (.) he lost small box//he has (.) had a long walk to his house//when he walked (.) home he met a strange man on the road//he was afraid (.) and he (.) started to run (.)//he (.) this strange man started to run after (.) him// behind Peter//when Peter was near home he this man (.) this strange man (.) catch and told (.) and said him 'You lost your box'//it was surprise for Peter//and he said 'Thank you very much'

Learner 3 (L1 Spanish; 21 years old; studied English for 2 years)

One evening a little boy get out of the bus//he have three box (.)//he (er) lost one of them//he didn't realize//the night was very dark and the little boy have to walk a lot of (.) a long time (.) to arrive his house//a man was walking behind him//then the little boy was afraid about that//he start to run and the man ran after him as well// when the little boy was near her house (.) his house the man got him//and the man show to the little boy the small box//the the little boy was very happy because he thought the man who was walking behind him were a thief (.) or horrible man.

Learner 4 (L1 German; 23 years old; studied English for 1 year)

One evening the boy was going out of his bus//he has three cases//xx but he don't know what he was thinking and he (.)//on the way for his home it was very dark and windy and a lot of trees//there was not noise//and a man come behi comes behind him//and the boy stopped and saw this man and he was very angry//and he thinked I must run//and he runs and runs along the way//and the man behind him runs and runs and runs//and then he stopped this boy (.) and said 'xx you losed one case//I want to give it to you'//'Oh' said the boy//and the boy was very lucky (.) very happy//and he said 'thank you'

Learner 5 (L1 Farsi; 43 years old; studied English for 3 years)

Boy s getting out (.) boy getting out in the bus (.) getting off the bus//and he has got three parcel in his hand//he must walking twenty minutes//(er) he going to the home//and (er) evening and the moon is shining and he's going (.) very fast to the

Table 4.7 (*continued*)

house//after (er) ten minute walk he's heard somebody in (.) back (er) him//and he's stop and watching the man//and after that he's saw the man is dark (.) suit and dark (er) hat//and he's right run away//he's run away and the man is run away//the *mani is shouting 'wait a minute//wait a minute//I have to speak to you//wait a minute'//and he's stop and he's (er) he's stop because he's (er) nearly get home// he's watched the man and the man say //'Sorry you dropped the parcel and I (er) and I after you give it to you this parcel'//and the boy he say 'Thank you very much//thanks//I'm sorry before I was afraid//thank you'*

Key:
(·) pause
// utterance boundary
' ' direct speech
xx words that were unclear and could not be transcribed

Table 4.7 Transcription of oral naratives

4 articles
5 regular past tense
6 irregular past tense

Your analysis should involve the following steps:

1 Identify the obligatory occasions for the use of the six morphemes and calculate the level of accurate suppliance of each morpheme by each learner.
2 Identify instances of oversuppliance of each morpheme and then calculate a target-like use score for each morpheme for each learner.
3 Determine the overall accuracy order for the six morphemes using the group score method.
4 Carry out an implicational scaling for the six morphemes and calculate the coefficient of reproducibility.

When you have finished your analyses consider these questions:

1 Does the accuracy order you have found correspond to the 'natural order of acquisition' as shown in Figure 4.1?
2 What problems did you experience in carrying out this analysis? How did you deal with each problem?

Final comment

Obligatory occasion analysis has served as the principal tool for analysing samples of learner language where the purpose is to describe the order of acquisition. The regularities in L2 development that this type of analysis has revealed constitute one of the major findings of SLA. The order that learners follow constitutes one of the most important 'facts' that any theory of L2 acquisition must account for (Long 1990b). This fact must also be taken into consideration in language pedagogy, in particular in making decisions about whether (or perhaps when) to provide form-focused instruction.

A limitation of obligatory occasion analysis is that is it is target-oriented. That is, it tells us whether or not learners have acquired target language forms. It is incapable of describing the interlanguage forms that arise as learners approximate to target language norms. For this reason, it sheds little light on the actual processes involved in acquiring a second language. In the next chapter we will consider another type of performance analysis that fares much better in this respect.

Notes

1 Krashen (1977a) argued that Rosansky's analysis was invalid as there were insufficient obligatory occasions for several of the morphemes. He argued that in studies where there was a minimum of seven obligatory occasions, the standard 'natural order' was obtained. However, Hakuta's study met this criterion so the differences he found cannot be so easily dismissed.

2 Other studies have reported a relationship between input frequency and accuracy order but they have not examined the input to the actual learners whose accuracy orders were investigated. Larsen-Freeman (1976), for example, reported significant correlations between the accuracy orders of ESL learners and the frequency orders of morphemes in the input of two ESL teachers who were not the learners' teachers.

3 Morpheme studies have typically been carried out on learner populations with very mixed proficiency levels. We know of no study where L2 proficiency has been used as a co-variant. The ordering for verb morphemes reported by Andersen (1978) was:

   copula → aspect (progressive) → tense (past) → subject-verb agreement (3rd person -*s*).

   A similar approach was adopted by J. D. Brown (1983), who grouped morphemes according to whether they were bound or free.

5 Frequency analysis

Introduction

Frequency analysis (Cancino *et al.* 1978) examines the various devices a learner uses in order to perform a specific grammatical feature and, therefore, can account for the inherent variability in learner language. For example, at one stage of development a learner might realize English irregular past tense by means of four linguistic devices:

1 the simple form of the verb (for example, *eat*)
2 over-generalized *-ed* (for example, *eated*)
3 double marking (for example, *ated*)
4 the irregular past tense form of the verb (for example, *ate*)

In frequency analysis, the analyst computes the frequency with which each of these devices is used by individual learners. By comparing the devices used at one stage of development with those used for the same linguistic feature at another time it is possible to describe the developmental route that learners follow. An advantage of frequency analysis is that it examines learner language in its own right rather than in relation to target language norms and thus avoids the *comparative fallacy* (Bley-Vroman 1983). Another advantage is that it captures the gradual and dynamic nature of interlanguage development (Huebner 1979).

Historical and theoretical background

We have seen that the morpheme studies came under attack in the late seventies and early eighties. Not all of the criticisms were directed at obligatory occasion analysis itself, which has continued to serve as a measure of accuracy. (See Chapter 7.) However, in one key respect obligatory occasion analysis (like error analysis) was found wanting. Bley-Vroman (1983: 15) pointed out that:

> ... any study which classifies interlanguage (IL) data according to a target language (TL) scheme or depends on the notion of obligatory context or binary choice will likely fail to illuminate the structure of the IL.

He went on to argue 'if researchers are to make serious progress in the investigation of interlanguage then the comparative fallacy must be avoided'

(1983: 16). In other words, learners' use of linguistic forms must be examined in their own right, not in terms of whether they correspond to target language forms. The question then arises as to how this can be achieved. The answer was frequency analysis, sometimes also referred to as *interlanguage analysis*.

Frequency analysis was closely linked to the study of variability in learner language. Learners sometimes produce errors and sometimes do not. In making errors, they do not always use the same non-target form. That is, the nature of the error varies from occasion to occasion. To describe the variability inherent in learner language, then, it is necessary to identify the *variants* that learners employ in the performance of a linguistic variable. Consider for example the linguistic variable 'third person present copula' in English. Ellis (1988) reports that the learners he studied used three variants:

zero copula (for example, *There church.*)
contracted copula (for example, *There's church.*)
full copula (for example, *There is a church.*)

Ellis shows that the learners differed in the frequency of use of these variants both horizontally, in accordance with the linguistic context, and also vertically, in accordance with their level of development. The learners were much more likely to use zero copula following a subject containing a noun (an open class element) than one consisting of a pronoun (a closed class element); interlanguage development, in contrast, consisted of the gradual replacement of zero copula by first full copula and then contracted copula. To study the nature of variability in learner language and, in particular, the relationship between horizontal and vertical variability, it is necessary to perform a frequency analysis.

Studies of variability, then, show that learners do not operate in accordance with categorical rules. That is, they do not have a clear rule for structures such as 3rd person copula, negation, or the definite article in English. In this respect they are both the same as and different from native speakers of the target language. They are the same in that native speakers also display variability—for example, they alternate in the use of full and contracted copula. They are different in that learners do not adhere to a categorical rule where native speakers do; they also typically employ a wider range of variants in the performance of a linguistic variable than native speakers. Put simply, learner language is much more variable than native speaker language use. This latter point is crucial because it implies that learner language cannot be effectively studied by comparing it to native speaker language use, even if variable target language norms serve as the basis for the comparison.

Frequency analysis is needed for another reason. It provides the methodological means for describing the stages of development that learners pass through on route to mastery of a linguistic structure. That is, it informs about the *sequence of acquisition*. Whereas 'order of acquisition' refers to the order in which learners acquire a number of different features such as the morphemes discussed in Chapter 4, 'sequence of acquisition' refers to the different stages in the acquisition of a single structure. Dulay, Burt, and Krashen (1982) use the term *transitional construction* to label features that manifest stages of development. They give as examples (for English) *wh*-questions, *yes/no* questions, embedded *wh*-questions and reflexive pronouns. A number of early longitudinal studies of L2 learners (for example, Ravem 1968; Wode 1976; Cancino, Rosansky, and Schumann 1978), which were carried out concurrently with the morpheme studies discussed above, documented the existence of such constructions and sought to identify the stages of development involved in the acquisition of each. Cancino *et al.*, for example, collected samples of spontaneous speech from six Spanish learners of English over a ten-month period. Initially they tried to account for the learners' acquisition of negatives by writing rules but found that 'the constant development and concomitant variation ... at any one point made the task impossible' (1978: 209–10). The solution was frequency analysis. They reported:

> The technique to which we turned was to catalogue the various negating devices (*no, don't, can't, isn't*, etc.) and for each sample to determine the proportion of each negating device to total number of negatives used by our subjects.

As a result of this procedure they identified a sequence of acquisition for negating devices that consisted of: (1) *no* + V, (2) *don't* + V, (3) aux-neg and (4) analysed *don't*[1] and disappearance of *no* + V. Subsequent studies of English negation for learners from different language backgrounds have found a very similar sequence of acquisition. (See Ellis 1994: Chapter 3.) Transitional constructions, however, are not limited to the acquisition of negatives and the other structures mentioned by Dulay, Burt, and Krashen (1982). Arguably, *all* constructions are transitional; that is, learners do not acquire any single structure straight off but pass through a series of stages before arriving at the target language form. Frequency analysis, therefore, serves as an important tool for describing how learners acquire the grammar of an L2.

The results obtained by studies that employed frequency analysis lent further support to the nativist claim that L2 acquisition is best explained in terms of learner internal contributions rather than environmental factors. The sequences of acquisition appeared to a large extent universal, uninfluenced except in relatively minor ways by learners' L1s.[2] They reflected a re-creation continuum of development rather than a restructuring one. (See Corder 1978.) That is, the stages of acquisition for structures such as negatives and interrogatives were best explained in terms of learners re-creating the stages of development evident in L1 acquisition rather than in terms of them systematically replacing L1 by L2 structures. The research pointed clearly to the view that learners' interlanguages constituted distinct linguistic systems that evolved gradually via a series of stages towards the norms of the target language. As Selinker (1984: 338) in his review of the current state of interlanguage studies put it, 'What is nice and clear, and most colleagues now accept this as fact, is that there exist patterns of regularity in IL data'. It was frequency analysis that revealed these patterns of regularity.

These early studies investigated naturalistic L2 acquisition. Later studies investigated the effects of instruction on the 'natural' sequences of acquisition. These were motivated by the same theoretical and practical concerns that informed studies such as Pica (1983). That is, they addressed the explanatory power of nativist accounts of L2 acquisition and they examined the extent to which form-focused instruction had a role to play in classroom language learning. Ellis (1984a) conducted a longitudinal study of three beginner classroom learners. Using similar techniques to those employed by Cancino *et al.*, he collected samples of spontaneous utterances from within the classroom and then submitted these to a frequency analysis. He found the same order of acquisition for negatives and interrogatives as that reported for naturalistic learners. Subsequent studies were experimental in design, seeking to establish whether instruction directed at specific target constructions enabled learners to 'jump' the early stages of acquisition. The results for *wh*-interrogatives (Ellis 1984a), for German word order rules (Pienemann 1984; Ellis 1989) and relative clauses (Pavesi 1986) suggested that the acquisition sequences were largely impervious to instruction. Reviewing these and other studies, Long (1988: 135) concluded that 'instruction does not... seem able to alter acquisition sequences, except temporarily, and in trivial ways, which may even hinder subsequent development'.

Frequency analysis has continued to figure in studies of L2 learners. It serves as the principal means for the analysis of data collected at different points of time (i.e. in longitudinal studies). A good example of its more recent use can be found in the European Science Foundation (ESF) study of adult migrant learners of a number of European languages. This was directed at providing a full account of the route of naturalistic interlanguage development. Klein and Perdue (1992) drew on the detailed findings of studies of different L2s to propose three general developmental levels in how learners organized their utterances. Initially learners' utterances were extremely simple, consisting mainly of unconnected nouns, adverbs and particles ('nominal utterance organization'). This stage gave way to a stage where learners began to use non-tensed verbs ('infinite utterance organization') and then to a stage where verbs are tensed ('finite utterance organization'). These stages were evident in all learners' learning all the languages under study.

The hypothesized immutability of acquisition sequences has continued to be tested in experimental studies. Spada and Lightbown (1993), for example, examined the effects of instruction on English interrogatives, basing their analysis on Pienemann, Johnston, and Brindley's (1988) six-stage sequence for this structure. They were able to show that the instruction assisted learners by helping them to produce questions at more advanced stages but did not seem to result in them skipping stages. For example, learners who produced stage 2 questions before the instruction were able to produce stage 3 questions after the instruction but not necessarily stage 4 or stage 5 questions. A subsequent study by Spada and Lightbown (1999) again indicates that instruction does not alter the natural route of acquisition. However, this study suggests that the instruction need not be 'fine-tuned' to the proximate developmental stage of individual learners. That is, even learners at an early stage of development were able to advance as a result of instruction directed at the target structure (representing the final stage). In this respect, these later studies suggest a more positive role for form-focused instruction than Long (1988) saw as possible.

Frequency analysis, then, has proved a valuable tool for investigating variability in learner language and for describing the sequence of language acquisition. The studies that have employed frequency analysis hold a central place in SLA research, contributing to some of its major findings. Whereas the morpheme studies fell out of favour as a result of the criticisms levelled at obligatory occasion analysis, studies of acquisition sequences based on frequency analysis have remained popular and have continued to contribute to theory development.

Nevertheless, frequency analysis is not without its problems. First, longitudinal studies of L2 learners are very time-consuming. However, pseudo-longitudinal studies overcome this practical problem. In such studies samples of learner language are collected from groups of learners of different proficiency levels at a single point in time. A longitudinal picture can be then constructed by comparing the devices used by the different groups ranked according to their proficiency. However, the validity of pseudo-longitudinal studies is dependent on the validity of the measure used to group the learners and, as Larsen-Freeman (1978) has pointed out, there is no widely accepted general index of L2 acquisition.

A second problem concerns how to operationalize 'stage of acquisition'. The procedure usually adopted (see, for example, Cancino *et al.* 1978) is to establish which device is most frequent in the learner's use of the L2 at a particular time. This feature characterizes the 'stage' the learner is at. However, Pienemann (1985) has suggested that stage of acquisition be determined in relation to 'onset', defined as the emergence of a feature in at least two 'creative' utterances in a learner's spontaneous speech.[3] However, this definition of 'acquisition' lacks rigour, not least because of the difficulty of determining what constitutes 'creative' as opposed to 'formulaic' speech. Arguably, an approach based on quantification is safer.

A third problem concerns the artificiality of defining the sequence of acquisition in terms of a set of stages. Researchers such as Huebner (1979) have pointed out that L2 acquisition is continuous and dynamic. (See Chapter 6.) Thus identifying discrete stages of development constitutes a reification of the data. Recently, sophisticated methods for analysing data using statistical tools such as VARBRUL (Young and Bayley 1996) and logistical regression (Berdan 1996) have been used to capture the complex but systematic nature of horizontal and vertical variability in learner language. These tools, however, all rely on frequency analysis.

Finally, it needs to be emphasized that frequency analysis serves as a tool for *describing* learner language and the sequence of acquisition. It does not provide an explanation. In this respect, of course, it is no different from obligatory occasion analysis.

Conducting a frequency analysis

We have already noted that a frequency analysis ideally requires longitudinal data. The procedure for carrying out a frequency analysis involves the following steps:

1. Select the linguistic variable you wish to investigate. This can be defined quite narrowly (for example, 3rd person copula *be*) or more broadly (for example, interrogatives). The choices of variable can be entirely data driven (i.e. the variable is chosen because the data affords plentiful examples of its use) or it can be theoretically motivated (for example, it is chosen to test a specific linguistic hypothesis).
2. Divide the data into periods of roughly equal length.
3. Go through the data and identify instances of use of the chosen linguistic variable.
4. Identify the different devices the learner uses to perform the linguistic variable by examining all the utterances. The analyst may like to consult previous research that has investigated the variable in question to establish putative devices but will need to check these against the data to ascertain whether they actually occur and also whether additional devices are evident.
5. Calculate the frequency of use of each device used in each period.
6. Determine the stages of acquisition by identifying which device is dominant in each period of development. This will enable the analyst to show how the learner shifts from the use of one device to another over time.

An alternative to steps (5) and (6) is to delineate the acquisition sequence in terms of the emergence of specific devices at different times. This approach eschews quantification and instead opts for the description and illustration of the stages of development. A good example can be found in the work of Andersen. (See, for example, Andersen 1984.)

We will now illustrate this procedure using the data shown in Table 5.1. These were taken from a longitudinal study of an 11-year old Punjabi speaking boy. (See Ellis 1984a.) The data for this study were collected from the learner's spontaneous classroom speech (i.e. they do not include any utterances elicited by means of a language exercise). We have extracted representative interrogatives from the data and arranged these chronologically into three periods, each period representing approximately four months.

English interrogatives constitute a well-researched transitional construction. (See Cancino *et al.* 1978; Ravem 1968; Wode 1978.) Ellis' (1984a) account of the general sequence of acquisition suggests a number of general devices that figure in learners' interrogative utterances:

1 Intonation questions (i.e. declarative utterances spoken with a rising intonation). Examples in the Table 5.1 include *My book?* (Period 1), *I go out?* (Period 2) and *They are twenty past one.* (Period 3).
2 *Wh*-questions used as formulae. A likely example in the data in Table 5.1 is *What's this?*. This occurs in all three periods.
3 *Wh*-pronouns used with a declarative nucleus. Examples from Table 5.1 are *What you doing*? (Period 2) and *What you say?* (Period 3).
4 Inversion in *yes/no* questions. Examples are *Are you a silly boy, eh?* (Period 2) and *Do you want pin?* (Period 3).
5 Inversion in *wh*-questions. Examples are *What's she writing?* (Period 2) and *Why are you coming?* (Period 3).

These categories can account for all of the utterances in Table 5.1.

However, coding the utterances in terms of these categories is not without problems. For example, it is not always easy to decide whether an utterance is an intonation question or an example of *yes/no* inversion. Consider the utterance:

Tomorrow is coming to school?

The learner has omitted the grammatical subject, making it impossible to decide whether the learner had intended to say:

Tomorrow I is coming to school? (intonation question)

or:

Tomorrow is I coming to school? (subject-verb-inversion)

In such cases, it is probably best to adopt a conservative approach by categorizing the utterances as belonging to the least advanced of the two categories (i.e. the category that appears developmentally earlier). Thus, we have coded this utterance as an intonation question.

Period	Utterance	Context
1	*My book?*	T had asked another pupil to bring his book
	Finish?	Checking if another pupil had finished.
	House?	Asking another pupil if her picture was of a house.
	Next week?	Asking when the spelling test would take place.
	What's wrong?	T had told him he was numbering his graph incorrectly.
	One colour?	Checking how many coloured crayons to use.
	Read?	Asking if he had to read.
	What's this sir?	Pointing at a word on the blackboard.
	In the locker?	Asking if he had to put his things in his locker.
2	*In the book?*	Checking if he had to write in his book.
	What you mean?	In response to another pupil who had said something he did not understand.
	In here?	Checking he was putting a book back in the correct place.
	Miss writing?	Checking if he needed to write.
	What's this?	Asking about a dictionary.
	What 'n'?	Another pupil was spelling out a name and he did not understand what she meant by 'n'.
	Drawing the picture?	Checking if he had to draw a picture
	What you doing?	To another pupil.
	What is that?	Pointing at a picture.
	Are you a silly boy, eh?	To another pupil.
	Here writing Friday?	Asking where he had to write the word 'Friday'.
	What's she writing?	Referring to the girl next to him who was writing.
	Clock drawing?	Checking if he needed to draw a clock.
	Tomorrow is coming to school?	Asking if he had to come to school the next day.
	What mean?	Asking what a word meant.
	I go out?	Asking if he had to leave the classroom.
	What colour window sir?	Asking what colour he should use for the window in his picture.
	What's go in there?	Pointing at a blank in a sentence.
	Who go first?	Referring to a game the class was playing.
3	*What's this?*	Referring to the word 'evening'.
	Where's next spelling test?	Looking for an old spelling test in his book.

Table 5.1 (*continued*)

Period	Utterance	Context
	Playing now bingo?	Asking if they were going to play bingo.
	Why are you sitting on the table?	To T who was sitting on a table.
	What you say?	Asking a pupil to repeat what he had said.
	Do you want pin?	Offering a pupil a drawing pin.
	I am sitting in the middle?	Asking if he had to sit in the middle.
	Where is the concert?	The pupils were going to a concert in the hall.
	What's this?	Checking a word on the blackboard.
	What you say?	He had not heard what another pupil had said to him.
	Writing cookie, yeah?	Seeking confirmation he had to write the word 'cooking'.
	Who is writing there?	Pointing at some writing on a desk.
	Where is the train station?	Referring to a map.
	What drawing after this?	Asking what he had to draw next.
	Why are you coming?	To researcher.
	Which nice?	Asking the T which picture he liked.
	They are twenty past one?	Checking the time he needed to write down.

Table 5.1 Interrogative utterances produced by an eleven-year old classroom learner over a twelve-month period

A less tractable problem is the difficulty in deciding whether an utterance constitutes a formula. Myles, Mitchell, and Hooper (1999: 50) describe this problem as follows:

> How do we know if a particular construction has been retrieved by the learner as an unanalysed whole or whether it is derived creatively from a rule or, indeed, whether and to what extent both processes can coexist in the learner's interlanguage at any one time?

They go on to suggest the following criteria for identifying formulae:

- Formulae have greater length and complexity compared with other learner output.
- They are spoken fluently without any hesitation.
- They are often overextended resulting in inappropriate use.

- They occur in the same form (i.e. no parts are substitutable).
- They tend to be well-formed and grammatically advanced compared to the rest of the learner's productions.
- They typically occur in routine contexts.

However, they note that 'chunk identification retains an irreducible intuitive dimension'. A quick inspection of Table 5.1 suggests that a number of utterances containing *What's*... and *Where's*... are either wholly or partly formulaic. To avoid the problem of identification we propose the following category:

wh-pronoun + ('*s*/*is*) + x

where x consists of any form other than a verb. This enables us to code utterances such as *What's this*?, *What 'n'?* and *Where bus station?* as belonging to the same category. This category differs from categories (3) and (5) above in one crucial respect—it does not involve a main verb. In the analysis of the data shown in Table 5.2, we have substituted this category for category (2) p. 99.

Our analysis of these utterances is shown in Table 5.2. It reveals that the predominant device in Period 1 is the intonation question. In period 2 we see this beginning to give way to interrogatives consisting of *wh* + declarative nucleus, which then becomes the principal device in Period 3. In Periods 2 and 3 we can also note the emergence of interrogatives with inversion although these are still in the minority. Clearly, this learner has some way to go to reach the target language norms but in general he seems to be following a sequence of acquisition very similar to that reported in the literature. It should be noted that intonation questions are commonly used by native speakers, especially as requests for confirmation (Vander Brook, Schlue, and Campbell 1980), a particular function that figured strongly in this learner's classroom speech. Thus, his continued use of this device, even after more developmentally advanced devices had emerged, was to be expected.

Interrogative device	**Period 1**	**Period 2**	**Period 3**
Intonation question	7 (78%)	8 (42%)	4 (24%)
wh + (*be*) + x	2 (22%)	3 (16%)	4 (24%)
wh + declarative nucleus	0	6 (32%)	5 (29%)
yes/no inversion	0	1 (5%)	1 (6%)
wh inversion	0	1 (5%)	3 (18%)
Totals	9	19	17

Table 5.2 Frequency analysis of interrogative utterances

An example of a study using frequency analysis

The study we have chosen as an example of frequency analysis is Berdan (1996). This constitutes a re-analysis of part of the data used by Schumann (1978) in his study of Alberto, one of the six L2 learners investigated by Cancino *et al.* (1978). Schumann (1978: 65) claimed that 'Alberto showed very little linguistic development during the course of the study'. In other words, Alberto had fossilized at an early, pidginized stage of development. Berdan set out to challenge this conclusion through a detailed analysis of Alberto's negative utterances that involved a study of the effects of both time and various contextual variables on the frequency of use of two negative devices—*no* and *don't*.

Berdan's analysis is very detailed, examining the effect of a number of factors. Here we will examine the results Berdan obtained for just three factors:

1 time (i.e. data collected at roughly 17 two-weekly intervals covering a 10-month period)
2 subject noun phrase (i.e. whether each negative utterances contained (a) no subject NP, (b) a 1st person singular pronoun, (c) some other pronoun or (d) another NP).
3 style (i.e. whether the negative utterances were produced in spontaneous conversation or by experimental elicitation).

A summary of Berdan's study is provided in Table 5.3.

The study demonstrates the importance of carrying out a fine-grained frequency analysis of learner language and of submitting the raw frequencies to searching statistical analysis. Whereas Schumann employed a standard frequency analysis of the kind illustrated in Table 5.2 and concluded that Alberto was not developing, Berdan carried out a detailed frequency analysis of the variability evident in Alberto's use of the two negative devices and, with the help of logistical regression, showed that Alberto had not fossilized. Berdan (1996: 237) comments: 'That Alberto evidences change is incontrovertible, and his change is in the direction of the target language'. Berdan was also able to show how linguistic context and style affected his choice of the more advanced *don't* over time.

There are lessons to be learned from this study. First, what analysts find in their data depends on what they decide to count! A simple frequency count of basic linguistic devices may fail to reveal significant patterning in the data. It is often necessary to explore a range of factors to discover patterning in the data. Secondly, using frequency analysis to identify discrete stages of development can be misleading. A better approach might be to adopt a method of analysis that acknowledges the variability inherent in learner language and that examines the continuous nature of L2 development. Frequency analysis in conjunction with powerful statistical techniques

Research question	Berdan investigated two research questions: 1 Is there language development in Alberto's negatives? 2 Is there systematic variation in Alberto's choice of negator?
Participants	Alberto was a 33-year old native speaker of Spanish from Costa Rica who had been in the United States for 3 months when the data collection began. He lived with another Cost Rican family and worked in a factory.
Data collection	Data were collected over a 10-month period, approximately once every two weeks. Three methods were used: 1 spontaneous speech recordings where Alberto and the researcher engaged in conversation 2 experimental elicitations (e.g. an imitation test) 3 pre-planned sociolinguistic interactions where subjects were taken to parties, restaurants, museums, sports events, etc.
Analysis	Among the analyses Berdan conducted were: 1 Frequency distribution of '*no + verb*' and '*don't + verb*' across the 17 two-weekly data collection points. 2 Frequency distribution of negative forms by subject noun phrase (no subject N P; 1st per sing. pronoun; other pronoun; other N P) 3 Frequency distribution of negative forms by style (conversation vs. elicited). Effects of time, subject noun phrase and style were investigated statistically using logistical regression.
Results	No uniform increase in the use of don't was apparent but overall it changes from the less likely to the more likely variant over time. Utterances with no subject N P were the least likely to employ *don't*. No significant main effect was found for style but *don't* increased significantly in elicited utterances over time (i.e. there was an interaction involving time and style).
Discussion	Berdan argues that the above analyses show that Alberto was in fact a language acquirer and had not fossilized as claimed by Schumann.
Implications	Berdan considers the methodological implications of his study, arguing that the method of analysis he used makes it 'possible to model language acquisition as continuous change over time' (p. 236) rather than as a series of successive stages.

Table 5.3 Summary of Berdan's (1996) study

can achieve this. Berdan's study illustrates the extent to which SLA studies employing frequency analysis have increased in sophistication since the early case studies of the 1970s.

Task: Carrying out a frequency analysis

Below in Table 5.4 are selected negative utterances produced by one learner of English as a second language (L1 = Portuguese). The learner was aged 10–11 years and was almost a complete beginner at the start of the study. The utterances cover a nine-month period. They represent the spontaneous speech produced by the learner in various classroom contexts.

Carry out a frequency analysis of the data to address these research questions:

Is this learner a language acquirer or has he fossilized?
To what extent does this classroom learner follow the same pattern of development for negatives as that reported for naturalistic learners?

To answer these questions you will need to:

1 Identify the linguistic devices the learner uses in his negative utterances over the entire nine-month period.

Notes:

- You should avoid identifying the different devices too narrowly. Broad categories reflecting basic linguistic strategies for performing negation will reveal the developmental trends in the data.
- You may wish to exclude some utterances on the grounds that they are formulaic.
- You may obtain a clearer picture if you group the data for the nine months into three three-month periods.

2 Calculate the frequency of use of each negative device.

You may also wish to undertake a more detailed frequency analysis to explore the role of contextual factors in the learner's variable use of negative devices.

Final comment

Frequency analysis was the methodological tool that led to the discovery that learners manifest distinct and, to a large extent, universal sequences of acquisition when acquiring the grammar of an L2. This constitutes one of the major findings of SLA (Lightbown 1985). No theory of L2 acquisition is complete if it cannot account for why these sequences appear. The results of research based on frequency analysis were also important for language

Utterance	Context
Month 1	
me no me	He doesn't have any crayons.
me no	He hasn't got a ruler.
no more	He doesn't want to play a game any more.
me no ruler	In response to the Q: 'John, have you got a ruler?'
Phoc no good	The teacher had just scolded Phoc.
Is not Captain Spock	He didn't think his picture really looked like Captain Spock.
Month 2	
we no school	In response to Q: 'John, Monday are you coming to school?'
don look please	He wanted Phoc to stop looking at his word bingo card.
no look, no good	Trying to stop other children from looking at his bingo card.
me no out of here	He didn't want to leave his seat.
me no thirsty	Said while looking at pictures of cups.
this one standing/ this one no standing	Describing the difference in position of two cups.
I don know	In response to Q: 'Where might he be going?'
Month 3	
not together	Describing a picture of a tree with part of the trunk missing.
a man no one leg	Describing a picture of a man vanishing through a wall.
foots no front walk	Describing a picture of a boy with feet pointing back to front.
umbrella no good	Describing a picture of a leaky umbrella.
a door no downstairs	Describing a picture of a house with the front door in the upstairs part.
no writing on the book	Describing a picture of a man reading a blank page.
a bicycle no pedals	Describing a picture of a bicycle with no pedals.
not finished	The teacher has just said that Phoc has not finished his drawing.
big square/not very big square	Describing a shape to another pupil.
no four, three legs	Describing a table with three legs.
Why don you play?	Asking someone why they don't want to play tic tac toe.

Table 5.4 (continued)

Utterance	Context
Month 4	
Not very very small	Answering query from teacher in describing game.
no very big	In response to the question:'Is it bigger?' in describing game.
me no out this one	Explaining that he was not the one who had torn some paper.
me no ruler	He didn't have a ruler.
its no there sir	Asking teacher to confirm he had drawn something correctly.
this one no?	The teacher didn't draw a mark on some card clearly.
Month 5	
Mariana no coming	Teacher Q: 'Where's Mariana today?'
I don't understand sir	Teacher had explained exercise to class.
me no play	Telling the teacher he wouldn't be playing football at break.
me no stay	Telling the teacher he wouldn't be staying after school.
sir don't sit in that one chair	The teacher was about to sit on a chair covered with chalk dust.
bicycle no pedal	Describing a picture of a bicycle with no pedals.
the bicycle has no pedals hasn't got any pedals	Repeating after the teacher.
the man is can't read it the book	Describing picture of a man reading a blank book.
me no drawing in here	He doesn't want to draw in his writing book.
Month 6	
not that one	Explaining that 'hangar' was wrong in hangman game.
sir, I don't know that big one	Looking at a picture of lorry, he didn't know the word.
me no match	Explaining that he doesn't use matches to light the cooker.
that one I don't know	Referring to spelling of 'bicycle'.
Month 7	
don't say that	Telling Mariana not to say something.
no speak Portuguese, only English	Telling Mariana not to speak Portuguese to him.

Table 5.4 (continued)

Utterance	Context
you did no read properly	To another pupil who had just read.
it's not	Correcting something pupil read.
mine, he cannot read	Criticizing pupils reading.
I'm not out	Denying he was out of the game.
She don't understand	A pupil had given wrong answer.
no sitting	Response to Q: 'Is something sitting or no?'
I don't know the colour	Response to Q: 'What colour do you wear clothes?'
no this is drawing?	Checking if he had to draw something on map.
Month 8	
In this one the man is not shouting	Describing a picture.
Especially the dog is not shouting	
No fruit	Correcting an answer after T had queried it.
Not climbing	Correcting his previous statement about some boys climbing.
is not the tree all right	Correcting another pupil.
don't draw anything	T told pupils not to draw and then asked if he was listening.
not this year	In response to Q: 'Aren't you going to Portugal?'
This man can't read because the light is green	Describing the picture.
Month 9	
the bicycle no go	In response to Q: 'What do you think would happen if a boy tried to ride this bicycle?'
I no throw paper on the floor	In response to Q: 'Who throws paper on the floor in the play ground?'
You don't?	A pupil had said 'I don't care'.
It's not smoking	Explaining that a pupil's money box doesn't contain cigarettes.
I not got a pen	Telling the teacher.
I said I don't want	i.e. he had told his parents he didn't want to go to Portugal.

Table 5.4 Negative utterances produced by one L2 learner over a nine-month period

pedagogy. If instruction is to be effective it was clear that it must be conducted in a way that takes into account the gradualness of acquisition and the inherent variability that accompanies interlanguage development.

Frequency analysis is best seen not as an alternative to obligatory occasion analysis but rather as complementary. Wode, Bahns, Bedey, and Frank (1978: 184) comment:

> ...the two approaches of morpheme order and developmental sequence focus on different aspects of the total process of L2 acquisition. Therefore, the conclusion cannot be to claim general superiority of one over the other. Morpheme order approaches if properly extended, may provide for the overall acquisitional order of different structural areas. However, ...developmental sequences of individual structural areas are indispensable to provide detailed insights into the mechanisms of the acquisitional process.

In particular, a focus on developmental sequence is necessary to demonstrate transitional stages leading to the final target language stage, learners' avoidance of the target form in specific linguistic environments and the influence of the learners' L1 at certain developmental stages. Frequency analysis is a powerful tool for achieving this.

Notes

1 'Analysed *don't*' is evident when learners begin to use different forms of the auxiliary *do* with both *n't* and *not* (for example, *does not* and *did not*).

2 The learner's L1 was shown to have some effect on the sequences of acquisition. It could speed up or slow down learners' progress through the stages. Also, the effect of the L1 could kick in at a particular stage if this provided the learner with evidence that the L2 was similar to the L1. For example, as Wode (1976) showed, when German learners of English discover that the verb *be* takes post-verbal negation (for example, *She is not a doctor*) this appears to trigger more widespread use of post-verbal negation with main verbs, as in L1 German (for example, *Mary stays not at home*).

3 Pienemann's decision to use 'onset' was motivated by his theory of L2 acquisition, which posited that the acquisition of different grammatical features was a reflection of the processing operations that underlie their production. He claimed that if learners demonstrated an ability to produce a particular feature in their creative speech then they had mastered the particular processing operation that the feature required.

6 Functional analysis

Introduction

The previous three chapters have examined the formal characteristics of learner language. That is, they have been concerned with methods of analysis that treat language as a formal system comprised of grammatical features. Language, however, is more than grammatical form. It is perhaps best conceptualized as a system of form–function mappings. That is, the grammatical forms that comprise a linguistic system are used to realize specific meanings. For example, plural *-s* in English constitutes a grammatical form that is used to realize the meaning 'more than one', past tense *-ed* is a grammatical form used to realize the meaning 'completed action in the past', and the article *a* is a grammatical form that indicates a referent is non-specific (as in *I saw a lion*). Of course not all the grammatical features in a language are functional in this way. Some features are entirely formal. For example, the distinction between *a* and *an* is not functional in English as it does not realize two distinct meanings; the choice of these forms is determined phonetically (i.e. we use *a* before nouns that begin with a consonant sound and *an* before nouns that begin with a vowel sound). In general, however, the features of the grammar of a language are functional, reflecting the fact that language is primarily a tool for communicating meaning.

It is possible to envisage a simple linguistic system in which each form is used to realize a single and distinct meaning. Such a system would be based on a 'one-to-one principle'. However, linguistic systems are not simple in this way. They are complex—that is, the same form can realize a number of different meanings, while a specific meaning can be performed using a variety of linguistic forms. The progressive form *-ing*, for example, realizes very different meanings in these sentences:

I am eating breakfast at the moment. (= ongoing action)

I am flying from Auckland to London next week. (= planned future action)

You are not exercising these days. (= critical comment)

Similarly, a function such as 'future time' can be performed using a number of different forms:

I will finish this book soon. (*will* + verb)

I am going to start on another book soon. (*going to* + verb)
I am starting on another book next month. (aux + verb *-ing*)
I start on another book soon. (verb simple form)

Multiple form–function mappings of these kinds afford speakers choices and are, therefore, the primary source of the variability in a language. For this reason, functional analyses have been employed by researchers who are interested in investigating variability.

If we view language as a system of form–function mappings, an interesting question arises: to what extent do the form–function mappings that comprise a learner's interlanguage system match those of the target language system? Or, to put it another way, do learners use grammatical forms to realize the same meanings as native speakers? To answer this question it is necessary to perform a functional analysis of learner language, comparing the results of such an analysis with accounts of form–function mappings to be found in a target language reference grammar.

Functional analyses are of two kinds, depending on what constitutes the starting point of the analysis. In a *form–function analysis* the starting point is a linguistic form. That is, the analyst selects a specific form to study (for example, plural *-s* or verb *-ing*) and then investigates the specific meanings that this form realizes in a sample of learner language. In a *function–form analysis* the starting point is a language function (for example, referring to future events) and the analyst then identifies the linguistic forms in the sample that are used to perform this meaning. As we will shortly see, researchers have employed both approaches.

Finally, a note on the use of the term 'function' is in order. As Huebner (1985) points out, this term has several meanings. (It is itself multi-functional.) He distinguishes the following meanings: *semantic function* (for example, specific/non-specific reference; future time; possibility), *semantico-grammatical function* (for example, subject/agent and object/patient), *pragmatic function* (for example, requesting, apologizing, complimenting), and *discourse function* (for example, topic/theme of an utterance).

Historical and theoretical background

The history of the study of learner language can be viewed in terms of a progression from purely formal analyses of the kinds examined in Chapters 3, 4, and 5 to form–function analyses and then to function–form analyses. Of course, all three kinds of analysis have continued to figure in SLA. Here, we begin with an account of form–function analysis and then move on to function–form analysis. We will incorporate a discussion of the theoretical perspectives that have both informed and been derived from these approaches to the study of learner language. In conclusion we will offer an evaluation of functional approaches.

Form–function analysis

Form–function analyses provide a much richer description of learner language than that afforded by frequency analysis; they account not just for what forms learners have at their disposal but how they use these forms to communicate. These analyses have demonstrated that variability is inherent in learner language and have given rise to new theories of L2 acquisition.

As we have seen, early studies (for example, the error analyses of the 1960s and the morpheme studies and longitudinal studies based on frequency analysis of the 1970s) focused more or less exclusively on the formal properties of learner language. This approach was criticized by Huebner (1979) for failing to take into account the functions performed by the linguistic forms under study. Huebner saw the learner's task as that of discovering what forms in the target language were required to express semantic functions, such as agent and object, or discourse functions, such as topic and comment. He portrayed learners' interlanguages as 'dynamic' in the sense that they consisted of a fluid system of form–function mappings as learners continually reassessed the meanings they realized through one specific form when they acquired new associated forms. Thus, in the 'dynamic paradigm', stages of acquisition are characterized in terms of configurations of form–function mappings rather than in terms of frequencies of use of different linguistic devices. We will illustrate Huebner's 'dynamic paradigm' from his own research.

Huebner (1979, 1985) conducted a longitudinal study of Ge, a Hmong learner of English. His aim was to show that even though Ge did not use articles in the same way as native speakers, nevertheless he did employ them in a systematic fashion by developing his own unique form–function mapping, which, over time, he reanalysed, bringing it more closely in line with the target language system. Huebner's analysis was based on Bickerton's (1981) 'semantic wheel' for noun phrases. This posits two binary features: (1) information assumed to be part of the hearer's knowledge (HK) and (2) specific reference (SR), which, when combined, afford four possible functional noun phrase types, as shown in Table 6.1.

Huebner conducted a form–function analysis. He began by identifying all the noun phrases where the learner used *da* (the learner's phonological version of English *the*) in oral data collected at three-weekly intervals. He then coded each noun phrase according to its functional type. As a result of this analysis he was able to show that the learner's development was characterized by stages consisting of different form–function mappings. First, *da* served to realize referential definites (except when the NP was the topic of the sentence, when zero article was used). Later, *da* was used to perform all four NP types. That is, during this stage 'flooding' occurred as a result of the learner's massive overuse of *da*. The later stages of development were characterized by the gradual elimination of *da* for performing functions that the definite article

Type of noun phrase	Forms used in English	Examples
Generic reference (+HK/−SR)	*a, the*, or zero article with a plural noun	***A lion*** *is a dangerous animal.* ***The lion*** *is a dangerous animal.* ***Lions*** *are dangerous animals.*
Referential definites (+HK/+SR)	This function can only be realized by means of *the*	*A lion appeared out of nowhere.* ***The lion*** *charged towards us.*
Referential indefinite (−HK/+SR)	This function can be conveyed by means of *a* or zero article with a plural noun	***A lion*** *appeared out of nowhere.* ***Lions*** *were basking in the sun.*
Nonreferentials (−HK/−SR)	This function is only realized by *a*	*I couldn't see* ***a lion*** *anywhere.*

Table 6.1 Four types of noun phrase (based on Bickerton 1981)

did not serve in English. Thus, *da* was first no longer used in non-referentials and some time later it was eliminated from referential indefinites. At this point, Ge was using *da* in much the same way as native speakers use *the*.

Further evidence of form–function mapping in learner language can be found in Young (1996).[1] This study examined the effect of a range of functional variables on Czech learners' choice of English definite and indefinite articles. Like Huebner, Young found clear evidence that the NP type influenced the choice of article. Thus, referential definites favoured the use of *the*, generics favoured zero article and *a(n)* and referential indefinites *a(n)* and zero article. Discourse function also had an effect. Whereas old/given information tended to be marked with definite articles, new information towards the end of clauses was typically realized by zero article. These various effects, however, were probabilistic, not categorical. That is, the learners tended to prefer one form over another to perform a particular function but also at times used an alternative form.

Variabilists such as Tarone (1983) and Preston (1996) have argued that learner language is essentially systematic. This claim is largely borne out by studies such as Huebner's and Young's, form–function analysis being the preferred tool for uncovering the underlying systematicity. Ellis (1985b; 1999), however, has argued that learners pass through a stage of *free variation*, defined by Matthews (1997: 136) as 'the relation between sounds or forms which have similar or partly similar distributions but are not described as being in contrast'. In fact, Huebner's study provides some evidence of this. As we have seen, Huebner found that at one stage of development, *da* flooded all the noun phrases his learner produced. However, *da* was not categorical at this stage. That is, the learner did not invariably use 'da' with nouns; on occasions he omitted it. What Huebner seems to be saying is that during this stage of the learner's development, he was unable to identify any functional constraints on the use of 'da'—that 'da' was used randomly and randomly omitted. Similarly, Young reports that, at lower proficiency levels, the Czech learners in his study overgeneralized the definite article with the result that there was no clear-cut form–function mapping. Acknowledging the existence of free variation, Young suggests that this arises when certain specific conditions are present, including, crucially, when there is no clear form–function relation between the form and meaning in the target language. Such is the case with *the*, which can be used to perform both referential definites and generics.

Ellis (1999) has incorporated the idea of free variation into a theory of L2 acquisition. He distinguishes two general aspects of acquisition; *item-learning* and *system-learning*. The former involves the accumulation of units that are connected only loosely in a network. The latter involves the extraction of rules from the items that have been acquired. Ellis argues that free variation is a reflection of item-learning and that it constitutes a necessary phase of acquisition because it allows learners to build up their resources without having to pay much attention to how the items are to be organized; it also permits items to be easily removed or assigned new functions. This idea of item-learning is compatible with a connectionist model of L2 acquisition (N. Ellis 1996, 2002), according to which learners bootstrap their way to grammar as a result of memorizing and subsequently analysing countless 'sequences' of language. Free variation can be seen as an inevitable outcome of this process.

Irrespective of whether free variation is integral to interlanguage, learners clearly pass through successive stages of development where form–function relationships are re-evaluated and restructured. The notion of 'restructuring' (McLaughlin 1990), then, is best understood not as the reorganization of elements within an entirely formal system but as the redistribution of forms and functions, such that old forms are redirected to perform new functions in the process of accommodating new forms. An important question is what drives this restructuring of form–function mappings. To address this question we need to consider function–form analysis.

Function–form analysis

Function–form analysis is motivated by the theoretical claim that interlanguage development is driven primarily by communicative need. This claim has been explored with reference to Givon's (1979) distinction between a 'pragmatic mode' and a 'syntactic mode'. The pragmatic mode arises typically in 'unplanned discourse' and occurs typically in the early stages of language acquisition. It is characterized by the use of topicalized constructions (for example, *My father—he sick*), by parataxis (i.e. the chaining of propositions and the use of co-ordination), repetition, the reduction and simplification of grammatical morphology, and a verbal style (i.e. short verbal clauses). The syntactic mode is evident in 'planned discourse' and arises later on as a result of 'syntactization' (i.e. the process by which a learner's interlanguage gradually incorporates grammatical properties). It features grammatical as opposed to topicalized constructions (for example, *My father is sick*), hypotaxis (i.e. the use of subordination), little repetition, full grammatical morphology and a nominal style (i.e. the use of several noun phrases with each verb). Whereas the pragmatic mode can function effectively for communicating in the here-and-now, when learners can draw on context to support what they want to say, the syntactic mode is needed to engage effectively in communication involving displaced activity, when no contextual support is available. As Widdowson (1990: 86) puts it, 'grammar ... frees us from a dependency on context and the limitations of a purely lexical categorization of reality'. The learner's need to communicate independently of context, then, drives syntactization.

This position has been examined in a number of empirical studies of L2 acquisition, most notably by Sato (1988, 1990) and Perdue (1993, 2000). Sato examined the predominantly naturalistic acquisition of English by two Vietnamese boys (Thanh and Tai). Employing a function–form analysis to examine their acquisition of past time reference and their encoding of propositions, Sato set out to test Givon's claim that acquisition involves a progression from a pragmatic to a syntactic mode. She found little evidence of development in the means used to express past time; the two learners continued to rely on context and lexical (adverbial) means over a ten-month period. Nor did the results of the analysis of propositional encoding provide conclusive evidence of the claim. Sato did find that the learners progressed from reliance on parataxis at the beginning of the study to greater use of hypotaxis at the end, but the simple juxtaposition of propositions continued as the primary means of linking ideas throughout. By and large, then, Sato's study lends very limited support to Givon's claim, possibly because of the cognitive and social maturity of the two learners and the fact that they were receiving some classroom instruction in English. However, the study serves as an excellent example of function–form analysis and of the importance of combining this with multi-level analysis to establish the inter-relationships between different levels of English (for example, phonology and syntax).

Klein and Perdue (1997) and Perdue (2000) propose a limited set of organizing principles involving the syntactic, semantic and pragmatic levels to explain the structure of learner varieties and how these evolve over time.

They base their claims on a series of longitudinal studies involving naturalistic learners of five European languages that comprised the European Science Foundation Project. Generalizing from the results of a series of function–form analyses of these languages, they propose a universal account of L2 development based on the idea of evolving 'language varieties'. The starting point is 'the pre-basic variety'. This is characterized by nominal utterance organization. Utterances are scaffolded (i.e. constructed over more than one turn) and context-dependent. To express temporality learners rely on lexis and chronological sequence. In time, this gives way to the 'basic variety', characterized by non-finite verbal organization. Utterances are now constructed in accordance with the general pragmatic principle that the 'controller' is mentioned first and the 'focus' last. The 'post-basic variety' involves a shift to finite verbal organization. When learners reach this stage of development their utterances are organized syntactically. Development from the pre-basic variety through the basic variety to the post-basic variety is driven by the learner's need to express what they want to say with greater clarity and efficiency. As Perdue (2000: 301) puts it 'the communicative limitations of (a) variety, in a sense, push the learner to further acquisition' but the properties of the learner's current variety constrain development such that 'new and even target-like forms that a learner acquires are not necessarily used in target-like ways (with target-like functions)'.

There are problems with this view, however. Foremost, is the definition of 'communicative need'. This is under-specified. How exactly do the communicative needs of learners change over time and how do these changes correspond to developments in their interlanguages? To date, no theory has attempted to explicate this. Ellis (1992, 1999) moves some way in this direction by distinguishing three kinds of need. He sees 'communicative need' as the most basic as it requires only formally simple L2 resources that are pragmatically organized. 'Expressive need' (i.e. the desire to have more than one linguistic device for performing a given function for purposes of variety) is required to explain why learners add resources even though there is no communicative need. 'Sociolinguistic need' (i.e. the need to use the L2 in socially appropriate ways) explains why learners continue to elaborate and restructure their systems towards target language norms. Ellis attempts to relate these different needs to identifiable stages in interlanguage development. ('Expressive need', for example, accounts for the replacement stage when free variation occurs). However, Ellis' account of the different types of need that learners experience, like other functional theories, operates at a very general level and does not allow for precise predictions of when learners will acquire specific L2 properties.

Function–form analysis has also been widely used in a different strand of SLA—the study of interlanguage pragmatics. This has borrowed from studies of native speaker linguistic action a number of areas of enquiry. Discourse sequencing and conversational management are two examples. It has focused in particular, though, on the linguistic means that learners employ to perform illocutionary acts such as complimenting (Wolfson 1983), apologizing (Olshtain and Cohen 1983) and requests (Olshtain and Blum-Kulka 1985). The study of illocutionary acts in an L2 has progressed from a peripheral area of enquiry in SLA to one that now occupies a more central position, driven in particular by Kasper's contributions (Blum-Kulka, House, and Kasper 1989; Kasper and Dahl 1991; Kasper 1996). This research has been primarily concerned with language use rather than language development, although this is now changing as studies examining the effects of instruction on pragmatic development are beginning to appear. (See the collection in Rose and Kasper 2001.) However, in contrast to the form–function studies considered above, which were all longitudinal in nature, the function–form studies of illocutionary acts have been almost entirely cross-sectional.

The study of illocutionary acts involves (1) the collection or assembly of learner utterances performing the target act, (2) the description of the linguistic 'strategies' used to realize the act and the comparison of the strategies identified with those used by native speakers, and (3) the identification of independent variables to explain learners' choice of strategies. (1) typically entails the use of clinical-elicitation instruments such as the discourse completion questionnaire (see Chapter 2) although a few studies have also used naturally occurring data. (2) is data-driven (i.e. the linguistic strategies emerge out of the analysis of the data) although there are now a number of well-established taxonomies of strategy for those illocutionary acts that have been thoroughly studied (for example, requests and apologies) to guide new studies. With regard to (3), both situational variables (for example, the familiarity and status of the addressee) and learner-internal factors (in particular, the learner's L1) have been examined.

A good example of a function–form study of an illocutionary act is Beebe, Takahashi, and Uliss-Weitz's (1990) study of pragmatic transfer in L2 refusals following requests, invitations and offers. Samples of learner refusals were collected from 20 Japanese learners of English as well as 20 native speakers of Japanese and 20 native speakers of English, using a discourse completion questionnaire. These samples were then analysed, resulting in the description of a number of semantic formulas. These are summarized with examples in Table 6.2. Results are presented in terms of the frequency of use of the different strategies, how the strategies were sequenced and the content of the refusals (for example, the specificity of excuses) by the three groups of participants and then discussed in terms of the differences that emerged. The study focused on identifying the role of the learners' L1 in their pragmatic behaviour. Beebe, Takahashi, and

Main strategy	Sub-strategies	Example
1 direct	a performative statement	*I refuse.*
	b non-performative statement	*No; I can't*
2 indirect	a statement of regret	*I'm sorry...*
	b wish	*I wish I could help you...*
	c excuse	*I have a headache...*
	d statement of alternative	*I'd prefer...*
	e set condition for future or past acceptance	*If you had asked me earlier, I'd...*
	f promise of future acceptance	*I'll do it next time.*
	g statement of principle	*I never do business with friends.*
	h statement of philosophy	*One can't be too careful.*
	i attempt to dissuade interlocutor	*Who do you think you are!*
	j acceptance that functions as a refusal	*Well, I guess, if you really want me to...*
	k avoidance	*Silence; topic switch; joke*

Table 6.2 Linguistic strategies for performing a refusal (summarized from Beebe, Takahashi, and Uliss-Weitz (1990)

Uliss-Weitz conclude that Japanese learners of English attempt to transfer their L1 strategies, particularly where content is concerned, when refusing in English.

Perhaps the main contribution of function–form analyses of illocutionary acts such as refusals has been to contribute to our understanding of the role of L1 transfer (see Kasper 1992) and, in particular, of the factors that constrain transfer. In accordance with earlier interlanguage studies of transfer (for example, Kellerman 1983), the studies suggest that pragmatic transfer depends crucially on the learners' perception of the language specificity or universality of specific L1 strategies. If a strategy is viewed as universal, it is likely to be transferred but if it is viewed as L1-specific, it is not. It is, of course, difficult to determine how learners perceive particular strategies from production data and for this reason recent studies have also incorporated transferability judgement questionnaires into their design (for example, Takahashi 1995).

Evaluating functional analysis

It should be clear from the above account that functional analyses of learner language have served very different purposes. Form–function analyses of the kind carried out by Huebner have fed into the mainsteam study of how learners' interlanguages develop, helping to flesh out the developmental progression evident in the acquisition of specific linguistic forms and, in particular, to account for the role that variability plays in development. Function–form analyses of the kind found in the European Science Foundation Project (Perdue 1993) have led to strong claims about a general pattern of L2 development and to the claim that acquisition is driven by communicative need. Function–form analyses of illocutionary acts have provided detailed information about learners' L2 pragmatic competence, thus helping to provide a more rounded account of learners' interlanguage. They have also contributed substantially to our understanding of the role of L1 transfer. Functional analyses, then, currently occupy a pivotal position in empirical enquiry and have significantly advanced the evolution of SLA.

There are, however, some obvious limitations to functional analyses. One, pointed out by Tarone (1988) and still largely true today, is that they do not take account of the role of psycholinguistic processes in L2 acquisition. It is unlikely, for example, that variability in L2 use can be fully explained without reference to the role of attention in production and acquisition. Thus, whether learners utilize form x or y to perform a particular function will depend in part at least on whether they are paying careful attention to what they say. Similarly, whether learners transfer an L1 strategy in the performance of an L2 illocutionary act may well depend on whether their language use reflects controlled or automatic processing. Another problem, noted by Mitchell and Myles (1998), is that most of the studies have focused on learners acquiring a language naturally and thus do not take account of the role of instruction.[2] Do adult classroom L2 learners, for example, also manifest progression from a pre-basic to a post-basic variety? Perhaps, though, the major limitation lies in the theoretical underpinnings of the research to date. Theory has tended to emerge loosely from descriptive research rather than to inform it in any tight way. This in itself, of course, does not matter (and in the eyes of some researchers might be seen as desirable) but, as we have seen, it has resulted in theories of very general scope that do not afford readily testable hypotheses. The one attempt to test hypotheses based on a functional theory (Sato's research) did not find much support for it.

Conducting a form–function analysis

Form–function analysis takes as its starting point a specific linguistic form and then examines the different uses of that form with a view to explicating the functions it maps on to. This method can be used to analyse learner language collected cross-sectionally but it is most revealing in longitudinal studies, where it serves to show how learners modify their use of the linguistic forms at their disposal over time by reorganizing the functions they perform. Form–function analysis, then, provides another tool for examining and explaining variability in learner language.

The following are the steps in a form–function analysis:

1 Choose the linguistic form(s) to be investigated.
The form chosen can be a target language form such as the English definite article *the* or an interlanguage form (for example, Huebner's examination of Ge's use of 'da' discussed earlier). In general, researchers have preferred to investigate interlanguage forms. In this way, they avoid the comparative fallacy (Bley-Vroman 1983) by treating interlanguage as a system in its own right.

2 Collect samples of learner language containing the chosen linguistic form(s) and identify all occasions of use of the form(s).
In general, researchers do not attempt to elicit use of the chosen form. Their preferred approach is to search through general samples of learner language for instances of the form. There is also a strong preference for naturally occurring samples, as eliciting data, even clinically, runs the risk of distorting the uses to which learners put the forms at their disposal. For example, Bahns and Wode (1980) found clear evidence of form–function distributions for *don't* and *didn't* in two German children's use of negative constructions in naturally occurring speech but not in data collected from structured interviews. As Hyltenstam (1984) notes, elicited data often lacks patterning.

3 Establish the functions performed by the form(s).
As noted earlier, 'function' can refer to semantic function, semantico-grammatical function, pragmatic function or discourse function. Typically, an analysis will choose one of these, although arguably a full account of the form–function mappings that comprise an interlanguage system requires a study of all four types of function.

4 Count the frequency with which each function is realized by the form.
A frequency analysis of the functions performed by the form reveals the patterning in the learner's use of the form. The researcher can see what the dominant function served by the form at one developmental point is. This can then be compared with the learner's use of the same form at a later time and also with the target language use. In this way the researcher can investigate how learners restructure their interlanguages and whether they reach a point where they conform to the norms of the target language system.

To illustrate this procedure we will analyse the data shown in Table 6.3. These consist of utterances produced by an 11-year old Pakistani boy (R).

Time	Utterance	Context
1	***Car*** *go up*	Describing a picture of a hump-backed bridge.
	Road *is lock*	Describing a picture of road that is closed.
	Look at ***a train***	Describing a picture of a level crossing.
	Train*'s come*	
	Bus *come*	
	Look ***line*** ***Line*** *very near*	Describing a picture showing electricity lines.
	Car *is stopping*	Describing a picture of a car stopping to let deer pass.
	Car *go in* ***a ship***	Describing picture of a car driving onto a ferry.
	Red light *is on*	Describing picture of traffic lights.
	Car *stop*	
	Writing with ***a pencil.*** *No writing with* ***a pen****.*	Getting organized to do a writing task.
	Gate *no there.*	Describing a picture of a railway crossing.
	Red triangle ***Blue square***	Doing an information-gap task involving describing a diagram.
	One man *is digging* ***a road***	Describing a picture
	I want ***a pin*** *I want just* ***one pin.*** *I can buy in* ***a shop.***	He needs a drawing pin to pin up his picture.
2	*I can see* ***a houses*** *I can see* ***a man*** *sewing* ***a ear***	Looking at slides of India—one slide shows a man cleaning ears with a needle-like instrument.
	He is taking ***a big stick*** *out*	Describing corporal punishment in his school in Pakistan.
	Sometimes take ***a bag*** *on the roof and sleep*	Explaining where he used to sleep.
	I write with ***a pen***	
	You can go in ***a big town****.*	i.e. to go swimming.
	Then you can see ***a swimming pool***	
	You can take ***a swimming costume***	= hire a swimming costume.
	One girl *is sleeping*	Describing a picture.

Table 6.3 (*continued*)

Time	Utterance	Context
	Draw ***a green big tree***	Information-gap task—describing a diagram.
	One red line *under the tree*	
	One bird *flying over the tree*	
	Can I have ***one paper?***	Asking for a piece of paper.
	One here peoples *stand*	Describing a mosque.
	My grandfather has got ***English book***	
	One road *is going straight like that*	He is drawing a map of his route to school.
	One park *near my house*	
	This is ***a good cars***	Commenting on a picture he has drawn.
	One ship *is going crash in the Falkland Islands*	Talking about a picture he has drawn.
	Is not ***good idea*** *to do that*	Commenting on action of another student.
	My dad's getting ***one car*** *today*	Commenting that his father will get a car from his employer.
	Half chicken *you bring,* ***half chicken*** *I bring*	Planning a meal.
	I can see ***a one man*** *is standing in the road*	
	Motor cycle *come and going to hit him*	
	Airplane *going that buildings*	Describing a picture.

Table 6.3 Utterances produced by an L2 learner (L1 = Punjabi)

The utterances have been selected from a large corpus of utterances covering a two-year period in R's acquisition of English. They were all collected within a classroom context, where R was interacting with the teacher and other students and are representative of R's spontaneous, un-modelled speech. Most of the utterances constitute R's attempt to describe pictures or diagrams (i.e. they perform what Halliday (1973) calls the 'referential function'). The utterances have been divided into two sets. Time 1 was at the beginning of the second year, while Time 2 was at the end of the same year. There is a gap of approximately six months between the two times. Ellis (1984a, 1992) provides detailed information about R and the data collection procedures.

The utterances were selected to provide obligatory occasions for noun phrases requiring the use of the indefinite article (*a/an*). The noun phrases, which are shown in bold, can be characterized as + specific reference/– hearer knowledge (see Table 6.1). That is, they constitute examples of referential indefinites. The learner utilized the following forms in the noun phrases:

- zero article(for example, ***Car** go up*)
- *a* (for example, *Look at **a train***)
- *one* (for example, ***One man** is digging a road*)

The question arises as to whether the distribution of these forms reflects their functional use. To answer this, a form–function analysis was carried out by examining the *discourse function* of each referential indefinite. The noun phrases were coded in terms of whether they realized:

- the topic of an utterance (defined as the part of the utterance seen as corresponding to what the sentence as a whole is about)
- the comment of the utterance (defined as the rest of the utterance).

Thus in the utterance:

Car go up

car is the topic and *go up* is the comment, while the utterance:

Look at a train

consists only of a comment (i.e. the topic is unstated but can be inferred as *I*—the speaker). Table 6.4 below shows the frequency of the use of the three forms in relation to discourse function.

At Time 1, zero article occurs in topic noun phrases, *a* never occurs, while *one* figures in a single utterance. In contrast, *a* is used in eight out of nine comment noun phrases. At Time 2, the picture is different. The learner demonstrates a preference for *one* to mark topic noun phrases, although he continues to use zero article with a minority of nouns. There is increased

	Time 1			**Time 2**		
Discourse function	zero	*a*	*one*	zero	*a*	*one*
Topic	12	0	1	4	0	7
Comment	1	8	0	2	12	2

Table 6.4 Distribution of forms in non-referential definite noun phrases according to discourse function

variability in the marking of comment noun phrases but *a* remains the preferred form.

This analysis then supports three frequently made claims about learners' interlanguages:

1 Forms are distributed systematically in accordance with function. In this case, the discourse function of non-referential definite noun phrases can account for the distribution of forms.
2 The patterning of forms and functions in interlanguage is unique. Thus, whereas the target language does not distinguish between the formal marking of referential indefinites in topic and comment noun phrases (i.e. *a* is required in both), this learner clearly does. The learner's need to distinguish topics and comments in this way may reflect language transfer.
3 The patterning changes from one time to another, thus supporting the claim that interlanguage is to be understood as a dynamic system of form–function mapping.

Of course, this analysis has focused on a small subset of the learner's language—referential indefinites. In this respect it is characteristic of the piecemeal approach of much of the published research. There are obvious dangers in isolating subsets in this way. In particular, it runs of risk of misrepresenting the nature of the systematicity in a learner's interlanguage by failing to take account of how form–function relations of one subset interlock with those of another. The above analysis, for example, tells us nothing about the functional distribution of the three linguistic forms in other types of noun phrase. Perhaps, though, the value of form–functional analyses such as the one above lies less in their descriptive adequacy than in what they reveal about the nature of interlanguage systems. They show convincingly that learners organize and restructure their interlanguages in terms of form–function relations.

Conducting a function–form analysis

If, as a number of researchers have suggested, interlanguage development is driven by communicative need, it would follow that L2 acquisition is best understood not by examining the forms learners have internalized (the underlying approach of form–function analysis) but by investigating what functions learners perform at different stages of development and the linguistic means they employ to realize them. In other words the starting point should be function rather than form.

Function–form analysis, then, is grounded in the claim that forms are acquired to enable learners to perform the functions that are important to them. Sampson (1982: 14), for example, argues that learners attend to an L2 form in the act of expressing an intention and that, therefore, 'the function draws the learner's attention to a form'. The need to perform a particular function motivates a learner to attend to a particular form, which is consequently acquired. Subsequent development takes place on two planes. Learners acquire alternative forms for performing the same function and also discover new functions that can be served by existing forms. Thus, as Sampson (1982: 19) puts it, 'function and forms are in a push-push or dialectal relationship'. It follows that a full understanding of how learners construct their interlanguages requires both a form–function and a function–form analysis.

The following are the steps in a function–form analysis:

1 Identify the specific function to be investigated.
As we have already noted, the function identified may be semantic (for example, temporality), semantico-grammatical (for example, agent), pragmatic (for example, illocutionary acts such as requests) or discourse (for example, topic/comment).

2 Collect samples of learner language where this function is performed.
As with form–function analysis, naturalistic samples are preferred. However, the study of the use and acquisition of illocutionary acts has been based largely on clinically elicited data (for example, through role-play or discourse completion tasks). There is a conspicuous lack of longitudinal function–form studies.

3 Identify the different linguistic forms used to perform the function.
In the case of illocutionary acts, these forms are sometimes referred to as 'linguistic strategies' and are given semantic labels. For example, the use of statements involving verbs such as *want*, *like* and *need* to perform requests (for example, *I'd like you to clean up now*) constitute a strategy labelled 'want statements'. (See Blum-Kulka, House, and Kasper 1989.) Despite these semantic labels the categories are clearly formal in nature as they are defined in terms of the specific linguistic forms used to realize the strategy. Illocutionary acts such as requests can also involve more than the performance of a head act (such as a need statement). For example, the learner may employ an alerter (for example, an attention getter), use one or more supportive moves (for example, checking on the hearer's ability to perform the act) and utilize various means for internally modifying the head act by means of down-graders (for example, *please*) and up-graders (for example, intensifiers like *really*). The identification of a complete set of linguistic forms for performing the function is data-led (i.e. the analyst must painstakingly examine all the data to provide a comprehensive account of the various forms employed). However, for a number of key functions (such as the illocutionary acts of requesting and apologizing), detailed taxonomies of the linguistic forms used by both L2 learners and native speakers are available.

4 Count the frequency of use of each form used to realize the function. This analysis can show what the dominant form used to realize the function is at a specific developmental stage and how this changes over time. A frequency analysis can also enable the analyst to explore the effect of independent variables on the choice of linguistic strategy. In the case of requests, for example, it can show to what extent the learner is sensitive to the level of imposition of the request and to the status/familiarity of the addressee. Comparisons of the realization devices used by different learners can also be undertaken.

Function–form analysis will be illustrated using the data collected by Ellis (1992). These consist of the requests produced by three learners over a two-year period, although only data for one of these learners ('R', the same learner who supplied the data for the form–function analysis above) will be analysed. The utterances were all spontaneously produced inside the classroom. Table 6.5 lists a selection of the head acts for the requests that R performed in six school terms.

School term	Utterance	Context
(1) November—December	*Sir, sir, sir pencil*	The teacher (T) had accidentally walked off with his pencil.
	Sir,colour	Asking the T for a coloured pencil.
	Sir, big triangle	Asking the teacher for shape.
(2) January—April	*Yellow cray*	Asking another student (S) for a crayon.
	Another paper, please	Asking the T for another piece of paper.
	Give me my paper	Asking the T to give him his piece of paper back.
	Get out	Another S was trying to sit in his place.
	Can I have this one?	He wants another S to help him read a word.
	Can I have pen please?	Asking T for a pen.
	Miss, I am like black colour.	Shouting out the colour he wanted.
(3) May—July	*Give it me.*	Asking another S to give him a card.
	Miss, pencil please	Holding up a blunt pencil.
	Give me the paper	Asking the T for a piece of paper.

Table 6.5 (*continued*)

School term	Utterance	Context
	You draw bus	Asking the T to draw a bus for him
	Can I have rubber please?	Asking another S for a rubber (eraser).
	Give me one pencil.	The T is giving out pencils.
	I need a ruler.	The T is giving out rulers.
	Can I have ruler?	Stretching to take a ruler from a S.
	Give it to him	Telling S to give some bluetack to another S.
(4) September—December	*Miss, give me my rubber*	The T had taken his rubber.
	Can I pencil?	He wanted the T to give him a pencil.
	Can I look?	He wanted to look at another S's picture.
	Shut up you very silly girl	To his sister (another S in the class).
	Can I have ruler please?	Asking the T for a ruler.
	You can draw for me.	Asking the T to do a drawing for him.
	Sir can you check again?	Asking the T to check what he had written.
	T, have you got flue?	To his sister.
	Can I have a see?	Asking to look at another S's puppet.
	Can you read from here?	Asking the T to read the next question on his worksheet.
	Can you make for me please?	Asking T to staple his papers together.
	I want see your pen.	Trying to take the pen from the researcher.
(5) January—April	*Can I have a read first?*	He wanted to read a book that another S had.
	Can you put this in your bag please?	To his sister.
	Can I take book with me?	Asking T for a book.
	Can you pass me a pencil?	To T—his pencil had fallen on the floor.
	I want to borrow this book	To his sister.
	Have you got my pen?	To T who had taken his pen.

Table 6.5 *(continued)*

School term	Utterance	Context
	Miss, can you check my homework?	To T.
	Put this in your book and closed it.	To another S who was reading a letter.
	Could you go over there?	Asking the T to move away.
	Could you put some in here?	Asking T to put some paper on his desk.
	Miss, I want some more easier one	Asking T for an easier reading book.
	Move sir	Asking the T to move.
(6) April—July	*Put it back inside*	Asking researcher to put piece of jigsaw back.
	You put it for me	He wanted the T to put a bean into a jar.
	Do it for me	Asking the T to show him what to do.
	Piece of paper please	To T.
	Can I have another one sir?	Asking T for another pencil.
	Miss, look my plants	To T while getting a potted plant from his locker.
	Can I have ruler?	To S.
	Can I borrow you pen, sir?	To T.
	Piece of paper, please.	To T.
	Can I borrow your scissors?	To another S.

Table 6.5 Requests produced by one classroom learner over two school years

To describe the linguistic strategies that R used to perform requests, the utterances in Table 6.5 were first inspected and a number of different realization devices identified. These were:

1 Object of the request (for example, S*ir, sir, sir pencil*)
2 Verb imperative (for example, *Give me my paper; You draw bus*)
3 Need statement (for example, M*iss, I am like black colour)*
4 Interrogative request:

 a *Can I have a __?* (for example, *Can I have a pen please?*)
 b *Can I* + verb (for example, *Can I look?*)
 c *Can you* + verb (for example, *Can you put this in your bag please?*)

d *Have you got ___?* (for example, *Have you got my pen?*)
e *Could you* + verb (for example, *Could you go over there?*)

These could have sufficed as a basis for the analysis. However, in order to avoid unnecessary duplication of taxonomies of strategies, the literature was checked to establish to what extent the linguistic strategies listed above could be accommodated in existing taxonomies. Blum-Kulka, House, and Kasper's (1989) taxonomy of strategy types for requests fitted the data well with the exception of 'object of request'.[3] With this addition, therefore, their taxonomy was adopted. Table 6.6 shows the final taxonomy and Table 6.7 the frequency of use of the different strategies in each of the six school terms.

A number of observations about R's use of request strategies can be made on the basis of this analysis. First, R does not use the full range of strategies identified by Blum-Kulka, House, and Kasper (1989). There are no examples of a performative (i.e. an utterance where the illocutionary force is explicitly named as in *I am asking you to...*), of an obligation statement (i.e. an utterance which states the obligation of the hearer to carry out the act as in *You'll have to...*), of a suggestory formula (an utterance which contains a

Strategy	Definition	Example
1 Object of request	An utterance where the object that is the focus of the request is named.	*Sir, sir, sir pencil*
2 Mood derivable	An utterance in which the grammatical mood of the verb signals illocutionary force.	*Give me my paper* *You draw bus*
3 Want statement	An utterance which states the speaker's desire that the hearer carries out the act.	*Miss I am like black colour.*
4 Query preparatory	An utterance containing reference to a preparatory condition (e.g. ability, willingness) as conventionalized in any specific language.	*Can I have ___?* *Can I look?* *Can you put this in your bag please?* *Have you got my pen?* *Could you go over there?*

Table 6.6 Taxonomy of request strategies

	Term 1	Term 2	Term 3	Term 4	Term 5	Term 6
1 Object of request	3 (100)	2 (28.5)	1 (11)	0 (0)	0 (0)	2 (20)
2 Mood derivable	0	2 (28.5)	5 (55.5)	3 (25)	3 (25)	4 (40)
3 Want statement	0	1 (15)	1 (11)	1 (8)	1 (8)	0 (0)
4 Query preparatory	0	2 (28.5)	2 (22)	8 (67)	8 (67)	4 (40)

Table 6.7 Frequency of use of request strategies (percentages shown in brackets)

suggestion to do x as in *How about* V*ing*...*?*) or of a hint (i.e. an utterance that can only be interpretable as a request by reference to the context).[4] In this respect, then, R's requests are limited in range. Secondly, it is possible to identify a developmental progression in R's use of request strategies over the two-year period of the study. Initially, R relies on object of request. A little later his preferred strategy is mood derivable while at the same time query preparatory makes an appearance. Later still, query preparatory becomes the dominant strategy. Also, he diversifies the linguistic forms he uses to perform this strategy, beginning with the formulaic routine *Can I have a*...*?* and advancing to interrogatives involving different verbs and a second person perspective (for example, *Can you*...*?*). Thirdly, the less polite strategies (i.e. object of request and mood derivable) never completely die out, reflecting perhaps the communicative norms of a relatively informal classroom setting.

The picture that emerges from this analysis is compatible with Sampson's claim that it is the learner's need to perform a particular function that motivates attention to form. First, R may have learned the names of common classroom objects (colour, pencil, paper, etc.) because of his need to request them in order to complete the classroom tasks he had been assigned. Secondly, he may have learned verb imperative requests because of the need to establish his needs clearly (the illocutionary force of *Give me pencil* is more explicit than *pencil*). Thirdly, query preparatory requests provided him with the means of softening the force of his utterances and thus satisfying the universal need to be polite. According to this interpretation, then, R's acquisition of linguistic forms was functionally driven. It is less clear, however, that he had any communicative need to diversify his query preparatory requests. It was for this reason that Ellis (1992) proposed that acquisition is also motivated by 'expressive need'. (See earlier comments.)

This example of a function–form analysis illustrates its value as an analytical tool in two ways: (1) it demonstrates the dialectal relationship between function and form in L2 performance, (2) it shows how communicative ability in an L2 develops progressively. The example also illustrates how a function–form analysis can be carried out rigorously providing that both the function under study and the linguistic strategies used to perform it can be reliably identified. It should be noted, however, that where this is possible in the case of a well-defined illocutionary act such as requesting, it is much more difficult to achieve with acts like criticizing, where the linguistic strategies are much less formulaic.

An example of a study using functional analysis

The study we have chosen as an example of functional analysis (see Table 6.8) examines the use of the negatives and, as such, can be usefully compared with Berdan's study of the same grammatical feature in Chapter 4. Whereas Berdan's analysis focused on the linguistic sources of variability in Alberto's use of negatives, Schachter (1986) focused on functional variability in the speech of another of the learners (Jorge) initially studied by Cancino *et al.* (1978). Like Berdan, Schachter was concerned with whether the variability evident in Jorge's speech, collected over a 10-month period, was random or systematic.

Schachter is concerned with the methodological difficulties involved in studying variability in learner language. She identifies four possible sources of variation: (1) situational factors, (2) the learner's processing capabilities, (3) the target language (i.e. the target system the learner is attempting to acquire is a variable not a categorical system), and (4) the analyst's procedural decisions. It is the last of these that she addresses through the re-analysis of Cancino *et al.*'s data. Schachter notes that Cancino *et al.* considered the variability in this learner's speech random. Jorge used four developmental negative forms (*no* V, *don't* V, aux-neg and analysed *don't*) more or less throughout the length of the study. However, Cancino *et al.* only examined the formal devices Jorge used to express negation. Schachter was able to show that when the functions performed by the negative utterances were taken into account, Jorge's use of the different devices was in fact far from random. In other words, the choice of negative device was functionally determined. Schacter argues that the analyst needs to search for 'deeper regularities'. Her study provides convincing evidence that one way of achieving this is via a functional analysis of learner language.

This study also raises a question we considered earlier in Chapter 4. What constitutes the 'onset' of a structural device? There we noted that Pienemann (1989) proposed that onset be defined as the occurrence of a new feature in two separate creative (as opposed to formulaic) utterances. Schachter, in contrast, proposes that onset requires 'several instances of a structure to appear on one tape' (1986: 127). Occasional uses of the structure prior to its regular use are characterized as 'the put-puts of a motor before it catches on with a roar'. The difference between Pienemann's and Schachter's definition of onset is in fact crucial for determining whether the variability in a learner's use of two forms is random (free variation) or distributional (systematic). Taking Pienemann's definition of onset, it is clear that the early instances of *don't* V and analysed aux are in free variation. Taking Schachter's definition, however, they are in complementary

Research question	Schachter's main purpose was to examine whether the variability in a learner's use of negative devices was random or systematic.
Participant	One learner—Jorge—a ten-year old Spanish speaker from Colombia. He had been living in the U.S. for one month before the data collection started and was attending an American junior high school. He was mainstreamed but had a one-hour ESL class each week.
Data collection	Schachter relied on the negative data from an earlier study (Cancino *et al.* 1978). Data were collected over a 10-month period, approximately once every two weeks. Three methods were used: 1 Spontaneous speech recordings where Alberto and the researcher engaged in conversation 2 experimental elicitations (e.g. an imitation test) 3 pre-planned socio-lingusitic interaction where a subjects were taken to parties, restaurants, b museums, sports events, etc.
Analysis	Schacter first provides an analysis of Jorge's syntactic development, using frequency analysis. She distinguishes two broad categories: 1 simple negative forms (i.e. *no*+x). 2 complex negative forms (i.e. emergence of a range of English-based negative forms such as *don't*+verb, *can't+ verb* and *never* V). Schachter then analysed the utterances in terms of seven functional categories; 1 non-existence (i.e. the learner claims a referent does not exist) 2 rejection (i.e. the learner indicates opposition to or rejection of an object 3 denial (i.e. the learner asserts that the actual or supposed predicate does not hold for a subject) 4 no information (i.e. the learner indicates he is not in a position to affirm or deny a predication) 5 correction (i.e. the learner indicates self- or other-correction or self-doubt) 6 affirmation (i.e. the learner asserts that a negative predication by another speak holds) 7 quantification (i.e. the learner hedges a denial) Schachter then established which negative forms were associated with each function.

Table 6.8 (*continued*)

Results	Schachter comments 'Jorge exhibits surprising regularity in his pairing of forms and functions, with a strong tendency to associate with each function a very limited set of syntactic forms and to associate with each form a very limited set of functions' (p. 131). For example, non-existence was performed primary by *no* N, rejection by *don't* V, no information by *I don't know* and affirmation by *no*.
Discussion	Schachter concludes 'what appears to be free variation in the use of specific forms to express negation is, in fact, to a large extent functionally determined' (p. 131). However, Schachter does note instances of what appear to be free variation, where a negative structure first appears and is used to perform the same function as a negative form acquired earlier. She likens this to the 'put-puts of a motor before it catches on with a roar' (p. 127).
Implications	Schachter suggests that her study indicates that 'deeper regularities' can be uncovered if the analysis of the data is complex enough. She argues that 'variation a challenge to further and deeper analysis' (p. 131)

Table 6.8 Summary of Schachter's (1986) study

distribution as by the time Jorge begins to make regular use of analysed aux it serves a different range of functions to *don't* V. Here then is an example of how very different interpretations can arise as a result of the analyst's operational definitions of key constructs. These interpretations can lead, in turn, to very different theoretical accounts of L2 acquisition. It is perhaps not so surprising that researchers argue over the existence of free variation.

There are some limitations evident in Schachter's study. She provides overall frequencies of use of the different formal devices serving each function but she does not show how these frequencies changed over time. Thus, unlike Huebner's (1985) study of *da* (see the introductory section to this chapter), this study does not afford a developmental account of Jorge's form–function mappings for negatives.

It is also worth noting that because functional categories are, by definition, notional they involve 'high' rather than 'low' inference. In the case of a form–function analysis the analyst is required to assign a meaning to each occurrence of the form under study. In the case of function–form analysis, the analyst must determine whether a particular utterance constitutes an exemplar of the function under study. Such decisions are not always easily made. For this reason, it is important to provide evidence of the reliability of the coding (for example, by calculating inter-coder reliability). Schachter's study (like other studies around the time it was published) failed to do so. For this reason the results must be treated cautiously.

Despite these limitations, Schachter's study is an important one. Combined with other studies referred to in the introduction to this chapter, it supports the claim that learners' use of the formal devices at their disposal are deployed systematically in accordance with the functions they are trying to perform. Schachter makes a strong case for functional analysis. Indeed, her study suggests that any analysis of learner language that does not examine the functional uses of formal devices will be seriously incomplete.

Task: Carrying out a functional analysis

Table 6.9 shows two interactions, one involving an American native-speaker of English and a Taiwanese non-native speaker, and the other two American native-speakers. Both interactions were elicited by role-play tasks designed to provide a context for performing 'date refusals' (Widjaja 1997). The role-play, entitled 'boyfriend', required Speaker A (male) to approach Speaker B (female) to explain that he was breaking up with Speaker A's friend and to seek a date with Speaker B.

Situation: 'Boyfriend'

Interaction (1): Non-native speaker–native-speaker

NS: Hey, Fei-fong, I'm really glad you are having coffee with me today.
NNS: Really?
NS: Yes, I really, I ah I know you're Su-ling's friend, so I wanted to talk to you um y'know about problems she and I have been having, and...
NNS: XXX
NS: Yeah, yeah, its too bad. We've talked about it a lot, but umm I think it's probably a good idea that we're going to break up, I think.
NNS: Oh, no.
NS: Yeah, I know. Su-ling's really a nice girl and like I said, I know she's your friend and everything, but we're um we're very different, so I think y'know its um...
NNS: Ummm you talk to her?
NS: Yeah. I talked to her a couple of times and y'know we've been going out for a couple of months, so we've tried to talk about the problems but...
NNS: You have better talk with her again because I don't understand this problem you have ended.
NS: I think its probably best we break up.
NNS: Ah, ah, I don't know.
NS: yeah, but but y'know I was wondering, umm, maybe after I finish talking to her and we break up, um, that maybe you'd like to go to a movie with me or something.

Table 6.9 (continued)

NNS: Oh, no, thank you. I have a boyfriend. Sorry, yeah.
NS: OK.
NNS: Maybe I have to go with my boyfriend.
NS: OK. Umm well umm, thanks for talking with me about XX. Bye.
NNS: Bye.

Interaction (2) Native-speaker–native-speaker

NS 1: Oh, I'm really glad that you have agreed to have coffee with me today.
NS 2: Oh, really? Yeah, its great. We haven't got together for a long time.
NS 1: Yeah, I know. It's been a long time. I kind of want to talk to you because I don't know whether Susan has told you. Things are not going too well with us. And umm it looks like we're breaking up pretty soon.
NS 2: Oh, really? It's a shame.
NS 1: Yeah—she's a really nice girl, but we just have different interests. Yeah, we talk about that a lot and decided this is what we're going to do.
NS 2: Sometimes things happen that way. I mean things just don't work out there can be two nice people.
NS 1: Yeah yeah I don't want to sound too much like a cad or anything, but I mean since the time Susan first introduced us, I've really liked you and I was wondering maybe sometime in the future you'd like to go see a movie with me or something?
NS 2: Well, Paul, I mean that... I'm really flattered, but I guess it would be kind of a tricky situation for me because y'know she's a really close friend, and you're too. I would feel really uncomfortable kind of getting into this sort of relationship thing, but I would like to keep you as a friend, and y'know, so we can keep hanging out like we normally do, and maybe we could do something.
NS 1: Ok, sure. Thanks.
NS 2: See you.

Table 6.9 Two interactions involve 'date refusals'

Carry out a functional analysis in order to answer this research question: What differences are there in the linguistic strategies used by the non-native and native speakers to perform a date refusal?
Your analysis will involve the following steps:

1 Identify the utterances performing the date refusal.
2 Describe the linguistic strategies used by the two speakers to perform the date refusal.[5]
3 Establish which strategies are used by the non-native and native speakers and present the results in a table.
4 Discuss the results in terms of the research question.

You might also like to try collecting some more data of your own using the same role-play situation.

Final comment

Functional analyses of learner language constitute powerful tools for examining both how learners make use of their linguistic resources to meet their communicative needs and also how communicative needs drive the process of L2 acquisition forward. Whereas form–function analysis draws on what Halliday (1975) has called 'functional grammar' (i.e. the view that the fundamental components of a language are functional rather than formal), function–form analysis draws on work in pragmatics, in particular that relating to speech acts. These two types of functional analysis are, therefore, complementary.

Both types of analysis support a functionalist view of language and of language learning, that is, a view that sees language not as a formal system but as a means for making meanings of various kinds. Learners bring to the task of learning an L2 an established set of functional concepts from their L1 and are driven to find appropriate linguistic means for performing these in the L2. As Bardovi-Harlig (2000) points out, this view has been more closely associated with European than with American researchers and, among some of the latter, it remains controversial. For theorists like Gregg (1989), for example, the goal of SLA enquiry needs to be grounded in a theory of linguistic competence that excludes any consideration of how language is actually used in behaviour. The kinds of functional analysis examined in this chapter are based on a very different view of language.

Notes

1 Other studies that examined functional determinants of articles are Tarone and Parrish (1988) and Parker and Chaudron (1987). Tarone and Parrish, for example, demonstrated that the discourse mode influenced the choice of NP types, with generics occurring frequently in an interview but hardly at all in a narrative and referential definites showing the opposite pattern.

2 This limitation is less true of interlanguage pragmatic studies. There is now a growing body of research that is investigating to what extent teaching learners how to perform specific illocutionary acts affects their use and acquisition of these acts. (See Rose and Kasper 2001.)

3 Blum-Kulka, House, and Kasper's (1989) taxonomy was based on the analysis of samples of learner language from relatively proficient learners' responses to discourse completion questionnaires. This can explain why 'object of request' does not figure in their taxonomy. It constitutes a developmentally early strategy and it is perhaps unlikely to occur in clinically elicited data. Other taxonomies of request strategies (for example, Takahashi 1995) also do not include object of request.

4 In the complete data (see Ellis 1992), R did use some of these other request strategies. However, they were very infrequent.

5 Widjaja (1997) grouped the strategies she identified into 'negative politeness strategies' (i.e. strategies designed to minimize the impoliteness of face-threatening acts) and 'positive politeness strategies' (i.e. strategies designed to maximize the politeness of polite illocutions). Thus 'excuse' is a negative politeness strategy, whereas 'future acceptance' is a positive politeness strategy.

7 Analysing accuracy, complexity, and fluency

Introduction

The performance analyses of learner language that we considered in Chapters 4, 5 and 6 address the use of specific linguistic features. In contrast, the type of analysis to be considered in this chapter provides a broader and more balanced picture of learner language. Researchers such as Skehan (1998a) and Robinson (2001) suggest that learners can have different goals when performing in an L2, sometimes focusing primarily on accuracy, sometimes on complexity, and on other occasions on fluency. This chapter considers how these constructs can be measured.

Accuracy refers to 'how well the target language is produced in relation to the rule system of the target language' (Skehan 1996b: 23). Learners who prioritize accuracy are seeking control over the elements they have already fully internalized and thus adopt a conservative stance towards L2 use. *Complexity* is the extent to which learners produce elaborated language. There are two senses in which language can be considered elaborated. First, as Skehan (2001) suggests, learners vary in their willingness to use more challenging and difficult language. Language that is at the upper limit of their interlanguage systems, and thus is not fully automated, can be considered more complex than language that has been fully internalized. Secondly, complexity can refer to the learner's preparedness to use a wide range of different structures. Complexity will depend on learners' willingness to take risks by experimenting linguistically. Finally, *fluency* is the production of language in real time without undue pausing or hesitation. Fluency occurs when learners prioritize meaning over form in order to get a task done. It is achieved through the use of processing strategies that enable learners to avoid or solve problems quickly.

Different ways of measuring each of these aspects of language have been developed. Accuracy can of course be measured by analysing the suppliance of specific grammatical forms in obligatory occasions but such a measure may not be representative of a learner's overall ability to use the L2 grammar and it also ignores lexis. Alternative measures based on error analysis, such as the percentage of error-free clauses or the number of errors per 100 words, are able to provide a more general measure of a learner's grammatical and lexical ability to perform accurately in the L2. Complexity is traditionally measured by examining the extent to which a learner employs subordination, the assumption being that the more subordination used the more complex the language produced. However, as we will see, there are a number of other measures available. Fluency requires an investigation of temporal variables such as rate of production (for example, the number of syllables produced per minute of speech) or the number and length of pauses and of hesitation phenomena (for example, the number of false starts).

Underlying these proposals for investigating learner language in terms of accuracy, complexity, and fluency, is a particular view of *L2 proficiency* and the assumption that learners may choose to prioritize one aspect of the L2 over another. The perspective that informs this approach to learner language is psycholinguistic rather than sociolinguistic or linguistic. We will begin by examining it.

Historical and theoretical background

The idea that L2 acquisition is a differentiated rather than a unitary phenomenon is well-established in SLA. In an early paper, Meisel, Clahsen, and Pienemann (1981) advanced the Multidimensional Model of L2 acquisition. This posited two dimensions or axes: (1) a developmental axis, which governed the order and sequence of acquisition of those aspects of grammar that were subject to processing constraints (for example, negatives or interrogatives), and (2) a variable axis, which governed non-developmental features (i.e. features that were acquirable at any time). They suggested that individual learners differ in their socio-psychological orientation to learning an L2 and that this influences, in particular, progress along the variable axis. Learners with a 'segregative orientation' are likely to engage in prolonged 'restrictive simplification' (i.e. they seek optimal results in communication by reducing the grammar to make it easy to handle). Such learners, it can be surmised, achieve communicative fluency at the expense of complexity and (perhaps) accuracy. In contrast, learners with an 'integrative orientation' may seek to complexify their grammatical system by adhering to target language norms. Such learners may prioritize accuracy and complexity over fluency.

Implicit in Meisel *et al.'s* model is the assumption that L2 learners experience difficulty in attending simultaneously to message content and linguistic form and thus need to choose which aspect to allocate primary attention to. Subsequent experimental research gives credence to this assumption. VanPatten (1990), for example, asked English-speaking learners to process information in a Spanish listening task under four conditions: (1) attention to meaning alone, (2) simultaneous attention to meaning and a specific lexical form (*inflación*) important for understanding the text, (3) simultaneous attention to meaning and a grammatical functor (the definite article *la*) and (4) simultaneous attention to meaning and a verb morpheme (*-n*). He then measured their ability to recall the content of the text. Overall, the learners' recall scores were highest in (1) and lowest in (4), with (2) and (3) intermediate. Furthermore, this effect was evident for all proficiency levels but was especially evident in the beginner learners. VanPatten concludes:

> ...conscious attention to form in the input competes with conscious attention to meaning... only when input is easily understood can learners attend to form as part of the intake process. (1990: 296)

VanPatten's study was concerned with input-processing but similar problems have been shown to exist in the case of output-processing. (See, for example, Ellis 1987.)

Why is it that L2 learners have this problem? The answer has been sought in theories of information processing that posit a limited capacity for processing input/output (for example, Skehan 1998b). In the case of input, limitations in working memory make it difficult for learners to process both the message content and to attend to linguistic form. These limitations relate to both capacity (i.e. how much information can be stored at a single time) and to activity (i.e. the need to exercise conscious effort and control over the information). Working memory extracts and temporarily stores information from both the input and long-term memory. In the case of the L2 learner, the demands on working memory are increased because the extraction of information from input and the activation of L2 knowledge from long-term memory rely to a much greater extent on controlled rather than automatic processing. As a result, working memory is overloaded making it difficult for the learner to simultaneously process for comprehension and for acquisition. Depending on context (and orientation), the learner opts to prioritize one or the other. A similar situation arises in the case of output. Here short-term memory functions as a buffer for the conceptualizing, formulating and articulating of speech acts. (See Baddeley 1986; Levelt 1989.) Learners need to access both encyclopaedic knowledge and L2 knowledge from their long-term memories and hold these in short-term memory in order to construct messages that represent their meaning intentions and that are pragmatically appropriate and grammatically correct. This task is extremely demanding, especially in online production (for example, free conversation) where the time available for planning is restricted. Not surprisingly, learners seek to simplify the burden on their working memories by giving priority either to the content of their messages or to linguistic norms, depending on context and orientation. Taken to extremes, this can result in language production on the one hand of the 'Me Tarzan, you Jane' type and of the 'My name is Stanley while, you, I assume, are the renowned Dr Livingstone' type on the other.

According to Skehan (1998b), the way L2 knowledge is represented in the human mind reflects the way it needs to be employed in production.

He distinguishes between exemplar-based and rule-based linguistic systems. The former consists of a large number of formulaic chunks of various shapes and sizes (i.e. from complete utterances to short phrases with one or more 'slots' open). Such fixed or semi-fixed sequences (referred to variably as 'chunks', 'composites', 'fixed expressions', 'formulaic language', 'frozen phrases', 'idioms', 'lexicalized sentence stems', 'prefabricated routines and patterns', and 'stock utterances') have been commonly noted in both native-speaker speech (see Nattinger and DeCarrico 1992) and in L2 learners' production (see Weinert 1995). For Skehan, their importance lies in the fact they conserve precious processing resources. Because they do not have to be computed, they can be accessed rapidly and relatively effortlessly. They enable language users to formulate speech acts when there is little time available for planning what to say. As Wray (2000) points out, they contribute to increased production speed and fluency and they can also be employed to 'buy time' while a speech act is planned. Language users also have access to a rule-based system. That is, they store knowledge of abstract rules that can be used to compute an infinite variety of well-formed utterances/sentences. The advantage of such a system is that it allows complex propositions to be expressed clearly, concisely and (as in the case of literature) in novel and creative ways. The disadvantage is that it is costly in processing effort, difficult to operate in online communication, especially where planning time is limited.

It should be noted, however, that the extent to which L2 knowledge is exemplar-based or rule-based remains a matter of considerable controversy. (See, for example, N. Ellis 1996 and the responses by Major 1996 and Ioup 1996, and *Studies in Second Language Acquisition* 24.2.) Skehan adopts the position that both systems are available to L2 learners; they move between them naturally in accordance with the processing demands of the particular task they are performing and individual difference factors such as their language aptitude and learning style. Such a position is attractive as it can account for the linguistic differences that have been observed in different types of learner discourse and is grounded in current information-processing theories.

The information-processing model outlined above, linked to the idea of a dual system of linguistic representation, serves as a foundation for investigating how the nature of the tasks learners are asked to perform affects their production. To this end, Skehan (1998b) proposes that learner production be examined in terms of an initial contrast between meaning and form, with form further distinguished with regard to 'control' and 'restructuring'. The three-way distinction that results is shown in Figure 7.1. Meaning is reflected in fluency, while form is manifested in either accuracy (if control is prioritized) or complexity (if opportunities for restructuring arise because of the learner's willingness to take risks). Skehan argues (1998b: 270) that these three areas afford 'effective indices for measuring performance on a particular task'.

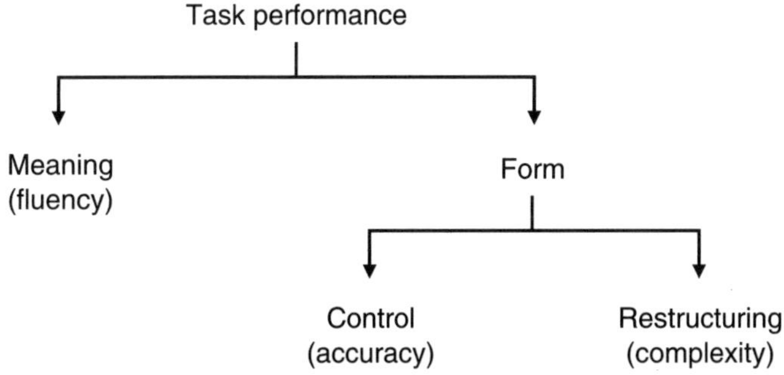

Figure 7.1 Skehan's three aspects of task performance

Much of Skehan's own research, in conjunction with Foster, has been directed at identifying the factors that influence how learners perform tasks. He distinguishes two sets of factors relating to (1) task features and (2) task implementation. In Skehan (2001), he summarizes the various task features he and Foster have identified and the effect they have been found to have on the accuracy, complexity, and fluency of learner production. For example, the feature 'familiarity of information' (i.e. the extent to which the task allows learners to draw on ready-made content schema) is seen as having no effect on form (accuracy and complexity) but contributing to enhanced fluency. In contrast, the feature 'dialogic' (i.e. the task requires learners to interact together rather than to perform a monologue) leads to greater attention to form, with a concomitant gain in accuracy and complexity but to the detriment of fluency. Task implementation factors include pre-task planning and during-task manipulations such as the inclusion a surprise element in the task. The provision of time to plan a task performance enables learners to overcome the limitations of their working memory and results in improved complexity and fluency, and, in some cases, also accuracy. (See, for example, Foster and Skehan 1996.)

Thus, task demands push learners to perform tasks in certain ways, prioritizing one or another aspect of language. The key question that arises concerns the nature of the trade-offs that occur when learners are confronted with demanding tasks. In the case of input-processing, the choice seems to lie between 'meaning' and 'form', as shown by the VanPatten study discussed above. In the case of production, however, the situation is more complicated. One possibility is that learners' basic choice is again between 'meaning' and 'form'. This is the view adopted by Robinson (2001). He distinguishes between resource-directing dimensions of task complexity (for example, the number of elements to be communicated or the absence/presence of contextual support) and resource-depleting dimensions (for example, whether or not learners are asked to perform a single or dual task). In accordance with his multiple-resources view of language processing, Robinson argues that complex tasks involving resource-directing dimensions result in greater attention to form with increments evident in both accuracy and complexity. Similarly, tasks with resource-depleting dimensions adversely affect learners' capacity to attend to both of these aspects of language. The choice then is between 'fluency' and combined 'accuracy/complexity'. Skehan's view is that learners not only have to choose between meaning and form but also between accuracy and complexity. He suggests that complex tasks may lead learners either to adopt a 'safety-first approach' by electing to use language for which they have already developed automatic processing or to adopt an 'accuracy last approach' where they attempt to utilize language requiring controlled processing but are unable to pay sufficient attention to it. In the former approach, complexity is sacrificed in favour of accuracy while in the latter the opposite occurs. Skehan and Foster (2001) note that these two contrasting accounts of trade-off effects may work differently for native and non-native speakers, with competition between complexity and accuracy only evident in the case of the latter. A third position is possible. Wendel (1997) argues that learners have to choose between fluency and form but that the aspect of form that is affected if they elect for fluency is always accuracy (i.e. fluency and complexity can co-occur but not fluency and accuracy).

It is probably premature to try to resolve these competing claims. Skehan and Foster (2001: 192) analyse the performances of learners on a variety of tasks to demonstrate that the three aspects of language—accuracy, complexity, and fluency—are distinct. They argue that the results 'do not sit well with the multiple resource pools view of attention'. Robinson's own research (for example, Robinson and Lim 1993; Robinson 2001) has failed to demonstrate that cognitively demanding tasks can have a dual effect on accuracy and complexity. Wendel (1997) and Yuan and Ellis (2003) found that pre-task planning aids both fluency and complexity but has no effect on accuracy. However, Yuan and Ellis also found that when learners had plenty of time for online planning (i.e. were not pressured to perform the task rapidly) both accuracy and complexity benefited, with fluency understandably reduced. Thus, there is some evidence to support all three claims.

The difficulty at arriving at a clear picture of what is traded-off with what and under what conditions is considerable. The research to date has employed very different tasks carried out under very different conditions. Further, these studies have also employed different measures of the three aspects of language. Thus comparison of results across studies is well-nigh impossible. Given the large number of task variables that can, singly or in varying combinations, affect performance, it may prove impossible to arrive at a definitive answer even if standard measures of accuracy, complexity, and fluency are agreed upon—an unlikely event!

Nevertheless, from our perspective here, the research that has drawn on measures of these three aspects of language is promising and useful. First, there has been substantial progress in operationalizing each aspect in terms of clearly defined measures. Secondly, the independence of the three aspects has also been established, both theoretically (as described above) and empirically in the task-based studies. Thirdly, distinguishing the three aspects is of obvious relevance to applied fields such as language testing and pedagogy. It affords a model of L2 proficiency that can inform both the design of tests (see Iwashita, Elder, and McNamara 2001) and language courses (see Ellis 2003a). It is likely, therefore, that we will see an increasing number of studies based on the analysis of learner language in terms of accuracy, complexity, and fluency in the years ahead.

Measuring accuracy, complexity, and fluency

The accuracy, complexity, and fluency of learner language of both oral and written production[1] can be measured. By and large the specific measures of accuracy and complexity that have been developed can be applied to both media. Obviously, however, fluency needs to be operationalized differently for oral and written language. We will proceed by examining the various measures that have been used to study each aspect, commenting wherever possible on their validity. Because different measures can produce different results researchers have preferred to use a number of measures of each aspect. One way of establishing concurrent validity is to examine the extent to which the different measures correlate with each.

Examples of the different measures will be provided by conducting analyses of two oral texts (see Table 7.1). These texts are taken from Yuan's (2000) study of the effects of pre-task and careful online planning on the accuracy, complexity, and fluency of oral narratives produced by a group of Chinese university students. The narrative task required the students to narrate a story orally, based on a picture composition from Heaton (1975). The story was about three boys who could not get on a bus because four big boys had pushed in front of them. They had to wait half an hour for another bus. However, they later passed the first bus, which had broken down on a hill. The three boys laughed at the four big boys as the bus passed. All the participants were required to begin their oral narratives by saying 'This morning, Tom, George, and Bill ...'.

Text A was produced by a learner from the pre-task planning group. He was given ten minutes to plan his performance of the task. He was given a sheet of paper to write notes on but was told not to write out the whole story. The notes were taken away before he started the task. When performing the task he was told to produce four sentences for each of the six pictures within five minutes. In this way, he was given time for pre-task planning but was put under pressure to perform the task rapidly (i.e. with limited opportunity for online planning). Text B was produced by a learner from the careful online planning group. This learner was required to carry out the task after seeing the pictures for only half a minute, but was given unlimited time to formulate and monitor his speech plans as he performed the task.

Text A (+ pre-task planning/– on-line planning)

the story's name is waiting for a bus // Tom Jack and George were waiting for er a bus er (4.0) // at the time they were waiting:: there come a truck //and {there was stretched} there was stretched a lot of dirty water on the ground // en so {when}when the bus came:: the dirty water was splashed {to them} er er (8.0) {to them} to them//{en then} en then when they were standing in the line:: there was a tall man:: push in front of the queue en (1.5) // and Tom was about to over on the ground // and {the} the number of the bus is twenty six // and then er (1.5) the bus conductor told them:: and the bus was full:: and can't carry any passengers // so er (2.0) it was {three o'clock} about three o'clock at the time //and then {they were waiting for another} they had to wait for another bus to come // they waited from three o'clock to three thirty // and then the bus {number} number thirty three {come} came {on the way on the way to (3.0) them} (1.5) er on the way to their school // the number twenty-six was driving before number thirty three // it was driving very fast bus // unfortuntely it {had} er er (1.5) was flat tire //so the conductor {got} get out of the bus:: and they change and change and change the tire // {and} but number thirty three {it is still} it is still driving //[and} and (2.0)Tom Jack and George {looked} stretched their hands out of the window // {and} (2.0) {and cried to} and shouted to er (1.0) the passengers on number twenty six // and they had a bad day // they had a bad day// but at last they {get} got a good result //

(Total speaking time = 2.65 minutes)

Text B (– pre-task planning/ + on-line planning)

this afternoon {Tom Tom} Tom and Jack and George mm {want to want to went to} went to water park (1.0) //and he must take {number} number twenty six bus on (3.0) {thirteen three bus} //{when he} when they (2.0) stand (1.0) on the{ bus} bus stop// en (2.0) {a truck come} a truck come here // then {the truck} (4.0) the truck {make them mm dirty make them dry make wet and} (2.0) and it make them very dirty //(4.0) {a moment ago} mm and the number twenty six bus {come} come here // when they want to {jump} jump to the bus // (5.0) and {the four} the four child (1.0) come here:: and {want to} want to come up first (2.0) // so {when when} when Tom Jack and George {want to go} want to come up the bus :: and the ticket {se} seller went (3.0) {tell them} tell them :: it {the bus is the bus the bus is filled} the bus is full (2.0) // young men cant {come come come down come} come up {so} (1.0) // {so (1.0) they must} so they must waiting for another bus // (2.0) {about} (1.0) about (1.0) seven thirteen (1.0) the number sixteen bus {come} come here //(5.0) so they come up the bus// (5.0) {though} though {they} they played :: but they can't come up the bus // they were very glad// (4.0) {after the bus }the bus drive very fast {when he come when he (2.0) when he come when he come when come in}:: when her drive in the {highways} highway// {em (2.0) about {three} three hours ago (2.0)} they saw :: the number {sixteen six twenty six} twenty six bus mmm was stopped beyond the wall // (1.0) they signed the number six twenty six bus // the tyre was broken :: and the driver is fix it // so (2.0) the customer in the twenty six bus and {must must stop must stop} must sit in the bus// (2.0) {in the} Tom Jack and Jill

Table 7.1 (continued)

(3.0) {come} come // and {they they all they were} (2.0) they were {held} held his hands // (1.0) mm mm {to make to make}(4.0) made the number twenty (2.0) six // {the other (2.0) the other} the other {bus} bus 's customer (2.0) {look at him} look at them // (4.0) they very glad // (6.0) {because they can come because they can} because they can {come come up them} come up them //

(Total speaking time = 3.06 minutes)

Key:
// boundaries of AS-units
( ) length of pause in seconds
{ } dysfluency
:: subordinate clause boundary

Table 7.1 Two oral narrative texts analysed into AS-units (Yuan 2000)

The analysis of learner language in terms of accuracy, complexity, and fluency requires a principled way of segmenting a text into units. This is easier to achieve in written language as the obvious unit is the sentence. However, it is more problematic in spoken language, especially dialogic, and so we will begin this section with a discussion of this issue. We will then consider different ways of measuring the three aspects of learner language.

A unit for measuring spoken language

One of the main problems in analysing oral production is deciding on a unit on which to base the analysis and then identifying this unit in the data. Foster, Tonkyn, and Wigglesworth (2000: 357) report the results of their survey of how SLA researchers have segmented written or spoken learner language:

> Our survey revealed a plethora of definitions of units of analysis, a paucity of examples, and a worrying tendency for researchers to avoid the issue altogether by drawing a veil of silence over their methods.

They criticize researchers for failing to define terms like 'utterance' and 'T-unit', arguing that without explicit definitions it is impossible to achieve accurate and comparable analyses.

The unit proposed by Foster *et al.* is the AS-unit, which they define as:

> . . . a single speaker's utterance consisting of *an independent clause or sub-clausal unit,* together with any *subordinate clause(s)* associated with it. (2000: 365).

This unit is primarily syntactic (rather than intonational or semantic) as syntactic units are easier to identify and are thus more reliable. However, they suggest that intonation and pausal phenomena will need to be taken into account to deal with 'awkward cases'. *An independent clause* is a clause that includes a finite verb. *A sub-clausal unit* consists of either a segment of speech/writing that can elaborated into a full clause by recovering elided elements or a minor utterance such as 'Thank you very much'. *A sub-ordinate clause* consists minimally of a finite or non-finite verb plus at least one other element (for example, subject or object). Also, in order to be certain that it is attached to the independent clause, the speaker should not have paused for longer than 0.5 seconds. Foster *et al.* go on to discuss how this definition can be applied to actual data, addressing how to deal with false starts, repetitions and self-corrections, topicalizations, and interruptions and scaffolding. Their definitions of these phenomena are shown in Table 7.2 together with their proposals for how they should be handled by the analyst. Readers are strongly advised to consult this article before undertaking an analysis of spoken learner language.

Phenomena	**Definition**	**How to handle**
False start	'an utterance that is begun and then either abandoned altogether or reformulated in some way' (p. 368).	Exclude from word count
Repetition	'the speaker repeats previously produced speech' (p. 368).	Exclude from word count unless repetition is for rhetorical effect
Self-correction	'the speaker identifies an error either during or immediately following production and stops and reformulates the speech' (p. 368).	The final version only is included.
Topicalization	The speaker states the topic of the AS-unit without incorporating it grammatically into the unit.	Include in the AS-unit unless they are followed by a falling intonation and a marked pause.
Interruption and scaffolding	A second speaker either interrupts the first speaker's utterance before he/she completes it or attempts to continue/complete it for the first speaker.	Include in the AS-unit produced by the first speaker providing this speaker completes his/her utterance or incorporates the scaffolded element into it.

Table 7.2 Handling dysfluency in the analysis of oral productions based on Foster et al.

Measure	Text A	Text B
Number of AS-Units	22 units	25 units
Total length of main pauses	28 seconds	90 seconds
Dysfluencies (total words)	42 words	127 words
Number of subordinate clauses	7 clauses	6 clauses
Total number of words (minus dysfluencies)	233 words	217 words

Table 7.3 Comparative analysis of Text A and Text B based on Foster et al.'s system

Table 7.1 above illustrates Foster *et al.*'s system of analysis as applied to the two texts. It shows (1) the AS-units, (2) the length of main pauses, (3) dysfluencies (i.e. false-starts, repetitions and self-corrections, and (4) the subordinate clause boundaries. Table 7.3 compares the two learners' narratives in terms of these measures. It reveals that both texts contain approximately the same number of AS units and subordinate clauses. However, they differ with regard to the number of long pauses and the total number of dysfluent words, with Text B markedly more dysfluent than Text A. All the subsequent analyses that we will discuss are dependent on this preliminary analysis in one way or another.

We will turn now to a consideration of how the accuracy, complexity, and fluency of learner language can be assessed. Two approaches are possible: (1) obtaining ratings (i.e. by providing general descriptors of different levels of accuracy, complexity, and fluency, which are then used to assess the performance of individual learners) and (2) calculating various discourse-based measures. Language testers have preferred (1) as ratings provide a practical way of assessing learner language and have high face-validity (i.e. they reflect how people in general might respond to a learner's ability to communicate). SLA researchers have typically employed (2) in order to obtain precise measures of the different aspects. A few studies (for example, Iwashita, Elder, and McNamara 2001; Wigglesworth 1997) have used both and compared results, finding some discrepancies. In the sections that follow we will consider only various discourse-based measures as only these require an analysis of learner language.

Measuring accuracy

Researchers have used a number of different measures of accuracy. The main ones are summarized in Table 7.4. We will comment briefly on each of these measures.

The number of *self-corrections* does not provide a measure of how accurately a learner uses the L2 but rather indicates the extent to which the

Measure	Definition	Study
Number of self-corrections	The number of self-corrections as a percentage of the total number of errors committed.	Wigglesworth (1997)
Percentage of error-free clauses	The number of error-free clauses divided by the total number of independent clauses, sub-clausal units and subordinate clauses multiplied by 100.	Foster and Skehan (1996)
Errors per 100 words	The number of errors divided by the total number of words produced divided by 100.	Mehnert (1998)
Percentage of target-like verbal morphology	The number of correct finite verb phrases divided by the total number of verb phrases multiplied by 100.	Wigglesworth (1997)
Percentage of target-like use of plurals	The number of correctly used plurals divided by the number of obligatory occasions for plurals multiplied by 100.	Crookes (1989)
Target-like use of vocabulary	The number of lexical errors divided by the total number of words in the text (excluding dysfluencies).	Skehan and Foster (1997)

Table 7.4 Measures of accuracy

learner is oriented towards accuracy. Frequent syntactical self-correction might be considered indicative of an integrative orientation (see earlier discussion) while a low-level of syntactical self-correction may reflect a more segregative orientation. Lexical corrections may be more indicative of a general need to get the message across. Fairly obviously, self-corrections need to be measured in terms of the learner's opportunity to self-correct. That is, a learner who makes few errors in the first place will have little need to self-correct, while a learner who makes many errors will have greater opportunity. For this reason, this measure ideally needs to be calculated in relation to the number of errors a learner makes. Self-corrections are also sometimes used as a measure of fluency. (See 'reformulations' in Table 7.8.)

Percentage error-free clauses and *errors per 100 words* serve as general measures of accuracy and for this reason have been widely used. Skehan and Foster (1999: 229) suggest that 'a generalized measure of accuracy is more sensitive to detecting differences between experimental conditions'. Such a measure is not without problems, however. First, in the case of error-free clauses, there is the problem of deciding what constitutes a 'clause', especially if the data is derived from interaction where elision is common. This problem disappears with errors per 100 words. In both measures, however, the analyst must decide how to handle clauses where the learner makes an initial error and then corrects it. It is probably best to count self-corrected clauses as error-free but this may depend on the purpose of the analysis. If the researcher is interested in a learner's ability to spontaneously produce correct language, it would be necessary to take account of all errors, irrespective of whether they were corrected. Further problems with both measures arise as a result of the difficulties of determining exactly what constitutes an error. Readers are referred to the discussion of this point in Chapter 3. An alternative to this measure is incidence of errors per AS-unit. Bygate (2001) suggests that this might produce a more sensitive measure of accuracy as it takes account of all the errors produced.

The next two measures, *target-like verbal morphology* and *target-like use of plurals* are more specific measures of grammatical accuracy.[2] Their validity as a general measure of accuracy rests on the extent to which learners' ability to use verb tenses/plurals correctly correlates with their overall grammatical competence. That is, an assumption is made that if learners are able to use one specific feature of grammar accurately, they will also be able to use others. The extent to which this assumption is justified is questionable, however, as learners do not acquire grammatical features concurrently. Rather, some features are acquired early and others late. For example, a learner may be able to use plurals accurately but be unable to produce other, later-acquired grammatical features such as regular past tense or possessive *-s*. Examining specific features is also dangerous because the learner's L1 may make a particular feature more or less easy. For example, learners whose L1 does not contain plural markers may be penalized by the target-use of plurals measure. Ideally, then, measures of specific grammatical features are best used alongside a more general measure, such as percentage of error-free clauses. However, specific measures of accuracy will obviously be required in the case of 'focused tasks' (Ellis 2003a) that have been designed to elicit production of particular linguistic features.

Ideally, the analyst needs to consider accuracy in relation to other levels of language than grammar. Measuring accuracy in pronunciation is a possibility but is especially problematic given the difficulty in determining what

Measure	Text A	Text B
Self-corrections	10	15
Error-free clauses	51.7%	6.5%
Target-like use of verb tenses	20/31 = 64.5%	9/34 = 26.5%
Target-like use of plurals	3/3 = 100%	3/6 = 50%
Target-like use of vocabulary	5/233 = .02	18/218 = .08

Table 7.5 The two texts compared in terms of measures of accuracy

constitutes the appropriate target accent to use as a baseline for examining the learner's pronunciation. However, with particular groups of learners, it might be possible to select specific phonemic contrasts that are common to all target varieties (for example, /l/ and /r/) for analysis). Measuring lexical accuracy is also problematic but has been more popular. *Target-like use of vocabulary* can be calculated in relation to the main unit of analysis (for example, the percentage of clauses without lexical errors) or in terms of the total number of words in the text (minus dysfluencies). Note that the lower the score, the more accurate the learner's use of lexis. As with grammatical errors, difficulties arise regarding the identification of lexical deviations. Skehan and Foster (1997: 195) suggest that only errors where a word used is 'nonexistent in English or indisputably inappropriate' be considered.

Table 7.5 compares Text A and Text B in terms of these different measures of accuracy. It is clear that Text A is much more accurate than Text B. This is evident in all the measures of grammatical accuracy and also in the measure of lexical accuracy. There are also more self-corrections in Text B suggesting this learner's general lack of oral proficiency in English. It is clear, then, that the various scores correlate closely, pointing to the concurrent validity of the accuracy measures.

Measuring complexity

Complexity measures can be grouped according to the aspect of language they relate to: (1) interactional, (2) propositional, (3) functional, (4) grammatical, and (5) lexical. Table 7.6 below provides definitions of the main measures that have been used together with citations of studies that have used each measure.

Number of turns per minute is an interactional measure and therefore applies only to dialogic discourse. It provides a measure of the extent of each speaker's contribution. Thus, a speaker's use of the L2 is considered to be complex if he/she contributes regularly to the interaction. One problem with this measure is that it does not take any account of the length of a speaker's contribution. Thus, a speaker who performs many short turns (for example, 'Okay', 'Yeah', 'I see') would achieve a high score even though the utterances produced were very simple. Thus this measure is perhaps best used

Measure	Definition	Study
Interactional		
1 Number of turns	The total number of turns performed by each speaker is counted. This can be then be expressed as a proportion of the total turns in the interaction. Alternatively, the average number of words for each speaker can be calculated.	Duff (1986)
2 Mean turn length	The total number of words (or pruned words) produced by a single speaker divided by this speaker's total number of turns.	
Propositional		
3 Number of idea units encoded	The total number of (a) major and (b) minor idea units in the text is counted. Major and minor ideas are established with reference to a baseline performance of the message (e.g. by a native speaker).	Zaki and Ellis (1999)
Functional		
4 Frequency of some specific language function (e.g. hypothesizing)	The total number of times a specific language function is performed by a learner is counted. This measure can be expressed as a raw frequency or relationally (e.g. in terms of total AS-units).	Brown (1991)
Grammatical		
5 Amount of subordination	The total number of separate clauses divided by the total number of c- (or AS) units.	Foster and Skehan (1996)
6 Use of some specific linguistic feature (e.g. different verb forms)	The number of different verb forms used.	Yuan and Ellis (2003)
7 Mean number of verb arguments	The total number of verb arguments (subjects, direct objects, indirect objects, adjectival complements, prepositional phrases) divided by the total number of finite verbs.	Bygate (1999)

Table 7.6 (continued)

Measure	Definition	Study
Lexical		
8 Type-token ratio	The total number of different words used (types) divided by the total number of words in the text (tokens).	Robinson (1995)

Table 7.6 Measures of complexity

alongside *mean length of turns,* or, in the case of written texts the total number of words produced or the total number of AS-units.

Calculating the number of *idea units* in a text provides a measure of propositional completeness (i.e. the extent to which a speaker/writer encodes the ideas needed to convey a given content) and thus may provide a measure of the extent to which learners have engaged in 'conceptualization' (Levelt 1989). An idea unit is defined as a message segment consisting of a topic and comment that is separated from contiguous units syntactically and/or intonationally. This measure works best when the elicitation task requires learners to communicate a pre-specified content, as for example when they are asked to tell a story based on pictures. A distinction can be made between 'major' and 'minor' idea units. Major idea units are those that are required to convey the essential content of the message. Minor idea units relate to details that embellish the message but are not essential. Major and minor ideas are best established by analysing the texts produced by fully competent speakers performing the same task.

Measuring the *frequency of use of a language function* that is linguistically and cognitively difficult or that provides evidence of a sophisticated knowledge of the conventions of a particular type of discourse can serve as an indicator of complexity. Nemeth and Kormos (2001), for example, examined the frequency of use of a number of functions associated with argumentation (for example, 'claims', 'counter-claims', 'supports' and 'counter-supports') in order to examine the effects of asking learners to repeat a task. In the case of narratives, the frequency of 'framing statements' (i.e. where the narrator comments on the story being told as opposed to simply relating events) can be used as an indicator of complexity. Brown (1991) measured complexity in terms of the extent to which learners hypothesized, reporting that tasks with open outcomes resulted in greater use of this function than tasks with closed outcomes.

The most commonly used measures of complexity are grammatical in nature. In L1 acquisition research, mean length of utterance serves as a general measure of grammatical complexity but is rarely used in SLA because of the large number of formulaic chunks that L2 learners employ.[3] Another popular measure found in L1 research is *the average length of*

T-unit, defined by Hunt (1965: 20) as 'a main clause with all subordinate clauses attached to it'.[4] This measure of subordination works well for analysing the complexity of L2 written texts but less well for oral texts, as these typically contain large numbers of sub-clausal units (see above). To deal with this problem, researchers have proposed other base units such as c-units, defined by Pica *et al.* (1989: 72) as 'utterances, for example, words phrases and sentences, grammatical and ungrammatical, which provide referential or pragmatic meaning', and the AS-unit discussed above. A measure of subordination based on these units serves as an effective indicator of complexity for those learners who have acquired some of the various subordinating devices (i.e. intermediate level learners and above) but fails to distinguish levels of complexity among more elementary learners who have not reached the stage where they employ subordinate constructions. For this reason, it needs to be complemented by a measure of some specific linguistic feature that occurs in all learners' use of the L2, irrespective of their developmental level. Researchers have used a variety of such measures—for example, *the number of different verb forms* used or the *ratio of indefinite to definite articles* (Wigglesworth 1997).[5] Finally, *the mean number of verb arguments* provides a measure of the communicative style of the speaker/writer. A low mean is indicative of a 'verbal style' while a high proportion suggests a 'nominal style'. A nominal style is considered more complex. It should be noted that these grammatical measures take no account of accuracy—for example, whether a subordinate clause is well-formed or not it still counts as an attempt at subordination.

It is also important to consider learners' use of vocabulary. This is because some learners may employ relatively simple grammatical structures but a wide range of different words. Lexical richness is also a measure of complexity. This is generally measured by calculating *type-token ratio*—the closer the type-token ratio is to one the greater the lexical richness. A problem with this measure is that it is influenced by text length; that is, it is easier to obtain a high type-token ration in a short text than in a long one. An alternative measure is Mean Segmental Type-Token Ratio. This requires dividing a learner's text into segments (for example, 50 words each) and calculating the type-token ratio of each segment.[6] The mean score of all the segments is then calculated. Other measures of lexical complexity are also possible—the number of different word families used, the ratio of structural to content words, and the ratio of lexical to copula verbs.

Table 7.7 compares Text A and Text B in terms of these different measures of complexity. Text A emerges as more complex on some measures especially on the functional measure (number of framing statements), the propositional measure and one of the grammatical measures (the ratio of indefinite to definite articles). On other measures, however, the differences are quite small. Also, Text B is a little longer than Text A and has almost the same type-token ratio. It can be noted, then, that the complexity measures

Measure	Text A	Text B
Text length	22 AS-units	25 AS-units
Number of major idea units*	8	6
Number of framing statements	4	0
Amount of subordination	1.32	1.24
Number of different verb forms	11	9
Ratio of indefinite to definite articles	.45	.087
Mean number of verb arguments	1.83	1.70
Type-token ratio	.52	.53

* 'Major idea units' are defined as the propositions essential for conveying the story-line depicted in the pictures. These were established by asking a native-speaker to give a 'bare-bones' summary of the story.

Table 7.7 The two texts compared in terms of measures of complexity

do not afford a totally consistent picture, suggesting that where this aspect of language is concerned multiple measures are desirable.

Measuring fluency

Measures of fluency have been of two principal kinds (Wiese 1984; Lennon 1990); *temporal variables* relating to the speed of speaking/writing and *hesitation phenomena* relating to dysfluency. Evidence that these constitute distinct dimensions of fluency is to be found in Skehan (1998b). He reports that a factor analysis of a range of fluency measures produced a two-factor solution—'breakdown fluency' (corresponding to temporal variables) and 'repair fluency' (corresponding to hesitation phenomena). Table 7.8 provides definitions of the main measures belonging to these two categories together with studies that have employed them.

The principal temporal variable is *speech/writing rate*. This is the only temporal variable that can be applied to both speech and writing. The other variables can only be calculated for speech. Speech rate provides a combined measure of two temporal aspects of spoken production; online planning time and rate of articulation. The difference between the speech rate of learners (even advanced ones) and native speakers is generally highly statistically significant (see, for example, Wiese 1984) but speech rate can improve markedly when learners spend a period of time in a country where the language is spoken (Towell 1987). *Number of pauses* and *pause length* provide an indication of the extent to which learners need to disengage from speaking in order to plan their spoken messages. Learners who spend less time pausing can be considered more fluent. Finally, *length of run* provides information about the extent to which learners are able to produce segments of a message without pausing. Length of run may reflect the extent to which learners access ready-made chunks of language (i.e. their exemplar-based

Measure	Definition	Study
Temporal variables		
1 Speech/Writing rate	This is usually measured in terms of the number of syllables produced per second or per minute on task. The number of pruned syllables (i.e. excluding dysfluencies) is counted and divided by the total number of seconds/minutes the text(s) took to produce.	Ellis (1990b)
2 Number of pauses	The total number of filled and unfilled pauses for each speaker.	Robinson, Ting, and Unwin (1995)
3 Pause length	This can be measured as either total length of pauses beyond some threshold (e.g. 1 second) or as the mean length of all pauses beyond the threshold. Pause length provides a measure of silence during a task.	Skehan and Foster (1999)
4 Length of run	This is the mean number of syllables between two pauses of a pre-determined length (e.g. 1 second). This measure discounts dysfluencies.	Wiese (1984)
Hesitation phenomena		
5 False starts	Utterances/sentences that are not complete (i.e. constitute fragments). They may or may not be followed by reformulation.	Skehan and Foster (1999)
6 Repetitions	Words, phrases or clauses that are repeated without any modification whatsoever.	Skehan and Foster (1999)
7 Reformulations	Phrases or clauses that are repeated with some modification.	Skehan and Foster (1999)
8 Replacements	Lexical items that are immediately replaced by other lexical items.	Skehan and Foster (1999)

Table 7.8 Measures of fluency

system). Dechert (1984: 169), for example, reports that one of the L2 learners he investigated in a story retelling task varied markedly in length of run depending on whether they employed 'small regular analytic chunks' or 'larger irregular Gestalt chunks'.

This list of temporal variables is based on Wiese (1984). However, the extent to which they all relate to the same temporal aspect of fluency is arguable. Rate, for example can be considered separate from pausing as it is possible for a learner to achieve a rapid rate of speech while speaking but still pause extensively. Length of run can also be seen as a distinct measure of fluency, capturing the complexity of the learners' 'unitization' of their spoken and written production.

Table 7.8 lists four hesitation variables (based on Wiese 1984). As studies have shown a high level of relationship among these, a valid measure of this aspect of fluency may be obtainable based on a single variable, for example, false starts. Skehan and Foster (1999: 230) suggest that hesitation phenomena are 'connected to moment-by-moment decisions during performance, reflecting adjustments and improvements that are feasible within the pressure of real-time communication'. It should be noted, however, that hesitation variables can be applied equally to speech and writing even though written language does not usually entail 'real-time communication'. Hesitation phenomena may be related to individual differences in learners. Krashen (1977b), for example, notes that some learners seem to monitor their performance whenever possible, and others do not monitor at all.

Table 7.9 compares Text A and Text B in terms of these different measures of fluency. It reveals clear differences in both the temporal and hesitation variables. The learner who produced Text A speaks faster, pauses much less, and has a higher average length of run than the learner who produced text B. He also made fewer false starts and repeated and reformulated less. In short, this learner performed much more fluently. All the measures of fluency point in the same direction.

Measure	Text A	Text B
Speech rate (syllables per minute)	88	71
Pause length (seconds)	28	90
Average length of run (syllables)	9.2	6.6
False starts	4	15
Repetitions	5	19
Reformulations	3	10
Replacements	6	7

Table 7.9 The two texts compared in terms of fluency

An example of a study of accuracy, complexity, and fluency

As we noted earlier in this chapter, the analysis of learner language in terms of accuracy, complexity, and fluency has figured strongly in studies of tasks. These studies have been conducted with a view to identifying how specific design features of tasks and/or implementational procedures influence L2 production. In particular, researchers have been interested in the effects of giving learners time for pre-task planning. This research views the opportunity to plan prior to performing a task as 'a pedagogical manipulation assumed to induce learners to focus on whichever formal and systemic aspects of the language are needed to accomplish a particular task' (Ortega 1999: 110). Thus, researchers have been motivated to study task planning in the belief that the focus-on-form that takes place incidentally during a task performance as a result of planning will assist both the performance itself and the process of L2 acquisition. They have investigated the effects of a range of planning variables (for example, the amount of time available to plan and whether it is detailed or undetailed) on accuracy, complexity, and fluency. (See Ortega 1999 for a review.)

We have chosen as an example of these planning studies one the earliest—Crookes (1989). This study was the first to employ measures of accuracy and complexity to the study of the effects of planning on L2 production. However, Crookes did not include any measures of fluency. The study is summarised in Table 7.10.

This is an important study, often cited by researchers. It provides clear evidence that planning affects the complexity of learner language. However, contrary to the findings of Ellis (1987), Crookes' study failed to show any significant effect of planning on accuracy. Subsequent research has also produced mixed results where accuracy is concerned, some showing that it has a definite effect and others no effect. Various factors may contribute to these mixed results (for example, the situation in which data are collected and the nature of the psycholinguistic processes involved in using language accurately). Researchers continue to probe for an explanation. (See Yuan and Ellis 2003.)

A feature of Crookes' study is the large number of measures used to assess complexity and accuracy (Table 7.10 lists only a selection). In this respect also the study led the way. Subsequent researchers have borrowed many of Crookes' measures and have also followed him in electing to use multiple measures. It is interesting (and comforting) to note that by and large the measures of complexity and accuracy converge; that is, the bulk of the complexity measures resulted in statistically significant differences between the planning conditions, whereas the accuracy measures did not. This suggests that the two sets of measures are indeed assessing different constructs.

Finally, a word on reliability. Despite the apparently objective nature of the measures Crookes used, considerable problems can arise in computing them, a point discussed further in the concluding section of this chapter.

Research question	The general hypothesis was 'planned speech will show more evidence of development than unplanned speech in a variety of aspects' (p. 370). This was broken down into a series of 'directional hypotheses' relating to the accuracy and complexity of learners' productions.
Design	Two groups of 20 learners each performed two tasks under two planning conditions.
Participants	40 adult ESL students (L1 = Japanese); intermediate and advanced levels
Data collection	Spoken data were collected using two tasks (1) a description of how to construct a Lego model and (2) an explanation of where to site a building on a map. Two equivalent versions of each task were used. The tasks were performed in a 'minimal planning condition' (i.e. the participants started as soon as they had they task instructions) and a 'planning condition' (i.e. the participants had 10 minutes to plan during which time they could make written notes, subsequently collected in before they performed the task).
Analysis	A large number of measures were used. The following are a sample: 1 Accuracy – number of error-free T-units – Target-like usage of plural *-s* – Target-like usage of *the* – Target-like usage of *a* 2 Complexity – words per utterance – number of subordinate clauses per utterance – words per subordinate clause – type-token ratio
Results	The main results were: 1 Planning resulted in greater accuracy than minimal planning on all the measures but only the difference for target-like usage of *the* achieved statistical significance. 2 Planning resulted in greater complexity, with the differences for most of the measures above proving statistically significant. Differences were also evident for the two tasks, with the effects of planning more evident in the Lego task.
Discussion	Crookes comments 'the general pattern of these results shows consistent, small- to medium-sized effects in favor of the planned condition and is tentatively taken here as supporting the position that planning is a process that can

Table 7.10 (continued)

	lead L2 learners to produce more developed speech in the short term' (p. 379). Crookes also considers factors that may have limited the effects of planning. He suggests that giving Japanese learners the opportunity to plan may have only a limited effect, as they are culturally disinclined to speak spontaneously even after planning. Also it is possible that the learners prioritized complexity at the expense of accuracy. He also suggests that choice of task may have more influence on learners' productions overall than planning.
Implications	Crookes rejects the view of some proponents of communicative language teaching that tasks should serve to provide opportunities for spontaneous, unrehearsed language use. He argues that there is a case for providing opportunities for planned language use in order to promote L2 development.

Table 7.10 Summary of Crookes' (1989) study of the effects of pre-task planning

It is obviously important, therefore, to ensure that the measures obtained are reliable. Crookes reports that he obtained satisfactory inter-rater reliability on a stratified random sample of the data[7] for segmenting the stream of speech into utterances and for the segmentation of utterances into T-units. However, he does not report the reliability of the specific measures.

Task: Carrying out an analysis of accuracy, complexity, and fluency

In Table 7.11 you will find two samples of oral learner language taken from Yuan (2000). Information about the learners, the task used and the conditions under which the task was performed was provided earlier. Text A involved an opportunity for pre-task planning but performance of the task was pressured. In contrast, in the case of Text B there was no opportunity for pre-task planning but it was performed without any time pressure.

Carry out a comparative analysis of the two texts in terms of the accuracy, complexity, and fluency of the learners' productions. To do this you should:

1 Prepare the texts for analysis by:
   a segmenting each text into AS-units
   b identifying dysfluencies
2 Calculate the following:
   a total AS-units in each text

b number of subordinate clauses
c total number of dysfluent words
d total number of fluent words
e total pause length

Text A (+ pre-task planning/ – on-line planning)

This morning Tom Jack and George want to m go to the park (1.0) and many people were waiting for the bus at the bus stop (1.0) just then four... older boys came here er (2.0) and on including the crowd (1.0) they are Tom (2.0) Jack and George er who were three little boys the ground was very bad and a bus (2.0) stopped at the bus stop mmm(4.0) and many and peoples people get got in the bus one by one (1.0) but the four boys came in front of the three little boys mm (3.0) one of them also pushed the boys the little boy and and three boys cannot couldn't get on the bus (1.0) it is about three o'clock at the afternoon and the four boys who got on the bus left at Tom Jack and George mm (4.0) the they didn't get them get on (2.0) the bus and they were very disappointed (1.0) and (1.0) three minutes later another bus came and three little boys got on the bus very happy (2.0) and on em (2.0) the bus on quickly went went away en after (4.0) a few minutes (2.0) the second the second bus caught up with the first one (1.0) the first bus got something wrong with it and the man was preparing it (7.0) and the second bus was passed passed the first one and the three little boys find the the four boys who is was the bus bus (1.0) they are very disappointed and mm (4.0) the three boys were very happy

(Total speaking time = 2.90 minutes)

Text B (– pre-task planning/ + on-line planning

Tom and Jack Tom Jack and George went through a street en (2.0) when en (1.0) he were is something in the shop en (1.0) here is here is here is a truck coming and and er the truck made the dirty water mm (4.0) the em (3.0) got off the dirty water made made the people made the people clothes dirty en en (4.0) and Tom Jack and George very very en (1.0) angry (4.0) en so when when he get get on the er bus they they find the boy getting getting his way (1.5) so they pushed the boy (4.0) out of here and (2.0) and and then the policemen (2.0) get off and (3.0) and tell them (2.0) give them a lesson en (2.0) and they find his mistake and (1.0) he want to (3.0) en (2.0) change (2.0) then he (2.0) when he got on the bus again en he (3.0) he en (3.0) he let line three in a line and and get on the bus in turn (7.0) and then when the bus (3.0) through the road (3.0) the tire is the tire was broken en (3.0) and no other the other car was passed away passed away and then (2.0) he had to en ask for help so (3.0) m so (3.0) make the driver (2.0) troublesome en then the bus before before them en (6.0) was the bus came back and to help them (5.0) help them (6.0) them they helped the bus to repair the tire

(Total speaking time = 3.45 minutes)

Table 7.11 Two samples of learner language from Yuan (2000)

3 Select and calculate measures of accuracy, complexity, and fluency. You should choose two measures of each. Compare the results of your analyses with another person's to establish inter-rater reliability.

What do your results show about the two texts?

How do your results for the two texts compare with the results of the analyses of the texts in Table 7.1?

What problems did you experience in carrying out these analyses?

Final comment

The measures that we have studied in this chapter are based on an information-processing framework and thus are appropriate for exploring the nature of the processes involved in producing L2 texts. They have been employed in both descriptive research of L2 productions (see Dechert, Mohle, and Raupach 1984 for examples of studies) and, increasingly, in experimental studies designed to investigate the effect of specific variables (such as pre-task planning) on learner language (for example, Foster and Skehan 1996b). As Skehan (1998a) points out they are 'generalized' in nature. Thus they are not as appropriate for testing fine-grained hypotheses as the measures we examined in the previous chapters. Their advantage, Skehan suggests, is in 'maximizing the variance which is available' (1998a: 275).

We conclude by pointing out two problems. The first problem concerns reliability. It is likely that, as a result of completing the task in the previous section, you discovered that calculating many of the measures is not as straightforward as you might have thought. The definitions of many of the measures require interpretation. For example, in identifying false starts it is necessary to decide exactly what constitutes an utterance that is 'abandoned before completion'. Determining how many false starts there are in an AS-unit such as the following

//to make to make (4.0) made the number twenty (2.) six//

is clearly problematic. At one level the whole unit is a fragment (i.e. structurally inchoate) but also within the unit there is an obvious false start, which itself contains a repetition ('to make to make'). Are there one, two or three false starts in this unit? To address difficulties such as these it is essential that the analyst makes explicit how such problems are dealt with and is consistent. It is also, obviously, necessary to demonstrate inter-rater reliability.[8]

The second problem concerns the sheer multiplicity of the measures that have been used. Given that different measures are frequently employed in different studies, to what extent is it possible to compare results across these studies? It would be desirable to determine (through careful research) which measures constitute valid and reliable measures of the constructs and then for researchers to stick to these. Given the vitality of the field, however, this is unlikely. Perhaps, though, the fact that measures of the same construct have been found to correlate highly, as in Crookes (1989), mitigates the danger of a proliferation of measures.

Notes

1 Although the measures of accuracy, complexity, and fluency can be applied to both oral and written language, the bulk of the research that has employed these measures has examined oral language only. Indeed, the theoretical background outlined in this chapter has been explicitly developed with oral production in mind and it is not clear to what extent it is explanatory of L2 written production. See Polio (1997) and Wolfe-Quintero *et al.* (1998), however, for specific suggestions about measurements of written language.

2 Other specific measures of accuracy can and have been used—for example, target-like use of articles.

3 Mean length of utterance is calculated by (1) identifying and then counting the number of morphemes in the sample, (2) counting the number of utterances produced by a speaker, and (3) dividing (1) by (2). Formulaic utterances like 'I don't know' (consisting of 4 morphemes) artificially inflate the morpheme total as they constitute single, unanalysed units for the learner.

4 Foster *et al.* (2000) point out that Hunt offers various definitions of a T-unit including one that includes 'non-clausal structures'.

5 Indefinite articles are generally acquired later than definite articles. Thus, a high ratio is indicative of a learner using a more advanced grammatical feature.

6 Malvern and Richards (2002) recommend another measure for calculating the type-token ratio. However, this is designed to work on a specific data base and for this reason is not considered here.

7 Five consecutive utterances were randomly selected for checking.

8 In fact, many published studies (for example, Foster and Skehan 1996) that have used measures of accuracy, complexity, and fluency have failed to report inter-rater reliability.

8 Interactional analysis

Introduction

The analyses considered in the previous chapters have all addressed characteristics of learner output. Although this output often arose in interaction, the samples of learner output consisted of isolated utterances and were analysed separately with minimal reference to their situational and/or interactional context. In this and the next two chapters, we examine the discourse in which learners participate. To this end, this chapter will draw on the theory and methods of *discourse analysis*. Chapter 9 will consider *conversation analysis,* while Chapter 10 will discuss *microgenetic analysis,* the method used by researchers working within a sociocultural theoretical framework.

Defining 'discourse analysis' is not easy. This is because the term has been very broadly defined and consequently can appear somewhat vague, covering a range of analytical practices (Allwright and Bailey 1991). Schiffrin (1994) points out that the definitions reflect two general approaches. In the first approach, discourse is viewed as 'language use'. This approach is functionalist in orientation, drawing in particular on speech act theory. It is based on the view that to understand the formal properties of language it is necessary to examine the functions they perform in human life. It is concerned with how utterances are situated in context. This approach to discourse analysis is reflected, in part, in the kinds of functional analysis we considered in Chapter 6 and is also evident in critical approaches to analysing learner language to be considered in Chapter 12. In the second approach, discourse is viewed as 'language above the sentence or above the clause' (Stubbs 1983). This approach considers discourse as text and seeks to identify the structural configurations of different types of text. It describes text in terms of 'constituents', 'relationships' and 'arrangements'.

In this chapter, we will adopt the definition of discourse analysis proposed by Shriffrin, namely that it entails the analysis of 'utterances'. This definition incorporates both approaches to discourse analysis in that it addresses the semantic and pragmatic aspects of discourse (i.e. what individual utterances mean in their contexts of use) and the sequential organization of utterances in texts (i.e. how utterances combine to form continuous text). In this chapter we will be concerned only with dialogic discourse (i.e. discourse that involves two or more participants communicating with each other). Reflecting this, we will refer to the particular kind of discourse analysis that we will utilize as *interactional analysis*.

The term 'interactional analysis' needs to be distinguished from 'interaction analysis'. The latter term refers to category systems used to code features of classroom interaction (for example, Moskowitz 1967). Such systems constituted discourse analysis of a sort in that they typically described functional aspects of classroom interaction (for example, 'teacher provides explanation') but they did not address its structural properties and, as Long (1980) pointed out, the choice of categories were not informed by any overarching theory of language use or acquisition. For these reasons, we will not consider interaction analysis in this chapter.

Interactional analysis, on the other hand, provides a means of describing the interactions in which learners participate. It tells us what kinds of function learners perform when they interact with other learners or native speakers in different contexts and the structural properties of these conversations. Arguably, this is interesting enough in itself and, in language pedagogy, is certainly important for achieving an understanding of how learners interpret the instructional tasks they are given. In SLA, however, interactional analysis serves as a tool for identifying those properties of interactions that have been hypothesized to contribute to L2 acquisition. We will begin, then, with an account of these properties, the theories from which they have been derived, and a brief review of the history of interactional analysis in SLA.

Theoretical and historical background

Interactional analysis has been widely used to describe the discourse involving L2 learners in both instructional and naturalistic settings. It has addressed both macro aspects of discourse (for example, Sinclair and Coulthard's (1975) framework for describing the structure of classroom interaction or van Lier's (1988) classification of the different types of classroom interaction involving L2 learners), and micro-aspects (for example, Hatch's (1978) description of topic-nomination sequences in conversations involving L2 children and native speaking adults). We will focus on three aspects of interaction, which have figured strongly in both the SLA and pedagogic literatures—the *negotiation of meaning, communication strategies,* and *error treatment.*

The negotiation of meaning

The term 'negotiation of meaning' refers to the conversational exchanges that arise when interlocutors seek to prevent a communicative impasse occurring or to remedy an actual impasse that has arisen, as illustrated in the following exchange, which took place in the context of L2 learners performing an information-gap task:

NS TEACHER	place the mushroom with the four yellow dots underneath the two mushrooms that are already there
NNS STUDENT	which one?
NS TEACHER	ok? place the mushroom
NNS STUDENT	what's a 'mushroom'?
NS TEACHER	it's another kind of plant
NNS STUDENT	a 'fungus'
NS TEACHER	yeah, a 'fungus'

(Pica 1992: 211)

The study of the negotiation of meaning has been closely linked to Long's Interaction Hypothesis (IH). This drew on Hatch's (1978) key insight that learners can learn a second language (L2) *through* the process of interacting rather than just manifesting what they have already learned *in* interaction. It is useful to distinguish early and late versions of the hypothesis.

In both versions the negotiation of meaning is the central discourse construct. Both versions also emphasize that interaction involving meaning negotiation only *facilitates* acquisition; it does not *cause* acquisition to take place. In other words, modified interaction can only 'set the scene for potential learning' (Gass, Mackey, and Pica 1998: 304). Furthermore, as Pica (1996) has pointed out, the Interaction Hypothesis does not claim that meaning negotiation is the only type of interaction in which the conditions that foster learning arise. She acknowledges that 'uninterrupted communication' (i.e. communication where there is no problem of understanding) can also contribute to acquisition, although, like Long, she maintains that learners' data needs are best met through negotiation.

The early version of the IH was closely associated with the Input Hypothesis (Krashen 1985). This claims that learners will acquire an L2 when they have access to comprehensible input and when their 'affective filter' is low (for example, they are motivated to learn and are not anxious) so that the comprehended input is made available to the internal acquisitional mechanisms for processing. Long (1983) adopted Krashen's view about the role of comprehensible input but stressed the importance of interaction as a source of this.

This early version of the IH was challenged on a number of fronts. First, the claim that comprehension promotes acquisition was questioned. A number of theorists (for example, Sharwood Smith 1986; Faerch and Kasper 1986) pointed out that learners can comprehend input by drawing on context and their schematic knowledge of the world in such a way that they do not have to attend to the actual linguistic forms in the input. This results in successful comprehension but not in acquisition. Secondly, Long's claim that interactionally modified input was especially beneficial for acquisition has been challenged. Krashen (1985) argued that simplified input that was not interactionally derived (i.e. premodified input) served equally well. However, a number of studies (for example, Pica, Young, and Doughty 1987) have been able to show that interactionally modified input results in better comprehension than premodified input, although one reason for this might simply be the extra time that learners gain to process input when they can negotiate for meaning. Doubts were also expressed as to whether learners always succeed in comprehending as a result of meaning negotiation. Hawkins (1985) showed that learners often fake comprehension in meaning negotiation sequences. Clearly, there are social constraints that influence the extent to which learners are prepared to negotiate to achieve understanding. Also, where vocabulary acquisition is concerned, Ellis (2001b) found that interactionally modified input was no more effective than premodified input. Ellis also noted that meaning negotiation can sometimes result in over-elaborated input that interferes with acquisition. Thirdly, it has been noted that some aspects of language (for example, inflectional morphology) are typically not subject to negotiation (Sato 1986), or, if they are, they are not actually noticed by learners (Mackey, Gass, and McDonough 2000). Fourthly, the claim that acquisition arises entirely through access to comprehensible input was challenged. Swain (1985; 1995) argued convincingly that comprehensible output also plays a role in L2 acquisition. (See below.)

The later version of the IH went some way towards addressing these criticisms. Long's (1996) updated IH emphasized that the role of negotiation is to facilitate the kinds of conscious 'noticing' that Schmidt (1990, 1994) has argued is required in order for learners to process input for 'intake'. Long writes:

> ...it is proposed that environmental contributions to acquisition are mediated by selective attention and the learner's developing L2 processing capacity, and that these resources are brought together more usefully, although not exclusively, during 'negotiation for meaning'. (1996: 414)

The later version of the IH also affords a much richer view of how negotiation can assist language learning. As in the early version, negotiation is seen as enabling learners to obtain comprehensible input, thereby supplying them with *positive evidence* (i.e. 'models of what is grammatical and acceptable', Long 1996: 413). Pica's detailed analyses of negotiation sequences have shown how negotiation can give salience to form-function relationships and also how it helps learners to segment message data into linguistic units. In the extract below, for example, the native speaker's modification helps the learner to segment a constituent ('above') in the input.

NS with a small pat of butter on it and above the plate
NNS hm hmm what is buvdaplate?
NS above
NNS above the plate
NS yeah

(Pica 1992: 225)

The later version of the IH also posited two other ways in which interaction can contribute to acquisition; through the provision of *negative evidence* and through opportunities for *modified output.* Long (1996: 413) defined negative evidence as input that provides 'direct or indirect evidence of what is grammatical'. It arises when learners receive feedback on their own attempts to use the L2. One of the major ways in which this takes place is through *recasts,* that is, utterances that rephrase a learner's utterance 'by changing one or more sentence components (subject, verb or object) while still referring to its central meanings' (Long 1996: 435). Long argued that recasts provide the opportunity for 'cognitive comparison' (i.e. for learners to compare their own deviant productions with grammatically correct input). A number of studies (for example, Long, Inagaki, and Ortega 1998; Mackey and Philp 1998) have investigated recasts in conversations involving L2 learners but with somewhat mixed results. We will come back to the subject of recasts below, when we consider them in relation to error treatment.

Long (1996) also incorporates a role for comprehensible output in the revised IH. Swain (1995) discusses four functions of output. First, it serves a consciousness-raising function by triggering 'noticing'. That is, producing language helps learners to notice their problems. Secondly, producing language enables learners to test out hypotheses about the L2. One way this occurs is through the modified output that learners produce following negative feedback (discussed further in the section on error treatment). Thirdly, output allows learners to reflect consciously about L2 forms. This can occur in the context of communicative tasks where the content is grammar (i.e. when learners negotiate for meaning as they grapple with a grammar problem). Fourthly, output can also help learners to achieve greater fluency by increasing control over forms they have already partially acquired. De Bot (1996) views this function as the most likely way output aids acquisition. A number of studies have investigated what opportunities for modified output arise in meaning negotiation sequences (for example, Oliver 1998) and, to a lesser extent, whether such output contributes to L2 acquisition (Mackey 1999; Van den Branden 1997). These studies provide some evidence that it does.

The later version of the IH emphasizes the contributions of negative feedback and modified output, as well as comprehensible input. It also recognizes that interaction works by connecting input, internal learner capacities, and output via selective attention. While this is obviously a major advance on the early version, there are, nevertheless, a number of caveats. First, there are methodological problems associated with the analysis of meaning negotiation sequences, which will be discussed later. Secondly, a theory based on a single type of interaction (negotiation sequences), which constitutes only a small part of the total interaction a learner experiences, can obviously present only a very partial account of L2 acquisition. Long (1996) does point out that the updated version of the IH is not intended to constitute a complete theory but this raises the question as to just how important meaning negotiation is for acquisition. Thirdly, the IH ignores sequences where there is no communication breakdown but there is nevertheless attention to a learner error through negative feedback. These sequences, labelled *negotiation of form* by Lyster and Ranta (1997), have a similar interactional structure to negotiation of meaning exchanges and have been observed to occur frequently in some classroom settings. Like negotiation of meaning exchanges, they also create a context for modified output. Finally, there is the question of individual differences. To what extent does the IH account for all learners, including those (such as young children) who may be less able or less inclined to engage in meaning negotiation. As Gass, Mackey, and Pica (1998) have pointed out, individual differences need to be looked at carefully in future research.

The later version of the IH is also implicated in Long's views about the importance of *focus on form*. Long (1991: 4–5) defines this as follows:

> Focus on form ... overtly draws students' attention to linguistic elements as they arise incidentally in lessons whose overriding focus is on meaning or communication.

Focus-on-form, then, is a discoursal phenomenon, although, presumably, it is intended to imply a cognitive correlate. (See Doughty 2001 for a discussion of the psycholinguistic aspects of focus on form.) According to Long, it typically arises when participants negotiate a communication problem. That is, it constitutes a kind of corrective feedback on learners' attempts to express themselves and thus involves attention being drawn to some specific linguistic form. For this reason, it will be dealt with in the section below on the treatment of error.[1]

Communication strategies

Whereas the negotiation of meaning is 'listener-oriented', communication strategies are 'speaker-oriented'; that is, they are used by learners to compensate for lack of L2 knowledge or their inability to access the L2 knowledge they have. There are a number of category systems offering taxonomies of communication strategy. Most of the strategies so identified relate to lexis, although, potentially they can apply to any level of language (i.e. phonological, grammatical, or pragmatic). Examples of the communication strategies that have been identified are 'avoidance' (where the learner gives up a topic or abandons a specific message) and various 'achievement' strategies such as 'paraphrase' (i.e. the use of approximation as when 'worm' is substituted for 'silkworm', word coinage or circumlocution), 'conscious transfer' (i.e. the deliberate use of the L1, for example, by literally translating an L1 expression), 'appeals for assistance' and 'mime' (see Tarone 1981). These taxonomies have been data-driven rather than theoretically informed and perhaps for this reason have tended to proliferate.

Faerch and Kasper (1983), however, usefully located such communication strategies within a general model of speech production. In their account, communication strategies are seen as part of the planning stage; they are called upon when speakers experience some kind of problem with their initial plan that prevents them from executing it. Bialystok (1990) offers a somewhat different psycholinguistic account. She suggests that communication strategies can be distinguished according to whether they are 'knowledge-based' or 'control-based'. The former involve the speaker adjusting the content of a message by exploiting knowledge of a concept, for example by providing a definition or paraphrase. The latter involve maintaining the original content of the message and manipulating the means of expression by going outside the L2, for example by using the L1 or mime.

A third psycholinguistic model of communication strategies, somewhat similar to Bialystok's, has been developed in the Nijmegen Project (Kellerman, Bongaerts, and Poulisse 1987; Poulisse 1990). The model rests on two archistrategies labelled 'conceptual' and 'linguistic'. Conceptual strategies involve the manipulation of the concept to be communicated. They are two broad types. Analytic strategies involve the use of identification of features of a referent as reflected in circumlocution, description and paraphrase. Holistic strategies involve the substitution of a superordinate, subordinate, or coordinate term for the term that is problematic. The distinction between analytic and holistic strategies is continuous rather than dichotomous. Linguistic strategies involve the manipulation of the language by recourse to the L1 or through morphological creativity. The model is summarized in Table 8.1. Kellerman (1991) claims that these distinctions reflect key differences in mental processing.

A key issue in the study of communication strategies is what motivates learners to use one type of strategy rather than another. Poulisse (1997) suggests that learners seek to conform to two general principles of communication—the Principle of Clarity and the Principle of Economy. (See Leech 1983.) The former requires speakers to be informative and clear while

Archistrategies	Communication strategies
Conceptual	1 Analytic (circumlocution, description, and paraphrase)
	2 Holistic (the use of a superordinate, coordinate or subordinate term)
Linguistic	1 Transfer (borrowing, foreignerizing, and literal translation)
	2 Morphological creativity

Table 8.1 A typology of communication strategies (based on Poulisse 1990: Chapter 7)

the latter requires them to be brief and economical. The problem facing learners is that they do not always have access to the language needed to be brief and economical. They may, for example, not know the L2 word to label a referent. Thus, they may need to sacrifice economy in order to achieve clarity (for example, by using a circumlocution). However, Poulisse argues that learners do try to adhere to the two principles and this motivates their choice of strategies. For example, they are likely to first try using their L1 (which satisfies both principles) and only subsequently apply other strategies. These may involve the progressive provision of more information (through approximation, word coinage, paraphrase, etc.) until they have achieved their goal. If a choice has to be made between being clear and saving effort, learners weigh up the importance of the goal, sometimes opting for clarity and sometimes for economy (for example, by avoiding the problem).

Whereas strong claims have been advanced regarding the usefulness of meaning negotiation for facilitating language acquisition, considerable uncertainty exists about the role of communication strategies. In general, communication strategies are seen as important for understanding L2 communication rather than for explaining acquisition. However, a number of researchers have suggested ways in which such strategies might aid acquisition, particularly lexical acquisition. Corder (1978) suggests that achievement strategies will foster acquisition but that avoidance strategies will not, a view endorsed by Faerch and Kasper (1980). They suggest that learners may incorporate some of the strategic solutions to problems into their interlanguage systems. Tarone (1980) argues that achievement strategies may be beneficial in that they help learners negotiate their way to the correct target language forms. They may also assist acquisition by helping to keep the conversation going, thus securing more input for learners. Kasper and Kellerman (1997) suggest that communication strategies are also an important vehicle for producing pushed output, which, as we have seen, some researchers claim contributes to acquisition. More specifically, they suggest that they help to develop semantic connections in the learner's mental lexicon and skill in word formation. Skehan (1998a) adopts a very different stance, however, arguing that learners who are adept in using communication strategies to overcome their linguistic problems may fossilize because they do not experience any communicative need to develop their interlanguage knowledge resources. Of course, language acquisition involves more than the development of linguistic competence. Even if communication strategies do not contribute to linguistic competence, they may contribute to the development of strategic competence (i.e. the ability to overcome problems and to communicate efficiently).

The treatment of error

The study of the treatment of learner error has been motivated by both pedagogical considerations and theoretical interest in the role of negative evidence in L2 acquisition.

Much of the early research (see Chaudron 1988 for a review) sought to describe the options for responding to error available to teachers. The taxonomies developed by Allwright (1975), Long (1977) and Chaudron (1977) testified to the complexity of error treatment as an interactional phenomenon in the language classroom. Three general characteristics of teachers' error correction practices are (1) its imprecision, (2) its inconsistency, and (3) its indirectness. Imprecision is evident in the fact that teachers use the same overt behaviour (for example, 'repetition') to both indicate that an error has been made and to reinforce a correct response. Nystrom (1983) has commented: 'teachers typically are unable to sort though the feedback options available to them and arrive at an appropriate response'. Inconsistency arises when teachers respond variably to the same error made by different students in the same class, correcting some students and ignoring others. Such inconsistency is not necessarily undesirable, however, for, as Allwright (1975) has pointed out, it may reflect teachers' attempts to cater for individual differences among the students. Indirectness is evident in teachers' preference for correction strategies that mitigate the illocutionary force of the correction. Seedhouse (1997) has shown that teachers rarely make it clear to learners that they have committed an error, generally preferring indirect strategies such as recasts.

Teachers' treatment of error has also been compared with the strategies for dealing with error in non-instructional settings, where *repair* is the preferred term. This is considered in greater detail in Chapter 9. Whereas error-treatment in the classroom typically consists of other-initiated repair and other-repair (that is, teachers generally decide what errors to repair and carry out the repair work themselves), in naturally occurring conversations it consists of self-initiated repair and self-repair (that is, it involves a 'self-righting mechanism' (Schegloff, Jefferson, and Sacks 1977)). Another difference between error treatment in classroom and natural settings is that it occurs much more frequently in the former. Chun, Day, Chenoweth, and Luppescu (1982) found that only nine per cent of ESL learners' errors were corrected in conversations with native speakers.

More recent research into error treatment has been motivated by theoretical claims about the role of negative evidence in L2 acquisition. If L2 acquisition is seen as relying on inductive learning procedures rather than on an innate language acquisition device, as claimed by some SLA theorists (for example, Bley-Vroman 1989; Felix 1985), then positive evidence (available through the input to which learners are exposed) may be insufficient to ensure that learners achieve full target-language competence. Negative evidence, in the form of error treatment, may also be needed. Cognitive accounts that stress the need for conscious attention to linguistic form in order for learning to take place (see, for example, Schmidt 2001) also recognize the importance of negative evidence. Long's revised Interaction Hypothesis and his claims about the role of 'focus on form' in language learning, for example, suggest that negative evidence derived from the reactive feedback that arises in the course of the negotiation of meaning plays a crucial part in enabling learners to notice the gap between their own interlanguage formulations and target language constructions.

From this theoretical perspective, the crucial questions become 'Does error treatment enable learners to notice their errors and to learn from them?' and 'Do some types of error treatment work better than others in this respect?' This has led to two lines of research. In one, researchers have examined the extent to which learners modify their output in the uptake move that follows the treatment of an error. Consider the negotiation sequence quoted earlier in this chapter from Pica (1992: 225). Here, the learner responds to the error treatment by correctly segmenting 'buvdaplate' in the uptake move ('above the plate'), suggesting that she has noticed the word boundaries and perhaps learned something from the exchange. One outcome of this interest in learners' modified output in correction sequences has been the development of taxonomies of uptake moves, an example of which is shown in Table 8.2.

In the second line of enquiry, researchers have sought to build on the earlier atheoretical taxonomies of error treatment by proposing a basic distinction between implicit (for example, recasts) and explicit (metalingual explanation) methods of feedback. In theories of L2 learning such as the Interaction Hypothesis, recasts are seen as the interactional means of engaging learners' attention to form in the context of message-centred communication and, thereby, of promoting acquisition. Studies of communicative classrooms have shown that recasts are the preferred means of treating learner error. However, the extent to which recasts promote successful uptake (i.e. repair of the error) appears to be variable. Some studies, such as Lyster and Ranta (1997), report relatively low levels of uptake (typically students responded to a recast with a topic continuation move

A	**Repair** 1 Repetition (i.e. the student repeats the teacher's feedback). 2 Incorporation (i.e. the student incorporates repetition of the correct form in a longer utterance. 3 Self-repair (i.e. the student corrects the error in response to teacher feedback that did not supply the correct form). 4 Peer-repair (i.e. a student other than the student who produced the error corrects it in response to teacher feedback).
B	**Needs repair** 1 Acknowledgement (e.g. students says 'yes' or 'no'). 2 Same error (i.e. the student produces the same error again). 3 Different error (i.e. the student fails to correct the original error and in addition produces a different error). 4 Off target (i.e. the student responds by circumventing the teacher's linguistic focus). 5 Hesitation (i.e. the student hesitates in response to the teacher feedback). 6 Partial repair (i.e. the student partly corrects the initial error).

Table 8.2 Different kinds of uptake (Lyster and Ranta 1997)

rather than repair); others, such as Ellis, Basturkmen, and Loewen (2001a), report much higher levels. So far, very few studies have examined whether error treatment sequences have any effect on learning, but Loewen (2002) found that when correction led to successful uptake, learners were more likely than not to supply the correct form subsequently in tests.

Final comment

As the above account shows, interactional analysis has played a major role in research relating to L2 learners' interactive behaviour and its impact on learning. In the earlier research, the focus was on gaining insights into specific learning and instructional events. This research, with its emphasis on the detailed micro-analysis of learner and teacher behaviour, arose as a response to the perceived problems of global method studies, which, by-and-large, had ignored classroom processes in favour of an exclusive examination of learning outcomes. (See Allwright 1988.) In this tradition, researchers used interactional analysis to establish whether instructional activities resulted in the kinds of behaviour they were designed to elicit. This line of research continues today but increasingly the detailed study of discourse involving learners has been marshalled to test hypotheses derived from theories of L2 acquisition. It has become the primary means of examining key aspects of the 'linguistic environment' and, thereby, of the role that this plays in acquisition. It has been used to investigate the contextual factors that influence interaction in a second language, for example, whether the interaction is between an L2 learner and a native speaker or between L2 learners, and, in the case of the latter, whether the learners are of similar or different proficiency. It has also been used to investigate the design features of tasks that promote specific kinds of interaction, especially the negotiation of meaning. (For a summary of this research, see Ellis 2003a: Chapter 3.)

Interactional analysis has figured in both interpretative accounts of learner interactions (as in van Lier 1988), where the emphasis has been on understanding why interactions take the form they do by relating them to their wider social context, and in confirmatory research designed to test specific theoretically-derived hypotheses about the role of interaction in L2 acquisition (for example, Long, Inagaki, and Ortega 1998). The former have typically involved holistic and illustrative descriptions of interactional sequences, while the latter has employed taxonomies of interactional categories that lend themselves to quantification.

Conducting an interactional analysis

Interactional analysts working with L2 data have drawn on a variety of different approaches. Our aim in this section is to offer a general guideline for analysing problem-solving interactions rather than to focus on a particular approach. However, we believe it will assist us in this enterprise if the reader has some familiarity with the specifics of the different approaches. To this end Table 8.3 summarizes four of the major approaches in terms of their goals and, in broad terms, their descriptive apparatus. The key terms relating to each approach are shown in italics. A fifth approach (conversation analysis) is dealt with in detail in Chapter 9. It is important to recognize that none of these approaches was concerned with describing interpersonal interactions for their own sake but addressed broader issues drawn from philosophy, linguistics, sociology and anthropology.

It should be obvious by now that interactional analysis does not constitute a well-defined method for analysing data. Thus, while it is possible to identify a number of general principles that guide how to conduct an interactional analysis, it is not possible to identify a definite set of procedures, as was the case with the other types of analysis we have considered. In part this is because interactional analysis is still in its infancy. There are, for instance, relatively few agreed terms for labelling the components of interactions. Each of the approaches outlined in Table 8.3 has developed its own terminology. This situation is in obvious contrast to grammatical analysis, where metalingual terms are well-established. But, in part, it is because interactional analysts have chosen to investigate a wide range of features of interaction (for example, specific speech act sequences such as requests,

Approach	Goal	Descriptive apparatus
Speech act theory (Searle 1976)	To explain how particular communicative acts (utterances) achieve their purpose (i.e. perform actions)—for example, how a request, even an indirect one, comes to be understood as a request—and to develop a theoretical basis for classifying communicative acts.	Searle identifies two kinds of meaning in a speech act; *locutionary meaning* (the propositional meaning of an utterance) and *illocutionary force* (the communicative function performed by an utterance). He also distinguishes *direct speech acts* and *indirect speech acts.*
Interactional sociolinguistics (Gumperz 1982)	To demonstrate how the meaning, structure and use of language in face-to-face encounters is culturally relative by examining the verbal signs used in interaction by different speech communities and thus to show how cognition and language are affected by social and cultural factors.	The basic approach involves (1) identifying specific utterances for analysis, (2) uncovering the situated meaning of this utterance by comparing it with other utterances and interactions. (2) precedes by describing the *contextualization cues* (i.e. the verbal and non-verbal signs that signal a speaker's meanings). These cues enable speakers to determine both what general kind of communicative activity they are engaging in and the specific illocutionary force of an utterance. Misunderstandings arise when speakers do not share contextualization cues.
The ethnography of communication (Hymes 1974)	To analyse patterns of communication as part of cultural knowledge in order to understand how people in a particular speech community communicate with each other.	Hymes proposed a classificatory grid (known as SPEAK) to identify the components involved in communication: S setting/scene P participants

Table 8.3 (continued)

Approach	Goal	Descriptive apparatus
		E ends (goals and outcomes) A act sequence (message, form and content) K key (tone, manner) N norms of interaction (including relationship to cultural belief system) G genre
A linguistic approach (Sinclair and Coulthard 1975)	To describe the structure of verbal interaction in classrooms, utilizing established linguistic techniques (i.e. Halliday's model of systemic grammar).	Classroom interaction is described in terms of a hierarchical set of ranks such that each unit is composed of units from the rank below it: – lesson – transaction – exchange – move – act Only units at the rank of *exchange* and below are described with any precision. A common structure for exchanges is that of Initiation, Response and Feedback (often referred to as IRF).

Table 8.3 Four approaches to interactional analysis

question-answer sequences, turn-taking mechanisms, topic-initiating devices, ways of closing conversations), with each feature involving different categories and structures. Thus, in order to explain how to do interactional analysis and to illustrate the procedures involved, it is necessary to focus on a particular type of interaction in order to delimit the features to be analysed. In the account that follows, we address the negotiation that interlocutors engage in when confronted with a communicative problem.

The data (see Table 8.4) that will be used to illustrate the general approach to interactional analysis comes from a communicative task performed by two undergraduate male students (L1 = Korean). The task required one learner to describe a route on a map to the other learner so that

1	L1: look at the bus station	
2		L2: mmhm
3	L1: right right upper-side	
4		L2: *right upper side*?
5	L1: yeah	
6		L2: *is it next to the card store*?
7	L1: right	
8		L2: okay
9	L1: and uh you can see river street	
10		L2: river street
11	L1: you walk down down street	
12		L2: down street
13	L1: yeah	
14		L2: *um?*
15	L1: to river street	
16		L2: okay
17	L1: and then come left you come left to sixth street	
18		L2: sixth street mm (1.0) uh okay
19	L1: and	
20		L2: turn left?
21	L1: yeah you can find uh shopping center	
22		L2: right
23	L1: uh enter the shopping center you can then	
24		L2: all right
25	L1: you can then (1.0) go out the shopping center	
26		L2: uh huh
27	27 L1: and then go through the sixth street and you can find pop-lar street	
28		L2: *mm what is it?*
29	L1: pop-lar	
30		L2: *poplar street I don't have that it's not on here so you have to tell me other street*
31	L1: it's the intersection between xxx sixth street three hundred east	
32		L2: I don't have that information here [laughs] all I know is that out of shopping center

Table 8.4 (*continued*)

		you mean back to that on sixth street am I on sixth street now?
33	L1: no no no	
34		L2: no I have different
35	L1: down street	
36		L2: down street
37	L1: to the station can you find the station	
38		L2: station?
39	L1: yeah	
40		L2: *what station?*
41	L1: I don't know	
42		L2: [laughs] no
43	L1: subway station	
44		L2: subway station
45	L1: do you have uh um railroad?	
46		L2: no
47	L1: no?	
48		L2: no
49	L1: mm	
50		L2: all I know is that I'm in the shopping center and I'm lost
51	L1: [laughs]	

Note: Italicized utterances indicate where negotiation is taking place

Table 8.4 Learner–learner interaction

the second learner could draw the route on his map. The two maps were not identical, however, thus creating a number of referential problems that needed to be addressed. (See Yule and McDonald 1990 for an example of a study based on this kind of task.)

Interactional analysts can approach the kind of data shown in Table 8.4 in two ways. The first constitutes a data-driven approach; that is, the analyst inspects the data with a view to identifying structural and functional features of the interaction that are relevant to a specific research question and seeks to describe them, guided by one of the approaches shown in Table 8.3. In this case, then, the description emerges from the discourse. The second approach is more theory-driven. Here the analyst identifies a pre-defined descriptive framework deemed to be of theoretical significance and applies this to the data, adapting the framework, if necessary, to ensure a good fit with the data. We will focus here on the theory-driven approach, drawing on the theoretical framework provided by the Interaction Hypothesis.

A general approach to analysing the interaction in Table 8.4 will involve the following steps:

1. Defining the object of the enquiry (i.e. the particular aspect of interaction to be studied). The object of the enquiry is best expressed as a research question.
2. Identifying instances of the object of the enquiry in the data (for example, identifying all the negotiation of meaning sequences).
3. Establishing a descriptive framework for analysing the object of the enquiry. In a theory-led approach this will involve utilizing an existing framework and, if necessary, adapting it to fit the data. Each category in the descriptive framework needs to be made 'operational' so that it can be reliably identified in the data. This will involve providing both a functional definition and an indication of the linguistic forms used to realize it.
4. If required by the research question, quantifying instances of the categories.

We will now illustrate this general procedure with the data in Table 8.4, discussing problems as they arise.

Step 1: Defining the object of the enquiry

In our illustration of this procedure, we will take as the object of the enquiry negotiation sequences. The analysis will serve to answer the following research question:

> To what extent are the two learners successful in negotiating the communicative problems that arise when they perform the task?

We define 'communicative problems' as involving interactional events where the participants do not immediately understand each other and thus engage in interactive work to resolve the difficulty. This work will typically involve the negotiation of meaning. By 'successful', we mean that the participants are able to work cooperatively to resolve their problems.

Step 2: Identifying problem sequences

The identification of problem sequences can proceed with reference to a notional definition of 'communication problem' (as above) or with reference to a formal/structural definition of a negotiation sequence. Given that the aim of step (3) in the procedure is to provide a full structural analysis of negotiation sequences, we propose that the initial identification be undertaken notionally. Subsequently, however, the sequences so identified will need to be confirmed by means of a formal/structural analysis. Thus the identification of problem sequences undertaken in this step is necessarily provisional.

Also, even a notionally-based identification will require the analyst to make use of linguistic signals of communication difficulty. To this end, it is useful to distinguish the conversational roles of the two speakers. In a task such as the one used to collect the data in Table 8.4, the design of the task itself imposes roles on the participants. Learner 1 is provided with a map with the route marked on it and consequently takes the 'initiating role' in the interaction through a series of directives. Learner 2 is asked to mark the route on his map and consequently is assigned a 'responding role'.[2] In other words, it is Learner 2 to whom the job of signalling communication difficulty falls. Thus, the analyst can search through the data for points where Learner 2 demonstrates non- or incomplete understanding of his partner. Learner 2's utterances that signal communication difficulty are shown in italics in Table 8.4.

Two problems of identification now arise. The first concerns what kind of problem gets negotiated. A careful study of the data suggests that the negotiation identified through the signalling moves of Learner 2 addresses two different kinds of problem: (1) failure to clearly understand what Learner 1 has said (as in turn 4) and (2) failure to relate the information provided by Learner 1 and understood by Learner 2 to the task at hand (as in turn 28). (1) constitutes what Long (1983) terms 'negotiation of meaning'; (2) involves what Rulon and McCreary (1986) have called 'negotiation of content'. The analyst must decide, therefore, whether to focus narrowly on the negotiation of meaning or to also include negotiation of content. We will address both types of negotiation.

The second problem concerns the boundaries of a negotiation sequence. In some cases, this seems fairly clear. For example, turns 13, 14, 15, and 16 in Table 8.4 constitute an apparent sequence. It is less clear, however, whether the signals of communication difficulty produced by Learner 2 from turn 28 onwards involve a series of separate sequences or whether they all belong to a single, extended sequence initiated by Learner 1's mention of 'pop-lar street' in turn 27. This is a problem that we cannot resolve at this stage of the analysis, as it calls for the kind of structural analysis to be undertaken in the next step. At this stage of the analysis, therefore, we will tentatively identify three negotiation sequences centred on Learner 2's signals of communication difficulty in turns 4, 14, and 28.

Step 3: Establishing a descriptive framework

This is the key step in the analytical procedure. It will serve to confirm the identification of negotiation sequences and it will provide the basis for answering the research question.

Varonis and Gass (1985) outline the structure of negotiation sequences in terms of the following categories:

1 trigger (i.e. the utterance that causes the communication problem)
2 indicator (i.e. the utterance that demonstrates a communication problem has occurred)

3 response (i.e. the utterance that attempts to address the communication problem identified in the indicator)
4 reaction (i.e. the utterance that indicates a speaker's uptake to the response).

See Table 8.5 for an example. This framework works quite well in the case of sequences such as that shown in Table 8.4. But even here there are some minor problems. In what sense can 'yeah' be considered a 'trigger'? We can assume that Learner 2 understands both the propositional and illocutionary meanings of this word (i.e. that Learner 1 is stating that he should indeed progress 'down street'). The problem would seem to rest not so much in what Learner 1 has said but in what he has *not* said (i.e. he has not stated where Learner 2 needs to go next). Clearly, then, 'trigger' needs to be defined not just in terms of what learners say but also what they do not say, especially if negotiation is held to include content as well as meaning. In the case of the other negotiation sequences in the interaction, the framework begins to creak somewhat. Consider the first negotiation sequence in the interaction. The trigger that starts the sequence is Learner 1's turn 3 ('right right upper-side'). This elicits an indicator from Learner 2 ('right upper side?') and a response from Learner 1 ('yeah'). But Learner 2's next utterance ('is it next to the card store?') is not a 'reaction' as it does not indicate uptake of Learner 1's response; rather, it seems to constitute a further indicator. Indeed, Learner 1 does provide a response to this utterance ('right'), which is then followed by Learner 2's reaction ('okay'). To deal with this kind of sequence, Varonis and Gass point out that the reaction is an optional element in a negotiation sequence, that a speaker's response can double-up as a further trigger, and that, as a result, it is possible for one negotiation sequence to consist of several negotiation 'exchanges'. An 'exchange' here consists minimally of a trigger, indicator, and response. Potentially, this embedding of negotiation exchanges in a sequence can become very complicated, as the negotiation sequence starting with Learner 1's turn 27 illustrates. The reader might like to see if Varonis and Gass's framework can be applied to this lengthy sequence.

Utterance	Utterance
trigger	L1: yeah
indicator	L2: um?
response	L1: to river street
reaction	L2: okay

Table 8.5 Analysis of the structure of a negotiation sequence (based on Varonis and Gass's 1985 framework)

Acts	Definition	Example
Clarification request	Any expression that elicits clarification of the preceding utterance.	A: She is on welfare. B: What do you mean by 'welfare'?
Confirmation check	Any expression immediately following the previous speaker's utterance intended to confirm that the utterance was understood or heard correctly. A confirmation check is interrogative in form. Often it includes a question tag.	A: Mexican food have a lot of ulcers? B: Mexicans have a lot of ulcers because of the food?
Recast[3]	An utterance that rephrases the previous speaker's utterance 'by changing one or more sentence components (subject, verb or object) while still referring to its central meanings' (Long 1996; 435). A recast is declarative in form.	A: I am going to the cinema. B: you went to the cinema.
Other repetition	An utterance that repeats the previous speaker's utterance without changing any sentence component. A repetition has the same form as the preceding utterance and may or may not be accompanied with emphasis on the word causing the problem.	A: She is having three children. B: She *is having* three children . . .

Table 8.6 Acts for performing the indicator move of negotiation sequences

Once a basic framework, such as Varonis and Gass's, has been identified, it is possible to develop a finer-grained analysis of the various structural components. This is what has happened in the negotiation literature. In particular, analysts have focused on the indicator, identifying various strategies or, to borrow the term used by Sinclair and Coutlhard (1975), 'acts', for performing this element. In this respect, the analysis resembles the function-form analysis discussed in Chapter 6. Table 8.6 identifies the various acts that can figure in the indicator move. The negotiation sequences in Table 8.4 contain examples of clarification requests (for example, in turns 14 and 28) and of confirmation checks (for example, in turns 4 and 38). There are no examples of recasts. There are a number of repetitions (for example, in turns 10, 12, 18). However, these do not function as indicators of communication problems but rather as continuing moves demonstrating that Learner 2 has understood what Learner 1 has said.

In addition, analysts have developed fine-grained systems of categories to account for the response move of negotiation sequences. This response move contains what researchers have referred to as 'uptake'. Table 8.2 provided an example of the system of categories developed by Lyster and Ranta (1997) to account for student uptake to teacher indicators in a classroom context. This system cannot be directly applied to the negotiation sequences in Table 8.4, however, as it was developed to account for whether the linguistic errors occurring in the trigger move are repaired following the indicator move. The negotiation sequences in Table 8.4 are not triggered by linguistic errors but rather by Learner 1 failing to provide the information Learner 2 needs to locate the route on his map (i.e. they involve negotiating content rather than meaning). Thus, Lyster and Ranta's system needs to be adapted. Table 8.7 below shows the categories needed to account for the response moves.

We will conclude this account of how to establish a descriptive framework to account for the structural and functional properties of face-to-face interaction by proposing a number of general principles to guide the analyst:

1 As far as possible make use of existing descriptive frameworks, adapting these when they clearly do not fit the data being analysed. Utilizing existing frameworks allows for a comparison of the results of the analysis with those of previous studies.
2 Attempt to develop the framework as a 'system' rather than a list. A system involves a hierarchy of categories, such that higher-order categories are defined in terms of lower-order categories (as in Sinclair and Coulthard 1975).
3 Ensure that all interactional categories are fully operationalized. This requires providing formal as well as notional definitions of the categories. Formal definitions can be constructed by (a) specifying the distribution of each category (i.e. in terms of the category that can precede or follow the category being defined) and (b) the linguistic exponents of the category.

Acts	Definition	Example
Acknowledgement	An utterance responding to a confirmation check by confirming or disconfirming that the previous speaker has understood correctly. This typically consists of 'yes' or 'no'.	L2: right upper side? L1: yeah.
Provision of information	An utterance responding to a request for clarification by providing new information.	L2: um? L1: to river street
Repetition	An utterance that repeats the whole or part of the trigger in response to a request for clarification.	L1: you can find pop-lar street L2: mm what is it? L1: pop-lar

Table 8.7 Acts for performing the response move of negotiation sequences

4 Ensure that the categories in the system account for all the data. That is, every utterance relating to the interactional phenomenon under investigation must be assigned a description based on the system.
5 In accordance with the conventions of linguistic description, ensure that the categories are mutually exclusive. That is, no utterance should be assigned to more than one of the categories in the system. (Note that, in this respect, interactional analysis differs from the inductive content analysis discussed in Chapter 11, where the multiple coding of features is often desirable.)
6 Ensure that the system of categories developed is economical in the sense that it does not include unnecessary categories for addressing the research question. This is largely a matter of deciding the level of delicacy to be incorporated into the system (i.e. how many levels of categories to include).

Step 4: Quantifying the data

The descriptive system outlined above provides a basis for quantifying the data in Table 8.4. This necessitates deciding at what level in the system to undertake quantification (i.e. at the level of 'sequence', 'exchange', 'move', or 'act'). The analysis shown in Table 8.8 is at the level of 'exchange'. It shows the frequency of the 'exchanges', of the different 'moves' that make up the exchanges and of the 'acts' that comprise two of the key moves (the indicator and the response).

The analysis reveals the extent of the negotiation in this interaction. In 51 turns there are 7 exchanges. Clearly, the interlocutors are working co-operatively to achieve mutual understanding. Learner 2 uses a mixture of clarification requests and confirmation checks to signal his difficulties, while Learner 1 responds with acknowledgements (after confirmation requests) and by providing information (after clarification requests). However, despite this interactive work, they struggle to solve their problems. In several instances, negotiation extends across more than one exchange as the first effort to overcome a communication problem fails; that is, Learner 1's response moves constitute additional triggers. When they encounter referential problems resulting from the differences in their maps, their attempts to resolve them founder despite their persistence in negotiation. In short, this analysis suggests that the learners are successful in creating an interactive relationship that is conducive to negotiation but are not very successful in negotiating solutions to the referential problems.

Quantification of negotiation sequences is common. It has served as a basis for comparing the extent to which negotiation occurs under different conditions (for example, according to the setting in which the interaction takes place, the kind of task used to elicit interaction and the social roles of the interlocutors). However, it should be noted that not all analysts feel that quantification is the best way to present the results of an interactional analysis. Many prefer to present the results of their analysis discursively, describing the key features that have emerged and illustrating them by providing sample sequences from the data.

Category	**Frequency**
Exchange	7
Trigger	7
Indicator	7
Request for clarification	3
Confirmation check	4
Recast	0
Repetition	0
Response	7
Acknowledge	3
Provide new information	3
Repetition	1
Reaction	4

Table 8.8 Frequency of different categories in the negotiation sequences

An example of a study of interactional analysis

Much of the research based on interactional analysis has examined adult learners but there have also been a number of interesting studies involving child learners, who have often been overlooked by SLA researchers. We have chosen one of these latter studies for a detailed examination. Oliver (1998) reports a study of children aged 8 to 13 years. Altogether there were 128 NNS children and 64 NSs, making it one of the largest studies employing interactional analysis to have been completed.

Research questions	Oliver investigated four questions relating to the negotiation of meaning: – whether primary school children negotiate – what strategies they use to negotiate – whether there are similarities and differences between children and adults – what the potential is for negotiation strategies to contribute to L2 acquisition
Participants	8–13-year old children; 128 NNSs with varied L1s and 64 NSs. The NNSs had all arrived in Western Australia in the last 2 years and had insufficient proficiency to participate in regular mainstream classes. The NSs were taken from mainstream classes; children experienced in foreigner talk were excluded. Three types of age and gender-matched pairings were formed; (a) NNS-NNS, (b) NNS-NS and (c) NS-NS.
Data collection	The pairs performed one-way and two-way communicative tasks on two occasions. The one-way task involved the NNSs describing a simple black outline picture for their partners to draw. The two-way task involved positioning objects in an outline of a kitchen. The children sat opposite each other with a barrier in between. The interactions were audio-recorded and the first 100 utterances from each pair's performance of a task were transcribed. Video recordings were used to check the accuracy of transcriptions.
Analysis	200 utterances for each dyad were analysed (100 from each task). The following negotiation strategies were coded (in each case percentages were calculated by dividing the number of strategies by the number of utterances and multiplying by 100): 1 Percentage of clarification requests NNS A little line in the leave. NS A what?

Table 8.9 (continued)

	2 Confirmation checks NNS 1 Where does the um, glasses go? NNS 2 The glasses? 3 Comprehension checks NNS You know what, you know? 4 Partial, exact, expanded and total self-repetitions NNS How long centimetres? How long centimetres? 5 Partial, complete, expanded and total other-repetitions. NNS 1 two foot? NNS 2 two foot and a leg?
Results	The children used a substantial number of negotiation strategies, especially self- and other-repetition. Comprehension checks were infrequent. A comparison of the negotiation strategies used by the children and those used by adults in Long (1983) showed that the children used fewer clarifications requests, confirmation requests, comprehension checks and self-repetitions than adults but more other repetitions. The children were able to negotiate meaning successfully (i.e. achieve mutual understanding). There were also many cases in which the children modified their own output successfully. Instances of the children providing explicit corrections were rare.
Discussion	Oliver argues that the results show that children of the 8–11-year old range do negotiate for meaning using a variety of strategies but that they 'tend to focus on constructing their own meaning, and less on facilitating their partner's construction of meaning' (p. 379). Children appear to benefit from opportunities to negotiate meaning in the same way as adults.
Implications	Oliver notes the need to demonstrate that negotiation leads to acquisition. She also notes the need to examine other age groups. However, the fact that both children and adults participate in negotiation suggests that environmental explanations cannot explain age differences in ultimate achievement.

Table 8.9 Summary of Oliver's (1998) study

The study is a model of how to carry out an interactional analysis. Oliver provides explicit definitions of the various interactional categories she uses together with examples of each category taken from the data. Also, crucially, given the high-inference nature of these categories, she addresses the problem of reliability with great thoroughness. Transcriptions based on an audio-recording were checked against a video-recording. Inter-rater reliability of the transcription was also checked (with 91 per cent agreement). Similarly, inter-rater reliability of the coding of the different categories was measured (with 94 per cent agreement).

Oliver's study is of interest because there is some doubt as to whether young children typically engage in meaning negotiation when they experience a communication problem. (See, for example, Scarcella and Higa 1981.) The study provides convincing evidence that children of this age do negotiate. This finding is of theoretical importance, for, as Oliver points out, it suggests that environmental explanations are inadequate to explain the well-attested age differences in ultimate achievement in an L2. (See Long 1990b.) It should be noted, however, that Oliver did find substantial quantitative differences in the negotiating behaviour of her children and that reported for adults in Long (1983). The fact that children negotiate less than adults yet typically achieve higher levels of L2 proficiency might be seen as evidence against the Interaction Hypothesis. However, Oliver's commitment to the IH prevents her from discussing this possibility.

This is a descriptive study. It documents with great care the negotiation strategies that children *use*. Like many such studies, it also attempts to relate the descriptive findings to L2 *acquisition*, drawing on the claims of the IH to do so. Oliver demonstrates an awareness of the risks entailed in this, noting that to demonstrate a causal relationship between negotiation and acquisition it would be necessary to conduct an experimental study involving pre- and post-tests. She might also have noted that evidence of acquisition can be obtained from descriptive data. This could be done by showing that linguistic forms used incorrectly and negotiated are subsequently used correctly by the same learner. Demonstrating that acquisition has taken place need not involve testing, as researchers operating within a sociocultural framework have shown. (See Chapter 10.)

Task: Carrying out an interactional analysis

Table 8.10 provides a number of short interactions extracted from lessons in a private language school in Auckland, New Zealand, catering for adult learners of L2 English.[4] The interactions all occurred in the context of a variety of communicative tasks designed to cater for 'fluency' rather than 'accuracy' (Brumfit 1984). However, in performing the tasks both the teachers and the students seized opportunities to attend to form, either to

Reactive FFEs

Episodes 1-4 come from an activity in which students must decide which prisoner, out of four potential candidates, to release on probation. They are given information about the prisoners' crimes and other relevant factors. They have to choose a prisoner and explain why they would release him/her. Episode 5 comes from a discussion activity and the student is commenting on the personal nature of the questions.

T = Teacher, all other letters represent individual students

Episode 1

C I I fink this is very
T I THink, try, try get get your tongue between [th]
C I THink =
T = think
C um this description is made by the people of the jail, so when they say it i-she is a difficult

Episode 2

E when he 18 years old he m- if he doed it
T did it
E uh did it
T yeah
E must go to the prison? went to the prison

Episode 3

H he was depression in prison because
T oo this is, what part of language is this
H depressed
T depressed great excellent well done
H he was depressed in prison because he wife divorced with him and take the two sons away from he

Episode 4

Rich she has um big family with uh sick mother and many niece and nephews, nephews
T nieces
Rich nieces and nephews
T good

Episode 5

B you're asking too much personal question <s>
T (laughs)

Table 8.10 (continued)

(Ss talking, T writes 'too much personal questions' on the board)
(Time elapsed 3.09)
T B you ask, you ask us, you ask too much personal questions, what's wrong with that?
B too many
T good, very good
T <why>
B <too much> because your face <budge> but I can't see the difference
T you can't see the difference
B no

T why
R too many personal questions too many is for like like uh question maybe not < > <offer price I think>
T okay okay you ask too many personal what's special about personal questions, is it countable or uncountable?
R countable
T it's countable, yeah
B personal questions is countable?
T yes one personal question two personal questions three personal questions what about you'd when you use for beer, what would you use
R too much beer
T you drink too much beer it's the it's just as simple as that () cause beer is beer is well beer's not a very good example because you can have one beer two beers but um you eat you eat too much cheese, okay
B uhuh
T you eat too much cheese yeah so cheese is uncountable, it's just a substance, you drink too much milk, okay too many personal questions

Teacher-initiated FFEs

Episodes 6–9 come from the prisoner activity. Episode 10 comes from an activity in which students are discussing their precious possessions (e.g. the student's cat).

Example 6

E its five years <little bit> a long time for a for an accident, because it was an accident =
T = not if you're a doctor, you kill someone it's manslaughter, you know manslaughter? accidental killing, if you kill someone by accident
J mm
E <what is this? can you write>
T it's called man slaughter
E manslaughter
J manslaughter
(T writes 'manslaughter' on the board)
T so that's when you kill someone but you don't intend to do it, yeah

Table 8.10 (continued)

Example 7

T she doesn't have to do the job, if you can't take the heat, get out of the kitchen,
J mm
T have you heard that saying, do you understand that
J <yes>
T if you can't if you if you can't take the heat
J take the heat
T if you can't take the heat get out of the kitchen
J oh, mm

Episode 8

T so if he's committed theft, what is he
H um he was in prison for two years,
T yeah that's where he was, what do we call the person who commits theft
B thief
T thief
H thief
T yeah okay

Episode 9

what's a what's a doctor who looks at people with psychiatric problems called
B [psychi<>=
Ss [psy<>=
T = a psych- a psychiatrist okay

Episode 10

T you could call it a ginger cat or orange cat
F ginger
T you know how to spell it?
F °yeah°
(T writes ginger)

(See appendix to Chapter 9 for transcription conventions.)

Table 8.10 Sample 'focus on form' episodes

resolve communication problems through the negotiation of meaning or simply to address linguistic features that were proving problematic in some way by means of negotiation of form. It is these interactions, reflecting a 'focus-on-form' (Long 1991), that serve as the basis for this task. You might, then, like to begin by reviewing the arguments that have been advanced for 'focus on form' earlier in this chapter.

The episodes in Table 8.10 are of two kinds. 'Reactive episodes' arise when a student produces an utterance that is problematic (the trigger) and this is then addressed interactionally. 'Teacher-initiated episodes' occur when the teacher anticipates a problem and attempts to address it. A quick examination of the data will show that the two kinds of episode are very different from a discourse point of view.

For each episode in Table 8.10, you are asked to address these questions:

1 What is the form that is being focused on?
2 How is the focus-on-form accomplished?

You will need to develop a set of categories for coding each episode. To answer question 1 you will need to consider the linguistic level (pronunciation, vocabulary, etc.) of the form that the episode addresses. To answer research question 2 you will need to carry out an interactional analysis. Where possible you should use categories taken from the literature (for example, those relating to the negotiation of meaning) but you may need to modify these to ensure a good fit with the data. You should also note that you will need a different set of categories to account for how the focus-on-form is accomplished in the two kinds of episode, reactive and teacher-initiated. The categories you develop should be explicitly defined and illustrated from the data. They should also be inclusive, that is capable of accounting for all the data.

Final comment

Interactional analysis has proved a tool of great value in providing an 'internal view' of language pedagogy. It has helped to show how external prescriptions about teaching methodology translate into interactional events and how these shape the language that learners' produce in instructional settings. Interactional analysis has also contributed to a growing understanding of how the linguistic environment (interactionally defined) contributes to language acquisition. Currently, the Interaction Hypothesis and associated constructs such as focus-on-form shed light on a substantial body of research directed at investigating how interaction creates opportunities for acquisition and under what conditions these opportunities are utilized by L2 learners.

Nevertheless, the view on discourse and communication that this chapter has drawn on has not been without its critics. Firth and Wagner (1997: 291), for example, criticize 'the mindset that views learners/non-natives as inherently defective communicators'. They dispute the use of the terms 'native' and 'non-native speakers' that underlie work on the IH, arguing that it is not possible to treat them as clearly distinct groups as if they are homogeneous. They argue for a more complex model of interaction that takes into account the inherent variability in interactions involving L2 learners as a result of such variables as the interactants' local agendas, the social and individual identities that are constructed in actual encounters, and 'the demands and contingencies that become relevant in the minutiae of the talk itself' (1997: 295). They call for a more 'holistic approach' to the analysis of interactions that acknowledges the complexity of social behaviour and its relationship to the individual and that is more 'critical' of key constructs.

In studies of interactional phenomena, one can detect an ongoing struggle between the need to parcel out some aspect of interaction that will lend itself to detailed and thorough analysis and the need to view interaction in all its complexity. This chapter has explored methods of analysis that focus on the micro rather than macro aspects of discourse. Clearly, as Firth and Wagner argue, there is a need for a broader approach. They acknowledge, however, that there is no existent methodology for pursuing the reconceptualization they advocate. In later chapters, especially Chapter 10, where we consider sociocultural approaches to analysing learner language and Chapter 12 where we look at critical approaches, we will describe methodologies that afford a broader and more holistic perspective. In so doing, however, we do not wish to suggest that the psycholinguistically-oriented approach to the analysis of interaction adopted in this chapter is invalid. In line with the rationale for this book, we wish to promote an eclectic and pluralistic approach to examining interactions involving learners.

Notes

1 In a subsequent publication (Long and Robinson 1998), Long acknowledges that 'focus on form' can be 'pre-emptive' as well as 'reactive'. However, the thrust of his own research and that of other researchers drawing on his views about 'focus on form' (for example, Doughty and Varela 1998) is to treat focus on form as a reactive phenomenon. Long also seems to view focus-on-form as deriving exclusively from the negotiation of meaning. However, as the research on the treatment of error in communicative classrooms has shown, it often occurs in the context of the negotiation of form (i.e. attention to form occurs even though no breakdown in communication has occurred).

2 Although Learner 1 acts as the initiator and Learner 2 as the responder there are instances in the interaction when these roles seem to be reversed. In turn 6, for example, Learner 2 seizes the initiative by asking a question.

3 The distinction between a 'recast' and a 'confirmation check' has not always been clearly made. Oliver (2000), for example, admits that in her coding of data they overlap. This is because confirmation checks that rephrase the preceding utterance were coded as recasts, irrespective of whether they were interrogative or declarative in form. This demonstrates one of the problems with interaction analysis, namely that researchers

fail to ensure that their categories are tightly defined and mutually exclusive.

4 The episodes were those used for the study of focus-on-form in communicative language teaching. (See Ellis, Basturkmen, and Loewen 2001a.)

9 Conversation analysis

Introduction

In the previous chapter we presented an interactional analytic approach to analysing the interactions in which L2 learners participate. In SLA, interactional analysis serves as a tool for identifying those properties of interactions which have been hypothesized to contribute to L2 acquisition. In SLA, though more recently, conversation analysis (CA) has the same goal. CA has its roots outside the SLA domain, in sociology, where initially it was concerned with casual, mundane conversations between friends and acquaintances. Now, all forms of spoken interaction, including those in institutional contexts such as classrooms, doctors' surgeries, and courtrooms are also targets of analysts' attention. Participants in all these forms of conversation, institutional or not, are occupied with at least the following in order to accomplish their talk: they will take turns at talk, usually one at a time; their talk will be sequentially ordered (i.e. coherently linked together into definite sequences of action); and it will be organized in such a way that it will accomplish some action—the talk will *do* something. Participants will, if necessary, also repair problems they experience in the interaction. Furthermore, they will do all of the above while orienting to (that is, taking note of) co-participants' immediately preceding and following talk.

These interactional arrangements and the work that conversational co-participants do to accomplish them are the concerns of CA. It is obvious to see, therefore, why those involved in SLA theory and research, and particularly those wanting to know more about the intricacies of learner language, would be interested in utilizing what CA has to offer as an analytic tool: language learners engage in conversations with other language learners and target-language speakers (including language teachers). A CA approach to analysing learner language aims to provide a detailed, turn-by-turn explication of what it is that they do in these conversations. This micro-analytic methodology gets to the finer details of their collaboratively produced conversations, more so than the interactional approach presented in Chapter 8. It is an empirically based approach which aims to develop a participant's perspective rather than an analyst's perspective on what is going on in the talk. As the participants display their interactional work to each other, however, they also make it available to any interested analyst.

What they do, therefore, is observable and thus available for analysis by non-participants in the talk.

Those using CA in SLA research have argued that this approach allows analysts to explicate not only how learners *use* language in their interactions but also how they *learn* language when interacting (Markee 2000). By showing how learners orient to a locally managed turn-taking system when doing conversations (which includes repairing them when problems arise), CA can contribute to our understanding of the 'processes through which new linguistic knowledge emerges from conversation and becomes incorporated into learners' evolving interlanguage systems' (Markee 2000: 78). Turn-taking and repair, therefore, are actually used by learners as resources for L2 learning. CA aims to show how this is done.

In this chapter, we present some of the published evidence which has led to these claims. We also provide a practical framework for conducting conversation analyses on learner language data, one based closely on the major CA methodological tenets. We begin by summarizing both the historical background of CA and the arguments put forward by SLA theorists and researchers for its use in SLA studies.

Historical and theoretical background

Conversation analysis arose primarily from the ideas and pioneering research of sociologist Harvey Sacks who lectured at the University of California in the 1960s and 1970s until his death in a car accident in 1975. His lectures were tape-recorded, transcribed and circulated by Gail Jefferson, one of his students, and were eventually published in 1992 (Sacks 1992). Sacks' ideas were mainly influenced by two theoretical initiatives in sociology.[1] The first of these was the work of Goffman (1959), which emphasized the ritual nature of face-to-face interaction: 'His argument was that we 'perform' our social selves, managing the ways we appear in everyday situations so as to affect, in either overt or tacit ways, how others orient to us' (Hutchby and Wooffit 1998). The second, more powerful, influence can be found in ethnomethodology, the work associated particularly with Garfinkel (1967). Ethnomethodology (see Heritage 1987; Maynard and Clayman 1991) refers broadly to the study of the commonsense methods participants use to make sense of everyday activities in the world around them and of the ways in which their understandings are incorporated into action.

Sacks took these ideas further by focusing on *talk*, specifically the 'methods and procedures used to accomplish everyday conversation' (Travers 2001: 84); that is, how participants understand and are understood by others. Sacks believed that ordinary conversation is a deeply ordered, structurally organized phenomenon. Conversation is not haphazard and coincidental and it is not accomplished by subjective, independent contributions; instead, participants concertedly accomplish a social order in their conversations. The 'machinery' (Benson and Hughes 1991) for doing so is what CA aims to discover (Hutchby and Wooffit 1998: 14):

> Principally it is to discover how participants understand and respond to one another in their turns at talk, with a central focus being on how *sequences* of action are generated. To put it another way, the objective of CA is to uncover the tacit reasoning procedures and sociolinguistic competencies underlying the production and interpretation of talk in organized sequences of interaction.

Furthermore, for conversation analysts, talk is the embodiment of social *action*. Participants do things with talk, they perform actions (for example, make requests, issue invitations, complain). As Hutchby and Wooffit (1998: 14) put it, 'the actual object of study is the *interactional organization of social activities*'.

From the start, Sacks believed that analysts can best develop a thorough understanding of these social activities by studying detailed transcripts of tape-recorded conversations. The recordings may not capture everything that actually happened in a communicative event, but, as Sacks (1984) points out, what they do capture at least did happen. The goal, then, is to explicate from these recordings the ways participants produce and interpret the talk in their conversations *from their perspective*; that is, how they orient to what they accomplish together, as opposed to any assumptions of an observing analyst. With each turn at talk, the speakers display for each other their understanding of the interaction. Writing about the orderly nature of this process, Schegloff and Sacks (1973: 290) disclose why their conversational data achieved this orderliness:

> ...because they had been methodically produced by members of society for one another, and it was a feature of the conversations we treated as data that they were produced so as to allow the display by the co-participants to each other of their orderliness, and to allow the participants to display to one another their analysis, appreciation and use of that orderliness.

Turn-taking in organized sequences, consequently, is the primary focus of CA. Speakers display their understanding of a turn (the prior turn) in their own turn which follows it (the next turn). In Extract 1, for example, D clearly displays to M in line 4 that she had understood M's 'hello Debs?' in the prior turn (line 3) to be a selection to contribute.[2] The next turn, by M in line 5, displays her perception that D's response in line 4 was not particularly helpful. A third participant suggests an answer to M's question, and then, in line 7, M signals, as evident in the rising intonation, that the answer supplied by E in the prior turn (line 6) might be in need of some repair. It is clear from this illustration that CA adopts a hearer's perspective of conversation, what Hutchby and Wooffit (1998: 15) call a 'next-turn proof procedure,... the most basic tool used in CA'.

Extract 1

1 M where again did you say?
2 (2.0)
3 M hello Debs?
4 D I didn't say
5 M do you know?
6 E Oakley street
7 M Oakley?

As the turn-by-turn unfolding of the interaction takes place, and as the interactants display their understandings to one another in this sequential way, they also make them available to the analyst, and thus 'analysis can be generated out of matters observable in the data of interaction' (Heritage and Atkinson 1984: 1).

So far in this chapter, we have been referring specifically to ordinary conversation as the analytic focus of conversation analysts. This is the kind of talk which people engage in when they are just being ordinary; mundane, informal conversations with friends, acquaintances, and family members. Ten Have (1999) uses the expression 'pure CA' to refer to the analytic practices which focus on analysing this type of talk. In contrast, what he calls 'applied CA' aims to understand talk used in a wider range of situations, particularly institutions such as medicine, education, and the legal system. In these institutional situations, participants typically have designated roles (for example, teacher) with related tasks that have a particular purpose. Furthermore, 'institutional interaction generally involves a reduction in the range of interactional practices deployed by the participants' (Heritage 1997: 164). In other words, participants are somewhat constrained by the institutional contexts of their interaction. There are some aspects of talk which do not have a place in classrooms or law courts, and there are others which necessarily constitute that talk. The asymmetrical distribution of questions and answers in classroom settings would be an example. The interactions in these contexts have an institutional purpose, and their sequential, turn-taking machinery reflects this. Early studies of institutional interaction aimed to compare institutional talk with that of ordinary conversation, though it has been argued (see Sacks *et al.* 1974; Schegloff 1992) that ordinary conversation is the fundamental domain for the analysis of interaction. It is what other types of talk are measured against, since, CA purists would argue, it is the 'predominant form of human interaction in the social world and the primary medium of communication to which the child is exposed and through which socialization proceeds' (Heritage 2001: 2741).

The domains of CA now include a whole range of interactions in a number of disciplines (for example, sociology, linguistics, anthropology, SLA), including both ordinary conversation and institutional interaction. A more inclusive term *talk-in-interaction* (Schegloff 1987) has therefore been coined to cover this range, even though the term 'conversation analysis' continues to be used for the field as a whole.

The organization of talk-in-interaction

The following three types of organization are usually identified by analysts of talk-in-interaction: turn-taking, sequence organization, and repair. Although these are sometimes distinguished in theoretical discussions about CA and sometimes when actually doing an analysis, they are obviously interconnected. Any analysis would necessarily consider all three.

Turn-taking

This phenomenon refers to both the construction and distribution of turns: what shapes turns take, where they start and end, what their content is, how they are acquired and given away, and how long they are. In terms of their construction, turns at talk are constructed out of units (*turn constructional units*, or TCUs) which can be sentences (or clauses), phrases, or even single words. The following short interaction has examples of these. Line 3 is, for example, a full sentence TCU, line 5 is a single word TCU, and line 10 is a phrasal TCU:

Extract 2 (McHoul 1990: 369)

T ... and what else will it be like Tom
(3.7)
T How else would that be diff'rent from surrounding areas
TOM Would probably be a lot flatter
T Yes
TOM And eh
(2.4)
TOM (sea)
(1.0)
TOM (Lotta) sand round there

Participants orient to TCUs in talk by the teacher and the student in the above extract, for instance. The TCUs' projectability (the route they take) allows the hearer to predict 'where they are heading', what sort of units they are, and where they will end. Therefore, it is possible for the hearer, as the potential next speaker, to determine when the current speaker's talk has come to a possible completion point. This point is referred to as a *transition relevance place* (or TRP), and it marks the place in the current speaker's turn at which the next speaker can legitimately take the floor. So, at the end of each TCU (i.e. at the TRP) there is the possibility for a change of speaker.

This, of course, does not mean that a next speaker will take the floor, or that the current speaker will stop talking. Sometimes, a next speaker does start to talk at a TRP even though the current speaker continues after the end of a TCU. When this happens, and it happens often in conversation, an *overlap* occurs. Extract 3 demonstrates overlapping talk starting at the end of the first TCU in line 1.

Extract 3 (Drew and Heritage 1992: 33)
1 HV He's enjoying that [isn't he.
2 F [° Yes, he certainly is = °

(See the appendix at the end of this chapter for an explanation of these and other transcription conventions.)

In their classic 1974 article, Sacks, Schegloff, and Jefferson present a set of rules which describes how turns at talk are allocated, or distributed, at each TRP. These rules are paraphrased by Hutchby and Wooffitt (1998: 49–50) as follows:

Rule 1

a If the current speaker has identified, or selected, a particular next speaker, then that speaker should take a turn at that place.

b If no such selection has been made, then any next speaker may (but need not) self-select at that point. If self-selection occurs, then first speaker has the right to the turn.

c If no next speaker has been selected, then alternatively the current speaker may, but need not, continue talking with another turn constructional unit, unless another speaker has self-selected, in which case that speaker gains the right to the turn.

Rule 2

Whichever option has operated, then rules 1a–c come into play again for the next transition relevance place.

These are the turn-taking rules which participants actually orient to when they engage in talk-in-interaction, rather than being a set of prescriptive rules which determine what participants ought to do when they interact. Furthermore, 'they account for the vast range of turn-taking practices in conversations involving any number of participants, in any set of relationships, speaking in whatever context and with whatever topics in play' (Hutchby and Wooffitt 1998: 50).

Sequence organization

Sequence organization refers to the normative, ordered relationship between turns. We have already covered what is meant by the *ordered* nature of talk-in-interaction; the way in which turns are coherently linked together in sequences of talk. The *normative* aspect of their relationship refers to the fact that one turn normally expects or requires a particular next turn. For example, an invitation requires an acceptance or a declination and a greeting requires a return greeting. These pairs of turns are called *adjacency pairs*, and consist of a first pair part and a second pair part which may or may not be immediately adjacent to one another. In Extract 4 an embedded or inserted sequence (lines 2–3, itself an adjacency pair) comes between the two parts of the question-answer adjacency pair (lines 1 and 4):

Extract 4 (Sacks *et al.* 1974: 723)
M Whad are you doin'.
2 L Me?
3 M Yeh, [you goina go ta sleep like that?
4 L [Nothing

Not supplying a required second pair part (for example, not returning a greeting) or responding inappropriately can have consequences for the following sequence of talk, not to mention the relationship between the interactants.[3] Certain second pair parts are thus preferred over possible alternatives. This is known as the *preference* organization of talk. The preference has to do not so much with the psychological motives or inclinations of participants as it does with the structure of the turns. It is quite acceptable, for example, not to grant a request if the refusal is organized as a relevant dispreferred turn; that is, there would usually be some delay in doing the actual refusal, and it would no doubt be qualified or 'explained' to a certain extent. First pair parts, too, can be designed in order to elicit a preferred second pair part: for example, forming a request in such a way that it can hardly be refused. (See Pomerantz 1984.)

We have presented just a simple description of adjacency pair sequences here. Sequences are often far more complex. Sometimes, for example, they include a *pre-sequence*, pairs which have implications for sequences which follow (for example, a question-answer pair to establish contact before an announcement is made), different types of *sequence expansions* (for example, of the sort in Extract 4), and so on. To sum up, then, sequences are '*patterns* of subsequent actions, where the 'subsequentiality' is not an arbitrary occurrence, but the realization of locally constituted projections, rights and obligations' (Ten Have 1999: 114–15).

Repair

Sometimes the sequential organization of talk-in-interaction does not always unfold the way that participants expect it to. (See Chapter 8.) There may be problems with understanding or hearing, for instance, and the particular *trouble source* will then need to be repaired in some way. The repair can be initiated either by the current speaker, referred to as *self-initiated*, or it can be initiated by another speaker, *other-initiated*. The repair work itself can be carried out by the original speaker, *self-repair*, or by another speaker, *other-repair*. Various combinations of these repair trajectories, 'the routes by which participants accomplish repair' (Seedhouse 1997: 549), are given in the following four extracts (Schegloff *et al.* 1977, cited in Seedhouse 1997: 549–50):

Extract 5: self-initiated self-repair
1 N She was giving me a:ll the people that were go:ne
2 this yea:r I mean this quarter.

Extract 6: self-initiated other-repair
1 B He had dis uh Mistuh W.... Whatever k.... I can't
2 think of his first name, Watts on, the one thet wrote
3 that piece...
4 A Dan Watts.

Extract 7: other-initiated self-repair
1 B hhh Well I'm working through the Amfat Corporation.
2 A The who?
3 B Amfah Corporation

Extract 8: other-initiated other-repair
1 A Lissena pigeons
2 B Quail, I think.

Markee (2000) cites research which indicates that there is a preference for self- over other-correction in ordinary L1 conversations. He adds, citing further research, that this may not be the case with talk which includes L2 participants. Besides the dimension of *who* initiates and does repair, and what their preferences are, there is the dimension of *where* the repair is initiated and concluded. In some cases, repairs are completed in the same turn as the trouble source, as in Extract 5 above. In other cases, repair initiation occurs in the turn that immediately follows a trouble source, called *next turn repair initiators* (NTRIS), which are produced by other.[4] This speaker (i.e. other) may also offer a candidate repair in the same turn or allow the repair by the prior speaker (i.e. self, the first speaker whose turn contained the trouble source) in the following (third) turn.

As Schegloff (2000: 209) points out, repair actions are not limited to correction and their sources are not limited to errors: 'there can be trouble grounded in other than mistakes—the unavailability of a word, such as a name, when needed (or of a name *recognition* on the recipient's side); hearing problems engendered by interference by ambient noise; an uncertain hearing or understanding in search of confirmation, and the like'. The one certain thing about repair, however, is that the ongoing trajectory of the talk-in-interaction is interrupted in order to deal with a problem in the talk.

Conversation analysis and learner language

Conversation analytic approaches have only recently begun to appear in SLA studies. In a recent review of CA's relationship with applied linguistics, Schegloff *et al.* (2002) identify the following research areas in which conversation analysts have been involved: native, non-native and multilingual talk; talk in educational institutions; grammar and interaction; and intercultural communication. Other areas, subcategories of those just mentioned, include teaching oral skills (Riggenbach 1999), validating oral language tests (Lazaraton 2002a), and the relationship between pedagogy and interaction (Seedhouse 1997). Markee's CA work (1994; 2000) has been directed at gaining a better understanding of L2 acquisition, more specifically at how learner talk-in-interaction (i.e. learner language in interaction) contributes to language learning.

Markee (2000: 45) proposes the following five criteria for a CA-oriented methodology for a social interactionist approach to SLA studies. As would be expected, they reflect the main theoretical and methodological principles of CA presented above. In proposing these criteria, Markee is not arguing that CA's contribution to SLA studies will or should result in another theory of SLA. Instead, he suggests, more conservatively, that CA has something to offer the enormous amount of work that already exists: 'I do claim that CA can help refine insights into how the structure of conversation can be used by learners as a means of getting comprehended input and producing comprehended output' (Markee 2000: 44). His focus on comprehended input, which comes from Gass's (1997) interactionist model of SLA, is consistent with a CA perspective of interaction: that is, it presents a hearer's perspective on what makes input understandable (as opposed to comprehensible input, which places the responsibility for understanding on the speaker).[5]

1 A CA-oriented methodology should be based on empirically motivated, emic accounts of members' interactional competence in different speech exchange systems.

We have already highlighted the fact that in order to understand what is going on in interaction, conversation analysts attempt to do so from the participants' perspective. With learner language analysis, therefore, we would be concerned with how the *learners* orient to the sequentially unfolding talk and the social practices it embodies. This emic (or insiders') account of the talk-in-interaction represents the very heart of CA. CA is thus empirically based in that the analyses and the understandings they generate emerge, first and foremost, from the speakers' own interpretation of events. This approach may possibly provide for a more varied, complex analysis than other interactionist approaches in SLA have so far produced (Wong 2000). Furthermore, they do so in a variety of different speech exchange systems, as a number have already done; for example, native-non-native speaker interactions (Wong 2000), and speech in more or less equal power exchange systems in both L1 and L2 settings (see Cameron and Williams 1997; Kasper 1985; McHoul 1978, 1990; Seedhouse 1997).

2 A CA-oriented methodology should be based on collections of relevant data that are excerpts of complete transcriptions of communicative events.

This point is a direct reference to one of the basic methodological principles of ordinary conversation CA. Short extracts or excerpts of talk are carefully and fully analysed, but these 'single cases' are examined in the light of the complete transcript of any communicative event, such as a whole lesson or series of lessons.[6] Contextualizing the single-case excerpt within the complete transcript affords a fuller account of the talk-in-interaction.

3 A CA-oriented methodology should be capable of exploiting the analytical potential of fine-grained transcripts.

The transcripts generated by conversation analysts capture more detail about what was said and how it was said in recordings of talk-in-interaction than transcripts usually used in SLA analyses. They are even narrower than the narrow transcriptions referred to in Chapter 2. Such a deep level of analysis and the resulting detailed transcript potentially allows analysts to 'investigate whether the moment-by-moment sequential organization of such talk has any direct and observable acquisitional consequences' (Markee 2000: 42). In other words, as Wong (2000) points out, the finer detail has the potential to provide a much richer dimension to the study of acquisition. In her study of repair in native-non-native interaction, for example, she shows that repair is done not only because of problems with a new word or linguistic structure (usually the assumption in SLA approaches to negotiation sequences), but also because of problems with noise interference, idiomatic uses of language, making inferences and discourse conventions.

4 A CA-oriented methodology should be capable of identifying both successful and unsuccessful learning behaviours, at least in the short term.

This is the main goal of the whole CA enterprise: to describe and explain how learners acquire language through being participants in talk-in-interaction. The aim, therefore, goes beyond the mere description of how learners accomplish and understand talk-in-interaction. Markee's (1994, 2000) in-depth study of the acquisition of definitions in an L2 classroom setting is one of the first to take on this assignment. Through his painstaking analysis of interactions involving one particular learner (though the complete database was much larger than this) he was able to demonstrate whether, when, and how she and her co-participants 'orient to the structure of talk-in-interaction as a resource for understanding and acquiring the word *coral*' (2000: 119), at least in the short term. We refer to an extract from this study in a later section of this chapter.

The rationale is that through resources within the structure of the talk-in-interaction, such as repair and sequential turn-taking, learners make opportunities for themselves to understand the language they hear and to produce language that is understood by others. This process involves some modification of the talk which consequently leads to learning new language. Markee adds that acquiring new vocabulary items is not the only preoccupation of learners during this process: 'When learners focus on vocabulary, they inevitably have to pay attention to, and also deploy, a broad range of semantic and syntactic resources' (2000: 45). It is much harder to demonstrate, however, whether syntax is actually acquired in this way. CA also has the potential to show how learners acquire target-like conversation patterns, though, as Wong (2000) cautions, these may not be acquired until problems in language knowledge have been resolved.

5 A CA-oriented methodology should be capable of showing how meaning is constructed as a socially distributed phenomenon, thereby critiquing and recasting cognitive notions of comprehension and learning.

This point makes the case that conversations are jointly constructed. Negotiations of meaning are thus achieved by participants as they do their interactional work together. Of course, interactionist SLA has always acknowledged this, but CA, because of its detailed level of analysis and because it takes a participants' perspective of the interaction, perhaps opens up areas of analytic interest which, in SLA, have not been sufficiently explored before. Furthermore, as Markee (2000) observes, because meaning is made socially as well as cognitively, a CA methodological contribution to the research work of SLA is warranted. However, the idea that 'cognition is not solely an individual but also a socially distributed phenomenon that is observable in members' conversational behaviors' (Markee 2000: 31), challenges somewhat SLA's preoccupation with being a cognitive discipline. Wong sums up this dilemma rather nicely by suggesting that within this convergent approach 'lies an emergent form of *inter*-language' (2000: 262), suggesting a merger of both 'interlanguage' in the traditional cognitive sense and in the sense that it is a socially achieved phenomenon.

Conducting a conversation analysis

Starting out

A number of introductory works on CA point out that there is no one right way to do CA (for example, Ten Have 1999). In some ways this is reassuring;

there is less chance of 'getting it wrong'. On the other hand, not having a set of specific guidelines makes the analytic task a little more challenging. Ten Have believes that the best way to become familiar with CA practices is to join a group of experienced analysts as an 'apprentice'. Working closely with them over an extended period of time would gradually equip a beginner with the skills necessary for satisfactory analytical work. However, this situation is not always possible for those starting out, and most have to make do with the available literature, including many examples of analyses, and perhaps the guidance of an instructor. In this chapter, we provide guidelines for the individual researcher, operating alone or with a colleague or two, but not part of an established research team. In the next section we provide a broad overview of the methodological practices of CA. A more specific set of analytic tools will be presented in the section that follows.

Methodological tenets

Schegloff *et al.* (2002: 5–6) sum up the methodological aims of CA as follows:

> For those trying to understand a bit of talk, the key question about any of its aspects is—*why that now* (Schegloff and Sacks 1973)? What is getting done by virtue of that bit of conduct, done that way, in just that place? This is, in the first instance, the central issue *for the parties to the talk*—both for its construction and for its understanding. And for this reason, it is the central issue for academic/professional students of the talk.

This central question is asked at each micro-moment of the talk-in-interaction. It is clear by now that it cannot be answered by focusing only on one targeted turn or lexical item in isolation. Any bit of the talk, any bit which attracts the question 'why that now', can only be understood in relation to the other bits which make up its sequential organization. What then, from a methodological point of view, guides the careful, detailed analysis of these bits of talk? The methodological tenets presented below summarize this work (Lazaraton 2002b: 37–8).

1 *Using authentic, recorded data which are carefully transcribed*
As we indicated above, Sacks believed that an understanding of participants' social actions can best be reached by examining recordings of their conversations. He further insisted that their interactions be naturally occurring; that is, the interactions should be recorded as they are constituted naturally in the normal everyday activities of the participants, and not the product of some pre-planned data-eliciting task, such as a role-play in a laboratory setting. These naturally occurring audio-recordings, and more recently

video-recordings, of participants' talk are the primary source of data used by conversation analysts. In SLA research, much of the CA data tend to be clinically elicited (see Chapter 2), for example, from pedagogic tasks, rather than being naturally occurring in the sense intended by Sacks.

The recordings make it possible for analysts to go back to the conversation time and time again. Doing so helps to ensure that during the transcribing process the transcription is both finely detailed and accurate. Repeated listening is also essential in order to develop a thorough analysis. Furthermore, it allows the same analyst or other analysts to check the analysis against the recorded conversations. As Sacks (1984: 26) says: 'Others could look at what I had studied and make of it what they could, if, for example, they wanted to be able to disagree with me'.

Before launching into an analysis of learner talk-in-interaction, however, the data have to be produced. As we have said above, the primary data in CA are the recordings of the talk. The transcripts of the recordings are not the data, but rather a representation of the data. As far as possible, therefore, the transcripts should be used together with the recordings during the analysis. The collection of the recordings follows the same procedures as those discussed in Chapter 2 and the procedures for producing the transcripts are similar to those described in several other chapters. (See Chapters 8, 10–13.) However, with CA, as many details of the interaction as possible must be captured in the transcript, well beyond the mere content of what is actually said. Transcribing accurately and in such fine detail requires a lot of practice, and as with CA more generally, initially working closely with an experienced analyst is an ideal way to gain such experience. Although the aim is to capture as many features of the vocal productions as possible, it is impossible to capture them all. A certain amount of hypothesizing is thus expected, though, of course, this should be kept to a minimum. A set of symbols commonly used in CA analyses has been generated to produce such a fine-grained representation of the talk. (See the appendix to this chapter for a list of these.)

Producing such a transcript obviously requires many visits to the original recording, *by the analyst*. For CA, there is no benefit to be gained for the analyst by recruiting the assistance of another transcriber to do the job. Transcribing is an integral part of the analysis itself. During the process, the analyst begins to notice aspects of the talk which may become an important part of the analysis. Hutchby and Wooffit (1998: 76) identify the following two categories:

- *The dynamics of turn-taking*: the beginnings and endings of turns, including precise details of overlapping talk, gaps, and pauses and audible breathing. Turn-taking in the transcript is shown as one turn following the other down the page, with precise places of overlaps and pauses indicated along the way.

- *Characteristics of speech delivery*: features of stress, enunciation (for example, vowel lengthening), intonation (for example, rising for a question at the boundary of a turn), and pitch.

Accurately capturing all these aspects of the talk in such fine detail is a skill which develops over time and only after much practice. The aim, nevertheless, even in the early stages of one's experience as a conversation analyst, is to engage as closely as possible with the recordings of the talk-in-interaction. The transcripts enable this to happen.

2 *Using 'unmotivated looking' rather than pre-stated research questions*
CA is an inductive approach to examining talk-in-interaction. It is data-driven rather than theory-driven. This means that research questions are not stated prior to analysing the data; instead, questions emerge from the data. Sacks (1984: 27) describes his practice as follows: 'When we start with a piece of data, the question of what we are going to end up with, what kind of findings it will give, should not be a consideration. We sit down with a piece of data, make a bunch of observations, and see where they will go'. This makes sense if one remembers that the aim of CA is to explicate both the understandings that are relevant *for the language learners* involved in the talk and the practices that organize those understandings. Analysts cannot know beforehand what the learners' understandings and practices will be in that particular context, and making prior assumptions would more than likely put blinkers on the analysis. However, as Ten Have (1999) reasons, it would be foolish to ignore completely the findings and insights accumulated over the past thirty odd years. He therefore proposes a moderate approach to the issue: start the analysis with the data at hand, but allow a limited amount of reference to earlier CA work.

3 *Employing the turn as the unit of analysis*
Conversation analysts achieve their analytic goals by focusing on turns and their sequential arrangements. We have already noted that CA adopts a hearer's perspective of talk-in-interaction; hearers' next turns display their understanding of prior turns. Through examining this sequential ordering analysts can explicate what is going on in the interaction. The three domains of research discussed above (turn-taking, sequence organization, and repair) are the focus of these turn-focused examinations.

4 *Analysing single cases, deviant cases, and collections thereof*
The standard procedure for unpacking the structure of talk-in-interaction is to start with a *single case* of the phenomenon at hand, say an extract of the opening of a telephone conversation (as in Schegloff's well-known 1968 study) or the repair work carried out in an ESL classroom task-based activity. The aim of single-case analyses is to provide a detailed account of the particular phenomenon so as to arrive at a thorough understanding of

how it works. The pattern or rule which is discovered is then put forward as a tentative explanation of that phenomenon. To develop the analysis, the single case is compared to a *collection* of similar cases of the same phenomenon (for example, telephone conversation openings) in order to 'test' the strength of the earlier findings. The question is: Does the single case analysis also account for a wider range of similar data?[7] In his (1968) study of telephone conversation openings, Schegloff discovered a *deviant case* in the 500th telephone call opening he analysed. In this case, the caller spoke first, whereas in the previous 499 cases the person who answered the phone spoke first. This deviant case was thus a departure from the previous pattern that Schegloff had found, and so he was forced to reformulate his rule for telephone conversation openings.[8]

5 *Disregarding ethnographic and demographic particulars of the context and participants*

A rather contentious issue which arises during the analysis of talk-in-interaction is whether or not to take into account the ethnographic or demographic particulars of the participants. What we mean by participants is fairly straightforward, but the concept of *context* is less easily explained. Very simply, for ethnographers, the context of an interaction includes cultural aspects of the participants' lives as well as their biographies and other demographic factors such as age, gender and ethnicity. (See Chapter 11.) This information is obtained from informants through interviews, questionnaires and observations, and is described in rich detail. Some conversation analysts make use of these data in their analyses (see Moerman 1988) believing that it is useful or even necessary for coming to a full understanding of the interaction. For those analysts doing 'pure CA', however, the mixing of ethnographic methods (and the use of the information they gather) and classic CA practices is rejected. Context for them refers to 'the immediate sequential environment of a turn' (Markee 2000: 28). In other words, the context is locally and concertedly constituted by the participants as they interact, and is thus relevant *to them* in the process of interacting. Furthermore, the evidence on which the analysis is based is right there in the available interactional data—in the activities in which the participants actually engage. It is not located in the filtered accounts of their subsequent tellings. With learner language, however, we are dealing with talk in an institutional context, most obviously if the talk occurs in a classroom. It would be impossible to ignore at least these demographic factors in this situation.

6 *Eschewing the coding and quantification of data*

When undertaking an analysis of a 'fresh' recording of talk, there is often the temptation to begin by referring to the concepts and patterns in CA which have been formulated by others who have previously worked in the field.

As we have suggested above, it is without doubt useful to consider their ideas, but the manner in which they are used is questioned within CA. The concepts and patterns should not be interpreted as laws which explain all instances of similar talk. If this were the case, analysts would simply wish to apply these laws in a mechanical way to a new set of data in order to determine their fit. Although this type of 'coding' acknowledges that any instance of talk-in-interaction 'is built on routines of various sorts', it ignores the fact that it is 'at the same time, a unique achievement here and now' (Ten Have 1999: 41). In other words, each interaction should be analysed independently as a distinctive social accomplishment, and existing descriptions of similar interactional patterns be used as suggestions for further analysis. It makes sense, therefore, that the quantification of the data, the counting of patterns and structures, does not have a place in the analysis, as Heritage (2001: 2744) remarks, 'statistical analysis has played little role in the field, largely because in the matter of interactional practices, as in the case of biological species, large numbers are not essential to establishing their existence'. Heritage does concede, however, that in institutional interaction, especially in applied fields like language learning, a more statistically focused methodology is being increasingly used. Although this practice is evident in SLA interactional research more generally, CA in learner language analysis tends to avoid the quantification of its data.

Analytic tools for conducting a CA

Instead of presenting at the start of this section one set of data for illustrative purposes, as we have in the previous chapters, we provide illustrative extracts from a number of different published sources. This is common practice in the CA literature (see, for example, Hutchby and Wooffitt 1998; Seedhouse 1997), and doing so will expose readers to a larger number of sample transcripts from a range of studies. For those wishing to read a composite illustrative analysis of only one extract, see Pomerantz and Fehr (1997) and Ten Have (1999),[9] or, for an analysis based on one large data set, see Markee (2000).

Pomerantz and Fehr (1997) propose a set of *tools for analysis* by which they mean a number of questions to ask and areas to consider when actually doing the analysis. They stress that these tools are not a blueprint for analysis, but rather a set of methodological suggestions. Their tools are designed specifically for the analysis of ordinary conversation, and not for institutional talk-in-interaction, however.[10] We have therefore conflated their suggestions with those of Heritage (1997), which are targeted more for the analysis of institutional interaction. By doing so we arrived at a set of six guidelines which we consider more appropriate for the analysis of learner language. Learner talk, like institutional talk, is after all goal oriented—in this case, to learn language.

1 *Select a sequence*

The first step is to select a sequence of talk-in-interaction for analysis. When analysing ordinary conversation a sequence is usually chosen rather arbitrarily, perhaps because something in the talk has been 'noticed' as interesting (Pomerantz and Fehr 1997). With learner language analysis noticing is also important, although it usually involves purposive noticing. In other words, there is some aspect of the learner talk-in-interaction which the analyst decides to focus on before the detailed turn-by-turn analysis actually starts. At the same time, however, the analyst should not harbour any pre-conceived ideas about what will be found; it is the talk-in-interaction itself that empirically reveals its structural organization. In order to set the limits of the sequence (where it starts and ends), its boundaries need to be set. Pomerantz and Fehr (1997: 71) suggest the following strategy:

> For the start of the sequence, locate the turn in which one of the participants initiated an action and/or topic that was taken up and responded to by co-participants. For the end of the sequence follow through the interaction until you locate the place in which the participants were no longer specifically responding to the prior action and/or topic.

A sequence thus refers to a stretch of talk-in-interaction in which the participants orient to a specific topic and/or coherent arrangement of related actions. Any one sequence may include a number of 'sub-sequences', such as short trajectories of talk which initiate and complete a repair, and adjacency pairs, for example. Conversation analysts represent these sequences in transcribed extracts or fragments of talk-in-interaction.

In Extract 9 the boundaries of the sequence are quite clear. The sequence is from an adult group-work discussion of a magazine article on the greenhouse effect. L10 indicates at line 377 that she has identified a word which she does not understand, and for which she requires a definition. Her request is taken up by L9 in line 379 after a four second pause. In what follows, the participants orient to a series of co-constructed repair sequences, which Markee suggests the participants use as a resource for both understanding and learning what the word 'coral' means.[11] One example begins at line 396 where L9 initiates repair (i.e. other-initiated repair) by repeating the word 'food' with rising intonation. At line 398, L10 responds to this initiation by repeating her claim that coral is 'food'. L9 interrupts her with an other-completed repair at line 399. She ends this turn with information of her own, namely, that coral is like a stone, which leads to L10's insistence in line 400 (and others which follow in the extract) that she now understands the word. The sequence ends with L10 uttering a final acknowledgement of understanding.

Extract 9 (Markee 2000: 170–1)

376		((L10 is reading her article to herself))
377	L 10	coral. what is corals
378		(4)
379	L 9	<hh> do you know the under the sea, under the sea,
380	L 10	un-
381	L 9	there's uh::
382		(+)
383	L 9	[how do we call it]
384	L 10	[have uh some coral]
385	L 9	ah yeah (+) coral sometimes
386		(+)
387	L 10	eh includ[ə]s (+) uh includes some uh: somethings uh-
388		(++)
389	L 10	[the corals,] is means uh: (+) s somethings at bottom of
390	L 9	[((unintelligible))]
391	L 10	[the] sea
392	L 9	[yeah,]
393	L 9	at the bottom of the sea,
394	L 10	ok uh:m also is a food for is a food for fish uh and uh
395		(+)
396	L 9	food?
397		(+)
398	L 10	foo-
399	L 9	no it is not a food it is like a stone you know?
400	L 10	oh I see I see I see I see I see I know I know (+) I see (+)
401		a whi- (+) a kind of a (+) white stone <h>[very beautiful]
402	L 9	[yeah yeah] very big yeah
403		[sometimes very beautiful and] sometimes when the ship moves
404	L 10	[I see I see I ok]
405	L 9	[ship tries ((unintelligible)) I think it was the ((unintelligible;
406		the final part of this turn is overlapped by L10's next turn))
407	L 10	[oh I see (+) I see the chinese is uh (+)] sanku
408		(++)
409	L 11	unh?
410	L v10	sanku
411		(+)
412	L 9	what
413	L 10	c[orals]
414	L 11	[corals]
415	L 9	corals oh okay
416	L 10	yeah

2 *Characterize the actions in the sequence*
As we said at the beginning of this chapter, participants' talk in their talk-in-interaction embodies social action; that is, they *do* things when they take turns at talk (for example, provide an answer, request information, agree, or disagree). Characterizing these actions is an important and very useful stage of the analysis. It helps the analyst to get a broad sense of what is going on; it provides an overview picture of what the participants together accomplish through their interaction. Pomerantz and Fehr (1997: 72) suggest that for each turn in the sequence the analyst asks, 'What is this participant doing in this turn?' They go on to say that there could be more than one action performed within a turn and that there is no one right characterization of these. At this stage, therefore, the characterizations should be treated as provisional. Further reflection on the actions or subsequent analysis may generate alternative understandings and so the characterizations will need to be changed.

The actions in Extract 10 have been characterized in Table 9.1; the transcript is on the left and the characterizations directly opposite each matching turn on the right.

In the above extract, the actions have not been characterized in isolation. The relationship between actions has also been taken into account (for example, asking a question in line 1 and giving an answer in line 2). In subsequent analysis, and especially with much longer extracts, such as Extract 9

		Extract 10 (Tsui 1995: 52)			**Extract 10 (characterizations of actions)**
1	**T**	After they have put up their tent, what did the boys do?	1	**T**	asks a question.
2	**L**	They cooking food.	2	**L**	supplies an answer which includes a grammatical error.
3	**T**	No, not they cooking food, pay attention.	3	**T**	negatively evaluates the response, points out the trouble source, and issues an instruction with regard to L's future behaviour.
4	**L**	They cook their meal.	4	**L**	responds with a revised answer.
5	**T**	Right, they cook their meal over an open fire.	5	**T**	positively evaluates the response, and repeats it with additional information.

Table 9.1 Characterizations of the actions in Extract 10

above, it may be necessary to focus on only selected sequences within the extract, mainly because there is always so much that could be examined and also because the analyst may be interested only in certain actions or topics (for example, the organization of repair). Further analysis of Extract 10 may, for instance, focus specifically on lines 2–4, which would reveal that in line 2 there is a trouble source, in line 3 repair is other-initiated, and in line 4 the self-repair is completed. Other aspects of this interaction (for example, T's evaluation procedures), though used in the analysis, are not its focus in this case.

3 *Consider how the speakers' 'packaging of actions'* (Pomerantz and Fehr 1997: 72), *including their selections of reference lexical items, provides for certain understandings of the actions performed and the matters talked about*

There are always alternative ways in which participants can produce their actions. For example, think of the different forms that greetings or invitations can take. By 'packaging of actions' Pomerantz and Fehr mean the way they are formed and delivered. Participants select (though usually not consciously) one form from a range of alternatives. At this stage, we ask why those forms are selected and not others, and what understandings (both the participants' and the analysts') are associated with those forms? Pomerantz and Fehr (1997: 73) offer the following set of questions that analysts can use to help 'identify the packaging of a given action and to understand its consequentiality':[12]

- What understandings do the interactants display (and you have) of the action?
- What aspects of the way in which the action was formed up and delivered may help provide for those understandings?
- What inferences, if any, might the recipients have made based on the packaging?
- What options does the packaging provide for the recipient (that is, its interactional consequences)?
- What are the circumstances that may be relevant for selecting this packaging over another for the action?

Extract 11 is a conversation between a native English speaker (NS), Beth, and Lin, a non-native English speaker (NNS). Wong was interested in the sequential organization of repair between NSs and NNSs, particularly the point at which repair is initiated by the NNSs. Although this repair is also accomplished through the turn-taking mechanisms of the talk-in-interaction, we focus here on the form of the actions.

Extract 11 (Wong 2000: 250)

1 BETH last week (.) um:: (0.2) I was- (.) doing some papers (.) of mine
2 LIN uh huh

BETH it was about six forty five sevenish
(0.2)
LIN oh::[(ng)
BETH [I thought oh::: I'm just so tired: I think I'll close my eyes
just- I'll just take a short nap
(0.4)
LIN mm hmm
BETH I woke up at eleven o'clock
LIN tchwow!
(0.4)
LIN *h you works the whole night?
BETH no no no no I- I- no no no no I mean- six- six thirty or seven
at night
LIN oh:::
BETH I mean I was already *tired* cause I'd been *teach*ing all *day*::

To illustrate this point, we focus on the repair sequence in lines 10–15. In line 10, Beth reports on the time she woke up from what should have been a short nap. This action perhaps represents the 'climax' of her story. It also represents the trouble source in the repair sequence. The trouble, to be revealed in a later turn, is that Lin understands Beth to be referring to eleven in the morning, that is, that she had worked through the night. This problem could have been prevented if Beth had packaged this or an earlier turn in a different way; for example, line 10 could have referred more generally to waking up in the middle of the night, or line 1 could have started, 'one evening last week'. Lin's immediate response in line 11 and the subsequent turn constructional unit (TCU) in line 13 is what interested Wong. Earlier work (Schegloff *et al.* 1977) on NS–NS next turn repair initiators (NTRIS) had shown that repair initiation is done as early as possible within next turn. Wong's analysis found that this was not always the case with Mandarin speakers, such as Lin. In line 11, Lin's action could be described as an immediate assessment of the previous action. Some sort of assessment was probably expected by Beth at this point, the climax of her story. Lin therefore obliges and saves face by doing so. In a sense, she 'claims' understanding at this point (Schegloff 1982, cited in Wong 2000). However, delayed within this turn is her repair initiation (line 13). With this action she asks for confirmation of her understanding, doubtful understanding, that is, as indicated by the rising intonation at the end of the TCU. The repair is completed by Beth in lines 14–15 with her reference to the time of day during which this event took place ('at night'). Lin chose to initiate repair after claiming she understood with her 'tchwow!' utterance. Even though she might have got away with this claim (packaged appropriately as an assessment), she chose to initiate the repair, thereby, suggests Wong, identifying herself not only as a speaker, but also as an NNS learner.

4 *Consider how the turn-taking organization provides for certain understandings of the actions and the matters talked about*

This stage involves a detailed turn-by-turn examination of the turn-taking processes in the sequence, specifically the timing and taking of turns (Pomerantz and Fehr 1997). In order to understand the actions and the matters talked about, Pomerantz and Fehr propose that for each turn the following are paid attention to (1997: 73–4):

- how the speaker obtained the turn; for example, Did the speaker self-select? Did the prior speaker select current speaker?
- the timing of the initiation of the turn relative to the prior turn; for example, Was there any overlap or interruption? Did the turn follow a gap or pause, or was it initiated at a transition relevance place (TRP)?
- terminating the turn; for example, Was the speaker definitely, possibly or not finished?
- selecting next speaker; for example, Who were the recipients and what were they doing during current speaker's turn, and how do we know?

Extract 12 (van Lier 1988: 206–7)

T okay so can we try and say now (Willy) can you say Brigitte
was phoning her boyfriend . . . while the children were
watching TV
L10 Brigitte was- Brigitte was phoning her- her boyfriend . . .
and- while the children were watching TV
T okay now.
L 9 Brigitte-
L ((unintelligible))
T [can we make that a bit faster . . Brigitte was phoning
her boyfriend while the children were watching TV
L 10 e:hh I can't say it so- so [so quickly
L L [((laughter))
T Brigitte was phoning
L 10 Brigitte was phoning
T her boyfriend
L 10 her boyfriend
T okay stop. say: her boyfriend
L 10 her boyfriend
T phoning her boyfriend
L 10 phoning her boyfriend
T w'z phoning her boyfriend
L 10 she was fa- phoning her boyfriend
T okay. Brigitte was phoning her boyfriend
L 10 Brigitte was phoning her boyfriend
T good. while the children were watching TV

L yes
L 10 while the children were . . [watching TV
T [watching TV
T good. much better. ((to L8:)) Brigitte was phoning her
boyfriend while the children were watching TV

The turn-taking organization in Extract 12 is very much determined by the nature of the classroom activity under way, in this case a teacher-led recitation sequence. In this type of activity, the teacher typically aims for a 'smooth running of the sequence, and with the learner's smooth, effortless production of the target utterance' (van Lier 1988: 206). This means that there is pressure on the learner to keep intra-turn pauses and hesitations to a minimum. Where they do occur (for example, the short hesitation at line 7, and the pause at line 27), they are pounced upon by the teacher to do a repair or to issue another prompt (for example, lines 9–10, and again in line 28). Opportunities for self-repair are thus very much reduced in such classroom language-instruction sequences. In fact, opportunities for any talk which does not conform to the targeted grammatical structure are limited. Even the moment of light relief (lines 11–12) is immediately followed by a prompt for further recitation. Overlaps, too, are infrequent. This is because in most cases the packaging of the chunks of talk are predetermined; that is, the form they take is determined by the grammatical structure that is receiving attention. Where there are overlaps (see lines 9 and 28 for examples) they are the result of the teacher prompting the learners to keep the recitation going smoothly. The only other overlap in the extract (lines 11 and 12) comes at a time when the recitation structure has broken down and 'ordinary' talk occurs.

In contrast, Extract 13 illustrates that intra-turn pauses occur more readily in group-work activity involving only learners. As opposed to the teacher-led recitation sequence, pauses here seem to give the learners time to do self-repair within the same turn (see lines 4–5).

Extract 13 (van Lier 1988: 199)
L 2 what were you doing- what were you doing while
I: . . . while I was having a bath
L 1 can you say again?
L 2 yes, what was you doing . . . what- what were you doing . .
when I was having a bath

Analysing turn-taking processes in such a way leads to an understanding of the 'overall structural organization of the interaction' (Heritage 1997). For example, the examination of the turn-taking mechanisms in Extracts 12 and 13 reveal quite different interactional organizations, a teacher-led recitation activity and a group-work activity involving only learners, respectively, and the talk-in-interaction produced in these two activities is thus quite different.

5 *Consider how the ways the actions were accomplished implicate certain identities, roles and/or relationships for the interactants in equal and unequal speech exchange systems*

Here we are concerned with the people involved in the talk-in-interaction. What can their talk tell us about themselves? The following questions are also relevant (Pomerantz and Fehr 1997: 74):

- Do the ways they packaged their actions implicate particular identities, roles, and/or relationships?
- Do the ways that the interactants took their turns (or declined to) implicate particular identities, roles, and/or relationships?

Ten Have (1999) questions the way in which Pomerantz and Fehr refer to identities, roles and relationships in such traditional, fixed categories. He believes that the focus of the analyst should first be on how their identities, roles and relationships 'are being (re-)negotiated at every moment during the talk' (Ten Have 1999: 106). Later the analysis could show how the local orientations relate to the more fixed categories. For learner language, and talk in other institutional settings, the identities, roles and relationships relevant to those contexts are perhaps more 'fixed' and certainly more easily recognizable.[13] In Extract 12, for example, the attributes of teacher and learner are discernable from the structure of their sequential contributions. They are, too, in a lot of other classroom interaction, for example, the initiation-response-feedback interactional structure referred to in Table 8.3. However, in other classroom situations, such as learner-only group-work, the talk may resemble more closely that of ordinary conversation, where the identities, roles and relationships are less easily defined and where the distribution of power is usually more equitable.

These contrasts are observable in the following three extracts. The interaction in Extract 14 takes place during a part of a lesson where the focus is on language, specifically formal correctness. Extracts 15 and 16 come from a phase in the lesson where the focus is on understanding the content of a set reading (and consequently less focus on formal correctness).

Extract 14 (Kasper 1985: 207)

1 L 1 everyone could see that it would break
2 T i stedet for (instead of)
3 L 1 instead of (. . .)
4 T can't you hear it sounds strange—to say that you will do something
5 instead of—you never end it—Henrik
6 H everyone could see that it would break instead
7 T instead yes ((explanation follows))

In the language-centred phase of the lesson, the trouble source is typically a linguistic error, as evident in Extract 14 (line 3). It is the shape of the repair sequences in this context that is interesting: other-initiated and other-completed repairs of learners' talk. T initiates repair at line 4 and then in the same turn delegates the repair work to Henrik, who completes the repair (line 6). Kasper (1985) points out that this repair structure is typically avoided in non-educational talk where the roles and relationships of participants are less clearly defined. Being teachers and learners in classrooms makes other-initiated and other-completed repairs more acceptable. In the content-phase of the lesson the repair work resembles more closely repair in ordinary conversation: other-initiated and self-completed repairs (as in Extract 15), completing repairs in passing (Extract 16), and a focus on content rather than linguistic correctness (see Extract 15, for example). During this phase of the lesson, then, the relationship between the teacher and the learners seems to be less of an 'educational' one. The focus is on talking about a book (as one might do in ordinary conversation) rather than on conducting a grammar lesson, and this difference is reflected in the talk.

Extract 15 (Kasper 1985: 212)

1	T	that's obviously the most important part of the letter—why Maj-Britt
2	M-B	he want to see her
3	T	oh he wants to see her to come along and say hi Elaine how are you
4	M-B	no he want to get her away

Extract 16 (Kasper 1985: 213)

1	T	if you look at the rest of the book what's typical of it—Erik
2	E	there are no conversations
3	T	not much

6 *Putting it all together*

The set of guidelines we have presented above could be considered merely a starting point in the analysis. Analysis is a slow, gradual process which requires repeated listening to the recorded conversation, continuous refinement of the transcript and constant searching for deeper understandings. Throughout this process the analyst's thoughts about the selected talk-in-interaction episode become clearer, and the analysis itself becomes more integrated, as opposed to moving systematically through the five stages presented above. Eventually it reaches the stage where it is probably a good idea to share the tentative analysis with others. Ten Have (1999: 124) proposes that this be done is what he calls a data session, an 'informal get-together of researchers in order to discuss some data'. Data sessions give analysts the opportunity to expose their data and their analyses to public scrutiny. This disciplined approach, which involves sharing analyses and calling for confirmatory or alternative interpretations, is one of the key principles of a CA methodological approach.

An example of a conversation analytic approach

Delayed next turn repair initiation

We introduced Wong's (2000) study in our discussion of Extract 11 above. We include further details about it here because it is one which exemplifies new CA research work within the SLA field. Furthermore, it focuses on adult talk in interaction outside the classroom. The study, including the report thereof, is a model of how to carry out a conversation analysis.

Research question	In typical CA style, there is no research question as such. The overall aim of the article is to explore 'the potential value of CA for the study of SLA through interaction' (Wong 2000: 244). In order to do this, Wong attempts to show how non-natives produce talk in a way different from native speakers of English. More specifically, she focuses on the site of their repair initiation when they interact with native speakers.
Participants	12 NS/NNS dyads; all the NNS participants were speakers of Mandarin as their native language. No further information is given about the participants, except that which is revealed in and relevant to the actual analysis; e.g. 'Chen had moved and neither informed Joan of the move nor of his new phone number' (Wong 2000: 257). This stance represents the classic approach to context in CA analyses; i.e. ethnographic descriptions of the participants are irrelevant to their co-construction of conversation.
Data collection	No details are given, though one must assume that the usual ethical and technical procedures were followed in the recording and transcribing of the data. Wong does disclose that the conversations amounted to roughly 150 pages of transcribed text.
Analysis	Following an inductive approach, Wong focuses on the details of participants' talk-in-interaction, in order to explore what is different about how NNSs repair their talk in conversations with NSs. Excerpts from the full database are used to illustrate her analysis and findings throughout the article. Thus, the typical CA approach to analysis is employed; the 'objective is one of describing the procedures by which conversationalists produce their own behavior and understand and deal with the behavior of others' (Heritage and Atkinson 1984: 1).

Table 9.2 (continued)

Results	Wong demonstrates that Mandarin-speaking NNSs do indeed sometimes initiate and do repair differently from NSs in NNS/NS interaction. Whereas in NS/NS conversations other-initiated repair is positioned as early as possible in the next turn (NTRI, see Schegloff *et al.* 1977), Wong's data show that with NNS the initiation is somewhat delayed (i.e. not as early as possible), although still within next turn. In other words, there is talk (by NNS, see Turn B below, and/or by NS, see Event C below) and/or silence between the trouble-source and the repair-initiator within the same, next turn of the recipient. (See also Extract 11.) *Delayed other-initiated repair sequence [NNSs]* Turn A Talk (which contains the trouble-source)[NS] Turn B Receipt [NNS] Event C Gap of silence (or minimal talk) [NS] Turn 1 Other-initiation of repair [NNS] Turn 2 Turn A (now treated as trouble source) Turn 3 Response to the repair-initiator [NS]
Discussion	The talk in Turn A is not in itself troublesome. Wong observes that at Turn B the NNS responds to the prior talk in a manner that displays a *claim* of understanding (not actual understanding). At Turn 1 the talk is understood differently from the way it was understood before; the troublesome or problematic nature of the prior talk is now displayed. The talk containing the trouble-source then becomes the focus of the talk which follows (i.e. after the repair initiation). Wong points out that this rendition of repair organization is different from that observed with NSs. She references native speaker data from Schegloff (2000) which show that where instances of delayed other-initiation of repair (OI) occur the talk prior to the repair-initiation within the same turn appears to have been spoken prematurely and is produced as a cut-off item (i.e. not in full). There is also a sense of disjunction between the turn initial segment (the cut-off item) and the OI. This is different from the NNS Turn B which is delivered in full, with final prosody, and which may be produced as a claim of understanding. In doing so, Wong argues that NNSs, in engagement with NS interactants, produce their talk (in this instance the organization of repair) in a way different from that of NSs, and thereby 'construct their identities as interactants who are talkers *and* learners (or NNSs)' (Wong 2000: 261).

Table 9.2 (continued)

Implications	Wong suggests that CA 'may provide a sound foundation for the study of interaction in SLA, because it is based on those features of the context which are relevant for the participants' (Wong 2000: 244). In other words, CA methodology has something to offer SLA: (a) CA offers a fine-grained analysis of data on a turn-by-turn basis from the interactants' perspective, rather than that of the analyst's. (b) The form that the interaction might take is an empirical issue, that is, an emergent feature of the jointly-produced talk-in-interaction. (c) Whereas interactive SLA approaches tend to focus on linguistic form, CA potentially presents a much fuller, more varied dimension to the study of SLA interactionist approaches because it looks beyond what is only considered formally correct or incorrect in the talk.

Table 9.2 Summary of Wong's (2000) analysis of repair initiation in native/non-native conversation

Task: Carrying out an analysis of a single case

Extract 17 provides a transcipt of talk-in-interaction recorded in a private language school in Auckland, New Zealand. The participants are the teacher and a number of adult learners of L2 English. We have provided a fairly broad transcription of the sequence, atypical of 'pure CA' practice, but in sufficient detail for the purposes of this task.

Extract 17 (Loewen: 2002: 389–90)

KAO yeah and she said she she'd been snatched
T she had been snatched?
KAO yeah
T .hh
KAO huh?
T snatched she had been snatched
KAO no no
T so lucky
LL ((laughter))
T sorry
KAO how how can I say she was snatched her bag uh
T mm so can anyone help her out anyone help her
A snatch her bag was snatched
TV yes yes
KAO her bag was snatched (nearly several) years ago when she was walking with her friend

17	T	great uh I should warn you that uh this morning in this building
18		there was a bag snatcher
19	M?	yeah
20	M?	really
21	T	yes
22	T?	oh

Analyse the episode in Extract 17 as follows:

1 Read it through a number of times to get a general understanding of what is going on.
2 Characterize each action on a turn-by-turn basis.
3 Identify the repair trajectories in the interaction. To do this you will need to find the place where repair is initiated and where it is completed.
4 Describe how the actions which accomplish each repair sequence are packaged; that is, what form do the actions take?
5 Consider next the turn-taking organization within the repair sequences: How are turns allocated? Who allocates them?
6 Now, using the information you have so far gathered in your analysis, and the understandings you have so far reached, provide full analyses of the repair sequences in this episode. Include answers to the following questions:
   a How would you classify the repair initiations and completions (self or other, for example)?
   b Are the repairs more typical of classroom interaction or ordinary conversation?
   c Does the way the participants accomplish the repair tell you anything interesting about their identities, roles and/or relationships?

Final comment

What CA provides for interactionist SLA is a hearers' perspective of the talk in which they engage, rather than an outsider, analyst's perspective on 'what is going on'. CA is a conservative methodological approach which looks for understandings of how participants accomplish social actions in the actual talk-in-interaction which they produce. The understandings, in other words, emerge from the data, rather than from any pre-conceived ideas about what ought to be there in the data. This empirical approach aims to discover how learners orient to the interactional machinery of which they are a constitutive part as a resource for learning language.

CA, being a rather new endeavour within the field of SLA, is not without its critics. One, highlighted by Markee (2000), is that CA is a behavioural discipline whereas SLA is preoccupied more with cognitive aspects of language learning. Another is that what CA has to offer is more a description of language use than an explanation of language acquisition. Markee counters the first of these objections by arguing that the social organization of talk-in-interaction also involves cognitive work; that is, cognition is a socially distributed phenomenon. Markee's own work of the acquisition of the word 'coral' is his answer to the second objection. After a detailed analysis of the talk in Extract 9 above, he presents a sequence where he shows how L10 demonstrates, during a class presentation, that learning has indeed taken place, at least in the short term. However, we know of no other CA research which has convincingly demonstrated L2 acquisition.

In SLA, quite often the distinctions between conversation analysis, institutional interaction analysis and interactional analysis (as presented in Chapter 8) are a little blurred. Over time, however, we feel that CA will establish for itself a niche where it 'successfully fills in important details of the SLA landscape that other methodologies would otherwise have left blank' (Markee 2000: 162).

Appendix: Transcription conventions

The transcription symbols presented below are an illustrative set of the major conventions used to depict details of the vocal production of utterances in talk-in-interaction.[14] They cover all of those used in the extracts included in this chapter. In most cases, we have remained faithful to the transcription conventions used by the original analysts, and since there is sometimes inconsistency, we present alternatives below (for example, for pauses). These are widely used in CA publications, and most are based on the system developed by Jefferson (1989).

T:	teacher
L1:	learner (identified as learner 1)
L:	unidentified learner
L L:	several or all learners simultaneously
L 2?:	probably learner 2
MARK:	participant identified by name
(1.5)	The number in brackets indicates elapsed time in tenths of a second.
...	three dots indicate a pause of about one second, two dots represent a slightly shorter pause
(+)	a pause of between 0.1 and 0.5 of a second
(++)	a pause of between 0.6 and 0.9 of a second
(.)	A dot in brackets indicates a very short gap in time of one tenth of a second or less within or between utterances
letter—why	dash also used to indicate a short pause

foo-	an abrupt cut-off of the prior word or sound
[	indicates the place where overlapping talk starts
]	indicates the place where overlap terminates
boy friend	underlining indicates speaker emphasis
?	rising intonation, not necessarily a question
yes,	a comma indicates a continuing intonation
end.	a full stop indicates falling (stopping) intonation
°isn't he°	degree signs indicate quieter (lower volume) talk
yea::r	colons indicate lengthening of the preceding sound; the more colons the greater the extent of the lengthening
hh	outbreath; more h's indicate longer outbreath
.hhh	inbreath; more h's indicate longer inbreath
<hhh>	another way of indicating inbreath; more h's indicate longer inbreath
*hh	also indicates inbreath
(hhhh)	laughter
includ[ə]s	phonetic transcription
((hands go up))	transcriber's comments including those about non-verbal actions
((unintelligible))	talk that is unintelligible
(sea)	unclear or probable item

Notes

1 Full and accessible accounts of the origins and development of CA within the sociological tradition can be found in Hutchby and Wooffit (1998) and Ten Have (1999).

2 See appendix for notes on transcription conventions.

3 There is clearly cultural variability with regard to the consequences of these actions, or lack of them.

4 See Schegloff (2000) for recent developments with regard to NTRIs.

5 See Chapter 8 for a theoretical discussion of interactionist approaches to analysing learner talk, particularly the section on the negotiation of meaning, which most obviously has implications for comprehensible and comprehended input.

6 This approach is a little different from the one we present below in our discussion of single cases and a collection of cases. In the latter, the collection could consist of similar types of talk (for example, bringing a lesson to a close, involving different teachers in different classrooms) which are not necessarily part of the same communicative event (for example, talk in one lesson).

7 Comparisons, of course, could also be made across dissimilar data, such as those made between ordinary conversations and interactions in institutional contexts.

8 In this chapter we focus only on the analysis of single cases.

9 These two references, however, do not focus on learner language data.

10 Ten Have (1999) has also produced a set of analytical guidelines for ordinary conversation, though not in the form of questions and areas to think about (i.e. tools). They do, however, overlap quite considerably with those of Pomerantz and Fehr (1997). One difference is not starting with the selection of a sequence, but rather to work through the turn-taking first: 'speaking-at-all precedes building relations between spoken utterances', he argues (Ten Have 1999: 108).

11 Markee (2000: 126–7) refers specifically to lines 394–416 as the evidence for the accomplishment of this learning.

12 Pomerantz and Fehr (1997) acknowledge that turn-taking organization is obviously a part of the packaging, but they, as we do, discuss it as a separate point.

13 This does not mean, of course, that identities, roles and relationships cannot change or be re-negotiated in these settings. (See Chapter 12.)

14 See further transcription conventions in Hutchby and Wooffitt (1998), Markee (2000) and Ten Have (1999).

10 Sociocultural methods of analysis

Introduction

A sociocultural approach to analysing learner language is based on a different set of metaphors to those we have been using so far. Dominant has been an 'acquisition' metaphor which specifies that learners on receiving language input acquire it for themselves; i.e. taking it in and possessing it (Donato 2000). This language knowledge is then stored in the mind and used for output when required. In this sense, social context is not integral to this metaphor. It is 'tacked on', simply the means for further input. Chapters 11, 12, and 13 illustrate this quite clearly. Sociocultural theorists, however, go further than this. The metaphor of 'participation' (Sfard 1998) rather than acquisition guides their work. Learning is a *socially situated* activity rather than an individual activity. Individuals obviously do play a role in learning, but what they will eventually be able to do by themselves, they first achieve collaboratively during social interaction.

In this view of language learning, 'the distinction between *use* of the L2 and *knowledge* of the L2 becomes blurred because knowledge is use and use creates knowledge' (Ellis 2003a: 176), or as Lantolf and Pavlenko (1995: 116) say, the sociocultural theoretical view 'erases the boundary between language learning and language using'. Sociocultural theory, therefore, offers a much more holistic perspective of language learning, where individual and social merge into one and where use and knowledge are indistinguishable. Consequently, Swain (2000: 112) believes that SLA researchers need to find new methodologies to 'unravel this layered complexity'. Analysts of learner language face a similar challenge. Furthermore, since sociocultural theory is a relative newcomer to the field (Mitchell and Myles 1998) at the margins of L2 research (Lantolf and Pavlenko 1995), there is as yet no established SLA methodology which can be clearly associated with a sociocultural perspective, although, as we shall see in this chapter, this is beginning to change.

In this chapter, therefore, we have focused our discussion on those areas of sociocultural theory which have received considerably more attention in the study of L2 learning, namely, collaborative learning in the *Zone of Proximal Development* (ZPD). Furthermore, and reflecting research to date, our emphasis is on the qualitative analysis of classroom interaction, rather than on interaction outside the classroom or on methods which are quantitative in nature, though mention of studies which incorporate these will be included where appropriate. Much of the reported sociocultural SLA research utilizes those analytic procedures which are presented in Chapters 9 and 11, i.e. methods associated with conversation analysis (see, particularly Ohta 2000; 2001) and inductive, qualitative research (for example, Storch 2002). Nevertheless, what a sociocultural perspective offers learner language analysis is not so much distinctive methodological practices as a fully articulated theoretical focus. In other words, its contribution has had less to do with *how* to look for evidence of language development than with *what* to look for. A range of effective methodological strategies have been employed, however, and we highlight some of these in this chapter (see particularly the work of Aljaafreh and Lantolf 1994; Lantolf and Aljaafreh 1995; and Swain 2000, which utilizes a microgenetic method of analysis, to be described below).

Theoretical and historical background

In this section we outline some of the key constructs in sociocultural theory, particularly as they relate to L2 learning.[1] Many of these stem from the ideas associated with Russian developmental psychologist, Lev Vygotsky. His research, conducted between 1925 and 1934 together with a number of colleagues, worked towards shaping these ideas into a sociocultural theory of mind, which has been developed more recently by others such as Cole (1996) and Wertsch (1985). As Lantolf (2000a: 1) points out, 'the most fundamental concept of sociocultural theory is that the human mind is *mediated*'. Lantolf (1994: 418) explains, '*mediation*, whether physical [for example, tools] or symbolic [for example, language], is understood to be the introduction of an auxiliary device into an activity that then links humans to the world of objects or to the world of mental behavior'. In the same way, therefore, that a physical tool links humans to the physical world, such as a garden spade provides the means to dig a hole, psychological tools such as language, link human mental activity to the social world. The tools mediate these connections: i.e. they promote the dialectical relationship between the mental and the social. In terms of development, sociocultural theory maintains that 'development does not proceed as the unfolding of inborn capacities, but as the transformation of innate capacities once they intertwine with socioculturally constructed mediational means' (Lantolf and Pavlenko 1995: 109). In other words, learning is mediated. The genetically endowed capacities with which we are born are 'modified and reorganized into higher order forms, which allow individuals to exercise conscious control over such mental activities as attention, planning and problem-solving' (Ellis 2003a: 175).

According to Vygotsky (1978), one way in which this occurs is through social interaction. In sociocultural SLA, language learning involves learners *appropriating* language both as a mediational tool (i.e. using the language to learn) and as an object (i.e. the language itself). In the classroom, they accomplish this by interacting with others who desire similar outcomes; i.e. language teachers and learners. They share the same goals. Goal-directed activity is an essential ingredient of the overall theoretical framework which informs sociocultural work, that is, *activity theory*. According to Lantolf (2000a: 8), activity theory comprises 'a unified account of Vygotsky's original proposals on the nature and development of human behavior'. Cole (1985) points out that the concept of activity was the basic unit of analysis that Vygotsky and his colleagues had been using 'in a partially articulated way' in their research. However, these were later refined by Leontiev in his theory of activity (Lantolf 2000a; Wertsch 1985).

In essence, activity theory provides a holistic perspective on human behaviour, addressing cognitive and social aspects of mediated activity. People do things because they are motivated to do them. According to Cole (1985: 151–2):

> Leont'ev conceived of activity as a nested system of coordinations bounded by general human motives. In contemporary ethnographic terminology, an activity is coextensive with the broadest context relevant to ongoing behavior. Activities are composed of actions, which are systems of coordination in the service of goals, which represent intermediate steps in satisfying the motive.... Actions, in turn, are composed of operations, the means whereby an action is carried out under specified constraints.

There are four interconnected concepts here: motives, goals, actions and operations. *Motives* can be biological, for example, needing to satisfy thirst, or they can be socioculturally constructed, for example, learning an L2 to get a job. Motives tell us why something is done. Activities are always directed at some *goal*; for example, learning to use the L2 effectively in the workplace. *Actions* are the goal-directed, concrete realizations of activities, and tell us what is done, or what course of action is followed. For example, in order to learn an L2 a learner may enrol in a language school. Finally, *operations* are the actual behaviours which accomplish the goal; i.e. specifically how it is achieved. Lantolf (2000a) cites Leontiev's example of the hunting practices of tribal cultures to illustrate these concepts. The activity is hunting (in our example, learning an L2), the motive is to satisfy hunger (getting a job), and the goal is to kill an animal (be able to use the L2 for communicative purposes on the job). The hunters perform a range of actions, such as scaring the animal, slaying it and carving it up—L2 learner's actions could include taking classes at a language school and seeking out opportunities to talk to native speakers of the target language—and these too can be operationalized in different ways.

As the developing child, or the language learner in our case, participates in social activities new knowledge is jointly constructed in dialogic communication.[2] The knowledge, therefore, is initially developed at an intermental level (i.e. it is distributed between the interacting participants and thus jointly owned) and is subsequently taken over or appropriated at an intramental level, as Vygotsky (1981: 163) outlines in his genetic law of cultural development:

> Any function in the child's development appears twice or on two planes. First it appears on the social plane, and then on the psychological plane. First it appears between people as an interpsychological category, and then within the child as an intrapsychological category.

Successful learning involves shifting control within activities from the social to the individual, from the external to within oneself. This does not mean, however, that this process, known as 'internalization', is simply 'the *transferal* of an external activity to a preexisting internal "plane of consciousness"' (Leontiev cited in Wertsch and Stone 1985: 163). Rather it involves the transformation of external processes to create internal processes. It is through internalization that higher forms of mental activity, including language knowledge, gradually come into being. Linguistic forms and functions are first used in collaboration with others during social interactions and subsequently internalized for independent use.

There is a shift, in other words, from *other-regulation* during social interaction to independent *self-regulation*. At an early stage of development, however, children are *object-regulated*. Since they are incapable of exercising control over the environment, their actions are very much determined by the environment. De Guerrero and Villamil (1994) were able to demonstrate object-regulation during a peer revision task in an ESL composition class at a Puerto Rican university. During the interaction students who exhibited object-regulated behaviour were: controlled by the draft of the composition; did not have the language or rhetorical knowledge necessary to carry out the task; did not ask many questions about the draft; did not engage in constructive dialogue with peers; and, confined their participation to echoing their peer's comments, laughing or joking. Although these students' behaviour fluctuated between the various forms of regulation, this is not always the case with very young children, who may not be able to carry out decontextualized actions independently.

However, with the appropriate, mediated help of another more experienced person learners can exert control over certain tasks, but only with this mediation (i.e. other-regulation). In the classroom, this person could be a teacher or more capable peers. Through dialogic verbal interaction, children eventually appropriate the 'regulatory means employed by others' (Lantolf 2000a: 14) and they become capable of independent strategic functioning; i.e. they have voluntary control over their own mental activity. In terms of L2 learning, self-regulation means that learners internalize language knowledge through participating in other-mediated interaction. It is within this context of the gradual internalization of shared sociocognitive activities (i.e. cognitive acitivity is derived from social activities) that Vygotsky introduced his concept of the zone of proximal development (ZPD).

Assisted performance and the Zone of Proximal Development (ZPD)

Vygotsky (1978: 86) defined the ZPD as 'the distance between the actual developmental level as determined by independent problem solving and the level of potential development as determined through problem solving under adult guidance or in collaboration with more capable peers'. There is thus a difference between what the child knows and what the child could potentially know with the appropriate help of another more expert person. There is no doubt a lot that the expert knows which is above the potential level boundary of the child's ZPD and thus no potential for internalization exists, even with mediation. In this case the help would be beyond the child's 'sphere of readiness' (Brown and Ferrara 1985). Furthermore, development will not occur if too much help is provided (i.e. not giving the child the opportunity to develop the ability to perform independently) or if the particular task is too easy (i.e. already within cognitive reach of the learner).

Even though two children may be at the same actual level of development, their ZPDs will vary individually if their potential levels of development are not the same. According to Vygotsky, potential level is more indicative of mental growth than actual development: 'the learner who is able to respond to such help [that provided by a teacher or more experienced peer] must be considered to be at a more advanced developmental level than the one who fails to do so, because the learner who responds to help can be expected to show a more rapid rate of actual development' (Aljaafreh and Lantolf 1994: 468). Consequently, Vygotsky's insistence that education 'should be aimed at the upper bound, rather than fettered by the lower' (Brown and Ferrara 1985: 298) has profound implications for instruction and learning. A further implication here is that each child should be supported in a unique way so that his or her individual development is maximized.

These challenges for L2 learning have been noted (see Aljaafreh and Lantolf 1994; Macdonald 2002; Washburn 1994). In spite of these, the ZPD has become the most prominent construct in sociocultural L2 acquisition work, and probably the most widely researched. Kinginger (2002) cautions, however, that as the construct becomes increasingly utilized by those with different interests, and as they adapt and reshape it to suit their own purposes, so the ZPD starts to take on a variety of different meanings. Her comments refer specifically to the teaching of foreign languages in the US, though they could easily apply to L2 instruction and learning in other contexts as well. Kinginger points to three common applications of the ZPD: (1) the skills interpretation, whereby the ZPD is invoked in an attempt to contextualize language teaching socially but without relinquishing the emphasis of skills acquisition; (2) the scaffolding interpretation, which addresses the nature of interaction between teacher and learner, focusing on the gradual handover of interactional control to the learner; (3) the metalinguistic interpretation, which emphasizes the role of reflection on language production during collaborative tasks, and associated with the work of Swain and colleagues (Nassaji and Swain 2000; Swain 2000; Swain and Lapkin 2000).

Despite these varied interpretations, progress has been made within sociocultural SLA. Ohta (2001: 9) has adapted Vygotsky's definition of the ZPD making it more suitable for the context of classroom SLA: 'For the L2 learner, the ZPD is the distance between the actual developmental level as determined by individual linguistic production, and the level of potential development as determined through language produced collaboratively with a peer or teacher'.[3] Ellis (2003a: 180) points out that this reformulation of the ZPD helps to explain a number of important phenomena about language learning:

> First, it explains why there are some structures that learners fail to perform no matter what the external mediation; learners [in collaboration with teachers and peers] are unable to construct the ZPDs that make the performance of such structures possible. Second, it explains why learners are able to perform some structures with social assistance but not independently; they are able to construct ZPDs for performing these even though they have not internalized them. Third, it explains how learners come to internalize new structures; they appropriate the structures for which, with the help of external mediation, they have created the necessary ZPDs.

On the surface, the ZPD may appear analogous to Krashen's i + 1; that is, that learners acquire language by 'understanding messages, or by receiving "comprehensible input"... that contains structures at our next "stage"—structures that are a bit beyond our current level of competence' (Krashen 1985: 2). However, Dunn and Lantolf (1998) have disputed such claims, arguing that the ZPD is not a place or a context or a stage in the 'natural order' of development. Furthermore, in Krashen's theory, the learner is 'fundamentally a loner who possesses a Language Acquisition Device (LAD) that does all the acquiring for the individual' (Dunn and Lantolf 1998: 423). In sociocultural theory, development takes place in interaction, and the ZPD is thus conceptualized not as something belonging to the individual learner, but as 'emerging' from the learner's participation in collaborative activity. In spite of this, the ZPD in the SLA literature is still very much referred to as an attribute of the learner.

Central in all of this is the kind of support provided to the learner. Aljaafreh and Lantolf (1994) point to three mechanisms of effective help in the ZPD. The first is that intervention should be graduated, starting with help which is more implicit and gradually becomes more specific until the appropriate level is reached. The point of this is to identify the learner's ZPD so that appropriate assistance can be given. Second, the help should be contingent. This means that help 'should be offered only when it is needed, and withdrawn as soon as the novice shows signs of self-control and ability to function independently' (1994: 468). Graduation and contingency operate simultaneously as the teacher (or more capable peer) and the learner work together to discover the learner's ZPD. As Aljaafreh and Lantolf point out, there is ongoing assessment of the learner's needs and abilities and the tailoring of help to suit these. The only way to achieve this is through collaborative interaction. This is the third mechanism of effective help; discovering the learner's ZPD is a dialogic activity. It is a joint activity undertaken by both interacting participants.

These collaborative dimensions of the learner's language development have most frequently been referred to by the metaphor of *scaffolding*; i.e. the dialogic process through which one interactive participant assists another in performing a task he or she cannot perform alone: 'in social interaction a knowledgeable participant can create, by means of speech, supportive conditions in which the novice can participate in, and extend, current skills and knowledge to higher levels of competence' (Donato 1994: 40). Wood, Bruner, and Ross (1976) identify the following functions of scaffolding:

1 recruiting interest in the task
2 simplifying the task
3 maintaining pursuit of the goal
4 marking critical features and discrepancies between what has been produced and the ideal solution
5 controlling frustration during problem solving
6 demonstrating an idealized version of the act to be performed

These functions cover the following components: providing affective support to the learner, maintaining focus on the task,[4] and promoting self-regulation. The term scaffolding has more recently fallen out of favour, however. As Ellis (2003a: 182) points out, 'dialogic mediation needs to be viewed as an "activity" that is jointly constructed by the participants involved and not as some kind of apparatus that one of the participants applied to conversation'. Swain (2000) prefers the term *collaborative dialogue* to foreground the dialogic nature of the collaborative activity, and activity in which participants are engaged in both 'problem solving' and 'knowledge building'.

For language teachers and language learners, working appropriately within the learner's ZPD is a pedagogical matter. The concern of SLA is to discover how such collaboration, when it occurs effectively, leads to language learning. In the next section, we look at some ways in which learner language has been analysed from a sociocultural perspective.

Conducting a qualitative microgenetic analysis

Wertsch (1985: 70–1) maintains that the ZPD 'is jointly determined by the child's level of development and the form of instruction involved; it is a property neither of the child nor of interpsychological functioning alone'. As such, it would be discordant to undertake an analysis of learner language alone, without consideration of its linguistic context. Just as the analysis of the language production of learners' interlocutors was unavoidable in Chapters 8 and 9, so too must it be integrated into the analysis in this chapter. From a sociocultural perspective, language learning takes place *in* interaction, and not merely *as a result of* interaction.

The analytic procedures we suggest are those which have been successfully employed in published studies. We have been selective in our choice of both the methods of analysis and the studies, drawing particularly on research which has included in its investigation the ZPD and socioculturally-specific collaborative dialogue. In this context, much of the work in L2 acquisition has been concerned with *microgenesis*; that is, the shift towards self-regulation which occurs during the moment-by-moment unfolding of a language learning acitivity.[5] A microgenetic analysis of collective activity, therefore, aims to discern internalization of L2 knowledge by learners as their interactions unfold utterance-by-utterance.

Procedures which work towards a microgenetic qualitative analysis of mediated learning within the ZPD, then, are the focus of the discussion that follows. We divide it into these sections:

- selecting relevant episodes for analysis
- determining patterns of interaction
- determining microgenetic growth

Although we present these aspects separately, they are obviously interconnected. Furthermore, any particular research question would determine where the analytic emphasis would lie. Consequently, our suggestions should be taken as a guiding framework, rather than as a set of prescriptions for conducting all sociocultural analyses.

For illustrative purposes, we will use the interactions in Episodes 1–3. The interactions all involve the same learner; a thirteen year old Pakistani girl (S) who had very recently arrived in London and was learning English in a Language Unit that catered for new arrivals with limited English. S, in fact, was a complete beginner. The three interactions involve S trying to describe a 'What's wrong card' depicting a man holding an umbrella with the rain falling inside the umbrella onto the person. T is an experienced ESL teacher. The one-to-one interactions took place at three different times: 6 weeks between interactions 1 and 2, and 8 weeks between interactions 2 and 3.[6]

Episode 1

1 T: What's that?
2 S: A man.
3 T: What's he holding?
4 An ___?
5 Don't you remember?
6 We were doing um ___ in the class.
7 Um ___ for ___
8 S: Um for
9 T: Remember Um ___?
10 Umbrella.
11 S: Umbrella.
12 T: You remember..umbrella.
13 S: Umbrella.
14 T: Now, but what's wrong?
15 S: No.
16 T: Yes, there's . . .
17 But can you tell me what's wrong?
18 S: ((laughter))
19 T: Where's the water coming?
20 Is it inside or outside?
21 S: Yes.
22 T: The water is ___?
23 Coming from ___?
24 S: Yes.
25 T: Inside the umbrella.
26 S: The umbrella.
27 T: Should the water be outside?
28 S: Yes.
29 T: Should the water be inside or outside?
30 S: ((laughing))

Episode 2

31 T: Look at this one.
32 S: Man and a . . .
33 T: What's it doing?
34 It's ___
35 It's raining.
36 S: Huh?
37 T: Raining.
38 S: Raining.
39 T: What's the man holding in his hand?
40 D'you know what this is called?
41 Begins with u . . . um ___

42 S: ((sounds of trying to remember)) Umbrella.
43 T: Umbrella, yes.
44 And where's the rain coming from?
45 S: Water.
46 T: Water yes. Where from?
47 Is it inside or outside the umbrella?
48 S: No.
49 T: Yeah, should be outside, yes?

Episode 3

50 T: That's a funny one.
51 S: A man . . . and raining.
52 T: What's he holding?
53 S: Umbrella.
54 Man in the rain.
55 T: Yeah, it's raining.
56 S: In the rain.
57 T: Yeah, now where is the rain coming from?
58 Inside or outside the umbrella?
59 S: Outside.
60 T: No.
61 S: Inside.
62 T: Yeah, but that's wrong, isn't it?
63 S: Wrong . . . outside.
64 T: Yeah, should be outside.

Selecting relevant episodes for analysis

Selecting episodes of relevant interaction for close analysis involves very much the same methods which were discussed in Chapters 8 and 9. The content and length of the episodes are essentially dictated by the research aim. In Nassaji and Swain's (2000) study, for example, their focus was on corrective feedback on inappropriate article use in English. In deciding on episodes for analysis, therefore, they chose interactions which contained an article error and the feedback directly associated with it. Episodes 1, 2, and 3 above are each clearly dealing with the same topic. The first lines of each episode (1, 31, and 50) signal the start of the activity, and the final line(s) in each case indicate some sort of closure.

Determining patterns of interaction

Since the relationship between the participants is of vital importance in any sociocultural analysis, the analyst should determine as far as possible what the nature of this relationship is. Applying labels such as 'more capable peer', 'student', 'expert' and 'teacher' may not be enough. Knowing more about how they approach the activity, the roles they assume, and the level of involvement and contribution of each member (Storch 2002), may help the analyst understand more deeply the dialogic process. At the very least, an awareness of the role relationships between participants provides for the analyst a context for interpreting the interaction. Storch's (2002) work on dyadic interaction in an adult ESL classroom identified four distinct role relationships: collaborative, dominant/dominant, dominant/passive, and expert/novice. Drawing on the work of Damon and Phelps (1989), Storch distinguishes these according to two indexes: equality and mutuality. *Equality* refers to the degree of control or authority over the task, and *mutuality* refers to the level of engagement with each other's contribution. Although Storch's study focused on adult peers, we feel that the categories of role relationships are useful for describing patterns of interaction in other learning contexts as well.

The four role relationship patterns are represented in Figure 10.1. The aim at this stage of the analysis is to place the predominant pattern of interaction evident in the selected episode into the appropriate quadrant. To do so the analyst needs to make decisions concerning the levels of equality and mutuality. The following are the relevant descriptors (Storch 2002):

Quadrant 1: Collaborative

- high equality, moderate to high mutuality
- working together on all parts of the task
- willing to offer and engage with each other's ideas
- alternative views offered and discussed
- resolutions acceptable to both participants

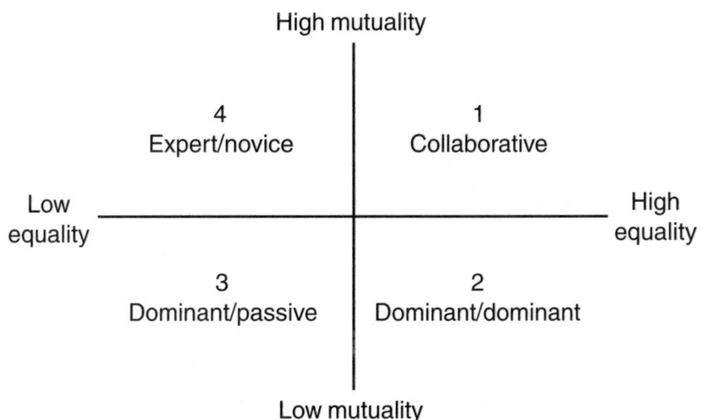

Figure 10.1 A model of dyadic interaction (Storch 2002: 128)

Quadrant 2: Dominant/dominant

- moderate to high equality, moderate to low mutuality
- unwillingness or inability to fully engage with each other's contribution
- high level of disagreements
- inability to reach consensus

Alternatively,

- high equality, low mutuality
- division of labour
- equal contribution to the task
- little engagement with each other's contribution

Quadrant 3: Dominant/passive

- equality and mutuality both moderate to low
- dominant participant takes authoritarian stance and appropriates task
- other participant adopts a passive, subservient role, with few contributions
- little negotiation

Quadrant 4: Expert/novice

- moderate to low equality, moderate to high mutuality
- one participant takes control of task, and actively encourages other participant to participate

The interactions in Episodes 1–3 would clearly fall into Quadrant 4, as would many others involving such obviously scaffold-like contributions by the teacher. It is clearly evident in these episodes that T has control; she determines what the task will be, starts the interactions by providing the initial instruction (lines 1, 31, and 50), and, through questions and other prompts dictates its direction. At the same time she encourages S to participate by offering many prompts (for example, lines 4, 7, 9, 22, and 23). Since there is high mutuality, the interaction also exhibits aspects of intersubjectivity: both parties are undeniably working together on this task, and contributing equally; of the 48 contributions, T makes 25 and S 23. Qualitatively, of course, their contributions are different; each is contributing to the task what she is able to contribute in order to realize the common goal.

Determining microgenetic growth

Having more or less determined the nature of the relationship between the participants, bearing in mind that these can change in different contexts, and even within particular interactions, the next step is to look for evidence of mediated microgenetic development within the learner's ZPD. The work of

Aljaafreh and Lantolf (1994; Lantolf and Aljaafreh, 1995) is central, and their analytic methods offer an exemplar for the close analysis of collaborative dialogue within the ZPD. The aim is to determine whether the learner shows evidence of shifting from other-regulation (reliance on the tutor) to self-regulation. In their 1994 study Aljaafreh and Lantolf determined this by considering the *frequency* and *quality* of help the learners received from the tutor, both in later episodes of the same tutorial and in episodes in later tutorials. They identified five levels of transition as the learners moved from intermental to intramental functioning; i.e. 'as they moved through the ZPD towards self-regulation and control over the target structures' (Aljaafreh and Lantolf 1994: 470). These levels differ according to: (1) the learner's need for *intervention* from the tutor, (2) the ability of the learner to *notice* the error, and (3) the ability of the learner to *correct* the error. The five levels are (Aljaafreh and Lantolf 1994: 47):

1 The learner is not able to notice or correct the error, even with intervention from the tutor.
2 The learner is able to notice the error, but cannot correct it, even with intervention.
3 The learner is able to notice and correct the error, but only under other-regulation.
4 The learner notices and corrects an error with minimal, or no obvious feedback from the tutor and begins to assume full responsibility for error correction.
5 The learner becomes more consistent in using the target structure correctly in all contexts. Noticing and correcting of errors, when they arise, do not require intervention. Thus, the individual is fully integrated.

Ohta (2001), in her extensive study of Japanese L2 development, examined the effect of corrective feedback in classroom learning. She also investigated the way students assisted each other through scaffolding, or how they *assisted performance*. Assistance was not only forthcoming when learners made errors, they were also assisted when they were *struggling*; for example, to produce or understand a word or grammatical structure.

So far, then, the analyst needs to be on the lookout for:

- the frequency of intervention by the tutor
- the quality of intervention (see the regulatory scales below)
- the need for intervention (i.e. when the learner is struggling or has made an error)
- the learner's ability to notice an error
- the learner's ability to correct an error
- evidence of the learner struggling

Observations about these would indicate on which of the five levels learners are within their ZPD. To put it simply, if they make no errors or are not struggling and no intervention is required, they have achieved independent control and thus are self-regulated or close to it; if they are able to notice and correct errors or overcome struggling with mediation from the tutor, they are other-regulated; and if they are unable to notice or correct errors or cannot resolve the cause of their struggling, even with tutor intervention, then they are probably object-regulated and very low in their ZPD. However, what specific evidence is required to make these claims? What if the interaction itself allows the analyst to decide the level of learners' regulation? Aljaafreh and Lantolf's (1994) Regulatory scale (see Table 10.1) lists specific types of help or regulation ranging from the most implicit (for example, levels 1, 2, 3) to the most explicit (for example, levels 10, 11, 12). Learners requiring help at the top of the hierarchy would be closer to self-regulation than those requiring the type of help towards the bottom, and as learners move from the bottom to the top, so they show evidence of microgenetic development.

Aljaafreh and Lantolf's (1994) scale emerged from their research on tutor sessions in which learners received corrective feedback on their written compositions. The levels on the Regulatory Scale, therefore, are obviously

0	Tutor asks the learner to read, find the errors, and correct them independently, prior to the tutorial.
1	Construction of a 'collaborative frame'[7] prompted by the presence of the tutor as a potential dialogic partner.
2	Prompted or focused reading of the sentence that contains the error by the learner or the tutor.
3	Tutor indicates that something may be wrong in a segment (e.g. sentence, clause, line): 'Is there anything wrong in this sentence?'
4	Tutor rejects unsuccessful attempts at recognising the error.
5	Tutor narrows down the location of the error (e.g. tutor repeats or points to the specific segment which contains the error).
6	Tutor indicates the nature of the error, but does not identify the error (e.g. 'There is something wrong with the tense marking here').
7	Tutor identifies the error ('You can't use an auxiliary here').
8	Tutor rejects learner's unsuccessful attempts at correcting the error.
9	Tutor provides clues to help the learner arrive at the correct form (e.g. 'It is not really past but some thing that is still going').
10	Tutor provides the correct form.
11	Tutor provides some explanation for use of the correct form.
12	Tutor provides examples of the correct pattern when other forms of help fail to produce an appropriate responsive action.

Table 10.1 Regulatory scale from implicit (level 1) to explicit (level 12) (Aljaafreh and Lantolf 1994: 471)

geared towards a writing task, and they focus specifically on the correction of grammatical forms. Ohta (2001), too, has developed a scale of assistance. In fact (see Table 10.2), there are two: assistance given to partners when they are struggling, and assistance provided when they have produced an error, though the former set (waiting, prompting, co-construction and explaining) can also be used when they make errors. The scale presents an array of mechanisms the learners used to assist one another, and these are arranged according to their level of explicitness, determined by how much information the assistance gives to the learner.

Although there is a lot of similarity with Aljaafreh and Lantolf's scale, Ohta's is different in that, firstly, it was generated from *peer* interaction in a classroom setting (as opposed to tutor-student interaction in a dyadic tutorial setting), and secondly, the assistance not only targets *written* forms, but all aspects of natural classroom conversation. Together, Aljaafreh and Lantolf's (1994) and Ohta's (2001) scales provide a very useful set of indicators which point to the regulatory level of the learners, and thus the position within their ZPDs. For the microgenetic analyst, therefore, this collection (a toolkit of indicators) is indispensable. The interactions in Episodes 1 to 3 demonstrate movement along both these scales.

The indicators of self-regulation which De Guerrero and Villamil (1994: 487) used in their analysis of 40 recordings of peer interaction during a written composition revision task included the following:

- The learner is capable of independent problem-solving. He/she can identify troublesources in the text, initiate revision, and provide alternatives for the text.
- The learner has internalized the task requirements and has a clear vision of the goals to achieve.
- The learner's attitude is one of self-confidence in terms of content, language use, task goals, and procedures.
- Prompts by peers are dealt with quickly and efficiently with little negotiation (because the learner already knows the answer) or firm rejection (because the learner considers suggestion inappropriate).

These indicators make a valuable addition to the sociocultural analyst's toolkit for determining microgenetic growth. An analysis of the three episodes follows.

Episode 1

If we focus our analysis on the vocabulary items, *man*, *umbrella*, *rain(ing)*, *inside* and *outside*, we see that learner S in Episode 1 is still very much object-regulated. Even with an enormous amount of explicit scaffolded help from T there is no evidence of progress. In line 3, T directly asks S to provide the vocabulary item, *umbrella*. In line 4, T frames the required

Methods	Level of explicitness	Description
1 When the interlocutor is struggling.		
A Waiting	1	One partner gives the other, even when struggling, time to complete an utterance without making any contribution.
B Prompting	2	Partner repeats the syllable or word just uttered, helping the interlocutor to continue.
C Co-construction	2–3	Partner contributes a syllable, word, phrase, or grammatical particle that completes or works towards completion of the utterance. This includes prompts that occur in the absence of an error, when the learner stops speaking, or produces false starts.
D Explaining	4	Partner explains in native language.
2 When the peer interlocutor makes an error, partners use the above methods (waiting, co-construction and prompting) as well as the methods listed below.		
E NTRI (without repair)	1–2	Partner indicates that the preceding utterance is somehow problematic (e.g. by saying 'huh?' or 'what?'). When the NTRI is in the form of a prompt, it more explicitly targets the error. The NTRI provides an opportunity for the interlocutor to consider the utterance and self-correct. This is the case even when the NTRI is triggered by comprehension difficulties rather than by a linguistic error.
F NTRI (provide)	3	Partner initiates and carries out repair (either fully or partially by providing a syllable, word, or phrase to the interlocutor. These may be in the form of recasts, which build semantically on the learner's utterance but change or expand it).
G Asking	4	Partner notices their interlocutor's error and asks the teacher about it.

Key: Level of Explicitness from least explicit (1) to most explicit (4).
NTRI = Next Turn Repair Initiator (see Chapter 9).

Table 10.2 Some methods of assistance occurring during classroom peer interaction (Ohta 2001: 89, slightly adapted)

Item	Episode 1	Episode 2	Episode 3
man	independent	independent	independent
umbrella	repeated	assisted	independent
rain(ing)	—	repeated	independent
inside	—	—	assisted
outside	—	—	assisted

Table 10.3 Summarized analysis of Episodes 1–3

item by giving an appropriate indefinite article, *an*, reminds S that this has been covered in class before (line 5) and then attempts to co-construct the item by providing its first syllable. This type of assistance (Ohta's level C—which we abbreviate O.C; and about level 9 in Aljaafreh and Lantolf—abbreviated AL.9) is certainly at the explicit end of both scales. In lines 10 and 12, T finally provides the *umbrella* item (AL.10, O.F). The question in line 17 affords S the opportunity to use the item *rain(ing)*, but she obviously does not know it, and T uses *water* instead, in line 19. Focus then shifts to where the water is coming from, *inside* or *outside* the umbrella. It appears as though S does not recognize these words either, even with co-construction attempts in lines 22 and 23 (O.C, AL.9). It is unlikely that S has internalized the items *inside* and *outside* by the end of the episode (even though she appropriately answers *yes* in line 28—this may be a lucky guess, however, since she uses *yes* inappropriately twice before in lines 21 and 24). In this episode, then, S is struggling. There is a strong need for intervention; the scaffolded assistance is frequent and explicit, though not too successful. Object-regulation is evident, and we could assume that this task is essentially outside S's ZPD. S's performance is summarized in column 2 in Table 10.3. She produced *man* independently, repeated *umbrella* when T used it, and did not produce and seemed not to understand *inside* and *outside*.

Episode 2

Six weeks later, development with these vocabulary items is evident, though the task itself is still not successfully completed. There is still a high frequency of intervention (i.e. much scaffolded assistance offered), but this time S's contributions show signs of other-regulation, which means that she is able to use the mediation provided by T to carry out the task. She once again uses *man* independently (line 32) but in the same line appears to have forgotten the word *umbrella*. The level of help offered in order for S to eventually produce the item (line 42) is much less explicit. In line 41, T attempts a short co-construction (*u*—O.C, probably with level 2 explicitness), waits (the short pause—O.A), increases the explicitness of the co-construction attempt (*um*) and then waits again in line

42 while S thinks of the appropriate word. S produces *rain(ing)* for the first time, by repeating it in line 38, and demonstrates her understanding of the item by associating it with *water* in lines 44–5. She still struggles with *inside* and *outside*, however (see Table 10.3). Nevertheless, with T's mediated support, the co-construction of the learner's ZPD has clearly begun.

Episode 3

After eight weeks, development is even more apparent. The episode itself is short, indicating that less intervention has been necessary for the task to be completed. In line 51, S immediately uses both *man* and *raining* independently, without any assistance. The same applies to *umbrella* (line 53). Mediation is required for *inside* and *outside*, however. In line 59, S provides the wrong answer to T's question in line 58. In line 60, T explicitly indicates this (similar to O.E, or to AL. 6), and S then produces the correct word in line 61. Finally, in line 63 she displays understanding of the words necessary to demonstrate task completion (i.e. there is something wrong with the picture, the rain should be on the *outside*). In line 64, T confirms her understanding and appropriate use of vocabulary. Self-regulation is therefore evident (see Table 10.3).

An example of a sociocultural analytic approach to analysing learner language

Nassaji and Swain's (2000) study makes use of Aljaafreh and Lantolf's (1994) Regulatory scale (see Table 10.1) to examine a tutor's oral feedback on the written compositions of two adult Korean learners of English. The students, who were enrolled in a five-week intensive writing class, were tutored weekly on the compositions they had written. The tutorial interactions were analysed in order to compare the effectiveness of corrective feedback on their acquisition of articles. One of the students (called the ZPD student) was provided with assistance which was within her ZPD; the tutor moved gradually and systematically through Aljaafreh and Lantolf's scale to negotiate the appropriate level of help needed. The other student (referred to as the non-ZPD student) was assisted by the tutor in a random manner; i.e. lists of prompts randomly generated from the regulatory scale were applied regardless of the student's ZPD.

It is the overall research design, and particularly the analytical procedures, which makes this study noteworthy. Qualitatively, the analysis consisted of a detailed analysis of relevant interactions produced within one tutorial, and of interactions across sessions. Quantitatively, Nassaji and Swain counted the number of article errors the students made in their

Research question	The study aimed to compare the effect of oral corrective feedback provided within a learner's ZPD on the learner's knowledge of English articles (*a, an, the*, ø) with the effect of providing feedback randomly and irrespective of a learner's ZPD
Participants	Two adult, female Korean speakers enrolled in an intermediate writing class in an intensive ESL programme in a university in Canada. One had been in Canada for six months and the other for two months.
Data collection	The two learners were randomly assigned to receive the ZPD error treatment procedure and the non-ZPD treatment procedure (see above). Each learner was tutored at four weekly tutorials on compositions they had written. These were tape-recorded and transcribed. At the end of the four weeks, the students each completed four task-based, cloze tests which were constructed from their own compositions. The tests were corrected versions of the compositions but with blanks for the articles they had originally got wrong.
Analysis	Analysis consisted of both qualitative and quantitative procedures. The qualitative analysis involved microgenetic analysis of relevant episodes (i.e. episodes which contained an article error and the feedback) to compare the amount of help the learner received within one tutorial session. A macrogenetic analysis was conducted to do the same across tutorials. Differences in the quality of assistance was also examined in these comparisons. In a process-product analysis of the data, the researchers compared the nature of the help provided in the tutorials with their performance in the cloze tests. The quantitative component involved determining the number of obligatory contexts (see Chapter 4) for the use of articles in each of the four compositions the students wrote as well as the correct instances of articles used in these contexts. Test scores were also ascertained.
Results	The quantitative analysis revealed that the ZPD student performed better on the tests than the non-ZPD student (82.8% versus 40%), and that while the ZPD student used articles less accurately in her first composition than the non-ZPD student, she did better

Table 10.4 (continued)

	than the non-ZPD student in her final composition (95.2% versus 68.7%). The qualitative analysis suggested that both microgenetic and macrogenetic development took place for the ZPD student, whereas the random prompts were not effective in helping the non-ZPD student. In addition, it was found that for the non-ZPD student more explicit help produced better results than less explicit help.
Discussion	The study clearly shows that when scaffolded support constructs a ZPD for a learner, learning results. The findings are therefore 'consistent with the Vygotskian sociocultural perspective in which knowledge is defined as social in nature and is constructed through a process of collaboration, interaction and communication among learners in social settings and as a result of interaction within the ZPD' (Nassaji and Swain 2000: 49).
Implications	Implications are presented in terms of ideas for further research, mostly based on the limitations of this study: e.g. replicating this study, focusing on language other than articles, and allowing varied negotiation of help in the ZPD (as opposed to dichotomizing help as negotiated versus random).

Table 10.4 Summary of Nassaji and Swain's (2000) study of the effect of random versus negotiated corrective feedback

compositions over time, and also looked for any improvement in their knowledge of articles using task-related cloze tests administered during their final tutorial. A combination of analytic procedures, therefore, was used to describe and measure learning. A summary of the study is provided in Table 10.4.

Task: An analysis of scaffolded interactions

Read the following two episodes of classroom interaction, and then answer the questions which follow. Episode 4 is a transcript of interaction recorded in a private language school in Auckland, New Zealand. The participants are the teacher and an adult learner (B) of L2 English. Episode 5 is a transcript of interaction between a high school ESL teacher and an intermediate English learner (P) who speaks Setswana, an African language, as his native language. They are working on a sentence from a paragraph he has written.

Episode 4 (Loewen 2002: 339)

B: I want to say for example the police uh didn't have any other option
T: yes
B: uh=
T: =fine
B: the police didn't have any other option uh (ano said) invade the bus the problem for me is this part that I know only in Portuguese
T: the police didn't have
B: another
T: any choice except
B: ah yes thank you [very much
T: [to okay that's alright, except to =
B: =except=
T: =to st- and the best word be there would be to storm the bus
B: to storm the bus [thank you very much
T: [yes, okay (laughs)
B: (that's beautiful)

Episode 5

T: that that bit again, there ((pointing to the line)).
P: 'and he asked who is going with me. [He'
T: [ok...
P: ok?
T: yes, good, what did he ask
P: 'who is going with me'
T: the whole sentence
P: 'He decide decided ((laughs)) to go and asked who is going with me'
(2.0)
T: the last bit =
P: =with him?
T: good him, and asked ___? ... asked ___?
P: ask?
T: um asked is right, look at the verb here ((pointing)), the tense.
P: present=
T: =tense, yes ... but this is like recorded speech ... read it now, asked ___
P: and 'and a:sked ...
T: think of the verb, the tense
P: 'and asked who was going with me =
T: =him
P: him, ya

1 (a) In terms of equality and mutuality, how would you characterize the role relationships between the interactants in the two episodes? i.e. In which quadrant in Figure 10.1 would you locate the two episodes? How are the episodes similar? How are they different?
   (b) Construct a 10-line hypothetical interaction between two language learning peers in which the role relationship is obviously of the dominant/dominant type.
2 (a) Provide a brief line-by-line description of what is happening in each line of Episode 5: for example,
   Line 1: T instructs P to read the line that she is pointing to.
   Line 2: P reads the designated line.
   Line 3: T stops P.
   etc.
   (b) On reading your descriptive notes, how would you on a general level describe the kind of assistance student P received?
3 Conduct a detailed analysis of the two episodes using the regulatory scales of Aljaafreh and Lantolf (1994) and Ohta (2001).
   (a) In each case, identify the levels of explicitness in the help provided to the learners.
   (b) What aspect of English is the target of T's scaffolding in each episode?
   (c) How successful are the learners in each interaction? How would sociocultural theory explain their (lack of) success?
4 Is there any evidence that B and P have moved towards self-regulation from performing these tasks?

Final comment

According to a sociocultural perspective, language learning starts with collaborative dialogue in social interaction between the learner and teacher or more experienced peers. Eventually the learner becomes self-regulated, the linguistic forms and functions being internalized. The ZPD is the 'dynamic region of sensitivity in which the transition from inter-psychological to intrapsychological functioning can be made' (Wertsch 1985: 67). In this chapter we have looked at a number of ways in which SLA researchers have begun to examine the ZPD, and have selected from their work a range of analytic tools which can be used to investigate micro-genesis. As with any analytic approach, how these tools are used depends on the research questions that analysts ask. Further specific selection may be necessary or they may need to be adapted in some way in order to meet the research objectives. The range of studies in Lantolf (2000b), Lantolf and Appel (1994) and the special issue of *The Modern Language Journal* (edited by Lantolf 1994), for example, demonstrate how this has been done.

A microgenteic sociocultural approach to analysing learner language affords a different perspective of interactional SLA. It has shifted the emphasis from viewing interaction as leading to language learning to interaction as being the place where language learning actually occurs. Although it has made a significant contribution over the past 20 years, the approach, however, is still relatively speaking, the 'new kid on the block' (Lantolf and Pavlenko 1995). Ellis (2003a) has pointed to the need for more longitudinal studies, for example, though acknowledges that these are starting to emerge (see Ohta 2001). He also argues that although researchers have documented what learners learn in terms of 'participation' they have been less successful at showing how learners progress from assisted to independent use of specific language features. Mitchell and Myles (1998) too have pointed out that evidence of learning has not been shown in spontaneous (unplanned) oral use of scaffolded items, particularly in the long term. This takes us back to the metaphorical distinction we introduced at the beginning of this chapter: that between the 'participation' metaphor of sociocultural SLA and the 'acquisition' metaphor which has dominated much other SLA work. These need not be 'competing' metaphors. It would be far more productive to discover what insights both approaches have to offer SLA and particularly learner language analysis.

Finally, the set of methodological procedures associated with sociocultural learner language analysis is perhaps within its *own* ZPD: 'an embryonic state ... the "buds" or "flowers" of development rather than the "fruits" of development' (Vygotsky 1978: 86). Drawing on the published research, we have provided a preliminary set of guidelines for undertaking a sociocultural analysis of learner language data. Further collaboration amongst researchers and theorists is necessary before these become fully developed.

Notes

1 More extensive overviews can be found in Lantolf (2000b), Lantolf and Appel (1994), Lantolf and Pavlenko (1995) and Ohta (2001).

2 Verbal interaction can also be monologic. Self-mediation through *private speech* is also possible. This self-directed speech has social origins but 'takes on a private or cognitive function. As cognitive development proceeds, private speech becomes subvocal and ultimately involves into *inner speech*, or language that at the deepest level loses its formal properties as it condenses into pure meaning' (Lantolf 2000a: 15).

3 Ohta includes in her definition both teacher and peers as collaborative partners. Her own work focused particularly on peer support (Ohta 2000, 2001). So too did the work of Donato (1994), who introduced the concept of collective scaffolding to describe this form of collaboration. (See also DiCamilla and Anton 1997.)

4 *Intersubjectivity* is achieved when the teacher and the learner are both on the same wavelength; i.e. they share a common motive and goal for performing a task.
5 According to Vygotsky's genetic method, development of the mind can only be observed and understood as it emerges over time. This included phylogenesis, the development of the human race across generations, and ontogenesis, 'how children appropriate and integrate mediational means, primarily language, into their thinking activities as they mature' (Lantolf 2000a: 3); i.e. their early childhood development.
6 The short lines (i.e. ___) in the interactions indicate a gap to be filled following a prompt by T. Other transcription conventions follow those described in the appendix to Chapter 9.
7 This level marks the beginning of the collaborative interaction. A collaborative setting or 'posture' (Aljaafreh and Lantolf 1994: 471) is constructed when the tutor is introduced as a potential collaborative partner. This is different from level 0 where the learner is expected to rely on him or herself.

11 Coding data qualitatively

Introduction

This chapter is about the qualitative coding of data. Qualitative data are data which have been gathered through methods such as naturalistic observation, open-ended interviews, introspection/retrospection and narrative inquiry, and typically take the form of field notes, interview transcripts, recall protocols and life-histories. (See Chapter 1.) Qualitative data is often referred to as 'rich', 'thick' or 'deep' data: put simply, it is data which represents the nature or attributes of something, in contrast with quantitative data which is data that can be measured or counted. In some cases, the analysis of qualitative data can also be quantitative. For example, diary entries of a particular classroom language learner could be examined for salient themes and these could be organized into patterns for the purpose of describing his or her reflections on selected aspects of the learning process. Alternatively, instances of the identified themes, in the form of key words and phrases, could be counted and then ranked, and then the numbers could be compared with numbers obtained from an analysis of the diary entries of other members of the class. Qualitative analysts have the task of reducing huge amounts of text to manageable units for further analysis. *Coding* is the technique used to achieve this.

Coding refers to organizing data into themes and categories so that they can be used for the purpose of ongoing analysis, interpretation and conclusion drawing. On a mechanical level, it involves assigning codes to units of data which represent the themes and categories that emerge from the data during analysis. LeCompte and Schensul (1999: 55) define *codes* as 'names or symbols used to stand for a group of similar items, ideas, or phenomena that the researcher has noticed in his or her data set'. This chapter is concerned with coding practices within an interpretive qualitative research tradition, and the focus is on the meanings expressed in the language produced by language learners.

Historical and theoretical background

Denzin and Lincoln (1998: 2) are exactly right when they declare that 'a complex, interconnected family of terms, concepts, and assumptions surround the term *qualitative research*'. This is certainly the case within the

ESOL/SLA field. Various labels have been assigned to different qualitative research traditions, which themselves have been arranged into an assortment of hierarchical orderings. Even when researchers are referring to the same approach, their reports exhibit personal preferences for one term over others; interpretative instead of qualitative, or ethnographic instead of naturalistic, for example. A quick survey of the literature produces labels such as 'descriptive', 'ethnographic', 'naturalistic', 'anthropological', 'inductive', 'interpretative', 'case studies', 'interaction analysis', 'critical discourse analysis', and of course, 'qualitative'.

Lazaraton (1995), in a special *TESOL Quarterly* issue on qualitative research in ESOL, lists even more. In her article, she provides an overview of recent qualitative research in applied linguistics and thereby attempts to work towards a definition of this research approach. One obvious reason why it is difficult to do so is that there is no one way of doing qualitative research and it is not associated with only one discipline or philosophy (see also Lazaraton 2003). Denzin and Lincoln (1998: 5), for example, indicate that it has multiple methodologies and research practices:

> Qualitative research, as a set of interpretative practices, privileges no single methodology over any other. As a site of discussion, or discourse, qualitative research is difficult to define clearly. It has no theory, or paradigm, that is distinctly its own.... Qualitative research is used in many separate disciplines.... It does not belong to a single discipline. Nor does qualitative research have a distinct set of methods that are entirely its own.

Each discipline has, of course, its own philosophy, theoretical and empirical literature, and recommendations for conducting research and reporting outcomes. Lazaraton (1995: 460), however, points out that the applied linguistics literature tends to blur these qualitative approaches. She then goes on to illustrate from a number of sources that the concern instead appears to be with contrasting (under various labels) qualitative and quantitative research approaches. She adds that since these sources do not clearly define and delineate qualitative research in the first place, 'some ambiguity and confusion remains in terms of understanding what counts as qualitative research and what does not'. Davis (1995) offers sound advice to avoid this confusion. She suggests that researchers simply state in their research reports what it is that they are doing and locate their research procedures within the theoretical, philosophical and methodological traditions associated with that approach.

This advice holds an important message worth bearing in mind for the remainder of this chapter: As with all research traditions, there is no one way of doing qualitative research. The methods chosen to analyse and interpret data should be those that will most appropriately answer the research questions. As Larsen-Freeman and Long (1991: 14) state, 'what is important for researchers is not the choice of *a priori* paradigms or even methodologies, but rather to be clear on what the purpose of the study is and to match that purpose with the attributes most likely to accomplish it'.

While it is true that there are different qualitative research approaches, each with its own set of distinguishing features, there are many features which they have in common. These common features stem from their roots in research practices in anthropology and sociology which are concerned with studying people living and interacting in their natural environments, the aim being to understand the 'patterned conduct and social processes' (Vidich and Lyman 1998: 41) of the society in which they live. It is the insider perspective that is important here; while maintaining a balance between sensitivity and objectivity, the researcher attempts to describe and explain how the participants live their lives from their own (*emic*) points of view. The terms *constructivist* and *interpretivist* are associated with the type of research that gives central consideration to the understanding of situation-specific meanings of actions, from the point of view of the actors. In other words, 'particular actors, in particular places, at particular times, fashion meaning out of events and phenomena through prolonged, complex processes of social interaction involving history, language and action' (Schwandt 1998: 221–2). It is the work of constructivists and interpretivists, that is, qualitative researchers, to interpret this meaning.

The following are other features shared, to a greater or lesser extent, by qualitative research approaches. (See Cumming 1994; Davis 1995; Denzin and Lincoln 2000 for the definitive overview, Johnson 1992; Lazaraton 2003; Seliger and Shohamy 1989; Strauss and Corbin 1998.)

1 They produce 'findings not arrived at by statistical procedures or other means of quantification' (Strauss and Corbin 1998: 10–11). This is because the nature of the research questions asked requires outcomes of a different kind. For example, research that attempts to understand the feelings, emotions, thoughts and experiences of language learners engaged in day-to-day communicative events lends itself to researchers actually observing them and talking to them as they do so. It is more difficult to understand these unobservable elements of human reality through a mathematical approach to analysis and interpretation.
2 This does not mean that qualitative and quantitative methods cannot be combined. A feature of some qualitative approaches is that they are flexible enough to allow this. It is quite possible, for example, to approach the analysis of qualitative data from a quantitative angle. Doing so often produces a different perspective on phenomena and brings about deeper interpretations of the meanings in the original qualitative data. Pease-Alvarez and Winsler (1994), for example, combined an ethnographic and a quantitative perspective in their investigation of the language practices and beliefs

of bilingual fourth-grade students in a school in the US. By quantifying the classroom observation field notes, the researchers were able not only to determine who the children spoke English and Spanish to, where, and during what type of classroom activity, they were also able to determine the extent (in percentages) of engagement with various interlocutors, and which locations and activities generated more or less English and Spanish.

3 The following set of related attributes all pertain to qualitative research: *naturalistic, longitudinal* and *holistic*. As we indicated above, the anthropological and sociological foundations of qualitative research have established the tradition of conducting qualitative research in the natural settings in which the participants live their lives, rather than removing them to artificial settings for closer inspection. The latter may save time and may allow researchers to focus on particular pre-specified variables, but qualitative researchers believe that it cannot result in a comprehensive, valid explanation of the participants' social meanings. The aim, therefore, is a holistic overview of the events, situations or people under study. A quick snapshot approach will not adequately achieve this. Connections need to be made between language learners and a wide range of the components which constitute their contexts, and sense needs to be made of how all these elements are arranged, integrated and related. Doing so obviously requires a lot of time. Qualitative studies, therefore, are necessarily longitudinal. Tarone and Liu (1995), for example, report on a study involving Bob, a young Chinese boy, who was observed in order to monitor his interlanguage development and use in a range of interactional contexts during a period of 26 months: with peers and teachers at school and with the researcher in the boy's home. And Maguire and Graves (2001) investigated how L2 writing intersects with identity construction by examining the 'discourses, texts, and voices' (2001: 561) of three eight-year-old Muslim girls while learning English over a three year period in Canada.

4 The data generated by qualitative research methods usually materializes as text: for example, interview transcripts, observation field notes, think aloud protocols, diary entries, written compositions, transcripts of classroom interaction. In qualitative research these texts are analysed from either a sociological perspective, where texts are treated as windows into human experience, or from a linguistic perspective, where texts are themselves the object of analysis. (See Tesch 1990.) In either case, the texts are composed of words, and so most analysis is done with words. This poses two challenges: firstly, there are usually many words, and whether they come in the form of single words, short phrases or free-flowing discourse, they need to be read, moved around and re-arranged—difficult work when the study

> has generated a vast number of words. Secondly, words are not numbers, as Miles and Huberman (1994: 56) have said, 'words are fatter than numbers'. Words often have multiple and sometimes ambiguous meanings. For them to be understood they need to be related to the linguistic as well as the social context in which they appear. Coding, the focus of this chapter, is one way of achieving this goal.

A distinction is often made between *deductive* and *inductive* orientations to qualitative research. In the former type of research, investigators begin with specific hypotheses or research questions and set out to prove or answer them, or they may have in mind a set of pre-defined, expected themes which they then go on to examine, ignoring other 'irrelevant' themes which they may come across in the process since they are not the focus of the study. A researcher, for example, may wish to interview language learners in order to examine the nature of their anxieties resulting from their perceptions of being less proficient than other students in a language class. Before the interview the researcher would determine the topics to be covered in the interview (these being generated from the theoretical and empirical literature, from the researcher's own experience as a teacher, or from concerns raised informally by the learners) and then ask questions only related to this topic in the interview. In this approach, therefore, the research starts with theory or a well-formed idea, which is used as an aid or tool in directing empirical investigation (van Lier 1988). An example of a study which took this stance was conducted by Barkhuizen (1999), who investigated high school students' perceptions of learning to spell in English. He was particularly concerned with their ideas about the purpose of learning how to spell correctly and why they thought the process, and the skill, was important (he predicted that they thought it would be after discovering this attitude and developing a conceptual framework of learner perceptions in an earlier study with similar students, see Barkhuizen 1998), and so he concentrated specifically on these issues during classroom observations, focus group interviews and in an open-ended questionnaire distributed to the learners.

Whereas deductive research is theory-driven, inductive research is data-driven. Inductive research has theory or an in-depth understanding as its goal (van Lier 1988). The theory or understanding is induced from the text data itself, that is, 'by examining the data first to see into what kind of chunks they fall naturally and then choosing a set of concepts that helps to explain why the data fell that way' (LeCompte and Schensul 1999: 46). In other words, in this *grounded theory* approach, the researcher begins with the data, and through its analysis (searching for salient themes or categories and arranging these to form explanatory patterns) arrives at an understanding of the phenomenon under investigation. These themes and patterns do not simply jump out at the researcher—discovering them requires a systematic approach to analysis based on familiarity with related literature and research experience.[1]

The inductive-deductive relationship should not be seen as binary but rather as two ends of a continuum. Qualitative research cannot be entirely one or the other. A researcher cannot, for instance, enter a research site or begin interviewing a participant without any idea of what to look for or what questions to ask. There must be some theory or idea or topic which guides data collection, analysis and interpretation, as Wolcott (1982: 157) says, it is 'impossible to embark upon research without some idea of what one is looking for and foolish not to make that quest explicit'. Qualitative researchers, therefore, use both induction and deduction throughout their analysis, and to classify a study as either only one or the other would be an oversimplification. A classic example of a primarily inductive study is that of Heath (1983) who explored the language and literacy practices of three communities in the Piedmont Carolinas in the US. Besides developing theories of language and literacy use within each of the communities, by comparing the language and literacy expectations of each group with those of the school, she contributed to our understanding of home/school cultural differences for explaining academic failure.

Inductive research has sometimes been referred to as *hypothesis-generating* research (Seliger and Shohamy 1989) because further research questions are suggested by the recurring patterns in the data. In other words, the data analysis raises questions which are then explored further in follow-up analysis, either with the same data-set or with fresh data generated by a new study. This iterative process by which the analyst becomes more and more 'grounded' in the data is typical of the grounded theory approach mentioned above. Another perspective on this matter is that inductive studies generate hypotheses which are then tested by 'harder', quantitative research procedures. From this perspective, qualitative inductive research plays a supportive, feeding role, whereby the questions it raises are fed into quantitative research designs for further investigation (see Henning 1986), without which generalization of the findings to other contexts would be very difficult. (See Chapter 1 for a discussion of external validity issues in qualitative research.) The early diary studies in SLA were used for this purpose. Bailey and Ochsner (1983: 188) provide a reason for analysing diary data: 'If we consider diary research as preliminary to more controlled, experimental studies, then our basic purpose is to generate new hypotheses. By combining these SL diary studies, we simply expand the data base: the more studies reviewed, the more hypotheses we may produce'. An alternative position on this issue is that qualitative research need not necessarily play a 'supportive' research role; i.e. the goal of qualitative research projects is to reach their own conclusions which explain the phenomena under study, not to generate questions which are then answered by other, quantitative studies. Generalization (or transferability) is achieved in the sense that qualitative studies seek to 'produce understandings of one situation which someone with knowledge of another situation may well be able to make use of' (Edge and Richards 1998: 345).

The distinction between deductive and inductive research also applies, of course, to the process of analysing the data using a coding system. With top-down, deductive coding, the analyst begins with a set of codes created before engagement with the data begins. Of course, these may change once the analysis gets underway, or codes may be deleted and others may be added. With bottom-up, inductive coding, the analyst develops the coding system only when the close analysis begins. Once again, the two approaches to coding can be placed along a deductive-inductive continuum, with researchers using both throughout the analysis. Inductive coding is the focus of this chapter and will be addressed in more detail in the next section.

Coding qualitative data

Although there are different approaches to analysing qualitative data, each using different or sometimes overlapping terminology to express what analysts do, they all follow a similar sequence. (See Table 11.1.)

This list simplifies the process somewhat, but it does indicate both the scope of an analysis and the types of procedures necessary for it to be satisfactorily completed. The sequence could be simplified even further: *coding for themes—looking for patterns—making interpretations—building theory*. This is the order we follow in this section, despite the fact that the procedures involved represent concurrent flows of activity throughout any qualitative study. The very early stages of coding, for example, obviously involve some interpretation, and even during the later stages of a study, codes may need to be revised or new ones added as previously undetected

1 Affixing codes to a set of field notes and transcriptions drawn from observations or interviews
2 Noting reflections or other remarks in the margins or in memos
3 Sorting and sifting through these materials to identify similar phrases, relationships between variables, patterns, themes, distinct differences between subgroups, and common sequences
4 Isolating these patterns and processes, commonalities and differences, and taking them out to the field in the next wave of data collection
5 Gradually elaborating a small set of generalizations that cover the consistencies discerned in the database
6 Confronting those generalizations with a formalized body of knowledge in the form of constructs and theories, and backing them up with copious illustration from the primary data.

Table 11.1 Typical sequence of a qualitative analysis (based on Miles and Huberman 1994: 9)

themes are discovered when the original data is revisited or new data is collected. Analysis is ongoing and recursive until saturation has been reached; i.e. further analysis yields no new themes or patterns. But the first step, coding, cannot begin at all unless there are texts to code.

Choosing a sample of texts

In qualitative inductive research, sampling decisions are crucial for later analysis. (See LeCompte and Preissle 1993.) In anthropological studies concerned with investigating the culture of groups, decisions about whom to observe and interview could backfire if representatives of those groups are not chosen. And even if appropriate representatives are chosen, what they say and why will still only reveal a slice of life of that particular group. For these reasons, sampling in qualitative research tends to be purposive rather than random; participants are chosen because they match the criteria identified by the researcher that are characteristic of the group under investigation. Random sampling, warn Miles and Huberman (1994: 27) 'can deal you a decidedly biased hand'. Sampling, of course, refers not only to selecting people, but also to documents, artefacts, video-recordings, field notes from observations and so on.

Sampling decisions can be made for other reasons as well: convenience for researcher or participants, time constraints, willingness of participants, restrictions set by authorities, or ethical considerations. Block (1994: 475), in his study of the perceptions learners have of the purpose of classroom learning activities and how these compare with those of their teachers, describes his sampling decision, whereby he purposively selected his sample of texts (students' diary accounts of an EFL class) to ensure a greater quantity of data: 'I shall discuss the data I collected on one single day of the study . . . I have chosen this day because it was in essence my best day as observer and data collector as I was able to collect 12 accounts as compared with seven on each of the other two days which I observed'.

Since SLA researchers are concerned with learner language, their aim when selecting samples is to obtain texts of the language that learners produce, and their decisions are usually guided by the research questions they ask. Sampling is therefore theory-driven; decisions are made either before data collection begins or progressively throughout the study, as in grounded theory, or both. Furthermore, as is typical of qualitative research, learner language research tends to focus on only one case—an individual or group of similar learners (same age, same class or school, or same community). For example, see Tarone and Liu (1995) who analysed the language of one boy, Block (1994) who focused on six students in one class, Barkhuizen (1999) who collected data from students in one school, and Pease-Alvarez and Winsler (1994) who studied three children in the same fourth-grade class.

Data management and reduction

During the early stages of analysis researchers are particularly concerned with data *management* and *reduction*. The former refers to creating some order in all the data that has been collected, what LeCompte and Schensul (1999) call 'tidying up'. This means: making copies of all important materials; putting field notes, interview and interaction transcriptions into order by labelling and indexing them; locating missing data; filing and storing the data in a safe place. Tidying up activities should not only begin once all the data has been collected, but should be maintained right from the start of the research project. Doing so will save a lot of time and frustration later on, and not doing so may lead to important information being missed during the analysis, with the result that ongoing, purposive data collection—what Strauss and Corbin (1998) call *theoretical sampling*—may be compromised. Even with single-case studies the amount of data which piles up can be very large. With large-scale ethnographies it can be positively overwhelming. For example, in Willet's (1995) study of the L2 socialization of four first-grade school children, she collected the following data: field notes from classroom participant observations, audiotapes of classroom interaction, field notes of school and community life, artefacts and documents from the school, notes from informal interactions with the children, the results from sociometric testing, and learning materials such as workbooks and readers.

It is no wonder, therefore, that data reduction is a necessary and welcome process. Reduction, through coding, summarizing, paraphrasing, focusing, writing memos and indexing, turns the large mass of data into smaller, manageable amounts of data, what Goetz and LeCompte (1981) refer to as 'crunched' data. This makes it easier for the researcher to work with the data, and thus facilitates access to the conceptual themes and patterns in the data which are the target of analysis. Data reduction is part of the analysis, and it continues throughout the duration of the study until the final report is written.

Open coding—the first level

In this and the following sections, we will be concerned with texts consisting of learner language. We acknowledge that qualitative studies of learner language typically incorporate data from other sources in order to contextualize the content of what learners say, as most of the studies cited in this chapter illustrate. However, our focus here is specifically on the coding of text actually produced by language learners, coding being the central activity of the analysis, as Miles and Huberman (1994: 56) say, 'Coding is analysis'.

In order to illustrate the stages of coding analysis we will use the data given in Table 11.2. The data comes from a study (Barkhuizen 1998) which

[RA] = Read Aloud
[OP] = Oral Presentation
[ST] = Speak/Talk in class
[DR] = Drama/plays
[LA] = Laugh At speaker/reader
[ER] = Emotional Reaction

[the number attached to each code indicates the grade of the learner]
[?] = TENTATIVE CODE

1 Other children in class like to laughed when you do not understand the word in the time you are busy reading for the teacher. I don't someone laughed me. I am very afraid for that.[RA8][LA8] [ER8]

2 I'am not shy to talk in English infront of people, but to read then I'am very shy.[ST8][RA8][ER8]

3 I dont like to read english in my class.[RA8?]

4 I do not like oral. I am a girl how afraid for very thing.[OP8][ER8]

5 I dont like to talk english infront of my friends.[ST8]

6 I dont like to play play's in the english class when you must talk english.[DR8]

7 What thing I do not like to english I dont like talk english because when I talk english some places I be wrong and other write.[ST8]

8 I love drama in the class when we read it.[DR8]

9 But the following I like is Drama workshop that what I like I really like about English.[DR8]

10 Oral is my favourite but I cant understand some people.[OP8]

11 I dont like oral because I am a very shy girl.[OP8][ER8]

12 I did hate english went I must go and stand in front of people I did hate to read and talk english. I don't like oral I hate it.[OP8]

13 When the teacher says we must do oral my points are very low.[OP8]

14 I like to read English books every Sunday and after school. What I not like about it is oral. Oral is so a clamsy thing.[OP8]

15 It is always hard delivering a speech in English.[OP8]

16 I dont like oral. I can do every thing in english not oral.[OP8]

17 I like to speak English in the class.[ST8]

18 When we are in the English class I dont to speak English because I dont no when I speaking my words right or wrong.[ST8]

19 I dont like to speak english.[ST8]

20 I dont like to speak english because you never no when you say something wrong, sometimes you speak english and you just say the rong words and all your friend are laughing.[ST8][LA8]

21 When I did come in the middle of the year I did understand every thing but I did hate to talk English because some of my words did not come out

Table 11.2 (continued)

prople out thats why I wrote ever english words wrong and I leave that school.[ST8]

22 I dont like to speak english in class in front of all my friends.[ST8]

23 I don't like to read aloud. When you read and there's a difficult word and you cant say it, everybody is looking at you. They laugh at you and you feel very shy.[RA9][LA9]

24 If you read for instens a English book in class ther are some of you class friends who will laught for you broken english.[RA9][LA9]

25 I also dont like to read aloud in the class.[RA9]

26 I dont like English because of Reading infront of the class.[RA9]

27 I don't like read infront of my classmates. I am a very shy person and that is the reason.[RA9]

28 Even reading infront of the whole class makes me nervous.[RA9]

29 I dont like oral. I dont like to speak infront of every body, and stand infront of the class.[OP9]

30 English is a good language, but there is always the bad things I don't like, for example I have to do oral in class I will speak at home, but not at school I am to shy. Even to read in front of the whole. I don't like it I will read in my mind.[RA9]

31 I don't like to talk in front of everybody. I will do English oral topics in front of the teacher table and talk to him/her.[OP9]

32 I dont like to perform before all the children in the class.[DR9]

33 I dont like English because of oral.[OP9]

34 The really thing I dislike in English is oral that makes me sick.[OP9][ER9]

35 I dont like to do orrels. That is not my hobbie. I dont like speaking English too.[OP9][ST9]

36 I don't like to talk oral topic in class. I'm afraid to speak English.[OP9][ST9]

37 I also dont like oral because I'am too shy to speak. I dont like to speak in front of the class.[OP9][ST9]

38 Oh when it comes to the point where you must do oral in front of the whole class makes me nervous.[OP9][ER9]

39 Many people like to justly you when you want to try to speak some words in english. They brake you down then you think you will never come ight.[ST9][LA9?][ER9]

40 In class when you speak with your English class teacher and the class is quite and you want to asked her something and you spoke some English words wrong out your class maites like to laugh for you and they shy justly you.[ST9][LA9]

41 The thing I hate about English is that when you talked with someone and this one used high words and you dont understand it then I am shy to say I dont understand because your friend are going to justly you.[ST9][LA9?]

Table 11.2 (continued)

42 dont like talk in english or communicated with people we dont understand Afrikaans. The reason why I dont like spoken english infront of people because I dont no what they will do or reac when I say something stuped its mean when I dont no what the meaning of a word is and I ask somebody to explain it to me.[ST9]

43 When it become that I must talk English with the teacher in class, I dont like it.[ST9]

44 I hate reading aloud in the classroom because of the children who likes laughing when you make a small mistake and I think the rest of us will feel more at ease if they would stop acting like small children because they are in grade ten and all of them are grown up by the time. [RA10][LA10][ER10]

45 I hate reading aloud in the English class out of books and paperclips. Sometime you would make a mistake and the whole class will laugh at you.[RA10][LA10]

46 I hate to read english out loud because I get nervous and started to say something incorrect then people laugh at me.[RA10][LA10][ER10]

47 The children like to make a joke out of you if you can't read well enough.[RA10][LA10]

48 What I like about English is to read infront of the class because I love reading but I don't like other people to laugh while I am reading.[RA10][LA10]

49 I dont like reading aloud because there is sometimes words that I cannot pronouns. The pupil like to laugh if I pronouns the words wrong.[RA10][LA10]

50 I hate to read aloud in the English class because some of us don't read very well and are nervice.[RA10][ER10]

51 What I hate about English is to read allowed in the classroom because their are some words that is difficult to pronounce and it emberres me a lot.[RA10][ER10]

52 What I hate about English is reading aloude because some times come across stang words and than I speak it don't out correctly and than my friend's makes fun of me.[RA10][LA10]

53 I like the English class sometimes, because when it comes to oral I like to listen to other pupils because of their faults that they make.[OP10]

54 The thing I like most about english is preparing oral to say to the teacher there at her desk.[OP10]

55 In class I like to do drama. I like to make jokes and performed the plays.[DR10]

56 What I would like in the classroom is to have more oral dramatic work because it will help me learn the language much better.[DR10]

57 The thing I do not like from English is oral. In oral theres nothing I can talk about. I felt worried when it becomes oral. I'am not a well English speaker that's why I hate oral. In front of the hole class if you talk a word rong they began to laugh at you as if you were a fool that why I hate oral. The topics that they are given for oral are very difficult so there are not time left for me

Table 11.2 (continued)

to prepare the oral topic. It is my nightmare. In the English lesson oral is my most problem.[OP10][LA10][ER10]

58 The thing of oral is making me sick, because I hate people laughing at me.[OP10][LA10]

59 I dont like reading and oral in the English classroom because it is hard to speak big word out, if I cant speak these word out I feel so upset. I decided I will never read, or do oral in the classroom the teacher can hit me but I will never do it.[RA10][OP10]

60 I does not like oral work because I hate to stand infront of all the people talking alow and the people is looking at me. I hate to make mistakes infront of the people.[OP10]

61 I likes to speak English in the English class because it makes your Oral Marks up.[OP10]

62 I hate to spoke the difficult words and it also makes me mad because my friends laugh at me.[ST10][LA10][ER10]

63 What I hate about English is speaking infront of the hole class. The reason I hate it is because I'm scared the class is going to laugh for me and don't like to be a joke infront of the class.[ST10][LA10][ER10]

Table 11.2 Coded units of data from students' compositions about English classes

investigated learners' perceptions of ESL learning in a South African high school. The focus was specifically on their perceptions of the learning activities in their ESL classes. In typical ethnographic style the researcher spent much time collecting data from the Grade 8–11 students, using a wide range of methods: students completed a closed-ended questionnaire, the researcher observed one class from each of the grades, he held individual interviews with each of the five ESL teachers and group interviews with six students in each grade, and he spent three weeks actually teaching in the school. Barkhuizen also asked students to write a composition about their likes and dislikes of ESL classes at school, the aim being to ascertain their perceptions of classroom learning activities. Between 25 and 40 compositions were collected from each grade. These compositions are the sample texts from which the illustrative data-set is drawn. The data are presented in a partially coded state, and we will refer to it as the *learner perceptions* (LP) data. How and why the numbered chunks of text were chosen is explained below.

Once the sample of texts has been collected, the analyst needs to decide on the basic units or items of analysis. Some of the options are single words, formulaic expressions, short phrases, complete sentences, utterances or even pieces of extended discourse. The chosen unit of text could represent a behaviour, an event, a thought, an opinion, a feeling or an attitude. In a top-down, deductive analysis, decisions about the units of analysis are made before the actual coding starts, and just like the codes themselves the units may change as the study progresses. In a bottom-up, inductive analysis the units will probably only be identified once a microanalysis of the data begins. In the LP data, short chunks of one or two sentences were used as the unit of analysis; each chunk expressing a perception about a learning activity. Each unit was identified by looking for a key word or phrase which expressed the perception and its length was limited to only the sentence or sentences in which that idea was expressed. The units are numbered for easy reference.

Deciding on units of analysis is not simply a mechanical process. Even this activity is theorizing in action; researchers are already starting to 'make sense' of the data. Once it has been established what is going to be coded, the actual coding can begin. *Codes* are names or tags assigned to *concepts* that represent at a more abstract level the experiences, ideas, attitudes or feelings identified in the data. The codes represent these concepts, which represent the *content* of the learner-language data. In order to arrive at the concepts, analysts need to read and re-read the texts very carefully. Strauss and Corbin (1998) refer to this line-by-line scrutiny of the data as *micro-analysis*. The text and notes in Table 11.3 illustrate these relationships:

Codes, therefore, are concepts. Coding takes place at the conceptual level. The example clearly shows how coding is also analysis; in order to assign codes to concepts, the concepts first have to be found in the data. Concepts are often referred to as *themes*, and this is the term we use in the rest of this chapter. Now, where do the themes come from? The most obvious starting point is the research question. As we have emphasized throughout this chapter, in inductive analyses researchers do not start their analysis with absolutely no idea of what to look for.[2] For example, Kumaravadivelu (1991) wanted to investigate ESL learners' perceptions of the nature, goals and demands of task-based classroom activities, and to compare them with those of their teachers. To do so he recorded interaction during the activities and he also interviewed both teachers and the learners. In his analysis of the data transcripts he was obviously guided by the research question, which led him to identify ten potential sources of mismatch between the perceptions of

Extract from a diary entry of an adult ESL learner

Things went well [**making progress**] today. I feel I can use the new anger expressions in class to my friends, but I don't feel happy about [**expressing an emotion**] saying those things to people I don't know.

Content = the meaning expressed by the words of the learner
Concepts = [**making progress**] [**expressing an emotion**]
Codes = PRO, EMO

Table 11.3 The relationship between content, concepts and codes

the learners and the teachers. The transcript extracts he presents in the report of the study illustrate the results of his focused analysis quite clearly.

In the LP data (see Table 11.2), the researcher was faced with over 100 compositions of 150–250 words each. As he read each composition line-by-line he had in mind the aim of the research question: learners' perceptions of ESL classroom learning activities. At each mention (the content) of an activity (a theme) a code was assigned to the unit of analysis (a short chunk of data) in which the theme was articulated. Some of the themes identified and their codes were as follows:

reading aloud [RA]
writing tests [TE]
writing examinations [EX]
using the dictionary [DT]
listening to the teacher [LT]
speaking or talking [ST]
drama/plays [DR]
writing compositions [CO]
reading poetry [PY]
oral presentations [OP]
writing business letters [BL]
group work [GW]
silent reading [SR]
doing comprehensions [CP]

We have explained where the themes come from, but what about the codes? Codes are letters (or less typically, numbers) which serve as mnemonic devices that identify and mark the themes in the text. They should be short, simple and easy to remember, and they should very clearly respond to and immediately signal the themes to which they refer. They are, after all, through their role in data reduction, supposed to make the analyst's life easier. It is a good idea, therefore, to keep them semantically close to the themes they represent. LeCompte and Schensul (1999) advise that codes must be kept at a low level of inference in order to minimize value judgements about classification of units. Inductive coding involves generating a list of codes during microanalysis. The list grows and the labels are revised as the researcher both discovers new themes and redefines old themes while working through new data and re-visiting previously analysed data.[3] In studies dealing with a lot of learner language text it is a good idea to manage codes by storing them in a codebook. (See Dey 1993; LeCompte and Schensul 1999.) Codebooks contain operational definitions of each code, inclusion and exclusion criteria and exemplars of units from the text data (for example, the chunks of text in the LP data). Just like codes, codebooks are dynamic and their contents and organization change as the study continues.

The mechanics of coding involve writing down the codes in the margins of the text alongside the corresponding theme.[4] Once the data has been coded at this level, researchers can begin to examine collections of codes to see how they are related to each other. A set of codes denoting similar themes/concepts are grouped together to form a *category*, a higher-level abstract explanatory concept. Categorizing the themes in this way makes the data more manageable to work with, thereby assisting the researcher to identify patterns within and between the different categories. Some of the themes from the LP data above could be categorized and coded as follows:

public oral production [PORP]
assessment [ASSM]
reading activities [READ]
writing activities [WRIT]

You might like to work out how the coded themes were categorized and which of them did not make it into the four categories. The coded data in Table 11.2 are all in the PORP category.

Looking for patterns

When researchers look for relationships between and within categories they are looking for *patterns*.[5] Patterns are linkages at the conceptual level, and so interpretation moves into a higher gear during this stage. Grounded theorists call coding at this level *axial coding* and stress its importance because of its role in building theory; 'sorting out the relationships between concepts and subconcepts' (Strauss and Corbin 1998: 142). But where do the patterns come from? How are the connections made between the categories? Ways in which patterns are discovered include the following (we once again refer to the LP data in Table 11.2 to illustrate these):

1 Perhaps the most common way to identify patterns is by the frequency with which themes occur. In the full LP data set almost all the students wrote about PORP activities.
2 Sometimes the informants themselves will alert the researcher to the existence of a pattern. A connection between the PORP activities is signalled by many of the learners' references to other learners laughing at their language errors (coded LA) when speaking or reading aloud. This pattern is obvious not only because laughing is mentioned frequently but also because it is overtly stated by the respondents: for example, 'I dont like to speak english because you never no when you say something wrong, sometimes you speak english and you just say the rong words and all your friend are laughing' (unit 20); 'What I hate about English is speaking infront of the hole class. The reason I hate it is because I'm scared the class is going to laugh for me and don't like to be a joke infront of the class' (unit 63).
3 Themes can also be linked because of their similarity. For a start, reading aloud [RA], oral presentations [OP], speaking/talking in class [ST] and drama/plays [DR] are linked because they all involve public oral production. They are also similar in that almost all learners expressed a negative perception of these activities. The PORP data is peppered with phrases such as: 'I don't like', 'I hate'. (See for example

units 11 and 12.) The data has not been coded for positive and negative perceptions. (See the task at the end of the chapter.)

4 The experience of the researcher also plays a role in identifying patterns. In the LP study the researcher's experience as an ESL teacher, a researcher and a teacher educator in the same educational system as the school provided him with insights into teaching and learning practices within that system. He was aware, for example, that although a communicative approach to ESL teaching was endorsed in the official syllabus documents, many teachers used structural, textbook-based approaches instead. In many ESL classes not much English speaking was taking place. When learners did speak, they found it difficult and embarrassing. The negative emotional reactions (coded [ER]) expressed by the learners, therefore, were not surprising to him. The ER pattern refers to comments about being afraid (for example, 1, 4), feeling embarrassed (2, 11)[6], nervous (38, 46), and even sick (34). The researcher's experience, in addition to helping him discover the pattern, also enabled him to interpret its significance with regard to the research questions asked.

5 Finally, consulting the literature in the field and the theories which inform their work, provides researchers with relevant ideas and expectations when they search for patterns in the data. In the case of the LP study, for example, Barkhuizen was aware of the relevant theories in the fields of education, SLA and ESOL teaching, and of research in communicative language teaching, and learner beliefs and attitudes.

The main functions of pattern coding are to reduce the large amount of data into a smaller, manageable set of categories, and to interpret the data in such a way that it can be explained. LeCompte and Schensul (1999: 98) provide an excellent analogy which sums up what pattern coding is all about:

> The pattern level of analysis is something like the middle stages of assembling a jigsaw puzzle; once the player has found all of the orange pieces and all of the blue pieces, for example, or all of the pieces with a particular pattern on them, he or she then can begin to assemble those pieces into a coherent chunk of the design portrayed in the completed puzzle. Furthermore, the player can begin to see how the orange chunks are related to the blue chunks, or where they fit into the overall picture.

We could add here that if the player tries a piece and it does not fit, that piece is not discarded. It may be a *negative case* for the time being, but sooner or later it will find its place in the puzzle. During the recursive analysis and interpretation process analysts come across negative cases, cases that refute or disconfirm a theme or a pattern. Although they may be the exceptions to the emergent rule, they do contribute to the interpretation by allowing researchers 'to establish the parameters or distribution of a construct' (Goetz and LeCompte 1984: 175), and therefore need to be accommodated. In the LP data, for example, negative cases would be those learners who actually liked speaking or reading aloud in class. (See units 17, 48, and 61.)

Data display

Miles and Huberman (1994) stress the importance of displaying data during the analysis in the form of Venn diagrams, tables, flowcharts, taxonomies, matrices, causal networks or conceptual maps. Visual displays are important for two reasons: firstly, they very quickly guide the reader of the research report to understand what may have taken the researcher a long time and a lot of work to figure out; secondly, the actual drawing of the visual displays forces researchers to clarify and articulate their interpretations. The act of constructing a display is an act of analysis and interpretation.

Figure 11.1 is a conceptual display of the arrangement of themes within the public oral production (PORP) category from the LP data. It represents the learners' perceptions of PORP activities. The researcher has placed PORP in the centre of the conceptual map, and linked it by means of solid lines to the four main themes in the category. Coming off each theme-bubble are two other bubbles: (1) 'al' which stand for alternative practices that are suggested by the learners; for example, see unit 54 where the learner suggests

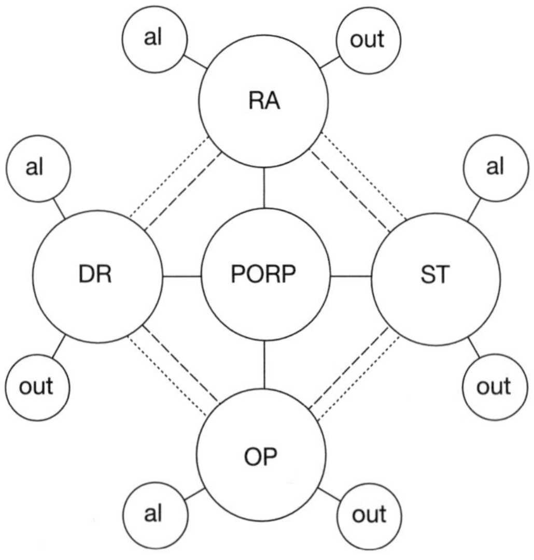

Figure 11.1 Conceptual display of PORP perceptions

that oral presentations should take place only with the teacher at his or her desk, and (2) 'out' which stands for outliers, or negative cases. The dotted lines (and there could be many more in Figure 11.1) represent the patterns, what the themes have in common, for instance. This conceptual display is only one possible configuration, and the themes and patterns could certainly be displayed in other sorts of visual formats as well.

Perhaps the most common form of display in qualitative research is the presentation of direct quotations from respondents. These need to be carefully chosen for both content and length so that they express with immediate impact the essence of the theme they represent. It is common to find direct quotations and other forms of visual display in the same research report. (See Maguire and Graves 2001 for an excellent example of this.) The combination increases the credibility of the research. At the same time, as we have said, choosing the quotations and drawing the diagrams compels researchers to refine and clarify their interpretations.

Interpreting the findings

The 'overall picture' is the aim of any study: to answer the research questions and to reach conclusions. In order words, the data which were collected for this purpose need to be described and explained. The results, therefore, cannot simply be presented as a list of themes; they have to be integrated into a set of conclusions. In a grounded theory approach, this is called theory building; presenting the findings as a set of interrelated themes and categories which explains the phenomenon under investigation. The work of making sense of the data is that of the researcher, not of the reader of the research report. Researchers must tell the readers what the results mean, and what possible implications they might have for future actions.

Tentative conclusions are drawn early on in the study, and recorded in memos (see Glaser 1978) or some other form of reflections on the analysis, such as a research diary or computer files. They remain tentative until they are verified. Verification could range from 'a fleeting second thought crossing the analyst's mind during writing, with a short excursion back to the field notes' (Miles and Huberman 1994: 11), to lengthy discussions with research colleagues who have also, independently, analysed the data. For example, in Leki and Carson's (1997) study of ESL students' perceptions of writing in an English for academic purposes class, the two researchers and a research assistant independently reviewed interview transcripts and then met to discuss the themes which each analyst had perceived. They then re-analysed the data with the collaboratively compiled set of themes in mind. They eventually reached their conclusions 'through repeated cycles of analysis and consultation' (1997: 48).

The analysis of the LP data as described in this chapter generated a theoretical framework which explains the cyclical development of language learner perceptions in their ESL classes: their perceptions of the activities led to attitudes towards them which in turn determine their levels of motivation and receptivity when they next engage in those activities (see Barkhuizen 1998). In typical inductive fashion, the framework emerged from the data through detailed, systematic categorization of coded themes and the search for patterns in those categories.

An example of an ethnographic analysis of academic listening

Watson-Gegeo declared in a 1988 article that 'ethnography has recently become fashionable in ESL, second language classroom, and educational research' (1988: 576). One year later Benson (1989) published his report of an ethnographic study which investigated an ESL student's listening activities at a US university. It is summarized in Table 11.4. Watson-Gegeo classifies ethnographic research as one type of qualitative research, and distinguishes it from other types, such as case studies, semiotics and life histories, by its concern with holism and because of the way it treats culture as integral to the analysis. Benson's ethnographic research is also naturalistic in that he observed and interviewed the main participant in his 'natural, ongoing environment' (Schatzman and Strauss 1973: 5).

Benson's study meets the criteria for being both ethnographic and qualitative. He collected an enormous amount of data over an extended period of time, and the data provided a rich description of the processes of the ESL student's academic listening. The content of the student's spoken words, in the form of interviews and recall protocols, and of his written words, in the form of lecture notes, assignments and examinations, provided the researcher with a picture of his listening proficiency and strategies. These data were triangulated with other data (interviews with the professor who taught the course, interviews with other members of the class, textbook analysis, classroom observation) in order to complete the analysis. The multiple perspectives gained from different data sources is one of the strengths of the study.

The main weakness of the study is not so much one of data collection or analysis, but rather has to do with the way in which the research methods are reported. We do not know *how* the data were analysed; whether or not coding took place, and if it did, what form it took. One would assume that some form of coding must have taken place, but it is not described. This, unfortunately, raises a number of questions about dependability and confirmability; reliability and objectivity in rationalist terminology (Edge and Richards 1998). Dependability requirements include scrupulous documentation of the research design and methods (including coding procedures) so that the conclusions reached are justifiable, and confirmability requirements include explicitly linking displayed data with the discussion and conclusions. Benson used direct quotes from the participant's interviews

Research question	The study sought to investigate a graduate ESL student's listening activities during one academic course at a US university in an attempt to provide a detailed picture of what he faced and how he successfully passed the course.
Participants	A graduate ESL student (Hamad) whom the researcher had taught in a preuniversity ESL programme. Hamad was a 26 year old Saudi who aimed to complete a master's degree in public administration in the US.
Data collection	Naturalistic inquiry, 'because of its holistic, humanistic, and cross-cultural perspectives' (Benson 1989), and because of its ability to comprehend experience 'from the native point of view' (Benson, citing Spradley 1980). Data collection consisted of three main stages: the selection of the informant, Hamad; a preliminary project which Benson termed a 'dry run'; and the main research itself. During the dry-run stage, the researcher gathered data through participant observation and key-informant interviews with both Hamad and the teacher of the public administration course in which he was enrolled. He also had access to the teachers' class outline and to Hamad's written work. During the third, main stage the researcher attended all class sessions for one of Hamad's elective courses, audiotaping four at random and videotaping one. There were five formal, taped interviews with the professor, Dr White, seven with Hamad (some in the form of lecture recall protocols), and one each with the 22 other class members. The researcher also examined Hamad's term paper, lecture notes, book report and final examination script, as well as Dr White's lecture notes.
Analysis	Procedures are not explicitly stated. From the style in which the report is presented, however, it is clear that the researcher analysed the data by searching for and developing salient themes and patterns in the data. No mention is made of coding, although we can assume some form must have occurred. In the article, representative excerpts from Hamad's interview transcripts, recall reports and written notes are given to illustrate the themes and patterns. The analysis was ongoing throughout the duration of the study.
Results	Note taking: 1 Fewer notes were taken by Hamad during interaction than during lecture-style teaching. 2 General (main) statements form the bulk of his notes. 3 Examples and metaphors were omitted and vocabulary could be a problem.

Table 11.4 (continued)

	4 Compared with a top L1 student, Hamad's notes lacked completeness but related content more strongly to human experience. 5 A Saudi Arabian viewpoint was evident. 6 Like all the students, Hamad carefully noted down series and lists. 7 Testability was a major consideration. Learning from lectures: 1 In recall protocols, there was no evidence of personal involvement with the material. 2 In a term paper, however, facts from a lecture were localized to facts with which Hamad was familiar; i.e. he avoided abstract elements of the content and foregrounded the human elements. 3 Interviews with Hamad and his written work reflect a generally reproductive learning conception.
Discussion	Typical of ethnographic research, the discussion is combined with the results. Discussion in this article elucidated and contextualized the points in the results section above.
Implications	Benson suggests four main principles on which an advanced listening course should be based: (1) the need for learning to take place; i.e. not only listening for comprehension, (2) the need for content to be related both to past experiences and anticipated academic involvement, (3) the need for all the skills to be practised, and (4) the need to encourage participation.

Table 11.4 Summary of Benson's (1989) ethnographic study of an ESL *students' academic listening*

and recall protocols, as well as excerpts from his written work, but we are not told how these extracts were coded or selected. No other type of display was included in the article.

This is a typical problem with the reporting of research which utilizes qualitative data collection and analysis methods.[7] Because there is usually so much data and because so many words are needed to present and discuss the results (as opposed to space-saving quantitative results), specific details of the study are often left out when research reports are submitted to academic journals for publication. Because these publications have space limits, statements such as the following are standard: 'for a detailed description of the methodology employed for the research see . . . ' (Benson 1989: 431, who refers to his doctoral dissertation) and 'standard procedures for analysing qualitative data were employed' (Schecter and Bayley 1997, who then cite a number of qualitative methodology textbooks). Benson's research, nevertheless, is a clear example of a study which used as its main source of data the spoken and written language produced by the focal participant, and although the analysis is only implicitly reported in the published article, it certainly was qualitative.

Task: An exercise in open coding

For this task you will be using the same data set which we used in this chapter to illustrate coding practices (i.e. the learner perceptions data in Table 11.2).

Carry out the following coding and display tasks:

1.1 Create an appropriate code and then code the data for *positive* and *negative* perceptions of speaking/talking [ST] aloud in class.

1.2 Identify patterns in the negative units: What do they have in common? What is the most frequently mentioned sub-theme? Code these patterns.

2.1 Create an appropriate code and then code the data for *positive* and *negative* perceptions of drama/plays [DR].

2.2 Identify patterns in the negative units: What do they have in common? What is the most frequently mentioned sub-theme? Code these patterns.

3 How are ST and DR different? How are they the same? Write short notes (a memo) describing your interpretations of the ST and DR data.

4 Draw a conceptual display (see Figure 11.1 for an example) of your interpretations.

Final comments

In this chapter, we have described an approach to analysing learner language which has as its aim the understanding of the content of what language learners say. Our concern has been with qualitative data and the inductive qualitative analysis of that data. Before choosing this approach to research, researchers most importantly need to consider the research problem: What exactly do they want to find out about learner language? And what is the best way of doing so? The research methods, in other words, must be the most appropriate ones for answering the research questions. Researchers also need to consider who they are: 'Some researchers are more oriented and temperamentally suited to doing this type of work' (Strauss and Corbin 1998: 11). Inductive qualitative researchers are typically those who are able to speculate and take chances with the data and who are also willing to step back and reflect on their findings and interpretations. They need to be bold enough to make objective analytic moves and, at the same time, be sensitive enough to really listen to the words and meanings of language learners. And, as we have pointed out a number of times in this chapter, with qualitative research there are a lot of words. Central to the effective management, analysis and interpretation of these words is coding, 'the heart and soul of whole-text analysis' (Ryan and Bernard 2000: 780). Good qualitative researchers, therefore, need to code well.

Notes

1 Miles and Huberman (1994) make a distinction between tight and loose research designs. A tight design would be evident in a study that has a pre-existent conceptual framework; that is, similar to a deductive orientation. A study with a loose design keeps pre-structuring to a minimum; similar to an inductive orientation. They point out that loose designs are appropriate for experienced researchers who have plenty of time to conduct their research, and recommend that inexperienced researchers veer towards studies with a tighter design; or at least those that employ an explicit combination of both.

2 For sociological qualitative research, Bulmer (1979) lists a number of different sources of themes, including: literature reviews, professional definitions, local commonsense constructs, researchers' values, prior experience and their general theoretical orientation.

3 With research approaches towards the deductive end of the deductive-inductive continuum, it may be possible to use a set of codes from an earlier study as a 'start list' (Miles and Huberman 1994), or researchers could create their own start list of anticipated codes. These will probably be revised as the analysis progresses.

4 Computer software can also be used to maintain code lists and to mark texts. (See Chapter 14.)

5 Some qualitative research methodologists refer to pattern coding as the grouping of themes into categories (the latter stages of our open coding), and others, particularly grounded theorists, take it a level higher where analysts 'look for answers to questions such as why or how come, where, when, how, and with what results, and in so doing they uncover relationships among categories' (Strauss and Corbin 1998: 127). This difference is not so important, as long as connections are, at some stage, made between the themes.

6 'Shy' is an inaccurate translation of Afrikaans 'skaam', which means 'embarrassed'.

7 For an example of one exception, see Leki and Carson (1997), who describe in detail their analysis procedures. They also include their coding categories, which are appended to their article.

12 Critical approaches to analysing learner language

Introduction

It is obvious that there exists a relationship between social context and language learning; learning does not and cannot take place in a social vacuum. But it is the nature and strength of this relationship which provide language learning theorists with a challenge. Tarone (2000: 182) raises this issue as follows:

> The central question has been whether a theory of SLA must account only for the psycholinguistic processes involved in acquiring an interlanguage (IL), or, alternatively, whether social and sociolinguistic factors influence those psycholinguistic processes to such an extent that they too must be included in such a theory. It seems very clear that SLA *is* a psycholinguistic process. But to what extent are those psycholinguistic processes affected by social context?

This chapter is about the social context of language learning and the place of learners within it. The perspective, however, is not one which considers the learners as unchanging, their relationship with context as static and unidirectional, and the context itself as apolitical. Instead, we present an account of language learning, as evidenced in the text produced by language learners, which sees learners as social beings positioning themselves and being positioned by inequitable relations of power. The sociocultural, political, economic and linguistic ways in which these positionings are constituted have significant implications for both language learning and the dynamic construction of learners' identities. It is, therefore, a complex, changing self which learners bring along to the task of language learning. A critical approach to analysing learner language attempts to understand what learners say about their learning by analysing both the surface level of the language they produce (i.e. the propositional content of what they say) and the deeper level meanings they express, often at a subconscious level (i.e. by reading between the lines, or digging beneath the surface). Both strategies require analysts to locate the text in the micro and macro social contexts in and by which they were constructed.

This task is obviously a multifaceted one, and has interested those involved in language pedagogy and teacher education (Kumaravadivelu 1999), bilingual education (Cummins 1996), language-in-education planning and policy (Pennycook 1998), literacy studies (Street 1997), and of course SLA (Peirce 1995). It is the last of these, and particularly the interconnectedness of language, identity and relations of power, that is the concern of this chapter.

Historical and theoretical background

What makes this chapter different from others in this book, is the political nature of the approach to learner language analysis which it describes. As in all the chapters, the goal is to understand how people acquire an L2. However, it has been argued that attempts at understanding this process will not be successful unless they make connections between learners, language, and the social context in which language is learned (Larsen-Freeman 2000). Furthermore, Pennycook (1999) notes that it might be important to critique work in SLA because it has emphasized the psychological domain of language learning at the expense of the social, economic, cultural, political, or physical contexts in which language learning takes place, but it is also important that these contexts are considered from a critical perspective.

On being critical

What is it, though, that makes a perspective *critical*? What stance do analysts of language learning processes have to take to make their investigations critical? There are no easy answers to these questions, as is evident in the varying and sometimes conflicting views of what critical theory has to offer. (See Habermas 1972; Kumaravadivelu 1999; Pennycook 2001.) What critical analysts have in common, however, is their consideration of the political and ideological contexts of language learning. Embedded in these contexts are the multiple relations of inequitable power in which language learners participate. Hidden in the interaction between participants, and often hidden from participants themselves (i.e. they are not consciously aware of them), are the common-sense assumptions (Fairclough 1985) which dictate the conventions of the interaction. In other words, it seems right and natural that the interaction happens the way it does. Fairclough (1989: 2) calls these assumptions *ideologies*, and adds:

> Ideologies are closely linked to power, because the nature of the ideological assumptions embedded in particular conventions, and so the nature of those conventions themselves, depend on the power relations which underlie the conventions; and because they are a means of legitimising existing social relations and differences of power, simply through the

recurrence of ordinary, familiar ways of behaving which take these relations of power differences for granted.

These 'naturalized' ideological representations are in fact illegitimate in the sense that they do not operate in the general interest; one participant's interests and power dominate another's interests and power. Critical analysts aim to uncover the hidden, taken-for-granted assumptions in order to expose the unequal relations of power at work, or in Fairclough's (1985) words, to 'denaturalize' or make clear the ideologies which were previously 'opaque' to the participants. Uncovering ideologies and thereby making participants aware of the reality of their condition is thus one of the aims of those operating from a critical perspective. Pennycook (1999, following Dean 1994), however, argues that this is not enough. He refers instead to a 'problematizing practice', which stresses the importance of the active, continuous nature of the endeavour. In other words, being critical does not mean only providing rational accounts of the ideological contexts of language teaching/learning conditions (i.e. thinking or theorizing about them) and thereby setting-up alternative truths. Rather, being critical means actively and constantly engaging in asking 'hard questions about cultural and social categories (for example, race, gender, ethnicity) and the way they may relate to language learning' (1999: 343). For example, it is not enough to examine the relationship between language learning and race; the meanings of race, language and learning must themselves be questioned.

But there is even more to the work of critical theorists and researchers. Their intention is not merely to question and to give an ongoing account of the social structures and practices with which language learning is involved. Their work has, in addition, a transformative agenda. Their intention is deliberately political: to resist and struggle against the exercise and the effects of illegitimate power. Those taking a critical perspective of language learning constantly keep an eye out for displays of unfair, oppressive behaviour and always strive to understand them and to change the conditions which led to them. Emancipation is the ultimate goal; working towards 'greater freedom and respect for all people' (Janks and Ivanič 1992: 306). However, the grandiosity of such aims, which call for liberation, emancipation, empowerment, and freedom, has been tempered somewhat by researchers such as Canagarajah (1993), who points out that critical work in TESOL has sometimes been overly over-determined, pessimistic, and even romantic. His study of students studying English in a Sri Lankan tertiary-level classroom (1999), shows that domination-resistance-empowerment relationships are too complex to be described in terms of monolithic, homogeneous categories. ('The dominant language', and 'disempowered students' would be examples of such categories.). His appeal is for an approach which is more local, plural, and personal—one which (1999: 2)

> provides for the possibility that, in everyday life, the powerless in post-colonial communities may find ways to negotiate, alter, and oppose political structures, and reconstruct their languages, cultures, and identities to their advantage. The intention is not to *reject* English, but to *reconstitute* it in more inclusive, ethical, and democratic terms, and so bring about . . . creative solutions to their linguistic conflicts.

The 'solutions', therefore, are *particularistic* in the sense that they are conceived and constructed socially by participants who, in their own circumstances, have a particular set of diverse and often conflicting ideological orientations to address. The result may not be their all-important (and perhaps too abstract and unattainable) emancipation; instead it may be the down-sized, but equally significant, answers to immediate problems encountered in situations where participants experience positions of domination and inequitable access. In Canagarajah's (1999) study, for example, the English students resist the cultural components of the US-English textbooks they use in class, but at the same time, and for socio-economic reasons, exhibit accommodative behaviour in declaring their strong motivation to study ESOL. Pennycook (2001) also calls for restraint when making claims and setting goals for critical applied linguistics, suggesting that the grand goals of awareness, transformation and emancipation be scaled down, and that applied linguists operate instead with 'some sort of vision of what is preferable', what he calls 'preferred futures' (2001: 8).

Finally, critical perspectives look at and interrogate their own way of looking. They constantly evaluate their own strategies and goals, and question the ideological bases from which they operate, or so they should. Pennycook (1999) argues for a 'self-reflexive' stance on critical approaches in order to prevent the situation where they remain as unchallenged as the ideas they aim to challenge. It seems reasonable to expect that those critically examining a social phenomenon would also critically examine their own ideas and their own social practices. Not doing so would be hypocritical and arrogant. In Morgan's (1997) study of identity and intonation in an ESL classroom he argues against systematic, objective research methods on the grounds that they could 'inadvertently parallel forms of political surveillance' (1997: 438) in the context of the research site, a Chinese community centre in Toronto. Data collection took place over only two days and consisted of notes made from memory immediately after lessons and from short phrases written down during classes. Some might argue that his 'research methodology' is flimsy and unsystematic and that his rationale for his approach somewhat unconvincing. He does, however, state his case: he has obviously thought deeply about his research approach, contrasting it with more mainstream methodologies, measuring its suitability for his own particular research setting, proposing the possibility that it may contribute to research into identity and language learning, and then writing about these reflections in the published research report.

Critical approaches in SLA

Since critical work in general focuses on issues on ethnicity, class, age, race, and gender, the role it plays in SLA is obvious: critical analyses make connections and expose relationships among language, language learning, language learners and the social contexts in which learning takes place. Central to this work is the notion of *power*. Put simply, who has it? Who does not? How is power distributed socially? What role does language play in this distribution of power? What role does or should language play in changing unequal relationships of power? How do power relations affect language learning, and how do they affect the social identities, wishes, desires, and histories of language learners?

It is only fairly recently that these questions have been asked in SLA. They have had a somewhat longer history in language education, particularly English language education. Kumaravadivelu (1999) provides a chronological overview of how language use has been conceived and investigated in the language classroom, for example. He begins by outlining the aims and practices of *classroom interaction analysis*. These typically involve the use of an observation instrument or scheme 'consisting of a finite set of preselected and predetermined categories for describing certain verbal behaviors of teachers and students as they interact in the classroom' (1999: 455). The most well-known schemes are FLINT (Flanders Interaction Analysis Categories) from general education and proposed by Flanders in 1970 (see Allwright 1988, and van Lier 1988, for descriptions and critiques of FLINT and other schemes), and COLT (Communicative Orientation of Language Teaching) developed by Allen, Fröhlich, and Spada (1984) and which has direct links to the communicative method of language teaching. These schemes, and numerous others (see Chaudron 1988), all share four limitations (Kumaravadivelu 1999: 455–6). First, they focus exclusively on the product of verbal behaviour of teachers and learners and give little or no consideration to classroom processes or to learning outcomes; secondly, they depend on quantitative measurements, thereby losing the essence of communicative intent that cannot be reduced to numerical codification; thirdly, they are unidirectional in that the information flow is generally from the observer to the teacher, the observer being a supervisor in the case of practising teachers or a teacher educator in the case of student teachers; and fourthly, they are unidimensional in that the basis of observation is largely confined to one single perspective, that of the observer, thus emphasizing the observer's perception of classroom interactional behaviour. The observation schemes certainly did contribute to a much better understanding of classroom language use. However, they provided only a limited, 'fragmented picture of classroom reality' (Kumaravadivelu 1999: 456).

In order to provide a more complete picture of classroom interactional life, observers widened their perspectives to include both the social context of the interactions and the perspectives of all participants on discourse in the classroom. These analytic approaches Kumaravadivelu (1999) groups together under the rubric of *classroom discourse analysis*. They took on a more ethnographic flavour (see particularly the work of van Lier 1988), endorsing qualitative interpretations of classroom events and language practices, in place of the rigid, quantitative codification procedures of the earlier schemes. The classroom was perceived as a 'minisociety with its own rules and regulations, routines, and rituals' (Kumaravadivelu 1999: 458) and interactions in the classroom were analysed as social events involving multiple participants using language above the level of isolated sentences; that is, language was analysed as discourse, as connected text. (See Chapter 8 and Ellis 1994 for reviews of this work.)

The descriptions of classroom learner language and classroom teaching/learning events which emerged from studies using discourse analytic approaches stayed very much inside the classroom, and although they focused on participants as individuals (rather than as a collective mass), they did so by drawing artificial distinctions between individual language learners and the classroom social context. Learners were simply people who used language for interactive, communicative or learning purposes during classroom learning/teaching social events. There was little discussion about the complex nature of the relationship between learners and context (and when there was, the focus tended to be on the immediate context of the discourse, typical of discourse analysis procedures, rather then the broader, macro-contexts that necessarily infiltrate the analyses of critical investigators), and there was certainly no consideration of how relations of power affect interaction and access to learning and speaking opportunities in the classroom. The same could be said for SLA research outside the classroom.[1] The work of Peirce (1995) begins to address these issues.[2]

Social identity theory

In Peirce's groundbreaking 1995 article, she criticizes SLA theorists for not developing 'a comprehensive theory of social identity that integrates the language learner and the language learning context'. She goes on to argue that 'they have not questioned how relations of power in the social world affect social interaction between second language learners and target language speakers' (1995: 12). It is this perspective on language learning that gives SLA theory a critical slant. In order to develop such a theory, theorists and researchers would unavoidably have to look beyond the walls of language classrooms and other language learning settings and events, beyond the bounds of static social relationships and unidimensional language learners, and beyond commonly accepted and unquestioned causal variables such as personality traits (introversion or extroversion, for instance) and motivational factors (for example, the influence of instrumental and integrative motivation). Peirce's commitment to discovering and explaining the connections among social identity, relations of power and the all-important concept of *investment*, places her work quite clearly in the critical domain.

McNamara (1997: 566) states that the 'centrality of the notion of social identity to current work on language learning reflects a renewed theoretical and political concern for the social dimension of language learning'. The wide array of articles in the special-topic issue of *TESOL Quarterly* edited by Norton (1997a) illustrates this point only too well. Norton's own work (1997b, 2000; Peirce 1995) presents perhaps the clearest and certainly most accessible account of the relationship between social identity and L2 learning. Norton sees *social identity* as the multiple ways in which people understand themselves in relation to others, and how they see their past and their future, as she explains (2000: 5):

> I use the term identity to reference how a person understands his or her relationship to the world, how that relationship is constructed across time and space, and how the person understands possibilities for the future. I argue that SLA theory needs to develop a conception of identity that is understood with reference to larger, and frequently inequitable, social structures which are reproduced in day-to-day social interaction. In taking this position, I foreground the role of language as constitutive of and constituted by a language learner's identity. ... It is through language that a person negotiates a sense of self within and across different sites at different points in time, and it is through language that a person gains access to—or is denied access to—powerful social networks that give learners the opportunity to speak.

Identity, therefore, is not constant, but multiple, fluid and often contradictory. In Norton's view of the relationship between social context and L2 learning, then, learners and their learning are socially constructed, so too are learners' social identities; language plays a central role in this process. Furthermore, a person is both 'subject of and subject to relations of power' (Peirce 1995: 15) in any particular social interaction. He or she takes up certain subject positions, but these positionings are changeable; they can be resisted and challenged. Language learners, therefore, become agents in their own empowerment (Rahman 2001).

Central to Norton's ideas on language learning is the concept of *investment*, which refers to learners' commitment to learning the L2, the level of commitment being tied to their perceptions of their relationship to the social world; in other words, it is an investment in the target language as well as in their social identity. Norton (2000: 10) explains:

> If learners invest in a second language, they do so with the understanding that they will acquire a wider range of symbolic and material resources, which will in turn increase the value of their cultural capital. Learners expect or hope to have a good return on that investment—a return that will give them access to hitherto unattainable resources.

Norton's study of adult immigrant learners of English in Canada (see Norton 2000 for a full account of the study) provided the data on which she bases her views of SLA theory. As her own study demonstrates, she recommends research which adopts qualitative methods and which emphasizes making sense of how L2 learners make sense of their experiences of learning the language. She also invites researchers (language learners and their teachers) to participate in collaborative classroom-based social research which collapses 'the boundaries between their classrooms and their communities' (Peirce: 1995: 26).

Toohey (2000) is one researcher who has accepted the invitation. Although she acknowledges the flimsiness of the classroom/community boundaries, she focuses her investigation on classroom activities and practices. The participants in her study were a small group of children from minority language backgrounds in Canada. During their time in kindergarten and Grades 1 and 2, Toohey examined, through observation and interviews, the practices of the school with respect to assigning identities to the children, how participation in physical, material and intellectual practices determined access to classroom resources (including conversations with peers and the teacher), and how discourse practices 'regulated children's access to possibilities for appropriation of powerful and desirable voices in their community' (2000: 3). Her findings are couched in a discussion of theoretical ideas which expose the intimate and complex nature of the relationship between language learners and their identities, their learning and their educational environments.

Identity and discourse

McKay and Wong (1996)—for a full summary of their study, see the end of this chapter—extend the early work of Peirce by introducing the concept of *discourse* into their critical exploration of language learner identity. Their ethnographic study of the English learning of four Chinese-speaking immigrant students at a junior high school in California examines the complex interrelationships among discourse, power, and identity construction in the social environment of each language learner.

The term 'discourse' as used in the social sciences is somewhat slippery. It has been variously defined and used by, amongst others, linguists, sociologists and more recently educationalists. (See Price 1999 for a sample of definitions, as well as his own critique of them.) Linguists have used the term to refer to text beyond the level of the sentence, and, for those interested in discourse analysis, to conversational phenomena such as turn-taking, holding the floor, and overlaps. In social theory, discourse refers, very broadly, to ways of structuring areas of knowledge and social practices (Mesthrie *et al.* 2000). According to Gee (1990: xix) discourses are 'ways of behaving, interacting, valuing, thinking, believing, speaking, and often reading and writing that are accepted as instantiations of particular roles by specific groups of people'. They are governed by and at the same time constitute the 'systems of rules implicated in specific kinds of power relation which make it possible for certain statements and ways of thinking to occur at particular times and places in history' (Mesthrie *et al.* 2000: 323).

In their study, McKay and Wong situate the focal students in a number of discourses which they identified during their research: colonialist/racialized discourses on immigrants, model-minority discourse (i.e. the 'good Asian student'), Chinese cultural nationalist discourses, social and academic school discourses, and gender discourses. The researchers discovered that these discourses interact with each other in complex ways as the students interact socially in the school setting, and it is during these interactions that the social identities of the learners are constructed. However, the students do not merely fill subject positions determined by power relations within discourses, they also deploy and participate in counter-discourses, which may construct for them more powerful positions or which may enable them to resist being positioned by more powerful others.

However, the McKay and Wong study clearly illustrates, as do several others in SLA (see all of those referred to above, as well as Goldstein 1995 and Thesen 1997), that there is no established methodology for critically *analysing* learner language. That is, there is no one accepted and agreed upon set of analytic methods which has been adopted by SLA/learner-language researchers. Instead, what the studies have in common is their research approach: an approach which places what the learner has to say or write in a social context which includes the relations of power in which the learner engages. Critical analysts, therefore, see language learners as social beings and the contexts in which they live their lives and learn their languages as ideologically fraught, that is, they are political. The unity of their approach is 'chiefly in the politics' (Toolan 1997: 99), rather than in the methods of analysis.

A number of the studies already mentioned (for example, Canagarajah 1999 and Norton 2000) and others (for example, Ibrahim 1999) label their research methodology *critical ethnography*. Critical ethnography is a research tool that has the potential to 'penetrate hidden meanings and underlying connections', and critical ethnographers are those who 'are actively engaged in dealing with powerful systems of discourse. They seek to deconstruct dominant discourses as well as counter-discourses by posing questions at the boundaries of ideology, power, knowledge, class, race and gender' (Kumaravadivelu 1999: 476). These aims, which we look at more fully later, echo to a certain extent those associated with *critical discourse analysis* (CDA): 'to systematically explore often opaque relationships of causality and determination between (a) discursive practices, events and texts, and (b) wider and social and cultural structures, relations and processes; to investigate how such practices, events and texts arise out of and are ideologically shaped by relations of power and struggles over power' (Fairclough 1995: 132). Fairclough and Wodack (1997: 271–80) identify eight key principles on which CDA is based:

1. CDA addresses social problems by exploring the linguistic character of social and cultural processes and structures.
2. Power relations are discursive; that is, power relations are exercised and negotiated in discourse, particularly language.
3. Discourse, including language, constitutes society and culture, as well as being constituted by them.
4. Discourse does ideological work; that is, ideologies (for example, relations based on gender and race) are ways of representing and constructing society which reproduce unequal relations of power.
5. Discourse is historical. Discourses are connected to those which were produced earlier, and also those which are produced synchronically and in the future, and these cannot be disregarded.
6. The link between text and society is mediated. CDA makes connections between social structures and processes and properties of texts. These connections are complex, and more often indirect; that is, they are mediated.
7. CDA is both interpretative and explanatory; that is, it goes beyond mere description.
8. CDA is a form of social action that aims to uncover opaqueness and power relationships in order to bring about change in communicative and socio-political practices.

What critical ethnography and CDA have in common is the critical stance they both adopt. They differ in that the former is primarily concerned with people and how they live their cultural lives within a particular community, and the latter is primarily concerned with text. This comparison suggests that a selective combination of the two would appear to be an ideal approach for critically analysing learner language. (See Figure 12.1.) This, of course, is an oversimplistic representation of what critical learner language analysis is all about, but it does capture its underlying rationale; an interest in language learners and the critical analysis of the texts they produce. Furthermore, it covers, albeit broadly, many of the rather uncoordinated and often unarticulated methods assumed by SLA critical researchers thus far. Another shortcoming of our representation is that it implies that

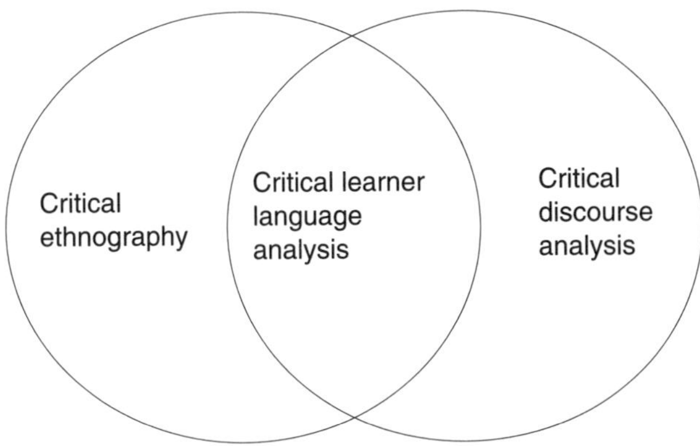

Figure 12.1 An approach to critical learner language analysis

ethnography and discourse analysis are 'non-critical' endeavours. Some would argue, as does Canagarajah (1999: 40), that all research methods should 'be sensitive to issues of power and difference'.

Criticisms of critical approaches

We end this section by noting some of the criticisms which have been levelled against critical approaches to the analysis of text. Critical researchers must be vigilant not to interpret meanings in texts arbitrarily. Naturally, it is essential for analysts to treat the words uttered or written by language learners as representative of the meanings they make out of their world, but they also have the important task of relating these words to 'larger historical processes and social contradictions, searching for the hidden forces that structure life' (Canagarajah 1999: 48). Doing so certainly presents a challenge for critical analysts, a challenge which makes it all too easy to slip into less rigorous, often unwarranted interpretations, or even possibly to make false interpretations which foreground their own political agenda. The subjective nature of critical inquiry, consequently, is susceptible to adverse comments about the validity and reliability of its findings. The goal is to balance the insider's view of reality (the language learner) with that of the researcher's perspective (Geertz 1983), and at the same time to utilize rigorous, ethical research procedures for both analysing and interpreting text data within their micro and macro contexts.

Stating the goal this way raises a number of problematic issues, many of which have been highlighted by critics of CDA (though the criticisms also apply to critical ethnography). Toolan (1997) points out that analysts need to be more critical and more demanding of the methods they use to analyse text, and they must strive for greater thoroughness and strength of evidence in their presentation and argumentation. In other words, the appeal here is for rigorous and meticulous use of analytic and interpretative methods (similar concerns are raised by Hansen and Liu 1997, in their commentary on methodological issues in the study of identity and language, and by Ramanathan and Atkinson (1999), in their review of ethnographic approaches and methods in L2 writing research).

Some, such as Toolan (1997) and van Leeuwen (1993), argue that the methodological diversity of critical research approaches is problematic, and strive instead for a systematic and focused framework in which to work. Diversity leads to a fractured, and therefore weakened, discipline. How are researchers to understand the important relationship between language learning and identity, for example, when they are working in different, sometimes incompatible ways? Without standardization, the results may be snapshots of different language learners in different contexts. But this is more like collecting butterflies than developing theory. Because of this, critical approaches to analysing learner language appear to have a decidedly unclear focus. There are those, however, who welcome the diversity of methodology. (See Chouliaraki and Fairclough 1999.)

Widdowson (1998: 149) warns that adherents of CDA (and one could add critical analysts of all text, including learner language) might be 'too anxious to make a political point, too quick to come to critical conclusions'. The danger here is that such a stance inevitably leads to sacrifices or unwise compromises:

1 A thorough grounding in relevant theory, both within the discipline and interdisciplinary, may not be achieved.
2 Appropriate analytic methods may not be selected, or methods may not be used rigorously enough.
3 Approaches which are considered 'non-critical' (for example, *descriptive* ethnography as opposed to *critical* ethnography) may be scorned and perceived to be irrelevant, resulting in missed opportunities for collaboration and the sharing of interpretations. If this is the case, critical researchers suffer the risk of being viewed as arrogant and their work as narrow in scope and lacking credibility.

Closely related to Widdowson's point is that there is sometimes the tendency by analysts to assume the *a priori* relevance of aspects of context in their analyses. Reporting on the debate which resulted from this observation by Schegloff (1997), Blommaert and Bulcaen (2000: 455–6) comment that 'analysts project their own political biases and prejudices onto their data and analyse them accordingly. Stable patterns of power relations are sketchy, often based on little more than social and political common sense, and then projected on to (and into) discourse'.

Pennycook (1994: 693) suggests that 'the kind of critical reception that critical research receives probably puts far greater emphasis on its being rigorous than does the adherence to methodological procedure or the bickering over statistical interpretation'. But what makes critical research rigorous in the first place? What is it that critical analysts should be *doing* when they disentangle texts? In other words, what are the tools of the critical trade and how are they used most effectively? In SLA the answer to these questions is not very clear. Many of the published research reports of studies which include analyses and interpretations of learner language data gloss over or fail to mention the analytic procedures which they employed, or they recommend to readers a list of secondary sources (and hence those not directly related to the particular study) for information on how the analysis was conducted. And where commentary is made about the analysis it is often in terms of research approach (i.e. broadly placing it within the critical domain) without getting down to the nitty-gritty of the actual analysis.

Conducting a critical analysis

A broad variety of learner language genres have been analysed in critical SLA research. The following, together with illustrative studies, are some examples: classroom interaction (Duff 2002), learner diaries (Norton 2000) and journals (Maguire and Graves 2001), classroom writing (McKay and Wong 1996), writing on the internet (Lam 2000), interview responses in both natural (Schecter and Bayley 1997) and educational settings (Thesen 1997), conversations recorded during field-work observations (Ibrahim 1999), informal conversations with the researcher (Kapp 2001), talk noted from memory after the event (Morgan 1997), and plagiarized text (Angelil-Carter 2000). In some of these texts, more typically in interviews and diaries, learners talk overtly about their actual learning experiences and ideological concerns. In the production of other texts, typically classroom writing and interaction, learners are engaged in learning tasks and activities and so do not address ideological issues explicitly. In these cases, it is up to the text analysts to discover them.

In examining the above kinds of text, the questions critical learner language analysts ask include the following: (a) *What* do language learners say?: i.e. the content of their talk or writing;[3] (b) *How* do they say it?: i.e. the linguistic forms they use; (c) *Why* do they say it?: i.e. the conscious and implicit ideological meanings they express when they talk or write; and (d) *When* do they say it?: i.e. particularly the opportunities they have or are denied to use the target language. The focus here is very much on the text that is produced, but the production of the text involves other elements too. Layder delineates a useful research framework, or 'resource map' (1993: 72), which incorporates both the micro and macro socio-historical context of the research and which identifies the participants as individual selves as well as social beings. He identifies four interconnected research elements, none of which is prime but all of which must be addressed. In terms of language learning, these are: the macro social *context* of the research, such as a nation with its political dispensations and language policies; the social *setting* in which learning takes place, such as schools and families; *situated social activity* which includes face-to-face interaction during communicative events; and finally the *self*, the language learner with his or her changing and multiple identities.

An adequate critical analysis of learner language text needs to take into account all of the above; both the wider and immediate contexts in which the text was produced, the producer of the text, and, centrally, the text itself. Critical analysts, therefore, ask social questions, personal questions and textual questions. As we suggested above, a good starting point for doing so can be found at the interface of critical ethnography and critical discourse analysis. Blommaert and Bulcaen (2000: 461) end their very thorough review of CDA with the following comment: 'a more ethnographically informed stance, in which linguistic practice is embedded in more general patterns of human meaningful action, could be highly productive'. Their view is that currently CDA is burdened by being too linguistic, as is evident in the strong influence of systemic-functional grammar on its analytic methods. (See Fairclough 1989 and Martins 2000.) A move towards a more ethnographic approach to CDA shifts the emphasis towards an approach to analysis which we are advocating in this chapter; that is, the place where CDA and critical ethnography meet. At this junction analysts benefit from the linguistic-discursive analytic tools associated with CDA and the qualitative methods associated with ethnography.[4]

Most important in the analysis, though, is what makes the analysis critical. As we have seen in the above section, learner-language texts, like all discourses, are socially constructed, politically motivated and historically determined. The fundamental aim for critical analysts is 'putting the forms of texts, the processes of production of texts, and the process of reading, together with the structures of power which have given rise to them, into crisis' (Kress 1991: 85). What makes critical analysis different from other forms of analysis is the interpretative and explanative challenge which this entails. Disentangling, deconstructing, or 'putting texts into crisis', requires analysts to go beyond the actual text for their interpretations, and to look to macro social contexts for understandings. This necessitates a certain amount of interpretative freedom (Canagarajah 1999), and it is precisely this freedom required to fill the space between text and macro context that makes it so difficult to prescribe a distinct set of analytic methods or tools for critically analysing learner language. As such, in this chapter, we are limited to demonstration and to offering a set of guidelines for analysing learner language critically, instead of a list of prescriptive steps (as is possible with some other methods described in this book).

However, even in our demonstration of a critical approach and in our presentation of a set of guidelines, we are perhaps flouting one of the underlying principles of critical work, i.e. that analysts should constantly be questioning their practices and the manner in which they present their work (Canagarajah 1996). By presenting these guidelines, therefore, we are giving form to an approach which should continuously be reforming itself, or as Pennycook (2001: 176) says, 'it needs to avoid any static model building' and instead be 'always in motion'. Notwithstanding these tensions, we hope that our suggestions in this chapter provide a theoretical context and a practical basis for analysing data critically.

Before suggesting possible ways of going about doing such an analysis, we introduce data which will be used for illustrative purposes (Table 12.1). The data (from Barkhuizen 2002) consist of a set of extracts from an interview conducted with an Afrikaans-speaking South African who at the time of the interview had been living in New Zealand for only seven months. Franz[5] is a white male and in his early 40s. He and his family lived on the North Shore of the city of Auckland, an area which has a large South African, Afrikaans-speaking community. The researcher had met Franz on a few occasions (for business purposes and socially), but only one 40-minute interview was carried out and audio-recorded. The interview formed part of a much larger data-set. Interviews were held with 28 Afrikaans speakers living in towns and cities across the full length of both New Zealand's main islands. The 15 males and 13 females were aged from 16–75 and had lived in New Zealand from 4 months to 14 years. One of the research questions was to explore, through narrative inquiry, the participants' perspectives of the interrelations of discourse and power in their social contexts (Afrikaans-speaking immigrants living in a so-called English-speaking country), and to discern their own articulation of their identities.

By itself the interview represents an example of what Hansen and Liu (1997: 573) refer to as 'onetime research'; that is, a one-off data collection activity. They rightly argue that such research is inadequate for the study of social identity, which 'is often context bound, and therefore onetime research yields only one view of a complex phenomenon'. The interview needs to be seen in the context of all the other interviews, the full range of research questions and the social problems they address, the history of Afrikaans in South Africa, the status of migrants in New Zealand, and the personal history of the researcher, himself a recent immigrant to New Zealand. Nevertheless, the illustrative examples we use in the rest of this chapter are indicative, however tentative, of some of the connections that can be made among what was said in the interview by the Afrikaans-speaker, the speaker himself, and the socio-historical context of his words.

A final comment about this data: Franz may not be the kind of person that critical methodologists typically investigate. He is disadvantaged in the sense that he is a recent migrant living in New Zealand, and is thus forced to deal with the economic, cultural, and personal difficulties that this move

F = Franz
I = interviewer

[On his expectations and concerns regarding moving to 'English' New Zealand, prior to the move, and on the time he has spent in New Zealand so far.]

F: Honestly, it was really the last worry for me to not be able to communicate. I knew there was a large contingent of Afrikaans speakers here, and I knew I would also be able to speak Afrikaans. I think that softens the blow a little bit. But because I had those English speaking clients, and exposure with her [his wife], we only spoke English only spoke English now and then if we didn't want the children to know what we were saying, till they started picking it up also. No, it wasn't really a concern, but I can tell you sometimes my English gets rusty and then I do stutter a little bit, I realize that. So if I speak to clients who are English speaking, even here now, while I'm talking to you now, I would maybe unrust and I think what happens is sometimes you are trying, there is a word missing, I look at my English vocabulary. If I speak to a Kiwi, sometimes there is a particular word that you wanna use and you can't recall it. The old computer can't find it in the memory bank. It is there and then you can just drop in an Afrikaans word. If you speak in Afrikaans to a South African English speaking person and you say, I can't think of an example now, I can't think of an example now, but you know what I'm saying. Sometimes you are talking and you would say, where is the 'knyprooster'? Because you can't get the English word for, for, I don't even know what it is now. Or 'waar is die... ' [where is the ...]?

I: tongs, I suppose it is?

F: but you can't do it when you speak to a Kiwi guy, because they have no idea what you're talking about. Like a braai, they don't know what a braai is, that is called a barbie [a barbecue], we are going to braai this afternoon. So, another thing is the accent here. With my work [financial adviser], I'm not sure, I am just working amongst South Africans now, I am finding enough clients now, but I feel a bit uneasy, 'cause I think eventually I will have to take the step and cross over, you know I will sometimes have to cross the bridge and maybe just arrive at the other side of the river for a while. Especially, it may dry up on this side, so I'm not really confident enough at this stage yet to, you know to try and conduct business with Kiwis and I think mainly because my language, because the accent, you know you stick out like a sore finger I think when you open your mouth. But there are so many foreigners in Auckland, so maybe that, I don't know yet, but in my subconscious I'm a bit, a little bit concerned about that.

Table 12.1 (continued)

I: Why does the accent worry you though?

F: I think because I'm a foreigner to them and I think we must not, I think we must be honest to ourself, because if you think back to when you were in South Africa, I mean, a Greek or a Portuguese, you would maybe rather do business with your fellow Afrikaans-speaking guy, before you do business, I think even if they were both qualified at the same level. If Jan van der Merwe [a stereotypical South African Afrikaans name] came to me and offered me his services, and maybe say a Greek guy, even though he's been in the country for long, if they were on equal footing I think Jan van der Merwe would have had the better chance to do business with me. And ag that was probably the same here. I don't think we have to kid ourselves about that. So I think you have to be good at what you doing. I don't know how many Kiwis are actually going to for instance South African medical practitioners. How many of their practices, maybe that is something you could find out? Because that would be interesting. Say, there is quite a couple of South African doctors here, do they attract a lot of Kiwi patients or not?

I: In the seven months you've been here, how much Afrikaans do you speak in the family?

F: All the time, all Afrikaans, just like in South Africa, no difference. But I can hear from the way they [his children] talking, only the short time that they have been attending an English school now, they actually learning very fast. And I can hear they sometimes speak English to us now. Sometimes if they start even after such a short time, they start using English words.

I: How old are they at the moment?

F: He is turning 10 next month and she is turning 8 years old.

I: What do you think is going to happen in the long run with their Afrikaans?

F: I think they are going to eventually speak more and more English and they will still, I think they will retain their Afrikaans as long, you know because we will probably speak it as long as we can. And we will probably speak more and more English, maybe we will get New Zealand friends later on.

I: Have you decided on a policy for the family? Have you actually spoken about it?

F: Ja, we decided we speak Afrikaans at home, because it is an extra language they can speak and they will be fluent in English anyway.

Table 12.1 (continued)

So because of they going to English schools. So, I think if we start speaking English, they would probably lose their Afrikaans ability to a large extent. So, you know I think it's in their interest, although Afrikaans you can't really use it much elsewhere in the world, but because there is such a large Afrikaans community, and well, I believe you can speak it in Belgium [laughs], so everyone go to Holland and Belgium because it sounds like Flemish.

Table 12.1 Extracts from an interview with Franz, an Afrikaans-speaking South African living in Auckland, New Zealand

entails. His situation is, however, fairly privileged when compared to the hardships experienced by, for example, refugees in the same country, often children separated from their families for months at a time, and living in centres which certainly do not match the comforts of Franz's rented home. Nevertheless, we have chosen to use this data in order to illustrate that it should be possible to employ a critical methodology for the analysis of any set of data, though we concede that the focus is typically on those who are very much more marginalized than Franz.

Norton's guidelines

Norton (2000: 21–2) summarizes ideas about research which she has gleaned from the work of educational researchers in cultural studies, feminist research, and critical ethnography. These ideas are not only 'highly productive for research on identity and language learning' (2000: 20), but also form a very useful set of guidelines for analysing learner language text. Where appropriate, we will consider these below in conjunction with Fairclough's (2001) proposed analytical framework for CDA, a framework which in a number of ways overlaps with the six research ideas listed by Norton (2000). It is modelled on Bhaskar's concept of 'explanatory critique' (Bhaskar 1986), and it presents a series of five stages for systematically working through the analysis.

The approach to analysis we propose could be managed largely by the qualitative procedures described in Chapter 11 together with critical interpretation and personal reflection. However, because of the CDA influence, the analytic task becomes more 'linguistic': 'CDA must rely ultimately always on quite precise analyses and descriptions of the materiality of language—on close linguistic description' (Kress 1991: 86). We have, therefore, also included ten questions which Fairclough (1989: 110–12) proposes provide a good starting point for a close analysis of the vocabulary, grammar and textual structure of texts. (See Table 12.2.) With regard to these formal features, Fairclough makes the point that any instance of a feature in a text represents a particular choice from among the options available in the discourse(s) in and by which the text was constructed. He goes on to say that 'in order to interpret the features which are actually present in a text, it is generally necessary to take account of what other choices might have been made' (1989: 110). So, what the language learner does not say is just as important as what he or she does say. We have adapted the questions to make them more applicable to the analysis of learner language. Norton's six guidelines provide the structure for the discussion which follows.

1 *The researchers aim to investigate the complex relationship between social structure on the one hand, and human agency on the other, without resorting to deterministic or reductionist analyses.*

This point clearly stipulates that in any analysis a connection needs to be made between individual language learners and social practices. First, who are the learners and what are their histories? What, for example, on a purely descriptive level, are their attributes, such as gender, age, nationality, language background, place of residence, level of education, and occupation? In making sense of Franz's narrative, it is vital to know that he is an Afrikaans-speaking South African who had very recently immigrated to New Zealand, that he is a married father of two children whose wife is unemployed, and that he was struggling to get started as a financial advisor in a new country despite the fact that he had many years' experience in South Africa.

Secondly, how do the learners and the text that they produce relate to both the immediate setting and situated activity (see Layder's 1993 framework above) with which they are engaged as well as to the wider socio-historical context? This is the difficult part. For a start, analysts need to be familiar with these contexts. The familiarity develops partly from empirical observation, life experience and reference to the relevant theoretical literature. Next, researchers must be aware of a social problem within these contexts, one that needs to be addressed with the aim of transformation. Fairclough (2001), in Stage 1 in his analytical framework, points out that critical research begins with a social problem rather than the typical research question. In the case of Franz, it was necessary for the researcher to understand the difficulties non-English speakers experience when moving to New Zealand: the lack of ESOL support; the negative attitudes felt towards South Africans, particularly Afrikaans speakers, because of their association with the pre-1994 apartheid regime; the powerful position which the Afrikaans language held during those days in South Africa; and the plight of all migrants moving to any new country (the expenses they incur, change of lifestyle, finding appropriate educational facilities, fitting in culturally,

A Vocabulary

1 What *experiential* values do words have (i.e. 'a trace of and a cue to the way in which the text producer's experiences of the natural or social world is represented'; experiential value is to do with knowledge and beliefs)?

Are there words which are ideologically contested?

Is there *rewording or overwording* (repeating words or using synonyms)?

What ideologically significant meaning relations (*synonymy, hyponymy, antonymy*) are there between words?

2 What *relational* values do words have (i.e. 'a trace of and a cue to the social relationships which are enacted via the text in the discourse')?

Are there euphemistic expressions?

Are there markedly formal or informal words?

3 What *expressive* values do words have (i.e. 'a trace of and a cue to text producer's evaluation (in the widest sense) of the bit of the reality it relates to'; expressive value is to do with social identities)?

4 What metaphors are used?

B Grammar

5 What experiential values do grammatical features have?

Is agency unclear?

Are processes what they seem?

Are sentences active or passive?

Are sentences positive or negative?

6 What relational values do grammatical features have?

What *modes* (*declarative, grammatical question, imperative*) are used?

Are the pronouns *we* and *you* used, and if so, how?

7 What expressive values do grammatical features have?

Are there important features of *expressive modality*?

8 How are (simple) sentences linked together?

What logical connectors are used?

Are complex sentences characterized by *coordination or subordination*?

What means are used for referring inside and outside the text?

C Textual structures

9 What interactional conventions are used?

Are there ways in which one participant controls the turns of others?

10 What larger-scale structures does the text have?

Table 12.2 Fairclough's vocabulary, grammar, and textual structure questions

confusing identity changes, for instance). Franz was one instance of the embodiment of the full range of these social, political and historical structures. He says, for example, in line 34, 'you know you stick out like a sore finger I think when you open your mouth', and again, 'I think because I'm a foreigner to them and I think we must not, I think we must be honest to ourself' (lines 39–40). The metaphors in line 34 and the use of 'us' and 'them' pronouns in the next example clearly shows that he feels out of place.

2 *The researchers assume that in order to understand social structures we need to understand inequitable relations of power based on gender, race, class, ethnicity and sexual orientation.*

It is clear from this point that the critical analysis of learner language really begins even before any data has been collected. It begins by studying the social practices, including language, operating in a particular group, and it continues by analysing the selected text for evidence of these practices, particularly issues of power, ideology and culture. Texts are socially constructed, and in them lies the substantiations of the social structural constraints such as class, gender and race. Analysts need to pick apart the texts in order to find them.

Fairclough's Stages 2 and 3 add another dimension to this aspect of the analysis. Stage 2 requires the analyst to identify obstacles to the social problem being tackled. This can be accomplished through analysis of: (a) the network of practices (the social order, or more generally, society) it is located within; (b) the relationship of the language (the text) to other elements within the particular practice(s) concerned; and, (c) the discourse (the language itself), which is accomplished by means of structural analysis (the way in which discourses and counterdiscourses are networked, or ordered, together), and linguistic analysis (see Table 12.2). The objective here is to understand how the problem arises and how it is rooted in the way social life is organized, by focusing on the obstacles to its resolution—on what makes it more or less intractable (2001: 236). In Stage 3, the analyst considers whether the social order (network of practices) 'needs' the problem. The point here is to ask whether those who benefit most from the way social life is now organized have an interest in the problem *not* being solved (2001: 236).

In South Africa, Franz's social position was a powerful one. He was a well-educated, white male, and so benefited from the socio-cultural rewards that South African society had to offer; it was easy, in other words, for him to maximize his economic, as well as his cultural and social capital (see Bourdieu 1977). In New Zealand, it has not been so easy. With regard to his work, he says 'I'm not sure', 'I feel a bit uneasy', 'it may dry up on this side' (referring to having only South African clients), 'I'm not really confident', 'I'm a bit, a little bit concerned about that' (lines 27–37). He cannot use Afrikaans, his mother-tongue, the same way he used to: 'my English gets rusty', 'sometimes you are trying [to speak English], there is a word missing' (line 12), and 'you can't do it ['drop in an Afrikaans word' (line 16)] when you speak to a Kiwi guy, because they have no idea what you are talking about' (line 23). And although he continues to use Afrikaans within his family, even that is becoming less frequent: 'And I can hear they [his children] sometimes speak English to us now' (lines 61–2), 'I think they are going to eventually speak more and more English' (line 68), and 'they would probably lose their Afrikaans ability to a large extent' (lines 78–9). Afrikaans, a clear symbol of Franz's power in South Africa, is not only less dominant in New Zealand, but he and his children are using it less and less. Franz's positioning in his world has changed, and because of this, the person he is, his identity, has also changed. One could ask whether or not these assimilative processes are beneficial to New Zealand society. Will Franz become a more productive member of the workforce if he becomes more proficient in English? Will his children become 'better citizens' if they, as they appear to be doing, steadily shift to English? One could also ask what obstacles (to use Fairclough's word) lie in the way of Franz becoming a productive member of society (i.e. to fulfil society's needs) as well as a person who feels good about himself and his family (i.e. to fulfil his own needs). We have mentioned some possibilities under the first point above. In addition to these, there exists a strange contradiction in New Zealand society, whereby on the one hand there are those who welcome immigrants and would like to see them settled and integrated into New Zealand society as soon as and as easily as possible, and on the other hand, there are those (for example, some politicians and some members of the general population who regularly express their thoughts in the media—particularly newspapers and talk-back radio—who feel threatened by the government's immigration policy and, more specifically, by the immigrants themselves. Franz is caught up in this contradiction between the needs (again using Fairclough's word) of the government and the feelings of some of the population. He admits this himself: 'I think because I'm a foreigner to them and I think we must not, I think we must be honest to ourself' (lines 39–40). His repetition of 'I think' here perhaps signifies the uncertainty he feels about his own position and needs in his new country.

Of course, this is not all that is happening to Franz. The above description sounds overly deterministic and it presents only a very broad, one-dimensional picture of Franz's experiences. Like one of the women in Norton's (2000) study who was able to position herself in relation to her co-workers in a way which allowed her to assume more power in the conversations she had with them (i.e. positioning herself as parent and them as children), Franz too was able to get on with his job by initially acquiring South African clients, 'I am just working amongst South Africans now' (lines 27–8), and thereby readily uses Afrikaans for business purposes. Furthermore, he was white (a distinct advantage in Auckland considering the frequently expressed negative attitudes towards, for example, the large Asian migrant population), rented a house in a safe middle-class suburb and his children went to a very good school. So at the same time as being a migrant feeling insecure in a strange country, he was a productive member of society living a comfortable life. There were no doubt a number of other constantly changing discourses in which Franz engaged and within which he negotiated his multiple, sometimes contradictory, identities.

3 *The researchers are interested in the way individuals make sense of their own experience.*

It is the insider perspective that is important here (Davis 1995; Strauss and Corbin 1998). The researcher attempts to describe and explain how language learners live their lives from their own (emic) points of view: 'particular actors, in particular places, at particular times, fashion meaning out of events and phenomena through prolonged, complex processes of social interaction involving history, language and action' (Schwandt 1998: 221–2). The analyst's job is to find out what these meanings are. The methods for interpreting and explaining learner language text (the data where the meanings are to be found) are similar to those associated with qualitative ethnographic research (see Chapter 11) and narrative inquiry (Clandinin and Connelly 2000), but with a critical edge. This does not mean simply adding a critical dimension to already established methodologies, however. Rather, doing a critical analysis means opening up a whole new array of questions and concerns about power, disparity and access (Pennycook 2001).

During the interview with Franz he put into words his own interpretations of his life; how he makes sense of his experience.[6] This is evident, for example, by his use of first person 'I' throughout the interview. By doing so he expresses agency quite clearly and together with the active form of many of his sentences situates his actions and his thoughts quite explicitly within the realm of his life experiences. Analysts interweave the learners' accounts, in which they often explicitly reference ideological matters, with their own interpretations of 'what is going on'. In other words, they integrate *their* perspectives with *learners'* perspectives represented in *text*, in which the learners may explicitly, but always implicitly, comment on issues of power and ideology in their discursive lives.

4 *The researchers are interested in locating their research within a historical context.*

This aim is consistent with one of the principles of CDA listed above; in order to understand the complexity of discursive practices, with learner language as the core in our case, we have to situate the learners and their communities in their changing historical contexts. Later on in Franz's interview,[7] he uses rugby as a vehicle for expressing his national identity as a South African, but one who is aware of the fragility of this status:

> I think if I was younger, if I was like twenty or twenty-five now, I would have made a more concerted effort maybe to say 'right, let me, you know,

> let me kiss the silver fern', you know to really become a supporter, but I mean I will surely support the All Black team except when they play against South Africa. But maybe, who knows, that comes naturally, but maybe in twenty years time I will start getting to a point where I can start supporting the All Blacks against South Africa.

This statement is loaded with meanings, many of which can only be explained with reference to the rugby playing history between the two nations, their team and national symbols, and the importance of rugby to the peoples of both countries. This short piece of text relates to many discourses about rugby between South Africa and New Zealand which have taken place over the years, particularly surrounding the Rugby World Cup and the disastrous South African tour to New Zealand in 1981, which for political reasons split the New Zealand nation in two. Franz, an enthusiastic rugby supporter, would necessarily change a major part of who he is and where he comes from were he to side with the All Blacks.

Canagarajah's (1993) account of a group of 22 students' perspectives of English language teaching at a Sri Lankan university begins with a section headed *Contextualizing the study* in which he outlines the history of English education in Sri Lanka (formerly Ceylon) since 1796. The historical colonial context, which the students themselves refer to in the study, provides an integral constituent for understanding the attitudes and beliefs of the participant students. Watson-Gegeo and Gegeo (1995) refer to both horizontal and vertical levels, or dimensions of context. Analysing horizontal context means analysing 'behavior, interactions, and events as they unfold in time, together with the immediate circumstances affecting them', whereas an analysis of vertical context requires 'examining events and behavior in light of both the long-term history of relationships in the immediate settings and the relevant larger historical processes related to vertical levels' (1995: 61). The experiences Canagarajah's students bring with them to their English lessons have been shaped by Sri Lankan society's various political dispensations in society at large, educational policies at schools, and socialization practices at home and in the community.

5 *The researchers reject the view that any research can claim to be objective or unbiased.*

When analysing learner-language text, analysts should always be self-reflexive. This means that they should constantly question their own position in relation to the project. (This is equivalent to Fairclough's Stage 5, which requires the analyst to reflect on where s/he is coming from, and her/his own social positioning.) They should reflect on their own subjective experience and knowledge as well as that of the language learner participants. Simon and Dippo (1986: 197) specify that critical ethnographers need to acknowledge that their work is 'constituted and regulated through historical relations of power and existing material conditions'. This is more than mere recognition of the subjectivity of any analysis; it is a challenge to analysts to become more aware of their own beliefs, values and personal histories, all of which are constitutive of the interpretation and explanation of the text data. Part of the analysis, then, is reflecting on what they are.

It would have been impossible for the analyst (Barkhuizen 2002) to ignore his own history in analysing Franz's interview. He too is a South African who has immigrated to New Zealand, and, although not a native Afrikaans speaker, he could empathize with the difficulties associated with moving to and settling in a new country. Furthermore, he has knowledge and experience of South African society, having lived most of his life in that country. He is able to speak Afrikaans and has insight into the history and politics of Afrikaners. An adequate explanation of Franz's words cannot be reached apart from the analyst's personal history—a different analyst would undoubtedly reach different conclusions.

6 *The researchers believe that the goal of educational research is social and educational change.*

This point has to do with educational change, but in the world of language learners there are other socio-institutional structures which have been targeted for transformation, particularly those involving immigration and employment. The transformative agenda of critical analysis has been discussed above in relation to critical theory. But in practice, what does it mean? From the analyst's point of view, there is a shift from focusing on the structure of the learner's social world to what is missing or what is wrong in that world, or as Fairclough (2001: 239) puts it, 'rather than focusing on how the network of practices [the social order] holds together, it focuses on the gaps and contradictions that exist'. (He labels Stage 4 in his analytical framework *Identifying possible ways past the obstacles.*) Kress (1991: 93) points out that 'if texts are the repositories of the effects of socio-cultural practices, then an adequate theory of text should turn texts into useful resources for socio-cultural analysis', and if this is the case, then the results of the analysis should be available as useful resources for sociocultural change. This, of course, relates directly back to the very first step: identifying a social problem at the start of the project. The analysis should contribute towards solving that problem.

Once again, there is no prescription for doing this; no easy step-by-step method for filling the gaps. Fairclough (2001: 239) addresses this question as follows:[8]

> How can critical analysis of texts and interactions contribute to emancipatory change? This requires critical reflection on how we are working, on how we write, on the meta-language we use for analysing semiosis, on where we publish, and so forth. For instance, as academics, when we identify and specify a problem, do we involve those whose problem it is? If we don't, are there ways that we could?

We have hinted at ways in which Franz's sense of insecurity and isolation as a foreigner could be addressed. More data than those gathered from a onetime interview would be needed to gain a fuller, clearer picture of what was happening in Franz's life. However, based on the data that we have included in this chapter (Tables 12.1 and 12.4), and considering also the experiences of the other Afrikaans-speaking immigrants in New Zealand who were interviewed (and no doubt the experiences of other language groups as well), we speculate that sources of change could, at the micro level, be located in the following: immigrant family counselling, ESOL provision, school-based workshops and meetings for the whole family, church activities (particularly Afrikaans church services) and recreational activities, such as gatherings for sports and entertainment. On the macro level, transformation could be accomplished through the development of settlement programmes for new immigrants and the changing of attitudes towards immigrants. Some of these proposals for change, of course, would be easier to achieve than others.

An example of a critical approach to analysing learner language: a contextualist perspective

McKay and Wong's (1996) longitudinal, ethnographic study of the English learning of four Chinese-speaking immigrant students at a junior high school in California is a classic example of a study which examines the complex interrelationship between discourse and power in the social environment of each language learner. They use discourse to refer to 'a set of historically grounded statements that exhibit regularities in presuppositions, thematic choices, values, etc.: that delimit what can be said about something, by whom, when, where, and how; and that are underwritten by some form of institutional authority' (1996: 579). Their investigation of the students' language learning experiences is very different from both product orientations to SLA research, which focus on the acquisition of the formal code with reference to native-speaker proficiency as the norm, and process orientations, which attempt to understand SLA by examining individual learners' reports on the strategies they use to accomplish successful learning. McKay and Wong's orientation, on the other hand, contextualizes the language learning by considering the social context in which learning takes place; specifically, they foreground the interrelations of discourse and power within that context.

In their study, McKay and Wong situate the focal students in a number of discourses which they identified during their research. The five most distinct and significant in the social language-learning lives of the students are the following: colonialist/racialized discourses on immigrants, model-minority discourse, Chinese cultural nationalist discourses, social and academic school discourses, and gender discourses. These discourses do not operate in isolation. Instead, they interact with each other in complex ways, each at times being more or less salient in the social interactions of the participants. Furthermore, it is during these social interactions that the social identities of the learners come into play; following Peirce (1995), McKay and Wong point out that 'when language learners speak, they are not only exchanging information with target language speakers, but they are constantly organizing and reorganizing a sense of who they are and how they relate to the social world' (1996: 579). In this sense, then, social identity is multiple and fluid, and it is this complex, changing self that the learners in this study bring to the task of learning English.

McKay and Wong point out, however, that it is not only the case that learners' identities, and hence their language learning, are shaped by discourses; that is, the relationship between discourses and identities is not unidirectional. Learners do not merely fill subject positions determined by power relations within discourses, they also exercise agency in terms of their positioning in these relations of power. They deploy and participate in counter-discourses, discourses which typically forge for the participants more powerful positions or discourses which enable them to resist being positioned by dominant others. One of the students, for example, Brad, was a Chinese mainlander; the other three students were from Taiwan, possibly considered by mainlanders as 'geographically marginal and less cultured' (1996: 598). He deployed a kind of Chinese cultural nationalist discourse by emphasizing this status in interactions with the other students. McKay and Wong point out that he did so to counter association with model-minority discourses; he felt that he could not measure up because of his poor performance at school, his perceived disruptive behaviour in class, and his lower socio-economic status in comparison with the Taiwanese families. Another student, Michael, was very proficient in sports, and he used this 'school sports discourse' to contradict the model-minority discourse, to which, like Brad, he could not always measure up because of his poor performance as an ESL student.

The link between the rather abstract concept of discourses[9] and the processes of L2 acquisition is made most evident through the concept of investment, which was introduced earlier. Put simply, through mobilizing and countering multiple discourses the learners invest, to varying degrees, in the target language as well as in their own identities. Michael, for example, was not particularly invested in acquiring written English 'because of the influence on immigrants of colonialist/racialized discourses as well as social school discourses, both of which place a premium on social English as an indicator of functionality in U.S. society' (1996: 592). Because of his success in school sports, he could more easily fit into the gender expectations of American school subculture and was able to establish friendships with students from various racial/ethnic groups. McKay and Wong believe that Michael directed his investment in learning English specifically on aural/oral skills because of the way he chose to define positively his social identity (i.e. his achievements in sports).

McKay and Wong's study makes a noteworthy contribution to social identity research and theory in the field of SLA. From a research methodological perspective the study is clearly ethnographic. (See Table 12.3 below.) The data collection procedures are described in detail, but there is no description of analytic methods. We assume that they are those typically associated with the analysis of qualitative data, such as observation field notes, interview transcripts and written records. Comments about analysis remain at a theoretical level, foregrounding a critical perspective to SLA research, at the expense of comments about analytical details at a mechanical, practical level, i.e. what the researchers actually did when organizing, interpreting and explaining the data. Nevertheless, this article is relevant here because the authors use actual learner language to provide evidence in support of their findings. They discuss the four focal students' English learning experiences in separate sections, and within these they display samples of their writing and extracts from written language assessment tasks, and they report on comments made by the students during informal conversations about their learning and their discursive practices. The analysis of learner language in this study has enabled the researchers to discover what the students have to say about their learning (i.e. by analysing the content of their language). At the same time, and in a less overt way, the learner language provides them with a window through which to interpret the students' negotiation of multiple discourses and multiple identities within the social context of their learning (i.e. by analysing how language is used).

Finally, McKay and Wong's article is one of the few critical accounts of L2 learning that are readable, informative and interesting. It is written in an accessible style and the stories of the four students are compelling enough to capture the attention of both SLA theorists and practising classroom teachers.

Task: An exercise in critical analysis

Table 12.4 includes extracts from the second half of the interview with Franz. Here he starts to talk explicitly about cultural and identity issues: how he sees himself as a non-native English speaker living in a new country. Tajfel (1974: 69) defines social identity as 'that part of an individual's self-concept which derives from his knowledge of his membership of a social group (or groups) together with the emotional significance attached to that membership'. Bearing in mind these definitions, and through careful analysis of the given text,[10] consider the following questions:

1 *Identity*

1.1 What identities does Franz foreground in these extracts? Quote short extracts from his actual words to support your answer.

Research question	There is no research question as such. Instead, and typical of critical research, the researchers start with a social problem (see Fairclough 2001): the difficulties associated with the English-language learning of immigrant Chinese students in an American school. By examining their learning they attempted to 'identify some of the multiple discourses in which the focal students were socially situated and to track the way they negotiated multiple, dynamic, and often contradictory identities' (McKay and Wong 1996: 580). They also related the students' development of English language skills to the coping strategies they employed while being positioned by and positioning themselves within relations of power.
Participants	Four Chinese-speaking students; two males and one female from Taiwan and one male from Shanghai. They all attended the same junior high school in California. All were recent arrivals in the U.S. with minimal English.
Data collection	Data collection took place over a two-year period. While the students were in the seventh and eighth grades they were followed by the researchers. They visited the students' classes 31 times over the two-year period, each visit lasting at least 5 hours. Writing samples were collected from three language assessment tasks, which were not part of the school curriculum, and from the writing portfolio of one of the students. Informal conversations were held with the focal students, their parents and their peers. Interviews were conducted with school personnel, including the principal and the ESL teachers.
Analysis	The method of analysis is not specified. Because the study is ethnographic in character, the analysis no doubt utilizes the procedures typically associated with the analysis of qualitative data. Analysis is implied in theoretical discussions of the interconnectedness of discourses, identities and language development (i.e. interpretations involve making connections between what the students write and say, and the discourses in which they participate in relations of power), rather than specifically described at a mechanical, practical level; i.e. what was actually done with the data (e.g. how it was organized, selected, coded, categorized and interpreted).

Table 12.3 (continued)

Findings	The following salient points emerge from the study (McKay and Wong 1996: 603–4): 1 'Learners are extremely complex social beings with a multitude of fluctuating, at times conflicting, needs and desires'. 2 'As subjects with agency and a need to exercise it, the learners, while positioned in power relations and subject to the influences of discourses, also resist positioning, attempt repositioning, and deploy discourses and counter-discourses'. 3 The learners' 'historically specific needs, desires, and negotiations' constitute the very fabric of their lives and determine their investment in learning English. 4 'Agency-enhancement and identity-enhancement, rather than investment-enhancement, appear to be paramount considerations' in their study. 5 The four language skills have different values for the learners and they are highly selective in their investment in any one or combination of the four. 6 The students' selection of coping strategies appears to be related to their identities and to their investment in learning English. The authors stress that it is necessary to 'understand the immigrant second-language learner as a complex social being, and the school, especially the ESL classroom, as a contestatory discursive site' (1996: 604), despite the caution that discourses and power relations are not amenable to quick intervention. Not doing so would make the task of educational change far more difficult than it already is.

Table 12.3 Summary of McKay and Wong's (1996) study of the English learning of four Chinese-speaking students in a junior high school in California

1.2 How do the short extracts you have chosen actually point to an identity? Why are they expressions of identity?

1.3 Do any of these identities seem to contradict each other?

1.4 Why is it difficult to decide on these identities?

2 *Textual features*

2.1 Consider Franz's use of pronouns in this text. How does he use them to express his affiliation to various language, cultural and national groups?

2.2 Identify examples of negative sentences/clauses (for example, 'as long as the people coming in haven't got too much of political

[Comments on using Afrikaans outside of the family domain]

F: I think one must be careful not to, because there are so many South Africans, you mustn't easily say, you must watch your words, you mustn't say 'Ek wens hierdie ou suurstof dief voor die tou wil nou vinniger maak' [I wish this old oxygen-thief ahead in the line would hurry up], they may turn around and say 'Jysal eendag een word' [You will be one one day]. I think that has happened to a lot of people here. I think the Kiwis, they understand, or they know that you're from South Africa, they, because they know the accent. There's a couple of new expressions, you now the Kiwi expressions, is interesting to me and there is some of them that I like, which I can relate to. Especially the one where they say 'no worries', it rolls easily off the tongue, and I like that one a lot. 'No worries', 'see you later', 'see you mate' and so on, so I think one will probably use those expressions more and more. They have got a distinct, you know, I know that they say 'car' [with a broad New Zealand accent], they don't say 'car', like us. 'Carpark', that doesn't sound right. And they mayor is a 'mare' [pronounces it in an exaggerated manner], I thought the mare is a female horse. I think one just has to get used to that.

I: So you are quite happy to make those sorts of adjustments?

F: Ja, I'll probably eventually also say 'the mare', listen to the mare's speech.

I: Language and culture are obviously very closely tied to each other. Before you left SA, did you have concerns about fitting in culturally?

F: I thought they were much similar than us, the ordinary New Zealander. I think they were also descendants from English settlers, from Europe. So it seems to me that there is a big inflow of Asians and I think if it is good for the economy, it is good, I mean if they bring money in, there is a lot of South East Asian countries which are becoming very affluent nowadays. And I think because countries are small, and I don't think there is all that much resources, so if that can kick-start the economy or keep the economy rolling, I think it is good for the country, yes. I don't know about problems, I think as long as the people coming in haven't got too much of political aspirations, you know I know the other day, similar to us, I don't think you wanna say, we should say they must bring in Afrikaans as a language here at school, I think you just looking for trouble if you wanna do that. I think you must practise your Afrikaans at your braai place or in your own time. Actually I make biltong [dried meat], I've got biltong hanging in my garage, so I do those things, I'm busy cooking 'boontjiesop' [bean soup] and make pap [thick porridge], so we do

Table 12.4 (*continued*)

it here. Although I think at this stage it feels to me that there is a bit of a difference between the cultures, between what we are used to and the Kiwis. But maybe that is just purely because I haven't, I don't know them well enough or I haven't got good Kiwi friends yet. But it feels to me that there is still a bit of a barrier between you know the way they operate, there is still a bit of us and them to me. I think I wouldn't like it to be like that, if I stay like that I think it will eventually evaporate. I hope so.

I: Language is very closely connected to who you are. Do you still feel Afrikaans, or do you feel you are changing a bit?

F: I am really with one foot. I am saying to the New Zealanders, they say 'are you from South Africa?', I would say 'yes, I am half New Zealander now, I'm half South African'. I think when you come here you have got so much other things to contend with, you know, finding a job, getting resettled, finding a house, finding a school for your children, you know, trying to get your money out at the best rates. There are millions of things that you have to think about, that you probably don't find time to ponder about 'am I eventually becoming and giving up my mother tongue or my culture'. I think about it now and then, I just think briefly about it, there is not really an answer to that. Because I will always have my roots. I had a client in South Africa, for instance, I had a couple of guys from Scotland and although they were in South Africa for thirty years, they still spoke with a very distinct Scottish accent, they were rolling the 'r' and the one guy still had pictures of all the castles, the Edinburgh castle and snow and he had this big table with a swords, it was something in the order of the knights of the castle. So I think the world is becoming at the moment, you know it is a global village so I think it is not happening to me alone, it is happening to a lot of other people as well.

I: Do you personally still feel you're the same person?

F: Ja, I think so. Because I was over forty when I came, so maybe in twenty years time when I've paid taxes here for twenty years, I will feel more like a Kiwi then, I think it is a long process really. I speak to a guy who was actually from England and he was in the States for a while. He is over sixty now and he has been here for over twenty years and he still thinks, he is much more of a Kiwi than me, but he still thinks a little bit as he is an Englishman. So, I think that is probably similar. I think for my children, they will be much more Kiwis. They will probably be proper Kiwis, because they will say 'yes, I grew up in South Africa, I remember about South Africa, still got relatives there'. So for me, I will still stay Afrikaner probably.

Table 12.4 (*continued*)

I: How do you feel about your children changing though?

F: I think that is the price that I have to pay for wanting them to come here for the reasons that I came here, you know, for better safety and so on. You can't have your bread buttered on both sides. I'm very thankful, I think if there wasn't an Afrikaans community here, to soften the, to make the ride easier, it would have been much more difficult. So I really take my hat off to the pioneers who came ten years ago. I think it must have been really difficult for them. For sure, if I went to Germany for instance now, where there were no South Africans and I was just exposed to Germans all the time, it would have been totally different experience. For sure. Or even in an English speaking country where you haven't got South Africans, it would have been much more difficult.

Table 12.4 Further extracts from an interview with Franz, an Afrikaans-speaking South African living in Auckland, New Zealand

aspirations', lines 33–4). What does Franz accomplish by expressing these ideas in the negative? How could they have been expressed in the positive?

2.3 Consider the vocabulary which Franz himself uses in the interview. How do his words express his perceptions of the social interactions in which he engages? Remember that 'power relations [which are often inequitable] play a crucial role in social interactions between language learners and target language speakers' (Peirce 1995: 3).

3 *Discourse*

3.1 What dominant discourses (in the entire interview; see Tables 12.1 and 12.4) is Franz situated in; that is, the discourses with which he engages? Quote evidence from the interview to support your observation.

3.2 Is there evidence of any counter-discourses which he deploys? Quote evidence from the interview to support your observation.

Final comment

This chapter is different from the others in this book in a number of ways: first, it introduces a *critical* element to analysis. Learner language text is examined not only for what it tells us about language development but also for what it tells us about the learners themselves and their social worlds. The text reflects the multiple and often contradictory discourses of that social world, a world in which learners engage in inequitable power relationships and in which and by which their own multiple identities are constructed. Secondly, it has not been possible to stipulate a prescriptive set of ordered procedures (chronologically or otherwise) for conducting a critical analysis. For a start there isn't one which has been proposed or consistently used in SLA learner language research. Furthermore, doing so would contradict almost everything we have said in this chapter: critical analysts are self-reflexive analysts; they constantly question and change their methods, and they reflect on and engage with their own personal histories during the course of the analysis. Finally, critical analyses require of their analysts very demanding interpretative and explanative work, the consequences of which have important implications for change. In other words, there is a lot of difficult interpreting to do. Besides the challenge of moving well beyond the text to look for answers to ideological concerns, a high level of responsibility and commitment to tackle these concerns is required. And if this all seems overwhelming, the words of Marcus (1998: 37) may be reassuring: 'You can't really say it all; all analyses no matter how totalistic their rhetorics, are partial'.

Notes

1 See particularly Beebe and Giles (1984) and Giles and Byrne (1982) on Intergroup Theory, a theory which takes into account the relationship between the learner's group (the ingroup) and the target-language group (the outgroup), and Schumann's (1986) Acculturation Model, which has as its main ingredient the learner adapting to a new culture. It was established to explain the acquisition of an L2 by immigrants in naturalistic majority-language contexts.

2 Bonny Norton Peirce is referenced as Peirce pre-1997 and as Norton from 1997 onwards.

3 In this chapter, we focus only on language forms (speech and writing), as is the case with most learner language analysts. Some analysts, especially in the field of CDA, are interested in other forms of meaning-making such as visual images (pictures, diagrams), gestures and facial expressions—what Fairclough (2001) references as *semiosis*.

4 See Chapter 11.

5 A pseudonym.

6 A broader research approach would have included other data such as multiple interviews, not only with Franz but also with work colleagues and members of his family, observation of family life, open-ended questionnaires and even diary entries.

7 See further extracts from the interview in the task section at the end of the chapter.

8 See also Canagarajah (1996).

9 The work of both McKay and Wong (1996) and Norton (1997b) has been critiqued for its static use of the notion of 'discourse'. (See Price 1999 and Thesen 1997.)

10 When introducing the first half of Franz's interview we mentioned that the interview represents only one aspect of his experience. Further ethnographic investigation would include, inter alia, both situational and macro contextual factors as well.

13 Metaphor analysis

Introduction

A metaphor consists of a comparison between two dissimilar notions where one notion is to be understood in terms of the other notion. In this chapter we will explore how the analysis of the metaphors that L2 learners use to talk about their learning can shed light on how they conceptualize the language they are learning, the process of learning itself and, in particular, the problems and obstacles they experience on the 'learning journey'. Metaphors provide 'windows' for examining the cognitions and feelings of learners. Because they are usually employed without consciousness on the part of learners they are arguably less subject to false-representation than learners' direct comments about learning. Our concern will be with the identification and interpretation of the metaphors that can be identified in learner self-report data. We will not consider how learners comprehend and produce metaphors.[1]

Historical and theoretical background

What Steen (1994) calls 'metaphorology' has undergone a remarkable revolution in the last twenty years or so. Traditionally, metaphor was viewed as a unique form of linguistic expression associated with literature, in particular poetry. It involved 'fancy language' that was in some way unusual or deviant. As such, it was largely ignored by linguists. At the end of the seventies, a number of publications, in particular Lakoff and Johnson's (1980) *Metaphors We Live By*, convincingly argued the case for metaphor as central not just to language but to human cognition as well. Lakoff and Johnson's arguments, subsequently repeated and developed in a series of publications throughout the eighties (for example, Lakoff 1986 and 1987; Lakoff and Turner 1989), are based on two principal contentions.

The first is that metaphorical use far from being special and rare is in fact very ordinary and commonplace. Lakoff and Turner (1989), argue that 'metaphor is a tool so ordinary that we use it unconsciously and automatically, with so little effort that we hardly notice it' (1989: xi). They note that people have the potential to construct and understand an infinitely large range of metaphors but, in fact, draw on a fairly well-defined and limited set. They refer to these as 'conventionalized metaphors', some of which are 'basic' in the sense that they are conceptually well-established, very widely used, and often realized linguistically by means of formulaic expressions. Basic metaphors are 'conceptually indispensable' according to Lakoff and Turner. Examples of such metaphors are 'People are containers' and 'People are machines'.

Lakoff and Turner's second contention is that metaphors are 'a matter of thought not language' (1989: 107). That is, people store metaphorical mappings as mental schemata which they draw on automatically in order to process metaphorical expressions in understanding and production. Such metaphors, therefore, are reflective of the modes of thought of the members of the linguistic community that employ them. Metaphor, then, is seen not just as a linguistic embellishment, but as a primary means by which people make sense of the world around them.

These contentions are not uncontroversial. It is not clear, for example, whether expressions such as 'input', a term in common usage in SLA, is best seen as metaphorical (i.e. a slot in the particular form of the 'People are machines' metaphor) or as polysemous, with the specific meaning attached to it in SLA as just one of several possible meanings. Glucksberg *et al.* (1992) have argued that many conventionalized metaphors cease to function as metaphors (i.e. they are no longer processed analogically). The 'analytic' methods used by Lakoff to investigate metaphor only demonstrate the existence of two semantic domains in a metaphor, not two conceptual domains. It is a moot point, then, whether a semantic mapping corresponds to a conceptual mapping.

In the eyes of many researchers, however, metaphor can serve as a tool for investigating how people view their world. In western thought (and perhaps in other cultures as well), for example, 'life' is viewed as a 'journey', 'love' as 'fire', and death as 'night'. But these conventional metaphors do more than construct particular realities; they also channel and constrain thought. As Lakoff and Turner (1989: 63) put it 'anything we rely on constantly, unconsciously, and automatically is so much a part of us that it cannot be easily resisted, in large part because it is barely noticed'. Highly conventional metaphors tend to lose their metaphorical power and be understood directly without awareness of their non-literal nature (Hoffman and Kemper 1987); they become 'literalized'.

Metaphor analysis has now become an accepted tool in both educational and applied linguistic enquiry. We will briefly consider three areas of research in which it has figured; (1) SLA researchers' conceptualization of their field of study, (2) teacher cognitions and (3) L2 learners' accounts of their own learning. In addition, research has been carried out into learners' metaphorical competence in an L2 (i.e. how they process metaphor) but this will not concern us here.

Several researchers have examined the metaphors that SLA researchers use to discuss L2 acquisition. Kramsch (1995) points out that the 'input-black box-output' metaphor is dominant in SLA. She notes that the choice of a metaphor drawn from the source domain of electrical engineering was expeditious because it linked SLA to an upcoming and prestigious field and thus ensured both respectability and funding. The metaphor was also useful to researchers in that its entailments led them to ask important questions such as 'what is the *nature* of input?' and 'what *counts* as input?' But Kramsch also notes that the metaphor soon took on 'a life of its own' (1985: 11) with the result that it limited the scope of SLA research and, also, ultimately reinforced the divide between researchers who study input and teachers who mediate it. Lantolf (1996) sees all SLA theories as inherently metaphorical. Like Kramsch, he claims that what he calls the 'mind-as-computer' metaphor has achieved an unhealthy dominance in the field of linguistics and SLA. He also warns against the dangers of literalized metaphors restricting thought and limiting theory development. He argues for an acceptance of theoretical pluralism in SLA, and suggests that to keep the field fresh and vibrant it is necessary to continually create new metaphors. Block (1999) also uses metaphor analysis to show how SLA has been 'framed' as 'monotheistic'. His analysis indicates that SLA has been characterized as problematic and anarchic because of the existence of multiple theories (as opposed to a single, widely-accepted theory), because of the application of multiple criteria for evaluating theories, and because of the absence of replication studies. Block argues the need to study the 'framing' function of metaphors. Ellis (2001a) analyses articles written by a number of well-known SLA researchers and identifies seven general metaphors they use to write about L2 acquisition. The most commonly used metaphor is that of 'Learner as machine'. As claimed by Kramsch and Lantolf, the 'Learner as container' is also widely used. These two metaphors project a view of the learner as passive and dehumanized. However, other popular metaphors—'learner as negotiator' and 'learner as problem solver' present learners as agents responsible for their own learning.

The general drift of these arguments is that SLA has become narrowly psycholinguistic because of the power of a limited set of metaphors to direct and constrain the field. The same point is made by Firth and Wagner (1997). However, they draw attention to a different metaphor, which has characterized the thinking of SLA researchers—the metaphor of the learner-as-defective communicator. They note that learners are typically viewed as non-native speakers who are 'handicapped' by the 'problem' of an under-developed competence. They suggest that this metaphor has enabled researchers to ignore the contextual and interactional aspects of language use and acquisition in favour of psycholinguistic aspects. Like Lantolf, they call for a widening of the research agenda to include approaches that view the learner more holistically by taking into account the social context in which learners learn, that adopt an emic perspective (i.e. (take the learner's perspective) and that are more critically sensitive to fundamental concepts such as 'native speaker' and 'interlanguage'. Interestingly, Ellis' (2001a) did find that Peirce (1995), whose approach accords with that recommended by Firth and Wagner, employed a very different set of metaphors to those found in mainstream SLA, for example 'Learner as struggler' and 'Learner as investor'.

Several studies have looked at how teachers conceptualize their work. Briscoe (1991), for example, shows in a case study of a science teacher struggling to change his style of teaching that 'the metaphors teachers use to make sense of their roles have a substantial affect on classroom practice' (1991: 197). The images teachers use metaphorically help to organize their belief sets and serve as an aid to reflection-on-practice. Block (1997) reports clear differences in the metaphors used by teachers to conceptualize what language learning involves and their actual roles in the classroom. Cortazzi and Jin (1999) examined the metaphors employed by teachers in their oral accounts of classroom experiences. They found that 'teachers' accounts of significant learning events are deeply and widely pervaded by metaphors' (1999: 157). For example, they discussed breakthroughs in their students' learning in terms of such expressions as 'it seemed to click' and 'it came on', reflecting the idea that students had to struggle to learn. Another common metaphor the teachers made use of was 'Learning is movement'. Cortazzi and Jin also suggest a number of reasons why teachers use metaphors, including those of 'identifying for themselves what they actually experience' and 'organizing systematic concepts'. De Guerrero and Villamil (2002) report the metaphors they elicited from 22 Puerto Rican teachers of English. The most common metaphors characterized teachers in the 'classical roles of leader, provider of knowledge, agent of change, nurturer and artist' (2002: 113). Other metaphors characterized learners according to how active they were (for example, 'player' vs. 'piece of clay'). The authors suggest that these metaphors were 'culturally sanctioned' and reflected the teachers' 'professional culture'.

There have been fewer studies that have examined the metaphors used by L2 learners. Cameron and Low's (1999a) *Researching and Applying Metaphor,* for example, contains no article dealing specifically with L2 learners' metaphors.[2] Oxford (2001) makes use of the personal narratives kept by 473 foreign/second language learners to identify the metaphors they used to talk about three teaching approaches. Metaphors characteristic of the 'autocratic teaching approach' included 'teacher as manufacturer', 'teacher as tyrant' and 'teacher as hanging judge'. Examples of metaphors reflecting the 'democratic/participatory teaching approach' were 'teacher as challenger and catalyst' and 'teacher as family member'. The third approach, the '*laisser-faire* teaching approach', was reflected in metaphors that emphasized the dysfunctional aspects of teachers such as 'teacher as blind eye' and 'teacher as bad baby-sitter'. Oxford reports that different groups of learners favoured different metaphors and also varied in the extent to which they employed metaphors to talk about teachers and teaching.

Ellis (2002) examined the metaphors used by beginner learners of L2 German in diaries that they kept over a six-month period. This Ellis (2002) study is examined in greater detail later in this chapter.

It is clear that metaphor analysis has gained in popularity as a method for examining how participants in the teaching-learning process construct themselves and the activities they engage in. The underlying assumption is that metaphor is not just a matter of language but of the mental representation of thought and feeling and, as such, its analysis can afford a person-oriented view of learners' cognitions and affective states. As yet, however, metaphor analysis has been little exploited as a means of studying learner cognitions.

Conducting a metaphor analysis

According to Cameron and Low (1999b: 88) metaphor analysis involves 'collecting samples of linguistic metaphors used to talk about the topic... generalizing from them the conceptual metaphors they exemplify, and using the result to suggest understandings or thought patterns which construct or constrain people's beliefs and actions'. In metaphor analysis, then, a key distinction is made between a *linguistic metaphor* and a *conceptual metaphor*.

Linguistic metaphors consist of the actual metaphorical expressions used by learners. For example, learners may refer to their progress in learning using such linguistic expressions as:

> 'Learning a language is like getting lost in a big forest.'
> 'I sailed through the lesson'.
> 'I shot off in the wrong direction'.
> 'I was lagging behind.'
> 'I was beginning to catch up.'

Linguistic metaphors can be analysed by identifying the *topic* and the *vehicle* of the expression. This is easy in the case of similes. For example, the *topic* of the first metaphorical expression above is 'learning a language' while the *vehicle* is 'getting lost in a forest'. It is more difficult in metaphorical expressions where the topic is not explicitly stated, as in all the other metaphorical expressions above. These mention the vehicles ('sailing through a lesson'; 'shooting off in the wrong direction'; 'lagging behind') but do make the comparisons explicit. The task of the analyst, therefore, is to identify the unstated topic. This is best done in general terms. For example, the topic in these expressions can be delineated broadly as 'learning a language'. In this way the expressions can be converted into similes: for example, 'Learning a language is like sailing or it is like a journey where you go off in the wrong direction'.

To establish the main conceptual metaphor that underlies a number of linguistic metaphors, the analyst needs to inspect the vehicles in the linguistic expressions carefully in order to identify what they have in common. The vehicles used in the above metaphors all relate to the idea of travelling or going on a journey or voyage. Thus the underlying conceptual metaphor can be stated as 'learning is a journey' or 'learner is a traveller'. Identifying what linguistic metaphors have in common conceptually necessarily involves interpretation and thus conceptual metaphors constitute high-inference categories. One way of establishing the validity of the conceptual metaphors identified in a particular sample of learner language is to illustrate them copiously by listing the linguistic metaphors from which they were derived. Not all studies that have employed metaphor analysis have done this, however. This is unfortunate because, as Cameron and Low (1999b) point out, many linguistic metaphors are 'fuzzy', involving complex constructs that can fit into more than one conceptual category.

The data for performing a metaphor analysis is of two basic kinds. They can consist of experimentally elicited metaphors or clinically elicited samples of learner language. (See Chapter 2.) In the case of experimentally elicited data, learners are explicitly asked to provide metaphors to describe their approach to learning an L2. Such metaphors often take the form of similes making the analysis easier. In the case of clinically elicited samples, the data will consist of learner discourses in the form of oral or written narratives, interviews or diaries. These discourses will need to be inspected to identify the linguistic metaphors used by the learners and then the underlying conceptual metaphors. These two methods share a number of features but also involve differences so they will be considered separately. Finally, the means of reporting the results of metaphor analysis will be considered.

The analysis of experimentally elicited metaphors

The method of analysis for experimentally elicited metaphors is described in detail by de Guerrero and Villamil (2002). It involves the following steps:

1. Construct a metaphor-elicitation instrument. This typically consists of a worksheet with an instruction and one or more prompts, as illustrated in Table 13.1. Metaphors are normally elicited in writing but they can also be elicited orally.
2. List the linguistic metaphors provided by the learners.
3. Break the metaphors down into analysable parts in order to identify salient features, common elements and similarities. One way of undertaking this is to examine the vocabulary the learners use.

4 Identify the underlying conceptual metaphors (i.e. categories) by assigning each of the linguistic metaphors (i.e. tokens) to a category. In some cases, it may be necessary to assign the same token to more than one category. De Guerrero and Villamil point out the need for a 'recursive process' involving the repetition of steps (3) and (4) in order to arrive at 'settled' category labels and tokens. It is important, though, to be aware of the problems of making the jump from utterance to conceptualization. As Low (1999) observes 'it is extraordinarily easy ... to make unwarranted assumptions about what metaphor users are actually thinking of' (1999: 65). Low argues that what is really needed is evidence to show that speakers actually behave or talk generally in accordance with the 'underlying metaphor model'. Such evidence has been rarely supplied.

5 Identify the entailments of each conceptual metaphor. Entailments are the key semantic elements found in a conceptual metaphor. They are identified by inspecting the Vehicles of the linguistic metaphors associated with a particular conceptual metaphor. For example, the entailments of the 'Learning is a journey' conceptual metaphor, as illustrated in the specific linguistic metaphors listed on p. 317 are 'ease/difficulty of learning', and 'progress in learning'.

What is your idea of a good language learner?

Think of three ways of completing the following sentence to reflect your ideas of a good language learner.

A good language learner is like ...

1 ______________________________

2 ______________________________

3 ______________________________

What is your idea of a good teacher?

Think of three ways of completing the following sentence to reflect your ideas of a good teacher.

A good teacher is like ...

1 ______________________________

2 ______________________________

3 ______________________________

Table 13.1 Example of worksheet for eliciting metaphors

6 The final step proposed by de Guerrero and Villamil involves identifying the participants' 'assumptions or theories underlying the metaphors' (2002: 1). This is necessarily an interpretative process but can be aided by asking the participants to comment on their choice of metaphors through the use of stimulated recall. (See Chapter 2.)

The analysis of metaphors in learner self-reports

Koch and Deetz (1981) propose the following procedure for analysing the metaphors in naturally occurring data:

1 Choose a representative corpora of texts.
2 Isolate metaphorical expressions in the texts and list them.
3 Decide which metaphors are worth analysing in accordance with the research purpose.
4 Reduce each metaphorical expression to the underlying conceptual metaphor by identifying its source (i.e. vehicle) and the target (i.e. topic) domains.
5 Sort these metaphors into coherent groups, thereby establishing the 'main metaphors' in the corpora. These metaphors are considered to be 'conceptual' (i.e. reflect ways in which the subjects view and interpret their world).
6 Consider the possible entailments of each main metaphor and examine to what extent these are or are not expressed in the corpora.

Steps 4–6 correspond to similar steps in the procedure for analysing experimentally elicited metaphors and so will not be discussed further. The discussion will now focus on steps 1–3.

Choosing a representative sample of texts

Low (1999) makes the point that certain genres are inherently more metaphorical than others. He gives as examples editorials and book reviews. However, little is known about the relative metaphorical density of the kinds of genres that figure in learner self-reports (for example, diaries, personal histories, interviews).[3] The researcher is faced with a choice; either to limit the sample of texts to be analysed to a specialized corpus involving a single genre or to employ a large corpus that includes different genres. Deignan (1999) favours the latter approach, arguing that only with a large corpus is it possible to identify the representative use of metaphors through frequency analysis and thus to tease out underlying beliefs and attitudes. Koch and Deetz (1981) point out that 'gathering data from a variety of sources helps insure that important metaphors are not omitted' (1981: 6). They also warn against designing instruments to specifically elicit the use of

6 October

Today we did something new (means of transport) and still every time we do something new I ***feel lost***. The teacher taught those students who would ***follow her*** because they've done German before. It seems to me that since German is a fairly structured language, therefore a systematic approach to teaching it would work. This teacher's way of teaching is very bitty. I am *3* ***lessons behind*** as far understanding them properly is concerned. We watched "Deutsch Direk" (BBC course book) second program and that was a lot simpler and ***easier to follow***.

15 October

I've not been able to keep my language learning diary up to date simply because I'm not up to date with what we've done in the lessons. The reason for this I think is that we'***ve been going too fast***. Students who have done German before have sort of ***kept up*** with the lessons.

28 October

One hour with a lang. assistant teacher. All we did was to practise the Present Perfect. Some of the other two seemed not to ***follow*** this as well as I think I did. I'm trying not to sound big headed but I feel as if I'm beginning to ***click into how German works***.
WATCH IT NEXT TIME I'LL WRITE MY DIARY AUF DEUTSCH.

12 December

Today is Friday.
Last Monday we read and some of us acted out a sort of story or don't know what because I didn't understand it all. It was the first part of "DIE GEFAHRLICHKEIT DER RASEMSPRENGER"(1). Tuesday, we didn't do anything at all with the language assistant because he'd spent a terrible night he said. Wednesday, we looked at the following structure with the Head of German. "I will Fotomodell werden, weil ich dann viel Geld verdienen." First of all, I didn't understand it at all until I translated one sentence. There was some reluctance on the part of the teacher to allow me to translate the sentence. Thursday, we went through some homework. I couldn't quite ***follow*** this and I couldn't understand why?
Friday, we had piece of German Christmas cake, it was rather nice. Later one we played a game; Ich packe meinen Kottie und lege hinein.
It was great practice having to use adjectives and nouns with the right declension. For the first time I realized that some nouns are declined as well. This ***threw me***. Another ***headache*** I thought.

I feel a lot, a lot better studying German. Now there are times when some of my classmates seem to ***be lost*** and I'm not. By the way, I'm finding it ***bit of a pain*** to have to learn each noun with its corresponding definite article.

Table 13.2 (continued)

9 January

This week we only had three sessions really. Two of 1hr. and one two hours. We are now ***tackling the simple past*** of "modal verbs."
I might be completely wrong but I am now finding German relatively easy. I think I'm ***cracking the grammar***. Somehow words are also beginning to ***fall into place***. I particularly like reading dialogues. I try to learn expressions by heart and then sort of activate them in my mind do that I can eventually produce them spontaneously.

10 January

As I think I've told you before, ***my morale goes up and down like a yo-yo***. One day I feel I am ***making good progress*** in German and next day I feel I'm ***getting nowhere***. This partly because I have other pressures to cope with and partly because it's a stage of learning a language I think. I also get very frustrated to have to dedicate most of the time to the other 4 subjects.

Table 13.2 Selected entries from Manuel's diary

metaphors. A minimum requirement is that the samples comprising the data to be analysed are described explicitly in terms of (1) the genre they represent, (2) the method of data collection and (3) their size.

The data to be discussed below constitute a specialized corpus. They consist of a diary written by Manuel, an adult learner taking an *ab initio* course in German at a tertiary college in London as part of a degree in languages. The diary was kept over a seven-month period. Manuel was requested to write entries as frequently as possible[4] and was given detailed instructions about what kinds of topics to consider together with examples taken from published diary studies. Altogether Manuel's diary contained 69,632 words. Examples of entries are shown in Table 13.2. The linguistic expressions we have identified as metaphorical are in bold.

Isolating the metaphorical expressions

The problems of identifying metaphorical expressions in learner reports are acute; they are discussed in detail in Cameron and Low (1999a). The analyst is first faced with the need to decide whether to limit identification to exemplar metaphors that are in some sense 'typical cases' and therefore uncontroversial. Cameron (1999b) lists the typicality conditions of such metaphors, the key ones of which are (1) the topic is explicitly stated and (2) there is a high degree of incongruity between topic and vehicle and (3) the producer intends to be metaphorical. A simile is an obvious exemplar metaphor. The advantage of limiting the analysis to such metaphors is that they can be easily and reliably identified. The disadvantages are that they may occur only sparingly in the data (there is only one obvious example in Table 13.2) and significant metaphorical expressions may be missed.

The identification of non-exemplar metaphors is much more problematic. This is because of the difficulty of determining exactly what constitutes the topic and the vehicle of such a metaphor. In verb- and preposition-metaphors, for example, the topic is usually not explicitly stated nor is the vehicle immediately apparent. For example, is 'behind' metaphorical in this sentence from Manuel's diary?

> I am 3 lessons *behind* as far understanding them properly is concerned.

The answer depends in part on whether the analyst considers 'behind' a polysemous item (i.e. referring literally to both 'location' and 'progress') or whether 'behind' is considered to refer quintessentially to location and its use to denote progress in a task as secondary and therefore metaphorical. Cameron (1999b) suggests that in order to interpret items such as 'behind' as metaphorical we need to be explicit about which meanings of the item that we consider literal. Thus, if we determine that the literal use of 'behind' is restricted to location, we can claim that its use to refer to progress is metaphorical. However, to be sure that 'behind' is metaphorical it is also necessary to determine exactly what is being compared to what. This necessitates a conceptual analysis. Thus, 'behind' can be considered metaphorical if the topic is deemed to be 'Learning a language' and the vehicle 'a journey'. In effect, then, it is not easy to keep the steps of identifying linguistic metaphors and then reducing them to conceptual metaphors distinct and sequential.

A further problem is the degree of difference between topic and vehicle that is necessary for a metaphor to be held to exist. Are the domains of 'Language learning' and 'a journey' sufficiently distinct? As Cameron (1999a: 21) points out this is 'ultimately a matter for decision by the researcher' while Low (1999) notes that metaphor researchers are likely to have a heightened sensitivity to metaphor, which may cause them to over-interpret the data. He comments 'the more the researcher reads (and reflects) on the text, the more metaphors tend to be identified' (1999: 50). This is an obvious threat to the reliability of the analysis. You might like to inspect the expressions in bold in Table 13.2 to see if you agree with us that they are metaphorical.

What can be done, then, to improve the reliability of the identification of metaphorical expressions? A basic requirement is that the analyst is fully explicit about the criteria and procedures used to identify metaphors. Low (1999) suggests that there are a number of ways in which researchers can supplement their own 'unilateral identification'. They can ask participants to review the text and mark all the metaphorical expressions they have used and then compare the expressions they and the participants have identified. The problem here, however, is that the participants may have an overly

The teacher taught those students who would **follow** her because they've done German before.

We watched "Deutsch Direk" (BBC course book) second program and that was a lot simpler and easier to ***follow***.

This week we did prepositions and even the students who have got "O" level German couldn't ***follow*** the couple of exercises we did.

I'm still finding it a bit difficult to ***follow*** these programmes.

I find modern listening exercise difficult to ***follow.***

Some of the other two seemed not to ***follow*** this as well as I think I did.

We went through some homework. I couldn't quite ***follow*** this and I couldn't understand why.

Table 13.3 Metaphorical expressions with 'follow' in Manuel's diary

narrow view of what constitutes a metaphorical expression. An alternative is for researchers to ask the participants what they meant by proposing a number of provisional interpretations. However, as Low observes, this may not work either as participants may not have had a specific meaning in mind. They are likely to experience special difficulty with metaphors that have become literalized. A better solution, again proposed by Low, may be to ask a third party (such as a linguist) to identify the metaphorical expressions in the sample. This has the advantage of affording a basis for determining reliability statistically by measuring the degree to which the researcher and the third party's identifications converge. But this method also has its disadvantages, not least that of ensuring that the researcher and third party share the same sense of what a metaphor is. However, Low is surely right in concluding that 'reliance on the researcher alone for views about what is metaphoric can be dangerous, and that both the metaphor users involved and third parties can prove to be valuable supplementary or alternative identifiers' (1999: 55).

Apart from the problem of determining what constitutes a metaphorical expression, researchers are also faced with the difficulty of ensuring that their analysis of metaphor is exhaustive (i.e. that they succeed in identifying *all* incidences of a particular metaphorical expression in their data). If the data are available in digitalized form, the researcher can use a concordancing program such as *Wordsmith Tools* (Scott 1997) or the 'find' function in a word processing programme to identify all the citations of a specific metaphorical item. Table 13.3 below shows the citations listed from Manuel's complete diary for 'follow'. These citations can then be inspected to determine which ones are metaphorical. Arguably all the citations in Table 13.1 are metaphorical expressions, representative of the 'Learning is a journey' conceptual metaphor referred to above.[5] As Deignan (1999) points out, concordancing is only a 'tool'; the researcher still has to decide what metaphorical expressions to look for in the data and how to interpret the results of the search. She comments 'There is no way of entering a speaker meaning or conceptual metaphor into a computer and being provided with a list of lexical items realising that particular meaning or metaphor' (1999: 197).

Selecting the metaphorical expressions for study

The researcher is next faced with the task of deciding whether to analyse all the metaphorical expressions that have been identified or limiting the analysis to selected expressions. If the goal of the research is to investigate learners' metaphorical competence in the L2, then, arguably, the researcher will need to undertake a comprehensive analysis. However, if the goal is to examine the conceptual and affective underpinnings of L2 acquisition the researcher will need to be selective, identifying those expressions that shed light on the research questions. If, for example, the research question is 'What problems do classroom learners experience in learning a foreign language *ab initio* in a classroom?' then metaphorical expressions relating to 'following', 'falling behind', 'keeping up', 'being thrown', 'getting a headache', and 'clicking into', all to be found in the extract from Manuel's diary in Table 13.2, are of obvious relevance. Further, the frequency with which such metaphors occur can serve as an indicator of the extent to which individual learners such as Manuel conceive of their learning experiences as problematic. Ultimately, however, the decision about what metaphorical expressions to include in the analysis is bound to be considerably subjective.

Reporting the results of a metaphor analysis

The results of a metaphor analysis can be reported qualitatively and/or quantitatively. In a qualitative approach, the researcher will need to (1) name each of the main conceptual metaphors that have been identified, (2) illustrate each conceptual metaphor copiously with metaphorical expressions taken from the data and (3) identify and illustrate each of the principal entailments of the metaphor. As in de Guerrero and Villamil (2002), a summary of the qualitative results can be presented in the form of a table, as illustrated in Table 13.4 on p. 326. In a quantitative analysis, information about the frequency of use of each metaphor is provided. This can be done in two ways. First, the analyst can report the frequency with which particular metaphorical expressions relating to each main conceptual metaphor are used. For example, in Manuel's diary the 'Learning is a journey' metaphor was realized by means of metaphorical expressions containing 'follow' on seven occasions. It would also be possible to quantify the frequency of specific entailments of each conceptual metaphor. Second, perhaps more usefully, the analyst can report how many learners in the

Main conceptual metaphor	Key metaphorical expressions	Metaphor entailments
1 LEARNING IS A JOURNEY	Progress/no progress Getting lost/stuck Keeping up Following/not following Catching up slowing down/speeding up	1 Progress is being made 2 Progress is not being made 3 Impediments to progress 4 Overcoming impediments
2 etc.		

Table 13.4 Metaphorical conceptualizations of one learner

study used each of the main conceptual metaphors. In this way, it is possible to see which conceptual metaphors were the dominant ones. Ideally, as shown in Cortazzi and Jin (1999), a combination of qualitative and quantitative reporting is desirable.

An example of a metaphor analysis

As we have already noted, whereas metaphor analysis has been quite widely used to explore teachers' conceptualizations of teaching (for example, de Guerrero and Villamil 2002; Oxford 2001), there are surprisingly few studies of L2 learners that have employed metaphor analysis (but see Block 1992). We have chosen a study by Ellis (2002) as an example. This study reports an analysis of the diaries kept by six *ab initio* learners of L2 German, one of whom was Manuel. It is summarized in Table 13.5.

Ellis' study reveals some of the strengths and weaknesses of metaphor analysis. Its main strength is that it affords a very different picture of what learners are thinking about their learning experiences to that provided by more traditional methods for investigating learner beliefs. The fact that learners (at least in his study) see classroom learning as a journey in which they have to deal with various cognitive and affective problems, that it involves suffering and struggle and that it is not something over which they have total control are not aspects of learning covered in closed-item belief questionnaires such as that of Horwitz (1987). Yet they seem to be quite central to learners' understanding of what is happening. In this respect, the claim that metaphor analysis can provide a window through which to view learners' conceptual systems is supported. Further, metaphor analysis is able to afford insights that may be missed by more traditional methods.

The weaknesses of Ellis' study are mainly those of metaphor analysis itself—in particular, the inherent difficulty of determining whether a particular expression is or is not metaphorical. Ellis attempted to overcome this problem by using third parties to assess the metaphoricity of

Research question	The study sought to investigate the belief systems of language learners. No specific research question is stated.
Participants	6 adult learners (4 female and 2 male) taking *ab initio* courses in German as a foreign language at two colleges in London. Five of the learners were selected from a larger group to keep a diary because they demonstrated a positive attitude to learning German in a pre-course questionnaire and because they expressed an interest in keeping a diary. One learner (Monique) volunteered to keep a diary.
Data collection	The participants kept their diaries for approximately 7 months. In a detailed set of guidelines, they were asked to record their reactions to the course, their teachers, their fellow-students and any other factors that influenced their learning. No attempt was made to elicit metaphorical expressions. The diaries were collected in weekly for photocopying and then returned to their owners. The size of the diaries varied from 40,960 words (Debbie) to 137,216 words (Monique).
Analysis	The procedure followed was; (1) identification of the metaphorical expressions in the diaries, (2) sorting these expressions in accordance with the conceptual metaphors they realized and then selecting the main conceptual metaphors, (3) identification of the key words in the expressions for each main conceptual metaphor followed by concordancing of these words using Wordsmith, (4) inspection of concordanced items by third parties (two applied linguists) to determine which of the items were metaphorical, (5) listing the entailments of the metaphorical expressions relating to each main conceptual metaphor.
Results	Ellis describes five conceptual metaphors and their entailments giving citation examples for the key words relating to each metaphor. The metaphors were: 1 LEARNING AS A JOURNEY (e.g. 'I got hopelessly lost'.) 2 LEARNING AS A PUZZLE (e.g. 'I think I'm cracking the grammar.') 3 LEARNING AS SUFFERING (e.g. 'The whole experience was a shock to my system.') 4 LEARNING AS A STRUGGLE (e.g. We were literally pulled to pieces.') 5 LEARNING AS WORK (e.g. 'The extra work paid off'.)

Table 13.5 (continued)

	Ellis also indicates which learners employed each metaphor (e.g. all 6 learners used the LEARNING AS A PUZZLE metaphor) and also the total number of metaphorical expressions in each main conceptual metaphor (e.g. 61 for LEARNING AS A JOURNEY).
Discussion	Ellis suggests the metaphors reveal two essential points about the learners' beliefs; (1) they all believed that learning German was problematic and that the problems they related were both cognitive and affective and (2) they constructed themselves as both agents of their own learning and as patients undergoing experiences they could not control.
Implications	Ellis considers the implications of his study in relation to the use of metaphor analysis as a methodological tool for exploring learner beliefs. He argues that metaphor analysis is effective in helping uncover learners' underlying conceptual systems and notes that the beliefs that emerged from the analysis are different from those reflected in questionnaires designed to investigate learners' beliefs.

Table 13.5 Summary of Ellis's (2002) metaphorical analysis of learner beliefs

expressions, which were first identified exhaustively with the help of a concordancing programme. Ellis describes how this was undertaken:

> Two applied linguists were given lists of the expressions relating to each conceptual metaphor and asked to consider which ones they considered metaphorical. Somewhat arbitrarily, I determined an expression was metaphorical if I and one of the applied linguists identified it as such. (2002: 166)

His reasons for adopting this procedure (not stated in the article) were that the three raters (Ellis and the third parties) rarely all agreed on which expressions were metaphorical! In part, this was because Ellis failed to provide an explicit definition of 'metaphor'. In part it was because what is and is not deemed metaphorical will always be, in part at least, subjective. By way of illustrating this, the reader might like to assess for him/herself the metaphoricity of the following expressions, all of which were counted as 'metaphorical' by Ellis:

> I find myself really stuck.
> It was quite difficult for me to grasp it all.

I was quite at a loss.
I'm not going to be defeated by a moody teacher.
The extra work paid off.

The key issue, then, is whether this uncertainty about what counts as metaphorical invalidates the study. The standard position adopted in social science research is that validity is not possible without reliability. A less stringent position might be that doubts about the metaphoricity of specific *linguistic* expressions need not invalidate the overall picture that an analysis of the multiple metaphors used by a learner can provide, as long as there is sufficient evidence to demonstrate the existence of key *conceptual* metaphors. Ellis sought to provide this evidence by listing citations for the key words associated with each main conceptual metaphor.

Task: Investigating a learner's conceptualizations using metaphor analysis

The data you will analyse in this task come from the personal learning biography of a Japanese learner of English, Chizu Kanada (Schumann 1997). The biography was written as an assignment mid-way through a graduate course on second language acquisition taught by Schumann. The students were asked to write approximately five-page autobiographical accounts of their language learning. Chizu Kanada, like the other students taking the course, had had extensive experience in learning a second language. We have selected the part of the biography in which Kanada discusses her experiences of English *outside* the classroom by interacting with other speakers of English.

Carry out a metaphor analysis to provide an answer to this question:

> How does this learner conceptualize the problems she experienced in learning English and the solutions to these problems?

To carry out the analysis you will need to:

1 Formulate a definition of metaphor to guide your analysis.
2 Identify the linguistic metaphors in the text. You may wish to work with a partner and to compare the metaphors you have identified as a way of demonstrating reliability.
3 Analyse each metaphorical expression in terms of its topic and vehicle. Again you will benefit by undertaking this with a partner.
4 Decide which of the metaphorical expressions are relevant to your research question.
5 Classify the relevant metaphorical expressions into categories representing the main conceptual metaphors.
6 Identify the main entailments of each conceptual metaphor and list the metaphorical expressions related to each entailment.

My first opportunity to interact with non-Japanese people came when I was seventeen. The local city office hosted a youth group from what was then West Germany, and my family volunteered to provide a week's room and board for two boys. They were seventeen and eighteen. I was extremely excited. I do not remember how well I communicated with them, but I do remember their English (their second or third language) was much better than mine. But I managed to establish friendships with them. Both the boys and my family enjoyed each other's company.

There was one boy in the group I especially liked. He did not stay with us, but I met and talked with him when all the participants in the program got together to socialize. He played European handball, a game I played passionately every day while in high school. I was excited to know that this completely different-looking young man played the same sport I did. I was eager to talk to him about handball and other things. I found him to be very gentle and thoughtful and I was very much attracted to him. After he left, I started to write to him, and our correspondence lasted for many years.

I feel that, from this point on, the motivation for my language learning moved decisively out of the classroom context and became centred around people. Certainly the prospect of becoming able to communicate with people like my German friend appealed to me immensely...

At the age of twenty one I went to Australia with a British organization. We stayed in Australia's Northern Territory for two and a half months and were engaged in excavation projects, the survey and protection of natural resources, providing community services, and the like. It was the first opportunity for me to be immersed in English and to use it quite literally as a survival tool. Here, too, as always, amidst the breathtaking landscapes and thrilling canoe trips, it was the people I met that made the most enduring impression on me. The many friendships I formed convinced me how precious a life tool my English could be.

This experience in Australia dramatically expanded my conception of English and its speakers. It made me see that the United States of America was not the only place where English was spoken. (I had internalized the quick and easy connection so commonly made in Japan between the English language and Americans). The people I was with were predominantly British, but there were also local Australians, including Caucasians, Asian-Australians and aborigines. They all spoke "English", but differently. This was most striking in their phonological variations. The reality of differences within English was an exciting discovery for me. I wanted to explore the linguistic and cultural forces that might account for such variety.

Table 13.6 (continued)

As soon as I came back from Australia, I was off to the United States. I spent a full academic year there as a visiting student and took courses that could be transferred to my home college in Tokyo. My experience there was of another order entirely from anything I had experienced hitherto. It was such a struggle, so arduous, with just enough fun and consolation to keep me going. But it was also during this year that a breakthrough occurred for me and my English ability. It was about the eighth month that I finally started to formulate English sentences without first translating them from Japanese. In other words, I no longer had to have an entire sentence down perfectly before I spoke it, but rather, I became able to speak as I thought. It was as if English had finally became part of my thought processes.

Until then I had been "writing" English sentences in my head. I actually visualized each letter of the alphabet in each word of the sentence I was formulating. I would then check for grammatical errors and, finally, produce it orally. The final stage of actually speaking was not easy, either, because it required a lot of care to say what I had "written" while adhering to the rules of pronunciation.

This pre-thinking in Japanese was a particular disadvantage in the classroom context. I would often find that the discussion had moved on to other subjects by the time I was ready to express my ideas. It was excruciating. My self-esteem was badly hurt because I was used to being an articulate student. I would often go to see a writing specialist who ended up being my counsellor as well. One day I burst into tears in his office as I was relating to him my problems with English. It was as if all the repressed frustration, depression, and humiliation surfaced at once. He asked me if I wanted to go home—to Japan. I remember being surprised at my own reaction because my answer was a defiant "no". I definitely wanted to stay, no question about it. After this incident, I learned to let myself burst open every now and again. I was able to make some good friends, a couple of whom were especially supportive and understanding.

When it came time to return to Tokyo, I felt I was leaving just as I was starting to function "normally" in English. I had a clear sense that I was beginning to reach a stage that was critical to my language development. At the very least, I was convinced that I needed to be in an environment where English was the principal mode of thinking and speaking: an everyday necessity. That was why I immediately started to look for ways that would take me back to an English speaking environment. I entertained the possibility of being a waitress at a Japanese restaurant in Bath, England; of becoming a graduate in English at a British institution; and of undertaking graduate study in comparative literature at a North American institution. As I look back on myself trying to find my way, I realize that English, my second language, came to be an integral part of not only my career choices but also my life path. My passion for English has had such a strong impact on my life; certainly at that particular point it was the central axis of my decision.

Table 13.6 (continued)

In the end, I chose to pursue a modified form of the third path. My two years at the University of British Columbia expanded my active vocabulary and greatly developed my thought processes in English. Learning patterns and a reasonable vocabulary base were gradually established. I learned mostly through reading books, and through classroom exchanges and conversations with friends. I recognized that I acquire new words most easily when I see them in written form and hear them in use, particularly when each encounter is temporally close to the other. I also learned a great deal, with the help of several editors, by writing academic papers and, later, specifically for the past four years, recommendation letters for students I was teaching Japanese to. The latter experience at Smith College and Northwestern University led me to familiarize myself with a range of new vocabulary, such as that of the classroom teacher, the counsellor, and the administrator.

Last summer, in my sixteenth year of learning English, I married a wonderful Canadian man. It made me think of how extraordinary the ramifications have been of my learning this second language. And as I got to know my new family, and begin making plans for one of my own, I am sure this linguistic life journey will continue to be as challenging and rewarding as it has always been.

Table 13.6 A Personal learning biography (Schumann 1997)

Conclusion

Block (1999), drawing on the work of Schön (1979), suggests that metaphors need to be viewed in terms of both process and product. As process, they provide the means by which new understandings can be created. Block suggests that metaphors encapsulate the processes of assimilating and accommodating new information and of managing the world. He refers to this as 'metaphorization'. Viewed as product, metaphors are linguistic artefacts that can be described, discussed and evaluated as a method for investigating how people conceptualize their worlds. The study of metaphor-as-process requires the analyst to adopt a diachronic approach to the analysis of metaphor, showing how learners' metaphorical usage changes over time and demonstrating the relationship between these changes and their developing understanding of learning. To the best of our knowledge there have been no studies of metaphor-as-process involving language learners. For this reason, this chapter has focused on metaphor-as-product. The study of metaphor-as-product requires the researcher to elicit or identify the linguistic metaphors that learners employ as the first step to uncovering the underlying conceptual metaphors and their entailments. These, it has been claimed, tell us how learners conceptualize their learning of an L2.

Two approaches to the analysis of metaphor have been considered—one involving the elicitation of metaphor and the other the identification of metaphorical expressions in learner reports. Metaphor elicitation avoids the thorny problem of analysts having to decide what is and is not metaphorical as it provides them with a set of ready-made metaphors, often of the exemplar kind (for example, similes). The danger is that learners will simply construct metaphors to conform to the demands of the elicitation task rather than choose metaphors that are a true representation of how they think and feel about learning. In contrast, the use of learner reports is more likely to guarantee the validity of the metaphors but poses analysts with the problem of reliably identifying the linguistic metaphors. There is, of course, no reason why the two methods should not be combined; the metaphors identified in learners' reports can be compared to the metaphors elicited from the same learners. However, we know of no study that has attempted this.

In both approaches, an essential step in the analysis involves establishing the main conceptual metaphors. As conceptual metaphors are high-inference categories, the reliability of the analysis is again threatened. Also, as Steen (1994) has pointed out, no analysis can demonstrate that linguistic metaphors have a conceptual basis in the minds of people. Thus, the validity of the conceptual metaphors the analyst has established may be open to challenge. Although various procedures are possible to ensure reliability and validity (see above), researchers opting for metaphor analysis need to do so in full awareness of the threats. Ultimately, researchers need to decide whether the rich insights that we think metaphor analysis can provide are worth the risks.

Notes

1 Gibbs (1999: 37) rightly points out the need 'to be quite careful to distinguish between the processes and products of metaphor understanding'.
2 Cortazzi and Jin (1999) do include in their article an account of metaphors elicited from L2 learners from different linguistic backgrounds. However, their study is primarily concerned with teachers' metaphors.
3 We speculate that the more 'personal' and 'presentational' the genre, the heavier the use of metaphors. Thus, we would anticipate that learners will be more inclined to use metaphorical expressions in personal histories and diaries than in interviews. However, this remains to be demonstrated.
4 There were periods when Manuel failed to make an entry. To make up for these Manuel wrote 'summary statements' covering these periods.
5 Some dictionaries (for example, Newbury House) explicitly acknowledge that the use of 'follow' with the meaning of 'understand' is figurative.

14 Computer-based analyses of learner language *by Michael Barlow*

Introduction

In this chapter we explore the insights to be gained into the nature of second language acquisition from the analysis of *learner corpora*, which are digital representations of the performance or output, typically written, of language learners. The use of learner corpora in SLA studies thus falls within the tradition of treating learner language as expression, as described in earlier chapters.

The way in which the emerging field of learner corpus analysis differs from other approaches to SLA is detailed in the following sections. First we examine the design and compilation of learner corpora, which is a crucial component of data gathering, since learner corpora are in some ways more complex as data sets than native speaker corpora and the appropriate encoding of information about the learners and the setting is a key prerequisite for ensuing analyses. Next we look at research on learner corpora, which, as Granger (2004) notes, is a relatively new development and consequently it is not possible to provide a comprehensive assessment of the place of learner corpora research in SLA studies at this time. Nevertheless, what we can do is review some existing research studies in order to present some of the findings coming out of learner corpus research and to illustrate different aspects of the analysis of learner corpus data.

One striking characteristic of learner corpus research is the prevalent use of frequency data, which might include the learners' over use or under use of lexical or grammatical forms or an analysis of the frequency of error forms. The emphasis on frequency, combined with the fact that learner corpora are quite large, means that software tools are an essential part of learner corpus research, and in the third section in this chapter we illustrate the application of corpus analysis software.

One impetus to compile learner corpora follows from the Error Analysis tradition of identifying, describing and explaining errors, and many of the issues related to error analysis and linguistic analyses based on categorization of errors described in Chapter 3 apply to the analysis of learner corpora. There are, however, some important differences in approach and also in procedure, since the analysis of learner corpora encompasses the techniques and many of the assumptions of *corpus linguistics*. Applying the methodology of corpus analysis (Sinclair 1991) to the investigation of learner corpora entails the collection of fairly large samples, typically hundreds of thousands of words or more of learner language. The general technique consists of trawling through learner corpora using searching software to reveal and quantify recurrent patterns, typically lexico-grammatical patterns, that characterize the learner language associated with different learners and different settings.

The links to corpus linguistics have influenced the models of grammar and acquisition processes typically used in learner corpus studies. This influence has been manifested in an emphasis both on lexis in grammatical descriptions and on frequency of occurrence of language structures as an important factor in research studies. (See Barlow 1996 and Kemmer and Barlow 2000 for a description of grammatical models influenced by the analysis of corpus data.)

Since the use of learner corpora is a new development, many of the results must be regarded as preliminary until a wider range of learner corpora are available for analysis, covering a range of proficiency levels and a number of L1-L2 combinations. The existing learner corpora tend to contain little in the way of analytical markup, i.e., annotations of the raw corpus data that code grammatical information, which means that the form-function or form-meaning part of the analysis must be completed manually, with all the practical and theoretical problems typically encountered when assigning language forms to abstract categories. Still more problematic is the uncertainty about the exact nature of the relationship between particular learner corpora and a more general characterization of interlanguage. A learner corpus often represents just a single genre, such as argumentative essays, and so some features of the learner's production may be closely associated with that genre rather than being more generally representative of interlanguage. (See Dagneaux 1995.) Thus while we might expect some aspects of the learner's production to be relatively invariant over a range of modalities and genres, other aspects of production are likely to be highly modality-specific or genre-specific. But, at present, the required range of learner corpus types is not available to provide the information necessary to assess the variability of different aspects of language production.

Design and compilation of learner corpora

Whether a learner corpus is to be used to help identify those aspects of the student's language that are due to L1 influence or those aspects that are due to developmental processes, then clearly the variables associated with the learners' production must be systematically encoded. While all corpora must be well-designed and well-documented, the recording of data concerning the individual learners and the tasks and settings associated with the learners' language production is all the more important for learner corpora because of the central importance assigned to knowledge of the characteristics of the language learners. In short, we may not care about the background of writers employed by the *New York Times*, but we need to know some basic information about learners and about the conditions under which their language is produced, if we are to draw any useful generalizations related to second language acquisition.

The collection of data for a learner corpus typically involves the sampling of language production (i.e., speech or writing) along with descriptions of the setting and a description of the variables for each learner (Granger 2002: 5), as shown in Table 14.1.

These variables may be stored in external files or database with an ID number linking the information in the database with the language production data. Alternatively, information concerning variables can be encoded as

Setting	***Task:*** A description of the nature of the task that provides the language sample. It could be a written prompt for an argumentative essay, a picture, or cartoon. Additional details may be furnished, depending on the particular nature of the task. ***Audience/Interlocutor:*** Identification of the person(s) interacting with the student, along with their role (teacher, tester, etc.). ***Time Limit:*** If the task is timed, what is the time allowed? ***Use of reference materials:*** Are dictionaries and other reference materials allowed?
Learner	***Mother tongue:*** The primary language of the student. ***Other languages:*** Languages that the student knows with an assessment of competence with respect to speaking/writing/listening/reading ***L2 level of proficiency:*** An assessment of the level of the student. Such assessments are sometimes difficult to equate across institutions and across countries. ***Location:*** The country or region that the students come from. ***Education:*** This variable may include general information about education as well as an indication of the nature of language classes. ***Age:/Sex:/***... and other attributes of the learner

Table 14.1 Examples of task and learner variables

Database format

ID	Sex	Proficiency	Mother tongue	Occupation	Age	Learning Context
028	male	intermediate	Dutch	Student	16	school
029	female	intermediate	French	Student	17	school
030	male	advanced	French	Student	18	school
031	female	intermediate	Dutch	Student	17	school

Tag format

<student id = "028">
<sex>male</sex>
<proficiency>intermediate</proficiency>
<language>Dutch</language>
<age>16</age>
<occupation>student</occupation>
<learning_context>school</learning_context>
</student>

Figure 14.1 Alternative representations of learner variables

tags or annotations within the corpus itself (Figure 14.1). The form in which this information is stored is not important in itself. The key point lies in structuring the data to allow retrieval software to reveal the links between a set of lexical or grammatical units in the learner corpus and the values of variables such as proficiency, age, L1, etc.

The most extensive and best-known collection of learner corpora is the International Corpus of Learner English (ICLE), a project started by Granger at the University of Louvain in 1990. The learner corpus consists of essays of about 700 words produced by Advanced EFL learners in a variety of countries. The aim is to compile a corpus of about 200,000 words per language or country (Granger 1998a: 10–11); currently there are seventeen international partners participating in the project (Granger, Dagneaux, and Meunier 2002: 11). The first release of the corpus on CD-ROM contains samples of English from Bulgarian, Czech, Dutch, French, Finnish, German, Italian, Polish, Russian, Spanish and Swedish learners of English, with data sets from Brazilian, Chinese, Japanese, Norwegian, Portuguese and South African learners to follow in subsequent releases. The Polish component of ICLE, called PICLE, can be accessed through a web-based search engine described in more detail below.

The ICLE subcorpora are typically made up of academic essays produced within a classroom-based EFL learning context. A learner profile questionnaire is used to collect information on a range of variables, both a core set of variables and a set of variables relevant for some subcorpora only.

Granger, Dagneaux, and Meunier (2002: 13) list the variables shared by all the subcorpora in ICLE as follows:

Learner variables
  age
  learning context
  proficiency level
Task variables
  medium (for example, writing)
  field (for example, general)
  genre
  length

The information on the relevant variables is stored in separate files, leaving the texts themselves with very little mark-up. The ICLE texts are not annotated with part-of-speech (POS) tags, but some preliminary investigations on the feasibility of tagging of learner corpora have been carried out (de Haan 2000; Meunier and de Mönnink 2001). The difficulty in applying standard taggers arises from misspellings and unusual word sequences in learner corpora, but with further work on the development of appropriate taggers, we can expect to see more learner corpora annotated with POS tags in the future.

While most learner corpora are based on writing, typically essay writing, there are some spoken learner corpora. While not generally referred to as a learner corpus, the ESF (European Science Foundation) Second Language Database consists of spoken data collected in France, Germany, Great Britain, The Netherlands and Sweden (Feldweg 1991). For the project, the spontaneous productions of forty adult immigrant workers living in Western Europe were sampled and transcribed. There are five target languages: Dutch, English, French, German and Swedish, and for each target language, there are two source languages.

A more conventional spoken learner corpus is the LINDSEI Project (Louvain International Database of Spoken English Interlanguage) (De Cock, Granger, and Petch-Tyson 1995). The first component of the learner corpus contains spoken transcripts of fifty French learners of English, yielding a corpus of around 100,000 words.[1]

The Standard Speaking Test (SST) Corpus was started in Japan in 1999 with the aim of creating a one million word spoken corpus of Japanese learners of English (Tono, Kaneko, Isahara, Saiga, Izumi, Narita, and Kaneko 2001), which is due to be released in 2004. The corpus data are collected from students taking an Oral Proficiency Interview and thus is based on the use of interviews and picture prompts to elicit speech in a situation that approximates a natural dialogue. A smaller test-based spoken corpus collected at the University of Bergen contains the output of 62 Norwegian pupils aged 14–15 who were asked to complete a variety of tasks such as role-play and describing pictures (Hasselgren 2002). These tasks were also carried out by 26 British pupils, providing an NS benchmark for the language of the Norwegian learners of English.

Commercially-based learner corpora, which are proprietary and thus generally unavailable to researchers, include the Longman Learner's Corpus and the Cambridge Learner Corpus. These corpora are large, about 10 million words each, and consist of the writings of a wide variety of students learning English around the world. The data in these corpora are analysed by lexicographers and materials developers in order to improve the usefulness of dictionaries and coursebooks for language learners.

There has been a considerable amount of work related to learner corpora in Hong Kong, such as the 25 million-word HKUST Learner corpus compiled by John Milton, the TeleNex Student Corpus, and the Chinese Learner English Corpus (CLEC). Other learner corpora described in Pravec (2002) and Nesselhauf (2004) include the Uppsala Student English project, which contains writings of Swedish undergraduates; the Learner Business Letters Corpus, consisting of business letters written by Japanese business people; and the Montclair Electronic Database (MELD), which is unusual in that it contains the language production of ESL learners rather than EFL learners.

Following in the EA tradition, one approach to the analysis of learner corpora is to annotate the learner language with error tags (Milton and Chowdhury 1994; Dagneaux, Denness, and Granger 1998). An error tag is an annotation added to the corpus to explicitly mark an error, as in 'The main feature of campus is (GA) the its conviviality' (Dagneaux, Denness, Granger, and Meunier 1996). In this example, the error tag GA is used to indicate a problem with article use and the target form 'its', signalled by $, has also been added by the annotator.

The identification of errors is, however, not at all straightforward since a sentence with errors can often be corrected in multiple ways, making the labelling of individual errors within the sentence quite difficult, as discussed in some detail in Chapter 3. For an error-tagged corpus to be useful for research purposes, clearly the assignment of error tags has to be consistent. The difficulties of tagging errors is compounded by the fact that following the corpus tradition of more is better, learner corpora tend to be quite large, perhaps containing millions of words. Such large data sets make error identification a time-consuming process, even with the aid of error taggers, since each error must be individually located and classified by a researcher.

An error-tagged learner corpus enables researchers to search for different types of error and may also allow searches of correct target forms in addition to the actual, possibly erroneous forms. As noted above, the marking of errors is not at all straightforward and involves some interpretation. A hierarchical error tagging system, developed at Louvain (Dagneaux, Denness, Granger, and Meunier 1996) assigns a major category type to

5.3 WORD MISSING: (WM)

This subcategory is for errors involving the omission of words
e.g. *We have a meeting* (WM) *0 on Monday.*
I do not (WM) *0 see why I should go there.*

The following types of errors should not be classified in this category:
(LP): where the missing word forms part of a set phrase:
e.g. (LP) *on equal footing $on an equal footing$*
(GA): for a missing article or misapplication of the zero article:
e.g. (GA) *He works in* (GA) *0 an office.*
(LC): missing connective or a word missing from a connective:
e.g. (LCLC) *on other hand $on the other hand$*

Figure 14.2 An extract from the Error Tagging Manual (Dagneaux, Denness, Granger, and Meunier 1996)

each error: grammatical (G), lexical (L), lexico-grammatical (X), formal (F), register (R), syntax (W) and style (S). Additional specifications include GV (grammatical verb error), GVAUX (grammatical auxiliary verb error), and GVT (tense error), among others. Documentation is available that defines and illustrates all the error codes so that the coding performed by different researchers is consistent. The extract from the Error Tagging Manual (Version 1.1) shown in Figure 14.2 illustrates the entry for the tagging of missing words.

The work on error-coding on the ICLE Project informed the development of markup software, called *TagEditor*, for use with the SST Corpus (Tono, Kaneko, Isahara, Saiga, Izumi, Narita, and Kaneko 2001). The software is used to facilitate the marking of errors, using XML tags[2] and to search the corpus in different ways.

Milton and Chowdhury (1994) describe the error-tagging of a corpus of Chinese learners of English. They make the interesting suggestion that the problem of multiple analyses of an error should, in some cases, be dealt with by encoding multiple alternative corrections within the tagging scheme (1994: 129).

Error tags are the most common type of annotation used to mark up learner corpora, but any aspect of linguistic structure can be coded explicitly using an appropriate annotation scheme. Burdine (2002), for example, annotated a corpus comprising interviews with French immersion students in order to show the occurrence of different communication strategies. In the following exchange, for example, a foreignization strategy <FOR> is followed by an unsuccessful attempt at correction <OC>: *c'est c'est facile à* <FOR> *marquer* </FOR> <OC> *à correcter* </OC>. Having identified the different communication strategies used by the students, Burdine is able to assess the relative frequency of different strategies as well as show the relationship between preferences for particular communication strategies and other parameters such as proficiency.

In this section we have focused on the structure of learner corpora, but as Altenberg (2002: 38) points out, in order to investigate and understand the nature of interlanguage, information must be gathered on not only the form and functioning of the interlanguage, but also the features of the learner's mother tongue and of the target language. Thus learner corpora, monolingual corpora and bilingual or parallel (translation) corpora all have a part to play. Parallel corpora can be used to establish equivalences or non-equivalences in lexis or grammar holding between two languages. For example, the word *line* in English and *ligne* in French take part in a variety of metaphorical extensions and occur in different phrases. Some of these uses are congruent in the two languages, while others are not. Using a parallel corpus, we can find, for instance, those uses of *line* in English which typically do not correspond to *ligne* in French. These include: *in line with, bring/fall into line, poverty line, down the line, the bottom line*, and *line of reasoning/argument/thought*. Data such as these provide background information on equivalences and non-equivalences between two languages, which can be used as part of the evaluation of the language of French learners of English and that of English learners of French.

Research on learner corpora

Research on learner corpora is often inherently contrastive and to some extent it follows some of the general concepts and aims associated with *contrastive analysis*. Granger (1998a: 12) refers to a new research paradigm of *contrastive interlanguage analysis*, which covers both NS/NNS and NNS/NNS comparisons. Studies which use native speaker corpora as a benchmark for the analysis of learner corpora (i.e. NS/NNS comparisons) provide evidence for the nature of interlanguage, focusing on the non-native aspects of learners' speech or writing. Alternatively, a comparison of different NNS corpora can be used to highlight aspects of language use and development shared by learners with different language backgrounds. In cases where differences emerge among learners with different language backgrounds, the analyst will explore the likelihood that the variation is due to L1 influence (Granger 2002: 13). In practice, many studies of learner corpora are designed to include both NS/NNS and NNS/NNS comparisons.

A comparison of learner corpora with NS corpora provides data on the properties of interlanguage, covering features which are typically overused or underused, in addition to those which are misused by language learners (Leech 1998: 20). Thus learner corpora studies often involve the counting of particular words or grammatical categories, a process which is not as simple as it sounds because of the ill-formed or variable nature of L2 production data. A further source of complexity is that automated counting routines are based on formal identity of linguistic items, not form-function identity. For instance, a count of the word *can* in an untagged corpus does not discriminate between *can* as a noun and *can* as a modal auxiliary. Furthermore, in some studies an even finer-grained functional categorization may be necessary to distinguish, for example, the ability uses of the modal *can* from the permission uses. The tabulation of form-function linguistic items in learner corpora can be time-consuming in cases where the corpora are not already annotated for the categories of interest. Yet such fine-grained analyses are often needed to give an accurate picture of the nature of interlanguage. For example, an investigation of essay-writing by Lin (2002) showed that the word *it* was used less frequently by Chinese learners of English than by native speakers. But when the different functions of *it* were examined, it turned out that some functions of *it* were underused by language learners (for example, *tough*-constructions such as *It is easy to please John*), while some were overused (for example, dummy *it*).

Once corpus-based data on particular characteristics of interlanguage have been analysed, it is possible to look for explanations for these features, which typically involve factors such as:

L1 transfer
Some forms or grammatical patterns found in the learner's language production may result from the intrusion of L1.

General learner strategies
To help deal with the complex task of speaking or writing in a second language, the learner may adopt some coping strategies such as the use of L1 forms, circumlocution, avoidance strategies, etc.

Paths of interlanguage development
Some aspects of interlanguage, such as the development of negation or the development of tense/aspect marking proceed in a series of stages which may be tracked using longitudinal studies of learner output.

Intralingual overgeneralization
Some features of the learner's language may be due to overgeneralization of an aspect of L2 grammar such as the use of *-ed* to mark past tense.

Input bias
The form of the learner's production may reflect the particular input received, such as the language used in coursebooks. (See Römer 2004.)

Genre/register influences
Researchers working with learner corpora have suggested that the writing of L2 learners contains a variety of informal patterns that are characteristic of spoken discourse.

We can distinguish two principal methodologies associated with learner corpus investigations. One is to use learner corpus data to test specific hypotheses about the nature of interlanguage generated through introspection, SLA theories, or as a result of the analysis of experimental or other non-corpus-based sources of data. In this case, text analysis software is used to extract data in a way that specifically relates to the hypothesis; the retrieved data are viewed as valuable only in so far as they confirm or disconfirm the hypothesis. One such study is exemplified in Tono (2000). His hypothesis is that the overall morpheme ordering data revealed by Dulay and Burt (1974) will be confirmed by an analysis of a written corpus consisting of English essays written by Japanese speakers. In his study, Tono found some differences in the morpheme acquisition order for Japanese learners in that the possessive *-s* morpheme was acquired relatively early and article usage emerged relatively late. Another instance of hypothesis-testing is Housen (2002) which aims to investigate the Aspect Hypothesis put forth in Andersen and Shirai (1996) and Bardovi-Harlig (1999). See below for further discussion of Housen's study.

An alternative is to investigate learner corpora data in a more exploratory manner and initiate analyses that yield patterns of data, which can then be inspected for unusual features. Such features may then be used to generate hypotheses about learner language. This general approach is illustrated in the section below on Corpus Analysis Software and in work such as Aijmer (2002). In her study, Aijmer starts out from the general observation that non-native speakers find it difficult to use English modal verbs appropriately. She then exploits different corpora to compare modal use by Swedish learners of English and by native-speakers and finds that there is a general overuse of modals by Swedish learners and a particular overuse of the modals *will, must, have (got) to, should* and *might*.

These two methodologies correspond loosely to the contrast between *hypothesis-driven* and *hypothesis-finding* approaches (Granger 1998b: 15), and to the general *corpus-based* versus *corpus-driven* distinction (Tognini-Bonelli 2001). In a corpus-based approach, a search is selected to find data that are relevant to a particular hypothesis. On the other hand, in a corpus-driven approach large amounts of data derived from corpus analysis are used in the formulation of grammatical descriptions.

In practice, researchers may well make use of a combination of approaches, but there are biases in practice such that broadly speaking the experimental/generative tradition favours hypothesis-driven, corpus-based approaches, while corpus linguists have a preference for a hypothesis-finding, corpus-driven methodology.

Table 14.2 provides a schematic overview of how a hypothesis-driven analysis of learner corpora might proceed; it is based on a study in Tono (2000). This contrasts with Table 14.3, which describes the stages in a topic-driven analysis of learner corpora.

1	***Initial hypothesis***	An analysis of a learner corpus will support the morpheme order results of Dulay and Burt.
2	***Corpus selection/ compilation***	Selection or compilation of learner corpora to use.
3	***Preliminary data analysis***	Tagging of relevant morphemes in the learner corpus. (e.g. *I have hardly had <ART> a </ART> bad dream.)*
4	***Further data analysis***	Searching for all instances of each morpheme tag and marking errors manually. (e.g. *Do I see <ER_ART> the </ER_ART> movies too much?*) Assessment and computation of frequency of errors, following Dulay and Burt's methodology.

Table 14.2 A hypothesis-driven learner corpus study

The most common form of learner corpora research involves contrasting an NNS with an NS corpus or with a corpus-based reference such as the Longman Grammar of Written and Spoken English (Biber, Johansson, Leech, Conrad, and Finnegan 1999). If a learner corpus is to be contrasted with an NS corpus, then a variety of issues arise, as they always do when corpora are compared. It is always possible to find fault with research relying on the comparison of corpora that have been compiled by different groups for different purposes. In such situations the corpora necessarily differ along several dimensions, making comparability of linguistic features open to question. Given that there is no perfect benchmark, an appropriate benchmark must be found for each study. One issue concerns the variety of NS English to be used. Is the reference corpus based on British, American or Australian English, for example? More important perhaps is the question of text type. A corpus such as the Brown corpus (Francis and Kucera 1967) or the American National Corpus (Ide, Reppen, and Suderman 2002) contain such a wide variety of different types of language that they are probably unsuitable for many studies (Granger and Tyson 1996). The problem here is that the combination of genres in the general corpus does not provide a good reference point for the learner corpus, which invariably consists of a single genre. Thus, using a general corpus introduces an additional variable, as any comparisons made would be based on one genre versus multiple genres as well as on learner language versus non-learner language.

In cases where the reference corpus is based on a single text type, such as a newspaper, variability in language use still occurs due to the styles of different writers and differences associated with different sections of the newspaper. Nevertheless, the variability is much reduced and the writing in a newspaper may be taken as a target that student writers may aim for. An alternative option is to use a reference corpus that is as close as possible in

1 Initial topic	Example: The use of hedges by language learners. (The identification of items of potential interest may be based on a preliminary learner corpus analysis as described below in Preliminary data analysis.)
2 Corpus selection/ compilation	Selection or compilation of learner corpora to use. Depending on the nature of the investigation, other types of corpora may be used: an NS corpus, a bilingual (translation) corpus, or a textbook corpus. See Contrastive studies below.
3 Preliminary data analysis	Analysis or identification of the item in a learner corpus: using word frequency lists, n-grams (e.g. 3-word sequences ordered by frequency), collocation lists, etc.
4 Further data analysis	Use of concordance searches on target forms to show the forms in their linguistic context. Sorting concordance lines may serve to group similar uses together. This format facilitates the identification of the range and frequency of form-function mappings. Coding of target forms.
5 Contrastive studies	Evaluation of the patterning revealed by learner corpus data analysis, typically based on one or more of the following: – Comparison of learners with different L1 – Comparison of learners in different instructional situations – Contrast of learner language with an L2 reference corpus – Comparison of different levels of proficiency – Longitudinal (or cross-sectional) analysis based on learner corpora – Evaluation of learner language based on L1–L2 equivalences revealed by analysis of a L1–L2 bilingual corpus and/or by analysis of L1 and L2 monolingual corpora – Comparison of different modalities or genres – Comparison with corpora representing input to the learners (textbooks, classroom talk, etc.)

Table 14.3 A hypothesis-finding, corpus-driven learner corpus study

genre and other dimensions to the learner corpus. In fact, most studies of ICLE subcorpora use the LOCNESS corpus as a benchmark. This corpus consists of essays written by British and American undergraduates.

Comparisons of learner corpora with a reference corpus have been carried out on a variety of lexical and grammatical topics: complement clauses

(Biber and Reppen 1998), direct questions (Virtanen 1998), causatives (Altenberg 2002), tenses (Granger 1999; Housen 2002), modals (Aijmer 2002; McEnery and Kifle 2002), hedges/certainty markers (Flowerdew 2000, Milton and Hyland 1997), adjective intensifiers (Lorenz 1998), formulae (de Cock 1998) and connectors (Altenberg and Tapper 1998).

A learner corpus study

An example of learner corpus analysis is Housen's 2002 study of the development of the English verbal system. This particular study is a quite complex analysis of the formal and functional development of the verbal system in learners. One goal of the investigation is to determine the applicability of the Aspect Hypothesis (Andersen and Shirai 1996; Bardovi-Harlig 1999), which suggests that the initial uses of verb morphology are constrained by the inherent semantics of the verbs used. Thus following this hypothesis, we might, for instance, expect the learners to initially use the morpheme *-ing* solely with activity verbs.

The patterns of language emerging from the study of actual production data reflect a variety of influences, including language processing, L1 influence, conceptual predisposition and frequency of forms in the input (Housen 2002: 108). The study is summarized in Table 14.4.

Housen's study can be seen as being in the tradition of research on the order of acquisition of morphemes, but in a corpus-based study such as this one considerable coding is required to identify the different verb forms embedded in the mass of corpus data. It is worth pointing out that in this particular study, the development of the verb by individual learners is not tracked and hence it is not possible to assess the variability in the developmental sequences followed by individuals.

Explaining patterns in learner corpora

Determining the source of the patterns detected in corpus analyses presents considerable difficulties. In some cases, researchers feel confident in attributing the patterns of interlanguage to transfer from L1, especially in cases of lexical patterns. For instance, Lu (2002: 51) found in a comparison of noun compounds used in a Chinese learner corpus (CLEC) that the phrase *we college students*, a translation of *wo men da xue sheng*, was used quite frequently.

The assessment of the source of grammatical patterns is much more difficult. In her investigation of modals in a learner corpus, Aijmer (2002: 60) points out that the overuse or underuse of particular modals may be due to L1 influences or to general learner strategies, but may also relate to the different distribution of modals in spoken and written modalities. Several researchers have found that the writing of English learners had the characteristics of more informal, spoken usage. For instance, Altenberg and

Research question	Housen (2002) investigates how second language learners of English acquire the forms and functions of the English verbal system.
Participants	23 Dutch-speaking and 23 French-speaking students, 9–17 years old. Also 8 native speakers, aged 11–13.
Data collection	The data were collected by interview and semi-guided speech tasks. The recorded data were transcribed, segmented, and annotated, forming the Corpus of Young Learner Interlanguage.
Analysis	1 The verbs were coded for morphosyntactic form (e.g. *-ing, -s, -ed, en*), agreement values, tense (past, present, etc.), aspect (imperfect, progressive, etc.), and inherent aspect (state, activity,etc.) 2 The learner transcripts were grouped according to proficiency level: Low, Lower Intermediate, Higher Intermediate and High. 3 The clauses in the transcripts were analysed for the underuse/overuse of inflectional verb categories (*V, Ving, Ved, Vs*). Underuse in this study measures the instances in which a particular form is omitted from an obligatory context. Overuse refers to instances of use of a form in inappropriate contexts.
Results	Based on the data, Housen described three formal stages. Stage 1. Invariant default forms. Verbs appear as invariant forms, typically the unmarked base form, but high frequency irregular *Ven* forms (e.g. *got*) also occur. Stage 2. Non-functional variation. The order of emergence of forms is *V0 > Ving; was > Ven > Ved; going + Vinf > have + V; Vs; will + V.* Stage 3. More target-like use of verb morphology to encode tense, aspect and agreement. The patterns of underuse and overuse decrease with increasing proficiency, although there is still variation among different verb forms. The results support the predictions of the Aspect Hypothesis for development of the *Ving* form, but not for the *Vs* form.
Discussion	The results reveal general patterns in the development of the English verbal system and also the variability in development.

Table 14.4 A study of the development of the English verbal system

Tapper (1998) found that formal connectors such as *therefore* and *thus* were underused, while more informal markers, *but* and *still*, were overused.

Altenberg (2002) undertakes an interesting contrastive study using parallel English-Swedish texts to analyse the range of causative constructions (for example, *make* causative, synthetic causatives, and other construction types) and to assess how the causative constructions correspond to each other in the two languages. As a result of his investigations on translated texts, Altenberg found that the English *make* causative is generally equivalent to the Swedish *göra* construction. Importantly, however, English *make* is in competition with a variety of other causative constructions, and many of the *göra* uses in Swedish are not translated using causative *make* in English. Thus, while there is a general equivalence between the two analytic causatives in English and Swedish, there are also some important differences which become apparent only after a detailed analysis of parallel texts.

What do Swedish learners of English do with respect to the production of English causative constructions? Not surprisingly, given the facts discussed above, Swedish learners of English tend to overuse the *make* causative, which Altenberg (2002: 52) suggests is due to transfer propelled by cross-linguistic similarity. He proposes that Swedish learners see the similarity between the prototypical causative construction in Swedish and the English construction, and tend to use *make* causatives in a way that mimics the wide functionality of the *göra* causative. This contrasts with the behaviour of French learners of English, for example, who do not overuse the English *make* causative.

Like NS–NNS studies, the analysis of NNS–NNS contrasts provides evidence of L1 influence on learner output, but such studies also provide evidence of general learner strategies, such as simplification, and other general aspects of L2 development that are unrelated to L1. Thus NNS–NNS comparisons can be seen as a way to increase our understanding of the characteristics of interlanguage and assess the influence of particular variables on the form of interlanguage. Aijmer (2002: 57) cautions that the results from a single study which point to the existence of learner strategies need to be followed up with more extensive investigations on a range of learners and on different types of data.

In order to fully understand the process of second language acquisition, it is necessary to trace the interlanguage of individual learners over time. In other words, it would be beneficial to carry out longitudinal studies to complement the kinds of investigations described above. Many learner corpora contain data from students at different proficiency levels, which can be used to suggest hypotheses about the paths of language development. Such 'quasi-longitudinal' data studies (Granger 2002: 11) can be checked using longitudinal corpora in which the progress of individual students can be tracked. Research by Housen (2002: 95), described above, suggests that the aggregate data on the development of the third-person singular morpheme *-s* broadly follows the patterns emerging from a longitudinal study (Housen 1995, 1998). It is also possible, however, that the aggregate view offered by the corpus as a whole will mask changes in the language of individuals or the differences in individual development paths. These longitudinal or quasi-longitudinal studies (Housen 2002; Tono 2000) have the potential to provide corpus evidence relating to the morpheme acquisition study of Dulay and Burt (1974). (See Chapter 4.)

Corpus analysis software

An example of a common type of data used in corpus linguistics is the word frequency list, which can easily be generated for any learner corpus and the results inspected for unusual patterns. But rather than simply examine a word frequency list of a learner corpus, we can compare the frequency of words in a learner corpus with a reference corpus, which might be another learner corpus or a native speaker corpus.

The screen shot in Figure 14.3 illustrates the data produced by the 'corpus comparison' command in the software program *MonoConc Pro* (Barlow 2002). In this example, the frequency of the words in a corpus, the French learners component of ICLE, are compared with the frequency of words in a reference corpus, in this case a corpus based on *The Times* newspaper.

MonoConc Pro - Fricle2 - [Corpus Comparison]

File Concordance Frequency Display Window Info

Current Count	Current Pct	Current Word	Reference Cour	Reference Pct	Pct Change	LL
834	0.3673%	europe	5894	0.0288%	0.3385%	2616.1633
5199	2.2896%	is	218353	1.0654%	1.2242%	2360.1252
333	0.1467%	harmony	213	0.0010%	0.1456%	2280.4646
298	0.1312%	ramsay	121	0.0006%	0.1306%	2189.1207
476	0.2096%	nation	1458	0.0071%	0.2025%	2170.6570
1237	0.5448%	people	21878	0.1068%	0.4380%	1998.9832
392	0.1726%	identity	869	0.0042%	0.1684%	1994.7478
1752	0.7716%	we	42847	0.2091%	0.5625%	1983.5640
0	0.0000%	"	78359	0.3823%	-0.3823%	1726.8397
481	0.2118%	countries	2876	0.0140%	0.1978%	1646.8850
166	0.0731%	pincher	0	0.0000%	0.0731%	1498.5349
279	0.1229%	imagination	706	0.0034%	0.1194%	1360.0693
1999	0.8803%	this	70430	0.3437%	0.5367%	1302.7413
564	0.2484%	was	161169	0.7864%	-0.5380%	1134.1905
0	0.0000%	pounds	50434	0.2461%	-0.2461%	1111.4413
589	0.2594%	european	8902	0.0434%	0.2160%	1098.1472
329	0.1449%	novel	2072	0.0101%	0.1348%	1097.1148
162	0.0713%	dreaming	115	0.0006%	0.0708%	1088.9699
0	0.0000%	1994	46906	0.2289%	-0.2289%	1033.6929
309	0.1361%	-	1976	0.0096%	0.1264%	1022.3139
641	0.2823%	life	12607	0.0615%	0.2208%	931.2360
13	0.0057%	date	46193	0.2254%	-0.2197%	896.7651

360 files in current corpus | 227,070 words, 12,993 types

Figure 14.3 The comparison of words in a learner corpus and reference corpus

The columns in the table in Figure 14.3 provide different kinds of data related to the words in the learner corpus. The leftmost column gives the count or frequency of each word in the learner corpus. In the next column these data are expressed as a percentage, i.e., the frequency divided by the total number of words in the corpus multiplied by 100. The third column lists all the words occurring in the learner corpus or reference corpus. The next two columns give the count and percentage for the word in the reference corpus.

The two rightmost columns provide comparative information for each word: Percentage Change and the Log Likelihood (LL) value, a statistical measure of difference (Rayson and Garside 2000) of words in two corpora.[3] Percentage change is simply (Percentage in current corpus) – (Percentage in reference corpus). A positive value for Percentage change indicates that the word is over-represented in the learner corpus; a negative value indicates under-representation.

The words shown in the screen shot in Figure 14.3 do not constitute a random selection; they represent those words which, according to the Log Likelihood value, are most distinct, based on a comparison of their occurrence in the two corpora. The next step is to examine the list more closely in order to eliminate those words that are not associated with learner language. The word *pounds*, for instance, does not occur in the learner corpus, but this under-representation occurs because the French learners of English happen not to be writing about British currency or weight. The words, *europe, harmony*, and *nation*, for example, are over-represented in the learner corpus, but this is due to the essay topics assigned to the students and again we can ignore such words.

After removing words which are not of interest, we are left with the selected data in Table 14.5. All the words listed in this table are significantly over-represented in the learner corpus and are candidates for follow-up investigations. We find various forms of the copula, as well as connectors such as *moreover, nowadays, because*, and *indeed*, and the modals *will* and *can*.

It goes without saying that results obtained in this manner are merely suggestive. The *Times* corpus is being used here as a representative of a target language, but clearly there are genre differences between a newspaper corpus and academic essays, and it may be these genre differences which are behind the difference in relative frequencies of these words. This may be the case for *is*, for example, but it may also be a fact that the French learners do overuse copula sentences or phrases such as *it is* or *there is* in their writing. Thus for each of these words, further investigations are needed in order to determine whether the overuse is a reflection of frequent syntactic or discourse patterns or whether it is simply a matter of lexical choice. Once this is determined, it is possible to take the next step and investigate possible reasons for the patterns found.

Word	Percentage Difference	Log Likelihood
is	1.22%	2360.12
people	0.43%	1998.98
we	0.56%	1983.56
this	0.53%	1302.74
will	0.40%	838.57
our	0.21%	811.08
they	0.37%	693.85
are	0.41%	677.17
moreover	0.05%	587.99
be	0.42%	577.98
not	0.37%	574.91
also	0.21%	572.66
can	0.23%	560.46
nowadays	0.04%	471.06
because	0.16%	452.60
think	0.11%	442.59
of	0.77%	419.51
to	0.70%	397.25
their	0.25%	378.56
it	0.36%	365.15
these	0.12%	328.59
indeed	0.06%	325.67
does	0.09%	319.61
that	0.38%	316.85

Table 14.5 Words over-represented in a learner corpus

Many variations on word counts are possible. For example, it may be profitable to count n-grams, for example, word pairs or word triples, etc., to see whether certain sequences appear to be overly frequent.[4] To briefly illustrate these kinds of data, Table 14.6 shows the rank order of the ten most frequent word pairs from the French, German, and Czech components of ICLE, and again these results are compared with data from the *Times* newspaper corpus.

Note that the same two most frequent bigrams occur in all the subcorpora and it is only in the third row that some differences start to appear. Looking at the table as a whole, we can see that further analysis of the bigram *will be* from the French subcorpus, the bigram *have to* from the German subcorpus, and the use of the copula in the Czech subcorpus might be fruitful as these results suggest an overuse of these forms in the learners' English. This methodology can be extended to trigrams, tetragrams, and so on. It should be noted, however, that the larger the n-gram, the more idiosyncrasies appear, due to the particular content being described.[5] It is also possible

French	German	Czech	Times
of the	*of the*	*of the*	*of the*
in the	*in the*	*in the*	*in the*
to the	*to be*	*it is*	*to the*
to be	*to the*	*to be*	*on the*
it is	*it is*	*do not*	*for the*
of a	*on the*	*to the*	*to be*
is a	*have to*	*It is*	*and the*
on the	*of a*	*is the*	*at the*
will be	*in a*	*is a*	*that the*
is the	*and the*	*is not*	*of a*

Table 14.6 Frequent bigrams in learner corpora and a newspaper corpus

French		German		Czech		Times	
The	10.2%	*The*	7.5%	*The*	7.5%	*The*	11.4%
In	5.0%	*I*	5.9%	*It*	7.2%	*It*	3.3%
This	4.9%	*But*	5.0%	*They*	5.8%	*He*	3.1%
But	4.2%	*It*	4.0%	*I*	4.8%	*But*	2.8%
It	4.0%	*In*	3.2%	*But*	3.5%	*In*	2.5%
He	3.4%	*They*	2.8%	*We*	3.5%	*I*	1.8%
They	3.1%	*And*	2.1%	*In*	2.8%	*A*	1.6%
We	2.8%	*This*	2.0%	*And*	2.6%	*They*	1.3%
As	2.1%	*There*	1.6%	*There*	2.6%	*This*	1.3%
She	1.6%	*If*	1.5%	*He*	2.2%	*In*	1.0%

Table 14.7 Common sentence-initial words in learner corpora and a newspaper corpus

to examine POS tag sequences rather than word sequences (Aarts and Granger 1998).

Another variant on word counts is shown in Table 14.7. This table illustrates the most common sentence-initial words in three learner corpora and in *The Times* newspaper corpus. We find that the same set of words tend to be used sentence-initially in all four subcorpora, but the use of *as* in the French subcorpus and the use of *if* in the German subcorpus stand out.

French	German	Czech	Times
It is	*It is*	*It is*	*It is*
On the	*In the*	*They are*	*In the*
This is	*There is*	*There is*	*It was*
As a	*There are*	*There are*	*He was*
In the	*On the*	*I think*	*There is*
He is	*When I*	*On the*	*But the*
In this	*This is*	*In the*	*This is*
There is	*It was*	*We can*	*It is*
Let us	*If you*	*This is*	*He is*
They are	*They are*	*It was*	*Yours faithfully*

Table 14.8 Common sentence-initial bigrams in learner corpora and a newspaper corpus

Following up on the data in Table 14.7, we can look at the most common sentence-initial word pairs and we find *as a* in the French subcorpus and *if you* in the German subcorpus (Table 14.8).

The advantage of performing these preliminary kinds of text analysis based on word frequency measures is that few, if any, assumptions are made about the nature of learner language. An initial examination of the results may reveal interesting data and can suggest hypotheses, which can be pursued by follow-up studies.

Different kinds of text analysis provide different views of language data (Barlow 2004) and one obvious problem with wordlists is that all the context of the words has been removed. Once a word or phrase has been selected for further study on the basis of wordlist data, the next step is typically to perform a KWIC (keyword in context) concordance search. As noted above, any of the words in Table 14.5 might be selected for a follow-up study. In this case, we can choose *indeed* and perform a concordance search for the word, as illustrated in Figure 14.4. Such a search will reveal all the instances, 81 in this case, of the keyword (or phrase) within its linguistic context, allowing for further classification on the basis of meaning, function, error type, etc. In other words, the text on either side of the keyword is used to classify each instance based on an error analysis or based on form-function mappings or whatever other level of analysis is deemed necessary. Such an analysis is necessary to determine which of the uses of *indeed* are being overused by the French learners of English. If the narrow context of a few words either side of the keyword is not enough for these classificatory purposes, then a wider context can be obtained by clicking on a particular line, as shown in Figure 14.4.

The analysis of concordance results is often aided by the ability to re-sort the concordance lines based, for instance, on the word preceding or

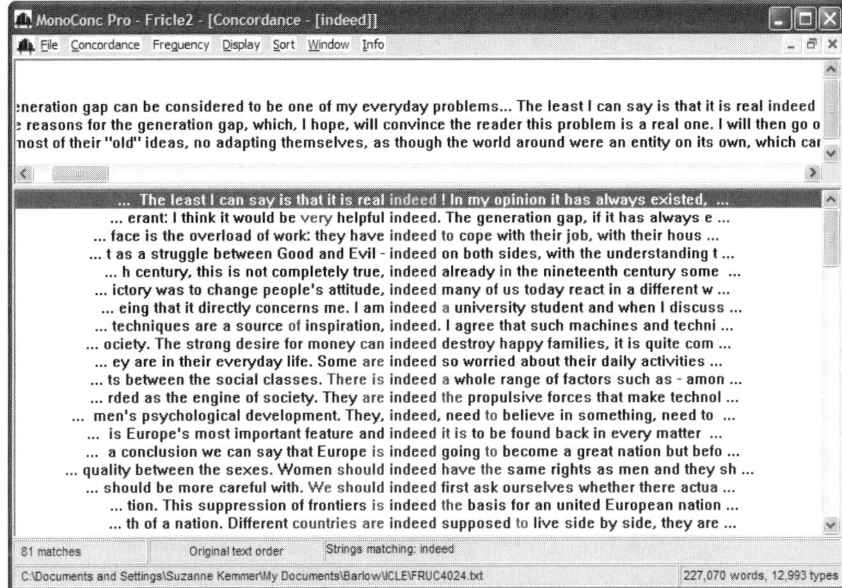

Figure 14.4 A concordance search for indeed *in a learner corpus*

the word following the keyword. Rearranging the lines in this way often highlights regularities in the data because repeated patterns stand out visually and this may make the classification of the concordance lines easier. The screen shot in Figure 14.5 shows the results of a search for sentence-initial *It is*. The concordance lines have been sorted 1st right, 2nd right, which alphabetizes the lines based on the word following *It is* and in those cases where the word is repeated, the lines are ordered secondarily according to the alphabetical order of the second word following *It is*.

In this section, we have discussed two uses of text analysis software. One is to generate wordlists and similar data structures that may reveal interesting patterns in the language used by learners. The second is to use concordance searches and sorting as an aid for in-depth analyses or classifications of errors, form-function mappings, or other linguistic functions. The fact that samples of learner performance data are stored in computer-based digital format means that it is simple to search for and extract particular lexical items (for example, *nevertheless, on the one hand*) and grammatical forms (for example, *have* + participle), along with as much linguistic context as is desired. Searches can be performed fairly easily and quickly, making it feasible to carry out multiple exploratory investigations.

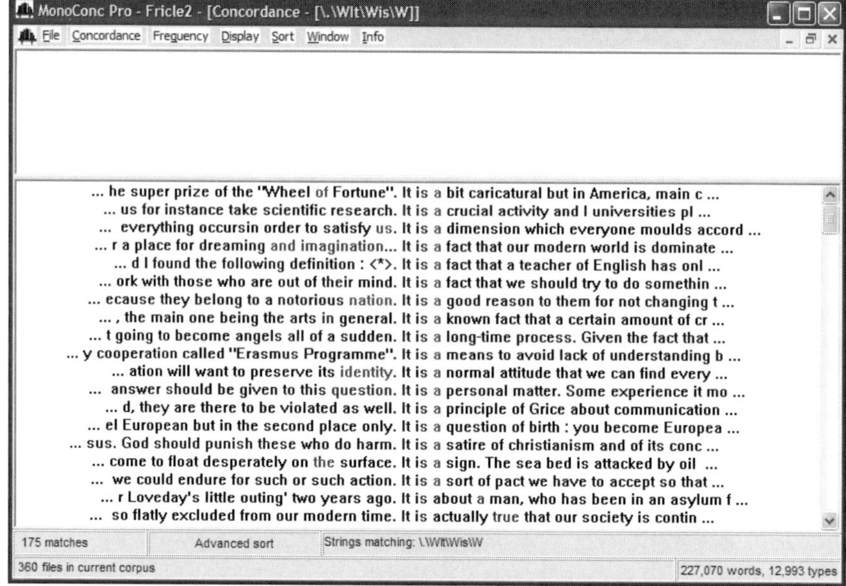

Figure 14.5 A concordance search for It is *sorted 1st right 2nd right*

Task: Analysing a learner corpus

You can examine the Polish component (350,000 words) of ICLE at the website http://elex.amu.edu.pl/~przemka/concord2/search.html

A preliminary analysis of Polish learners of English shows that the sentence-initial phrase *As a* is used quite frequently, as it is in French. Analyse the use of the sentence initial phrase *As a* in this Polish learner corpus to find out if the patterns of use are similar to those found in the French data where three main phrases used were *as a conclusion* (41%), *as a matter of fact* (29%) and *as a result* (10%).

To perform the analysis, carry out the follow steps.

1 Perform a KWIC search for *As a* (i.e. *As a* followed by space), remembering to search for *As a*, not *as a*.
2 How many instances occur in the corpus?
3 List the main sentence-initial phrases based on *As a* (*As a result*, etc.). Give the percentages for these phrases.
4 How do these percentages compare with the results for French, given above?
5 Describe how you would construct a follow-up investigation to test for overuse or underuse of these phrases.

Final comment

Learner corpora potentially provide a very rich source of data, which may be used to overcome some of the problems with EA noted in Chapter 3, such as the inability of the method to account for learners' avoidance of L2 forms. On the other hand, the size and complexity of learner corpus data means that in the absence of automatic analysis software, researchers must perform a considerable amount of manual coding of errors or form-function categories.

Most of the existing learner corpora are based on the writing of fairly advanced language learners. In order to play a central role in understanding SLA a wider range of learner corpora, including spoken learner corpora, will have to be created. As Granger (2002: 9) notes, 'learner corpora should not be seen as a panacea, but rather as one highly versatile resource which SLA/FLT researchers can usefully add to their battery of data types'.

Notes

1 Currently four subcorpora are complete (French, Chinese, Italian, Japanese) and a CD-ROM release of LINDSEI (with audio-synchronization) is planned for 2005. See http://www.fltr.ucl.ac.be/fltr/germ/etan/cecl/Cecl–Projects/Lindsei/lindsei.htm.

2 XML stands for Extensible Markup Language and is similar in many ways to the html tags used in webpages. See http://www.w3.org/XML for details. The following is an example of a sentence from a learner corpus with an error tagged using XML: *The main feature of campus is <GA> the "Corr = it"</GA> conviviality.*

3 This statistic is similar to the better-known chi-squared test, but is more reliable for low scores. The test compares the frequency of word A in corpus 1 with the frequency of word B in corpus 2, based on the assumption that the word occurrences follow a binomial distribution.

4 See De Cock, Granger, Leech, and McEnery (1998) for an analysis which takes distribution as well as frequency into account.

5 The n-gram data were produced by the software program *Collocate* (Barlow 2003), but it is also possible to write simple Perl scripts or use UNIX commands such as *sort, uniq, tail*, and so on, to produce such lists.

15 Conclusion

Introduction

In this book we have explored SLA by examining how researchers have analysed learner language. The variety of methods we have discussed is a testimony to the multidimensional nature of SLA. They reflect the broad range of research questions that SLA researchers have sought to address and the disparate theoretical underpinnings of these questions. The different methods are evidence, then, of the different conceptions of what it means to acquire an L2. In this final chapter, we explore these different conceptions and demonstrate how they are related to the various methods of analysis we have considered. We will do so in accordance with the general distinction that has informed this book—between learner language as a source of data for investigating what learners know and can do with an L2 (Chapters 3 through 10) and learner language as a source of information about the factors that influence L2 learning (Chapters 11, 12, and 13).

Learner language as evidence of L2 acquisition

Implicit in all the methods of analysis we have considered is the assumption that what learners say or write is indicative of what they know of the L2. This assumption, however, has not gone unchallenged. Some SLA researchers (for example, Sharwood Smith 1986) have taken the view that learner intuitions, tapped by means of grammaticality judgement tasks (see Chapter 2) constitute a more valid measure of what learners know (i.e. their linguistic competence). Such measures have been widely used by researchers interested in testing specific hypotheses based on a theory of generative grammar (for example, the principles and parameters model). Increasingly, however, even researchers working in this paradigm have seen the need to at least complement judgement data with learner-language data. (See, for example, White 1989.) Our own position, stated explicitly in Chapter 2, is that learner language should constitute the primary data for the study of L2 acquisition.

What then are the principal conceptions in SLA that underlie the methods of analysis discussed in Chapters 3 to 10? We will identify a number of key conceptions involving (1) choice of norms, (2) L2 competence/proficiency,

(3) the discoursal context of L2 acquisition, and (4) the relationship between L2 use and acquisition.

External and internal norms

It is possible to identify two different kinds of norm underlying the different methods: external and internal norms. In the case of conceptions based on external norms, learners are seen as 'targeted' on native-speaker norms. That is, acquisition is measured in terms of the extent to which learners employ target-language forms. Thus, the native speaker becomes a yardstick with which to measure acquisition. This is reflected most obviously in the idea of a 'criterion level' of accuracy (typically 90 per cent) as a means of determining whether specific features have been 'acquired'. Conceiving acquisition in terms of external norms is problematic for two main reasons. First, there is the question of the choice of external norms to serve as the point of comparison with learner language. As Davies (1991) has shown it is not easy to define who a 'native speaker' is.[1] SLA researchers have tended to assume that learners are targeted on some standard dialect but Beebe (1985) and Goldstein (1987) have pointed out that learners often choose speakers of non-standard dialects as their reference group. Second, and perhaps more seriously, Bley-Vroman (1983) has pointed out that analyses of learner language that are based on external norms may fail to reveal the inner systematicity of learner's interlanguages. He argues that, in order to avoid the 'comparative fallacy', researchers need to view interlanguage on its own terms by identifying the internal norms that learners establish at different stages of development. As Table 15.1 shows, error analysis, obligatory occasion analysis, the kinds of measures used to determine accuracy discussed in Chapter 7, and many of the interactional analyses presented in Chapter 8 are all predicated on external norms and are thus 'guilty' of committing the comparative fallacy. In contrast, frequency analysis, functional analysis, conversation analysis, and the methods of analysis based on sociocultural theory are all designed to examine learners' internal norms.

There is clearly a need to examine learners' interlanguages in terms of their internal norms. Only by so doing can the 'dynamic' aspects of interlanguage development be properly understood. However, we can also question the validity of the 'comparative fallacy'. As we noted in Chapter 2, learners are typically targeted on native-speaker norms and as such themselves perform 'cognitive comparisons' in the process of learning an L2. In this respect, then, an analysis based on external norms can be seen as psycholinguistically valid (James 1998). Davies (2003: 196) endorses such a view, noting that 'the native speaker must represent a model and a goal for learners of second languages'. Lardiere (2003) points out the learner's external linguistic environment, which serves as a primary source of data for interlanguage development in the eyes of many SLA theorists, also reflects

Methods of analysis	(1) Norms	(2) Competence/proficiency	(3) Discoursal context	(4) Type of L2 use
1 Error analysis	external	linguistic competence	decontextualized utterances	independently constructed utterances
2 Obligatory occasion analysis	external	linguistic competence	decontextualized utterances	independently constructed utterances
3 Frequency analysis	internal	linguistic competence	decontextualized utterances	independently constructed utterances
4 Functional analysis	internal	functional competence	decontextualized utterances	independently constructed utterances
5 Analysing fluency, complexity and accuracy	external	proficiency	decontextualized utterances	independently constructed utterances
6 Interactional analysis (e.g. corrective feedback)	external	linguistic competence	discoursal perspective	no inherent position
7 Conversation analysis	internal	linguistic and functional competence	discoursal perspective	no inherent position
8 Sociocultural methods of analysis	internal	linguistic and functional competence	discoursal perspective	co-constructed and independently constructed utterances

Table 15.1 Theoretical conceptions underlying methods of analysis directed at describing and explaining learners' interlanguages

target language systems. It follows that a legitimate line of enquiry is to examine in what ways learner language mirrors or departs from these norms. Ideally, when this is undertaken, researchers should, however, seek to compare how learners and native speakers perform the same task rather than just assume that native-speaker competence entails perfect mastery. None the less, in some of the best studies of learner language, both conceptualizations have been evident. Doughty and Varela (1998), for example, conducted both a target-language analysis (based on external norms) and an interlanguage analysis (based on internal norms) of samples of learner language in order to determine the effects of corrective recasting on learners' L2 development.

The nature of L2 competence/proficiency

SLA researchers, especially those committed to a psycholinguistic perspective, generally talk about 'L2 competence'. In contrast, language testers and teachers prefer to talk about 'L2 proficiency'. The two labels represent somewhat different conceptualizations of the products of L2 acquisition. Richards *et al.* (1992) define competence as 'a person's internalized grammar of the language' (1992: 68) and language proficiency as 'the degree of skill with which a person can use a language' (1992: 204). Taylor (1988) elegantly captures the key difference in pointing out that whereas the term 'competence' relates to what learners *know*, 'proficiency' incorporates both what they know and their *ability to use* their knowledge in actual communication. In other words, when we conceptualize L2 acquisition in terms of knowledge, we do so in a narrower, more restricted sense than when we conceptualize it in terms of proficiency.

Further, 'competence', even when this is narrowly defined in terms of 'grammar', can be viewed in different ways. Grammar is both form and function. Thus, competence can refer to the formal properties of a learner's interlanguage or it can refer to how forms and functions map onto each other. Early methods of analysing learner language (for example, error analysis, obligatory occasion analysis and frequency analysis) treated the learner's interlanguage as a system comprised of formal features (for example, plural *-s*, article *a*, *no* + verb, aux + neg + verb). Later, researchers developed methods for examining the evidence of form-function mappings in learner language, offering a much richer view of interlanguage and how this changed over time. This shift, of course, reflected a general shift in applied linguistics away from a concern for 'linguistic competence' in favour of 'functional/communicative competence'.

Only one of the methods we have examined in this book views L2 acquisition in terms of 'proficiency'—Chapter 7. There we considered learner language in relation to three aspects of language use (fluency, complexity and accuracy). Not surprisingly this approach to analysing language has been promoted by a researcher with a keen interest in language testing (Skehan), where traditionally 'proficiency' has been identified as the target for measurement. However, whereas testers have traditionally used rating scales to assess learners' performance on tasks, SLA researchers have preferred the 'more precise operationalizations of underlying constructs' (Skehan 2001) afforded by the specific measures of the three aspects of language use described in Chapter 7.

Again, whether researchers view L2 acquisition in relation to 'linguistic competence', 'functional competence' or 'language proficiency', will depend on their particular interests. Conceptualizing it as competence allows for very detailed linguistic descriptions of interlanguage development and for very specific hypotheses to be investigated, as evidenced in sample studies presented in Chapters 3, 4, 5, and 6. Arguably, too, in competence-oriented research that taps into learners' implicit knowledge system (i.e. by collecting naturally occurring or clinically elicited samples of learner language) the distinction between 'knowledge' and 'ability to use' becomes blurred. In contrast, conceptualizing L2 acquisition as language proficiency provides for a broader, more holistic account of L2 acquisition, which may afford a better union between SLA on the one hand and language testing/pedagogy on the other.

The discoursal context of L2 acquisition

Learner language can be conceived as comprising sets of decontextualized utterances (spoken or written) or as continuous discourse arising from learners' interaction with other learners or native speakers. In general, mainstream SLA has viewed it as the former: error analysis, obligatory occasion analysis, frequency analysis and functional analysis are all methods that operate on sets of discrete utterances, as reflected in the data sets provided for the data-analysis tasks in the chapters dealing with these methods. Of course, these methods have not entirely ignored the discoursal contexts of learner utterances, as these are often consulted in order to determine how individual utterances should be coded. For example, it is not always possible to identify whether or not an utterance is deviant without considering the broader context. Nevertheless, these methods do not take account of how individual utterances are discoursally constructed. In contrast, interactional analysis, conversation analysis and analyses based on sociocultural theory do so. The theories that underpin these methods of analysis differ in substantive ways but implicit in all of them is the view that the discourse helps to shape the utterances learners produce. As Hatch (1978) put it, linguistic knowledge is not so much a prerequisite for discourse as the product of it. From such a perspective, it follows that discrete utterances can only be properly understood and described in terms of the interactive work that learners engage in. There is also the important question of how learners acquire L2 pragmatic competence in its own right. Obviously this can only be answered by examining the discoursal context of learner utterances. Thus, whether the target of the enquiry is linguistic or pragmatic competence, a discoursal perspective on learner language is needed.

However, as we have seen in Chapters 8, 9, and 10, there is no agreement as to how such a discoursal perspective can best be provided. Apart from the different theoretical frameworks employed by interactional, conversation and microgenetic methods of analysis, SLA researchers differ fundamentally as to whether an atomistic approach that focuses on specific types of discourse, such as the negotiation of meaning, conversational repair work or collaborative dialogue, or a more all-encompassing approach that views learner discourse in relation to social context and seeks to account for it in more qualitative and holistic ways, is to be preferred. (See, for example, van Lier 1996 for a discussion of these approaches.) Linked to this debate is the question of whether learner discourse can be viewed in purely descriptive terms or whether a more critical, ideologically motivated perspective is required to understand how learners are positioned socially. In Chapter 8, for example, we noted Firth and Wagner's critique of mainstream studies of interactional phenomena in SLA on the grounds that they characterized learners as 'defective communicators'. In short, discoursal perspectives on L2 acquisition are multifarious, competitive and evolving.

The relationship between L2 use and acquisition

Finally, we turn to what is possibly the key to understanding the varying conceptions that underlie the different methods of analysis—how researchers have viewed the relationship between 'L2 use' and 'L2 acquisition'. Again, it is useful to point out what researchers have in common before highlighting their differences. All researchers who accept the primacy of learner language as data for investigating L2 acquisition accept that learners' use of the L2 in some way reflects their L2 competence/proficiency. The differences arise as to the *kind* of L2 use they see as fundamental.

In Chapters 1 and 2, we discussed different types of production data, pointing out that they can afford very different pictures of what learners know or can do. We argued that naturally occurring samples of L2 use provide the best evidence but that clinically elicited samples can also afford valid information. While not dismissing experimentally elicited data (as they may be required to investigate specific linguistic features that occur only infrequently in more spontaneous samples), we queried whether they can shed light on learners' implicit L2 knowledge—the description and explanation of which most researchers, irrespective of their theoretical affiliation, acknowledge as the principal goal of SLA studies. The priority we have assigned to naturally occurring samples (or failing those clinically elicited samples) is not especially controversial. Nevertheless, a quick trawl through SLA articles published in the last five years in *Studies in Second Language Acquisition* or *Second Language Research* will reveal the dominance of clinically elicited samples. This, in our view, constitutes a weakness in the research.

Greater controversy, which is theoretically motivated, lies in the interpretation to be given to what we will call 'co-constructed utterances'. These can be distinguished from 'independently constructed utterances'. The former consist of utterances that are discoursally constructed through the negotiation of meaning (or form), adjacency pairings, scaffolding, and the like. The latter consist of utterances that learners produce using their own linguistic resources without any interactional assistance. Consider, for example, this utterance:

Maria isn't coming to school today.

as it might have occurred in the following discoursal contexts:

Context A
LEARNER Maria no coming to school today.
TEACHER Oh, she isn't coming today.
LEARNER Yeah, *Maria isn't coming today.*

Context B
LEARNER *Maria isn't coming to school today.*
TEACHER Oh, why's that?
LEARNER She sick.

In Context A, the learner initially produces a deviant negative construction but subsequently corrects this by uptaking the teacher's recast. In Context B, the learner produces the correct negative construction independently. There can be no disagreement that the learner in Context B provides evidence of having acquired the English negative construction. But what about the learner in Context A? Some researchers (for example, Long forthcoming) have argued that learner uptake does not constitute evidence of acquisition and that only independently constructed utterances provide that. Other researchers, such as those working within sociocultural theory, have taken a radically different position. They have argued that participation *is* acquisition on the grounds that scaffolded production serves as the precursor of independent production. In other words, because other-regulation precedes self-regulation it constitutes a necessary stage in the process of acquiring new linguistic forms. It is not easy to see how these different positions can be reconciled until there is agreement on how to define 'acquisition' (i.e. as 'participation' *and* 'internalization' or just as 'internalization').

By way of summary, Table 15.1 identifies the underlying conceptions of the various methods of analysis treated in Chapters 3 to 10. It shows how the methods differ in their theoretical underpinnings. Thus, for example, a traditional method like error analysis is characterized as dependent on external norms, directed at describing linguistic competence and typically utilizing decontextualized, independently constructed utterances. In contrast, sociocultural methods of analysis are characterized as based on internal norms, directed at describing both linguistic and functional competence, adopting a discoursal perspective and utilizing both co-constructed and independently constructed utterances as evidence of acquisition.

Construct validity

In effect, this discussion of the underlying conceptions addresses the central question of construct validity. This concerns whether what is being measured is theoretically justified and can be effectively generalized. Because the different methods of analysis are underpinned by very different conceptions of what 'acquisition' means, it is clear that no one 'construct' is being measured. Rather different methods purport (explicitly or implicitly) to measure different constructs. This is itself problematic because it makes it difficult or even impossible to compare findings across studies that have employed methods of analysis based on very different constructs. It is self-evidently difficult to compare the findings of research directed at linguistic competence (for example, using error analysis) with those of research directed at L2 proficiency (for example, based on measure the fluency, complexity or accuracy of learners' productions). But it is also difficult, if not impossible, to compare results of a study based on external norms (for example, as with obligatory occasion analysis) with a study designed to identify learners' internal norms (for example, as with frequency analysis) even though both studies seek to investigate linguistic competence. Generalizability of results remains one of the central problems in SLA. At best, researchers can aim only to achieve construct validity in relation to the particular conception of acquisition that informs their own research.

Learner language as self-report data

As we have seen in Chapters 11 to 13, what L2 learners say about their learning provides researchers with a very valuable source of information about the factors that influence L2 acquisition. Those analysts who focus on the content of what learners say prefer data which are typically more qualitative in nature, in the sense that they take the form of extended texts, such as interview transcripts, written reports, diaries and open-ended questionnaires. As such, in the opinion of some researchers, the understanding and interpretation of these data require a higher element of risk; i.e. it is harder to get it right, and easier to get it wrong. (See the Final comment in this chapter, however.) Contributing to this situation are two principal conceptions underlying the methods of analysis in these chapters (i.e. coding data qualitatively, critical approaches and metaphor analysis): (1) learners being more or less aware of their learning and of the factors influencing their learning, and (2) the ideological contextualization of learning.

Direct and indirect accessibility

L2 learners are not always aware of how they learn or of the products of their learning. Furthermore, they are not always able to identify the factors which influence their learning; either those which promote learning or those which deny them opportunities to learn. At other times, they are able to articulate quite clearly their attitudes, beliefs, emotions and experiences. In this latter case, what they have to say is overtly displayed and thus directly available to analysts, whereas with the former case, the information is indirectly accessible through the interpretative work of analysts. With metaphor analysis, for example, the metaphors serve as 'windows' through which analysts examine the feelings and cognitions of learners. Meanings are thus *indirectly* accessible, and, as with other interpretive approaches (see Chapter 1), the analytic process involves a fair amount of flexibility, openness, and tolerance for ambiguity (Strauss and Corbin 1998) on the part of the analyst.

On the other hand, the numerous written comments by ESL students about their classes given in Chapter 11 point *directly* to the learners' perceptions of the usefulness of the learning/teaching activities in those classes. What the learners mean is overtly stated in their own words. Although meticulous coding for themes and searching for patterns is still required by analysts, there is perhaps less interpretative work required when learners' meanings are so directly accessible.

It makes sense to view the degrees of directness along a directness continuum: obviously, interpretative work is involved in qualitative coding, even when meanings are quite overtly displayed, and there may just as readily be times in metaphor analyses and in critical deconstructions of learner language texts when interpretations of data are made more accessible by the direct expression of ideological meanings by participants. In SLA, research which adopts inductive coding in its analysis would probably be more towards the *direct* end of this continuum, and metaphor and critical analytical approaches would be more towards the *indirect* end.

Ideological contextualization

Another continuum would be one which distinguishes analytical approaches which more or less take into account the contexts of learners' language learning experiences: that is, 'all relevant and salient micro and macro contextual influences that stand in a systematic relationship to the behavior

Methods of analysis	(1) Directness	(2) Ideological
1 Qualitative coding	more direct	less ideologically contextualized
2 Critical approaches	less direct	more ideologically contextualized
3 Metaphor analysis	less direct	less ideologically contextualized

Table 15.2 Theoretical conceptions underlying methods of analysis directed at describing and explaining learners' self-reports of language learning

or events one is attempting to explain' (Watson-Gegeo 1992: 54). However, authors such as Pennycook (2001) have argued that often these conceptualizations of context are 'limited to an overlocalized and undertheorized view of social relations' (2001: 5) and call for an approach which considers learner language (or any text) in its relation to broader sociocultural and political contexts. (See Chapter 12.) This certainly is the case in critical SLA. (See, for example, Norton 2000; Toohey 2000; Thesen 1997.)

As we indicated in Chapter 12, critical approaches to analysing learner language are explicitly ideological; their aim is to discover and transform the inequitable relations of power in which learners participate. These approaches involve constantly asking hard questions about gender, race, ethnicity, age, sexual orientation, class, culture, and identity—questions which address access, power, disparity, desire, difference, and resistance (Pennycook 2001: 11). Critical SLA is overtly political and its agenda is transparent and available for scrutiny. For critical SLA researchers, it is not possible to gain a full understanding of L2 acquisition without taking this stance. As such, there can hardly be an SLA which is not critical. Having a separate chapter on Critical Approaches in this book can, therefore, be seen as anomalous. However, in practice not all SLA work is critical, and so it becomes possible to place the three approaches in Chapters 11 to 13 along a critical continuum; those which more or less take into account the ideological context of learner language. (See Table 15.2.) Of course, the less ideological approaches have the potential to appropriate analytical procedures consistent with critical methodology.

Dependability

In the two sections above, we have pointed to the uncertain task of understanding and interpreting the content of what language learners say. In most cases, learners produce high-inference data which makes accurate analysis difficult. Reliability is thus constantly under threat. Instead of 'reliability', Lincoln and Guba (1985) prefer the term 'dependability', which means that analysts need to take care that all aspects of their analysis are fully documented, 'so that the decisions made and the conclusions reached are justifiable in their own contexts' (Edge and Richards 1998: 345). Although the three approaches to analysing learner-language data we have presented in Chapters 11, 12, and 13 involve an openness, a flexibility and a certain amount of risk-taking on the part of the analyst, they nevertheless have to produce accounts of that data which are dependable.

Final comment

The methods of analysis relating to learner language as language and as content might seem very different in terms of the degree of interpretation required of the researcher. Methods such as error analysis and obligatory occasion analysis may appear to be rigorous and 'objective' in comparison to methods such as inductive analysis or metaphor analysis. However, we have been at pains to point out that even the 'tighter' linguistic analyses in Chapters 3 to 10 call for all kinds of interpretive decision-making on the part of the researcher. For example, the very concept of 'error' in error analysis is problematic, creating problems of identification. For this reason, the need to demonstrate reliability or dependability, a point we have constantly emphasized throughout the book, is important no matter what the method of analysis.

Notes

1 Davies (2003) suggests that the only definition of 'native speaker' possible is a negative one—'to be a native speaker means not to be a non-native speaker' (2003: 213). Such a definition, however, cannot serve as a yardstick for measuring to what extent L2 learners have achieved native-speaker competence!

Bibliography

Aarts, J. and **S. Granger**. 1998. 'Tag sequences in learner corpora: a key to interlanguage grammar and discourse ' in S. Granger (ed.): *Learner English on Computer*. London and New York: Addison Wesley Longman.

Aijmer, K. 2002. 'Modality in advanced Swedish learners' written interlanguage' in S. Granger, J. Hung, and S. Petch-Tyson (eds.).

Aljaafreh, A. and **J. P. Lantolf**. 1994. 'Negative feedback as regulation and second language learning in the zone of proximal development.' *The Modern Language Journal* 78: 465–83.

Allen, J. P. B., M. Fröhlich, and **N. Spada**. 1984. 'The communicative orientation of language teaching: An observation scheme' in J. Handscombe, R. A. Orem, and B. P. Taylor (eds.): *On TESOL '83: The Question of Control*. Washington, DC: TESOL.

Allwright, R. 1975. 'Problems in the study of the language teachers' treatment of learner error' in M. Burt and H. Dulay (eds.): *On TESOL '75: New Directions in Second-Language Learning, Teaching and Bilingual Education*. Washington, DC: TESOL.

Allwright, R. 1988. *Observation in the Language Classroom*. London: Longman.

Allwright, R. and **K. Bailey**. 1991. *Focus on the Language Classroom*. Cambridge: Cambridge University Press.

Altenberg, B. 2002. 'Using bilingual corpus evidence in learner corpus research' in S. Granger, J. Hung, and S. Petch-Tyson (eds.).

Altenberg, B. and **M. Tapper**. 1998. 'The use of adverbial connectors in advanced Swedish learners' written English' in S. Granger (ed.): *Learner English on Computer*. London and New York: Addison Wesley Longman.

Andersen, R. 1978. 'An implicational model for second language research.' *Language Learning* 28: 221–82.

Andersen, R. 1984. 'What's gender good for anyway?' in R. Andersen (ed.): *Second Languages: A Cross-Linguistic Perspective*. Rowley, MA: Newbury House.

Andersen, R. and **Y. Shirai**. 1996. 'Primacy of aspect in first and second language acquisition: The pidgin creole connection' in W. Ritchie and T. Bhatia (eds.): *Handbook of Second Language Acquisition*. London: Academic Press.

Angelil-Carter, S. 2000. *Stolen Language? Plagiarism in Writing*. Harlow: Pearson.

Ary, D., L. Jacobs, and **A. Razavieh**. 1990. *Introduction to Research in Education*. Fort Worth: Harcourt Brace Jovanovich College Publishers.

Bachman, L. 1990. *Fundamental Considerations in Language Testing*. Oxford: Oxford University Press.

Baddeley, A. 1986. *Working Memory*. Oxford: Clarendon Press.

Bahns, J. and **H. Wode**. 1980. 'Form and function in L2 acquisition: the case of do-support in L2 acquisition' in S. Felix (ed.): *Second Language Development*. Tubingen: Gunter Narr.

Bailey, K. 1991. 'Diary studies of classroom language learning: the doubting game and the believing game' in E. Sadtano (ed.): *Language Acquisition and the Second/Foreign Language Classroom*. Singapore: SEAMEO Regional Language Centre.

Bailey, N., C. Madden, and **S. Krashen**. 1974. 'Is there a "natural sequence" in adult second language learning?' *Language Learning* 21: 235–43.

Bailey, K. M. and **Ochsner, R.** 1983. 'A methodological review of the diary studies: Windmill tilting or social science?' in K. M. Bailey, M. H. Long, and S. Peck (eds.): *Second Language Acquisition Studies*. Rowley, MA: Newbury House.

Baker, C. 1997. 'Survey methods in researching language and education' in N. Hornberger and D. Corson (eds.): *Encyclopedia of Language and Education, Volume 8: Research Methods in Language and Education*. Dordrecht: Kluwer.

Bardovi-Harlig, K. 1999. 'From morpheme studies to temporal semantics. Tense-aspect research in SLA: The state of the art' *Studies in Second Language Acquisition* 21: 341–82.

Bardovi-Harlig, K. 2000. 'Tense and aspect in second language acquisition: form, meaning and use.' *Language Learning Monograph Series*. Oxford: Blackwell.

Bardovi-Harlig, K. and **T. Bofman**. 1989. 'Attainment of syntactic and morphological accuracy by advanced language learners.' *Studies in Second Language Acquisition* 11: 17–34.

Barkhuizen, G. P. 1998. 'Discovering learners' perceptions of ESL classroom teaching/learning activities in a South African context.' *TESOL Quarterly* 32: 85–108.

Barkhuizen, G. P. 1999. 'Teaching and learning good English spelling: What's the point?' *Journal for Language Teaching* 33: 331–40.

Barkhuizen, G. 2002. ' "Maybe in twenty years time I will start getting to the point where I can start supporting the All Blacks against South Africa": Afrikaans speakers living in New Zealand.' Paper presented at the Language and Society conference, Hamilton, New Zealand, November 20–22.

Barlow, M. 1996. 'Corpora for theory and practice.' *International Journal of Corpus Linguistics* 1(1): 1–37.

Barlow, M. 2002. *MonoConc Pro*. Houston: Athelstan.

Barlow, M. 2003. *Collocate*. Houston: Athelstan.

Barlow, M. 2004. 'Software for corpus access and analysis' in J. Sinclair (ed.): *How to Use Corpora in Language Teaching*. Amsterdam: Benjamins.

Bayley, R. and **D. Preston**. (eds.). 1996. *Second Language Acquisition and Linguistic Variation*. Amsterdam: John Benjamins.

Beebe, L. 1985. 'Input: Choosing the right stuff' in S. Gass and C. Madden (eds.): *Input in Second Language Acquisition*. Rowley, MA: Newbury House.

Beebe, L. M. and **H. Giles**. 1984. 'Speech-accommodation theories: A discussion in terms of second-language acquisition.' *International Journal of the Sociology of Language* 46: 5–32.

Beebe, L., T. Takahashi, and **R. Uliss-Weltz**. 1990. 'Pragmatic transfer in ESL refusals' in R. Scarcella, E. Andersen, and S. Krashen (eds.): *On the Development of Communicative Competence in a Second Language*. New York: Newbury House.

Benson, M. J. 1989. 'The academic listening task: A case study.' *TESOL Quarterly* 23: 421–45.

Benson, D. and **J. Hughes**. 1991. 'Method: Evidence and inference for ethnomethodology.' in G. Button (ed.) *Ethnomethodology and the Human Sciences* (pp. 109–36). Cambridge: Cambridge University Press.

Berdan, R. 1996. 'Disentangling language acquisition from language variation' in R. Bayley and R. Preston (eds.).

Bhaskar, R. 1986. *Scientific Realism and Human Emancipation*. London: Verso.

Bialystok, E. 1990. *Communication Strategies: A Psychological Analysis of Second-Language Use*. Oxford: Basil Blackwell.

Biber, D. and **R. Reppen**. 1998. 'Comparing native and learner perspectives on English grammar: A study of complement clauses' in S. Granger (ed.): *Learner English on Computer*. London and New York: Addison Wesley Longman.

Biber, D., S. Johansson, G. Leech, S. Conrad, and **E. Finnegan**. 1999. *Longman Grammar of Spoken and Written English*. London: Longman.

Bickerton, D. 1981. *Roots of Language*. Ann Arbor: Karoma.

Birdsong, D. 1989. *Metalinguistic Performance and Interlinguistic Competence*. Berlin: Springer-Verlag.

Bley-Vroman, R. 1983. 'The comparative fallacy in interlanguage studies: The case of systematicity.' *Language Learning* 33: 1–17.

Bley-Vroman, R. 1989. 'The logical problem of second language learning' in S. Gass and J. Schachter (eds.).

Bley-Vroman, R. and **H. Joo.** 2001. 'The acquisition and interpretation of English locative constructions by native speakers of Korean.' *Studies in Second Language Acquisition* 23: 207–19.

Block, D. 1992. 'Metaphors we teach and learn by.' *Prospect* 7: 42–55.

Block, D. 1994. 'A day in the life of a class: Teacher/learner perceptions of task purpose in conflict.' *System* 22: 473–86.

Block, D. 1997. 'Learning by listening to language learners.' *System* 25: 347–60.

Block, D. 1999. 'Who framed SLA research? Problem framing and metaphoric accounts of the SLA research process' in L. Cameron and G. Low (eds.).

Block, D. 2003. *The Social Turn in Second Language Acquisition.* Edinburgh: Edinburgh University Press.

Blommaert, J. and **C. Bulcaen.** 2000. Critical discourse analysis. *Annual Review of Anthropology* 29: 447–66.

Blum-Kulka, S., J. House, and **G. Kasper** (eds.). 1989. *Cross-Cultural Pragmatics: Requests and Apologies.* Norwood, NJ: Ablex.

Bolton, K., G. Nelson, and **J. Hung.** 2002. 'A corpus-based study of connectors in student writing: research from the International Corpus of English in Hong Kong (ICE-HK).' *International Journal of Corpus Linguistics* 7: 165–82.

Bourdieu, P. 1977. 'The economics of linguistic exchanges.' *Social Science Information* 16: 645–68.

Briscoe, C. 1991. 'The dynamic interactions among beliefs, role metaphors and teaching practices: A case study of teacher change.' *Science Education* 75: 185–99.

Brooks, N. 1960. *Language and Language Learning: Theory and Practice.* New York: Harcourt Brace and World.

Brown, A. L. and **R. A. Ferrara.** 1985. 'Diagnosing zones of proximal development' in J. V. Wertsch (ed.): *Culture, Communication and Cognition: Vygotskian Perspectives.* Cambridge: Cambridge University Press.

Brown, J. D. 1983. 'An exploration of morpheme group interactions' in K. Bailey, M. Long, and S. Peck (eds.): *Second Language Acquisition Studies.* Rowley, MA: Newbury House.

Brown, J. D. 1988. *Understanding Research in Second Language Learning: A Teacher's Guide to Statistics and Research Design.* Cambridge: Cambridge University Press.

Brown, J. D. 2001. *Using Surveys in Language Programs.* Cambridge: Cambridge University Press.

Brown, J. D., T. Hilgers, and **J. Marsella.** 1991. 'Essay prompts and topics: Minimizing the effect of mean differences.' *Written Communication* 8: 533–56.

Brown, J. D. and **T. Rodgers.** 2002. *Doing Second Language Research.* Oxford: Oxford University Press.

Brown, R. 1973. *A First Language: The Early Stages.* Cambridge, MA: Harvard University Press.

Brown, R. 1991. 'Group work, task difference, and second language acquisition.' *Applied Linguistics* 21: 1–12.

Brumfit, C. 1984. *Communicative Methodology in Language Teaching.* Cambridge: Cambridge University Press.

Bulmer, M. 1979. 'Concepts in the analysis of qualitative data.' *Sociological Review* 27: 651–77.

Burdine, S. 2002. 'Means to an end: Communication strategies in French immersion.' Unpublished PhD Dissertation, Rice University.

Burmeister, H. and **D. Ufert.** 1980. 'Strategy switching' in S. Felix (ed.): *Second Language Development.* Tubingen: Gunter Narr.

Burt, M., H. Dulay, and **E. Hernandez Chavez.** 1973. *Bilingual Syntax Measure.* New York: Harcourt Brace Jovanovich.

Burt, M. and **C. Kiparsky**. 1972. *The Gooficon: A Repair Manual for English*. Rowley, MA: Newbury House.

Bygate, M. 1999. 'Quality of language and purpose of task: Patterns of learners' language on two oral communication tasks.' *Language Teaching Research* 3: 185–214.

Bygate, M. 2001. 'Effects of task repetition on the structure and control of oral language' in M. Bygate, P. Skehan, and M. Swain (eds.).

Bygate, M., P. Skehan, and **M. Swain**. (eds.). 2001. *Researching Pedagogic Tasks, Second Language Learning, Teaching and Testing*. Harlow: Longman.

Cameron, L. 1999a. 'Operationalising "metaphor" for applied linguistic research' in L. Cameron and G. Low (eds.).

Cameron, L. 1999b. 'Identifying and describing metaphor in spoken discourse' in L. Cameron and G. Low (eds.).

Cameron, L. and **G. Low** (eds.). 1999a. *Researching and Applying Metaphor*. Cambridge: Cambridge Applied Linguistics.

Cameron, L. and **G. Low** (eds.). 1999b. 'Metaphor.' *Language Teaching* 32: 1–20.

Cameron, R. and **J. Williams**. 1997. '*Senténce to ten cents*: A case study of relevance and communicative success in nonnative–native speaker interactions in a medical setting.' *Applied Linguistics*, 18: 415–45.

Canagarajah, A. S. 1993. 'Critical ethnography of a Sri Lankan classroom: Ambiguities in student opposition to reproduction through ESOL.' *TESOL Quarterly* 27: 601–26.

Canagarajah, A. S. 1996. 'From critical research practice to critical research reporting.' *TESOL Quarterly* 30: 321–30.

Canagarajah, A. S. 1999. *Resisting Linguistic Imperialism in English Teaching*. Oxford: Oxford University Press.

Canale, M. and **M. Swain**. 1980. 'Theoretical bases of communicative approaches to second language testing.' *Applied Linguistics* 1: 1–47.

Cancino, H., E. Rosansky, and **J. Schumann**. 1978. 'The acquisition of English negatives and interrogatives by native Spanish speakers' in E. Hatch (ed.): *Second Language Acquisition: A Book of Readings*. Rowley, MA: Newbury House.

Chaudron, C. 1977. 'A descriptive model of discourse in the corrective treatment of learners' errors.' *Language Learning* 27: 29–46.

Chaudron, C. 1988. *Second Language Classrooms: Research on Teaching and Learning*. Cambridge: Cambridge University Press.

Chaudron, C. and **K. Parker**. 1990. 'Discourse markedness and structural markedness: The acquisition of English noun phrases.' *Studies in Second Language Acquisition* 12(1): 43–64.

Chee, M., E. Tan, and **T. Thiel**. 1999. 'Mandarin and English single word processing studied with functional magnetic resonance imaging.' *The Journal of Neuroscience* 19: 3050–6.

Chomsky, N. 1959. 'Review of "Verbal behavior" by B. F. Skinner.' *Language* 35: 26–58.

Chomsky, N. 1965. *Aspects of the Theory of Syntax*. Cambridge, MA: MIT Press.

Chouliaraki, L. and **Fairclough, N.** 1999. *Discourse in Late Modernity: Rethinking Critical Discourse Analysis*. Edinburgh: Edinburgh University Press.

Chun, A., R. Day, A. Chenoweth, and **S. Luppescu**. 1982. 'Errors, interaction, and correction: a study of non-native conversations.' *TESOL Quarterly* 16: 537–47.

Clandinin, D. J. and **F. M. Connelly**. 2000. *Narrative Inquiry: Experience and Story in Qualitative Research*. San Francisco: Jossey-Bass.

Cohen, A. 1987. 'Using verbal reports in research on language learning' in C. Faerch and G. Kasper (eds.).

Cohen, L. and **L. Manion**. 1994. *Research Methods in Education; Fourth Edition*. London: Routledge.

Cole, M. 1985. 'The zone of proximal development: Where culture and cognition create each other' in J. V. Wertsch (ed.): *Culture, Communication and Cognition: Vygotskian Perspectives*. Cambridge: Cambridge University Press.

Cole, M. 1996. *Cultural Psychology: A Once and Future Discipline.* Cambridge, MA: Belknap Press.

Connor, U. 1996. *Contrastive Rhetoric: Cross-Cultural Aspects of Second Language Writing.* Cambridge: Cambridge University Press.

Connor, U. and **K. Precht.** 2002. 'Business English: Learner data from Belgium, Finland and the U.S.' in S. Granger, J. Hung, and S. Petch-Tyson (eds.).

Converse, J. and **H. Schumann.** 1974. *Conversations at Random: Survey Research as Interviewers See It.* New York: Wiley.

Corder, S. P. 1967. 'The significance of learners' errors.' *International Review of Applied Linguistics* 5: 161–70.

Corder, S. P. 1971. 'Idiosyncractic dialects and error analysis.' *International Review of Applied Linguistics* 9: 149–59.

Corder, S. P. 1974. 'Error analysis' in J. Allen and S. Corder (eds.): *The Edinburgh Course in Applied Linguistics Volume 3: Techniques in Applied Linguistics.* Oxford: Oxford University Press.

Corder, S. P. 1976. 'The study of interlanguage' in Proceedings of the Fourth International Conference of Applied Linguistics. Munich, Hochschulverlag. Also in Corder 1981. *Error Analysis and Interlanguage.* Oxford: Oxford University Press.

Corder, S. P. 1978. 'Language-learner language' in J. Richards (ed.): *Understanding Second and Foreign Language Learning.* Rowley, MA: Newbury House.

Corder, S. P. 1981. *Error Analysis and Interlanguage.* Oxford: Oxford University Press.

Corder, S. P. 1983. 'A role for the mother tongue' in S. Gass and L. Selinker (eds.): *Language Transfer in Language Learning.* Rowley, MA: Newbury House.

Cortazzi, M. and **L. Jin.** 1999. 'Bridges to learning: Metaphors of teaching, learning and language' in L. Cameron and G. Low (eds.) 1999a: *Researching and Applying Metaphor.*

Crookes, G. 1989. 'Planning and interlanguage variability.' *Studies in Second Language Acquisition* 11: 367–83.

Cumming, A. 1990. 'Writing expertise and second language proficiency.' *Language Learning* 39: 81–141.

Cumming, A. 1994. 'Alternatives in TESOL research: Descriptive, interpretive, and ideological orientations.' *TESOL Quarterly* 4: 673–703.

Cummins, J. 1996. *Negotiating Identities: Education for Empowerment in a Diverse Society.* Ontario: California Association for Bilingual Education.

Dagneaux, E. 1995. 'Expressions of epistemic modality in native and non-native essay writing.' Unpublished MA Dissertation, Départment d'Etudes Germaniques, Université Catholique de Louvain.

Dagneaux, E., S. Denness, and **S. Granger.** 1998. 'Computer-aided error analysis.' *System: An International Journal of Educational Technology and Applied Linguistics* 26: 163–74.

Dagneaux, E., S. Denness, S. Granger, and **F. Meunier.** 1996. *Error Tagging Manual Version 1.1.* Centre for English Corpus Linguistics, Université Catholique de Louvain, Louvain-la-Neuve.

Damon, W. and **E. Phelps.** 1989. 'Critical distinctions among three approaches to peer education.' *International Journal of Educational Research* 13: 9–19.

Davies, A. 1978. 'Language testing: Survey article Part 1.' *Language Teaching and Linguistics Abstracts* 11: 145–59.

Davies, A. 1991. *The Native Speaker in Applied Linguistics.* Edinburgh: Edinburgh University Press.

Davies, A. 2003. *The Native Speaker: Myth and Reality.* Clevedon. Multilingual Matters.

Davies, W. and **T. Kaplan.** 1998. 'Native speaker vs. L2 learner grammaticality judgments.' *Applied Linguistics* 19: 183–203.

Davis, K. A. 1995. 'Qualitative theory and methods in applied linguistics research.' *TESOL Quarterly* 29: 427–53.

Day, R. (ed.). 1986. *Talking to Learn: Conversation in Second Language Acquisition.* Rowley, MA: Newbury House.

de Bot, K. 1996. 'The psycholinguistics of the output hypothesis.' *Language Learning* 46: 529–55.

de Cock, S. 1998. 'A recurrent word combination approach to the study of formulae in the speech of native and non-native speakers of English.' *International Journal of Corpus Linguistics* 3: 59–80.

de Cock, S., S. Granger, G. Leech, and **T. McEnery.** 1998. 'An automated approach to the phrasicon of EFL learners' in S. Granger (ed.): *Learner English on Computer.* London and New York: Addison Wesley Longman.

de Cock, S., S. Granger, and **S. Petch-Tyson.** 1995. *Louvain International Database of Spoken English Interlanguage.* Université Catholique de Louvain.

de Guerrero, M. and **O. Villamil.** 1994. 'Social-cognitive dimensions of interaction in L2 peer revision' *The Modern Language Journal* 78: 484–96.

de Guerrero, M. and **O. Villamil.** 2002. 'Metaphorical conceptualizations of ESL teaching and learning.' *Language Teaching Research* 6: 95–120.

de Haan, P. 2000. 'Tagging non-native English with the TOSCA-ICLE tagger' in C. Mair and M. Hundt (eds.): *Corpus Linguistics and Linguistic Theory. Papers from the Twentieth International Conference on English Language Research on Computerized Corpora (ICAME 20) Freiburg im Breisgau 1999.* Amsterdam: Rodopi.

de Villiers, J. and **P. de Villiers.** 1973. 'A cross-sectional study of the development of grammatical morphemes in child speech.' *Journal of Psycholinguistic Research* 2: 267–78.

Dean, M. 1994. *Critical and Effective Histories: Foucault's Methods and Historical Sociology.* London: Routledge.

Dechert, H. 1983. 'How a story is done in a second language' in C. Faerch and G. Kasper (eds.): *Strategies in Interlanguage Communication.* London: Longman.

Dechert, H. 1984. 'Individual variation in language' in H. Dechert, D. Mohle, and M. Raupach (eds.).

Dechert, H., D. Mohle, and **M. Raupach.** (eds.). 1984. *Second Language Productions.* Tubingen: Gunter Narr.

Deignan, A. 1999. 'Corpus-based research in metaphor' in L. Cameron and G. Low (eds.).

Denzin, N. K. and **Y. S. Lincoln.** 1998. 'Introduction: Entering the field of qualitative research' in N. K. Denzin and Y. S. Lincoln (eds.): *The Landscape of Qualitative Research: Theories and Issues.* Thousand Oaks, CA: Sage.

Denzin, N. K. and **Y. S. Lincoln.** (eds.): 2000. *The Handbook of Qualitative Research.* Second edition. Thousand Oaks, CA: Sage Publications.

Dey, I. 1993. *Qualitative Data Analysis: A User-Friendly Guide for Social Scientists.* London: Routledge and Kegan Paul.

DiCamilla, F. J. and **M. Anton.** 1997. 'The function of repetition in the collaborative discourse of L2 learners.' *The Canadian Modern Language Review* 53: 609–33.

Donato, R. 1994. 'Collective scaffolding in second language learning' in J. P. Lantolf and G. Appel (eds.).

Donato, R. 2000. 'Sociocultural contributions to understanding the foreign and second language classroom' in J. P. Lantolf (ed.).

Dornyei, Z. 2003. *Questionnaires in Second Language Research: Construction, Administration, and Processing.* Mahwah, NJ: Lawrence Erlbaum.

Doughty, C. 2001. 'Cognitive underpinnings of focus on form' in P. Robinson (ed.): *Cognition and Second Language Instruction.* Cambridge: Cambridge University Press.

Doughty, C. and **E. Varela.** 1998. 'Communicative focus on form' in C. Doughty and J. Williams (eds.): *Focus on Form in Classroom Second Language Acquisition.* Cambridge: Cambridge University Press.

Doughty, C. and **J. Williams.** (eds.): 1998. *Focus on Form in Classroom Second Language Acquisition.* Cambridge: Cambridge University Press.

Douglas, D. 2001. 'Performance consistency in second language acquisition and language testing research: a conceptual gap.' *Second Language Research* 17: 442–56.

Drew, P. and **J. Heritage.** 1992. 'Analysing talk at work: An introduction' in P. Drew and J. Heritage (eds.) *Talk at Work: Interaction in Institutional Settings* (pp. 3–65). Cambridge: Cambridge University Press.

Dubois, J. 1991. 'Transcription design principles for spoken discourse research.' *Pragmatics* 1: 71–106.

Duff, P. 1986. 'Another look at interlanguage talk: Taking task to task' in R. Day (ed.): *Talking to Learn.* Rowley, MA: Newbury House.

Duff, P. A. 2002. 'The discursive co-construction of knowledge, identity, and difference: an ethnography of communication in the high school mainstream.' *Applied Linguistics* 23: 289–322.

Dulay, H. and **M. Burt.** 1973. 'Should we teach children syntax?' *Language Learning* 23: 245–58.

Dulay, H. and **M. Burt.** 1974. 'Errors and strategies in child second language acquisition.' *TESOL Quarterly* 8: 129–36.

Dulay, H. and **M. Burt.** 1980. 'On acquisition orders' in S. Felix (ed.): *Second Language Development.* Tubingen: Gunter Narr.

Dulay, H., M. Burt, and **S. Krashen.** 1982. *Language Two.* New York: Oxford University Press.

Dunn, W. E. and **J. P. Lantolf.** 1998. 'Vygotsky's zone of proximal development and Krashen's i + 1: Incommensurable constructs; incommensurable theories.' *Language Learning* 48: 411–42.

Edge, J. and **Richards, K.** 1998. 'May I see your warrant, please?: Justifying outcomes in qualitative research.' *Applied Linguistics* 19: 334–56.

Ellis, N. 1996. 'Sequencing in SLA: phonological memory, chunking, and points of order.' *Studies in Second Language Acquisition* 18: 91–126.

Ellis, N. 2002. 'Frequency effects in language processing: A review with implications for theories of implicit and explicit language acquisition.' *Studies in Second Language Acquisition* 24: 143–88.

Ellis, R. 1984a. *Second Language Classroom Development.* Oxford: Pergamon.

Ellis, R. 1984b. 'Can syntax be taught? A study of the effects of formal instruction on the acquisition of WH questions by children.' *Applied Linguistics* 5: 138–55.

Ellis, R. 1985a. *Understanding Second Language Acquisition.* Oxford: Oxford University Press.

Ellis, R. 1985b. 'Sources of variability in interlanguage.' *Applied Linguistics* 6: 118–31.

Ellis, R. 1987. 'Interlanguage variability in narrative discourse: Style shifting in the use of the past tense.' *Studies in Second Language Acquisition* 9: 1–20.

Ellis, R. 1988. 'The effects of linguistic environment on the second language acquisition of grammatical rules.' *Applied Linguistics* 9: 257–74.

Ellis, R. 1989. 'Are classroom and naturalistic acquisition the same? A study of the classroom acquisition of German word order rules.' *Studies in Second Language Acquisition* 11: 305–28.

Ellis, R. 1990a. *Instructed Language Learning.* Oxford: Blackwell.

Ellis, R. 1990b. 'Individual styles in classroom second language development' in J. de Jong, and D. Stevenson (eds.): *Individualizing the Assessment of Language Abilities.* Clevedon, Avon: Multilingual Matters.

Ellis, R. 1990c. *Instructed Second Language Acquisition.* Oxford: Blackwell.

Ellis, R. 1991. 'Grammaticality judgements and learner variability' in R. Burmeister and P. Rounds (eds.): *Variability in Second Language Acquisition: Proceedings of the Tenth Meeting of the second language Research Forum.* Eugene, OR: University of Oregon.

Ellis, R. 1992. 'Learning to communicate in the classroom.' *Studies in Second Language Acquisition* 14: 1–23.

Ellis, R. 1994. *The Study of Second Language Acquisition*. Oxford: Oxford University Press.

Ellis, R. 1999. 'Item versus system learning: Explaining free variation.' *Applied Linguistics* 20: 460–80.

Ellis, R. 2001a. 'The metaphorical constructions of second language learners' in M. Breen (ed.). *Learner Contributions to Language Learning*. Harlow: Longman.

Ellis, R. 2001b. 'Non-reciprocal tasks, comprehension and second language acquisition' in M. Bygate, P. Skehan, and M. Swain (eds.).

Ellis, R. 2002. 'A metaphorical analysis of learner beliefs' in P. Burmeister, T. Piske and A. Rohde (eds.): *An Integrated View of Language Development: Papers in Honor of Henning Wode*. Trier, Germany: Wissenschaftlicher Verlag.

Ellis, R. 2003a. *Task-Based Language Learning and Teaching*. Oxford: Oxford University Press.

Ellis, R. 2003b. 'Measuring implicit and explicit knowledge of an L2: A psychometric study.' Unpublished paper, Department of Applied Language Studies and Linguistics, University of Auckland.

Ellis, R. 2004. 'The definition and measurement of explicit knowledge.' *Language Learning* 54(2).

Ellis, R. 2005. 'Measuring implicit and explicit knowledge of a second language: A psychometric study.' *Studies in Second Language Acquisition* 27(2).

Ellis, R., H. Basturkmen, and **S. Loewen**. 2001a. 'Learner uptake in communicative ESL lessons.' *Language Learning* 51: 281–318.

Ellis, R., H. Basturkmen, and **S. Loewen**. 2001b. 'Preemptive focus on form in the ESL classroom.' *TESOL Quarterly* 35: 407–32.

Ellis, R. and **M. Rathbone**. 1987. *The Acquisition of German in a Classroom Context*. Ealing, London: Ealing College of Higher Education.

Ericsson, K. and **H. Simon**. 1987. 'Verbal reports on thinking' in C. Faerch and G. Kasper (eds.).

Faerch, C. and **G. Kasper**. 1980. 'Processes and strategies in foreign language learning and communication.' *Interlanguage Studies Bulletin* 5: 47–118.

Faerch, C. and **G. Kasper** (eds.) 1983. *Strategies in Interlanguage Communication*. London: Longman.

Faerch, C. and **G. Kasper**. 1986. 'The role of comprehension in second language learning.' *Applied Linguistics* 7: 257–74.

Faerch, C. and **G. Kasper**. (eds.). 1987. *Introspection in Second Language Research*. Clevedon: Multilingual Matters.

Fairclough, N. 1985. 'Critical and descriptive goals in discourse analysis.' *Journal of Pragmatics* 9: 739–63.

Fairclough, N. 1989. *Language and Power*. London: Longman.

Fairclough, N. 1995. *Critical Discourse Analysis: The Critical Study of Language*. London: Longman.

Fairclough, N. 2001. 'The discourse of new labour: Critical discourse analysis' in M. Wetherell, S. Taylor, and S. Yates (eds.): *Discourse as Data*. Milton Keynes: The Open University.

Fairclough, N. and **R. Wodak**. 1997. 'Critical discourse analysis' in T. van Dijk (ed.): *Discourse as Social Interaction: Discourse Studies*. London: Sage.

Fathman, A. 1978. 'ESL and EFL learning: similar or dissimilar?' in C. Blatchford and J. Schachter (eds.): *On TESOL '78: EFL Policies, Programs, Practices*. Washington, DC: TESOL.

Feldweg, H. 1991. *The European Science Foundation Second Language Database*. Nijmegen: Max-Planck-Institute for Psycholinguistics.

Felix, S. 1985. 'More evidence on competing cognitive systems.' *Second Language Research* 1: 47–72.

Firth, A. and **J. Wagner**. 1997. 'On discourse, communication, and (some) fundamental concepts in SLA.' *Modern Language Journal* 81: 285–300.

Fitikides, T. 1936. *Common Mistakes in English*. London: Longman.

Flowerdew, J. 2000. 'Computer assisted analysis of language learner diaries. A qualitative application of word frequency and concordancing software.' Paper presented at the 4th International Conference on Teaching and Language Corpora, Graz.

Foster, P. 1996. 'Doing the task better: How planning time influences students' performance' in J. Willis and D. Willis (eds.): *Challenge and Change in Language Teaching*. Oxford: Heinemann.

Foster, P. and **P. Skehan**. 1996. 'The influence of planning and task type on second language performance.' *Studies in Second Language Acquisition* 18: 299–323.

Foster, P., A. Tonkyn, and **G. Wigglesworth**. 2000. 'Measuring spoken language: A unit for all reasons.' *Applied Linguistics* 21: 354–75.

Fowler, H. 1906. *The King's English*. Oxford: Clarendon Press.

Francis, S. and **H. Kucera**. 1967. *Computing Analysis of Present-day American English*. Providence, RI: Brown University Press.

Freedman, S. and **K. Forster**. 1985. 'The psychological status of overgenerated sentences.' *Cognition* 19: 101–31.

Garfinkel, H. 1967. *Studies in Ethnomethodology*. Cambridge: Polity Press.

Gass, S. 1994. 'The reliability of second language grammaticality judgments.' in E. Tarone, S. Gass, and A. Cohen (eds.): *Research Methdology in Second Language Research*. Hillsdale, NJ: Lawrence Erlbaum.

Gass, S. 1997. *Input, Interaction and the Second Language Learner*. Mahwah, NJ: Lawrence Erlbaum.

Gass, S. 2001. 'Sentence matching: a re-examination.' *Second Language Research* 17: 421–41.

Gass, S. and **A. Mackey**. 2000. *Stimulated Recall Methodology in Second Language Research*. Mahwah, NJ: Lawrence Erlbaum.

Gass, S., A. Mackey, and **T. Pica**. 1998. 'The role of input and interaction in second language acquisition: Introduction to the special issue.' *The Modern Language Journal* 82: 299–305.

Gass, S. and **L. Selinker**. 1994. *Second Language Acquisition: An Introductory Course*. Hillsdale, NJ: Lawrence Erlbaum.

Gee, J. 1990. *Social Linguistics and Literacies: Ideology in Discourses*. Basingstoke: Falmer Press.

Geertz, C. 1983. *Local Knowledge: Further Essays in Interpretive Anthropology*. New York: Basic Books.

George, H. 1972. *Common Errors in Language Learning: Insights from English*. Rowley, MA: Newbury House.

Gibbs, R. 1999. 'Researching metaphor.' in L. Cameron and G. Low (eds.).

Giles, H. and **T. Byrne**. 1982. 'An intergroup approach to second language acquisition.' *Journal of Multilingual and Multicultural Development* 3: 17–40.

Givon, T. 1979. *On Understanding Grammar*. New York: Academic Press.

Glaser, B. 1978. *Theoretical Sensitivity*. Mill Valley, CA: Sociology Press.

Glucksberg, S., B. Keysar, and **M. McGlone**. 1992. 'Metaphor understanding and accessing conceptual schema; reply to Gibbs.' *Psychological Review* 99: 578–81.

Goetz, J. P. and **M. D. LeCompte**. 1981. Ethnographic research and the problem of data reduction: What do I do with the five drawers of fieldnotes? *Anthropology and Education Quarterly* 12: 51–71.

Goetz, J. P. and **M. D. LeCompte**. 1984. *Ethnography and Qualitative Design in Educational Research*. Orlando: Academic Press.

Goffman, E. 1959. *The Presentation of Self in Everyday Life*. New York: Doubleday.

Goldschneider, J. and **R. DeKeyser**. 2001. 'Explaining the "natural order of L2 morpheme acquisition" in English: A meta-analysis of multiple determinants.' *Language Learning* 51: 1–50.

Goldstein, L. 1987. 'Standard English: The only target for nonnative speakers of English?' *TESOL Quarterly* 21: 417–36.

Goldstein, T. 1995. 'Nobody is talking bad: Creating Community and Claiming Power on the Production Lines' in K. Hall and M. Bucholtz (eds.): *Gender Articulated: Language and the Social Constructed Self*. New York: Routledge.

Goss, N., Z. Ying-Hua, and **J. Lantolf.** 1994. 'Two heads may be better than one: mental activity in second language grammaticality judgements' in E. Tarone, S. Gass, and A. Cohen (eds.): *Research Methdology in Second Language Research*. Hillsdale, NJ: Lawrence Erlbaum.

Granger, S. (ed.). 1998a. *Learner English on Computer*. London and New York: Addison Wesley Longman.

Granger, S. 1998b. 'The computerized learner corpus: a versatile new source of data for SLA research' in S. Granger (ed.): *Learner English on Computer*. London and New York: Addison Wesley Longman.

Granger, S. 1999. 'Use of tenses by advanced EFL learners: evidence from an error-tagged computer corpus' in H. Hasselgard and S. Oksefjell (eds.): *Out of Corpora–Studies in Honour of Stig Johansson*. Amsterdam and Atlanta: Rodopi.

Granger, S. 2002. 'A Bird's-eye view of computer learner corpus research' in S. Granger, J. Hung, and S. Petch-Tyson. (eds.).

Granger, S. 2004. 'Computer learner corpus research: current status and future prospects' in U. Connor and T. Upton (eds.): *Applied Corpus Linguistics: A Multidimensional Perspective*. Amsterdam and Atlanta: Rodopi.

Granger, S. and **P. Rayson.** 1998. 'Automatic lexical profiling of learner texts' in S. Granger (ed.).

Granger, S. and **S. Tyson.** 1996. 'Connector usage in the English essay writing of native and non-native EFL speakers of English.' *World Englishes* 15: 19–29.

Granger, S., E. Dagneaux, and **F. Meunier.** 2002. *The International Corpus of Learner English. Handbook and CD-ROM*. Louvain-la-Neuve: Presses Universitaires de Louvain.

Granger, S., J. Hung, and **S. Petch-Tyson.** (eds.). 2002. *Computer Learner Corpora, Second Language Acquisition and Foreign Language Teaching*. Amsterdam and Philadelphia: Benjamins.

Gregg, K. 1989. 'Second language acquisition theory: the case for a generative perspective' in S. Gass and J. Schachter (eds.): *Linguistic Perspectives on Second Language Acquisition*. Cambridge: Cambridge University Press.

Gregg, K. 1990. 'The variable competence model of second language acquisition and why it isn't.' *Applied Linguistics* 11: 364–83.

Grotjahn, R. 1987. 'On the methodological basis of introspective methods' in C. Faerch and G. Kasper (eds.).

Grotjahn, R. 1991. 'The research programme subjective theories: A new approach in second language research.' *Studies in Second Language Acquisition* 13: 187–214.

Guba, E. and **Y. Lincoln.** 1985. *Naturalistic Inquiry*. Beverley Hills, CA: Sage.

Gumperz, J. 1982. *Discourse Strategies*. Cambridge: Cambridge University Press.

Habermas, J. 1972. *Knowledge and Human Interests* (trans. J. Shapiro). London: Heinemann.

Hakuta, K. 1974. 'A preliminary report on the development of grammatical morphemes in a Japanese girl learning English as a second language.' *Working Papers on Bilingualism* 3: 18–43.

Halliday, M. 1973. *Explorations in the Functions of Language*. London: Edward Arnold.

Halliday, M. 1975. *An Introduction to Functional Grammar*. London: Edward Arnold.

Han, Y. 1996. 'L2 learners' explicit knowledge of verb complement structures and its relationship to L2 implicit knowledge.' Unpublished EdD dissertation, Temple University, Philadelphia.

Hansen, J. G. and **J. Liu.** 1997. 'Social identity and language: Theoretical and methodological issues.' *TESOL Quarterly* 31: 567–76.

Hasselgren, A. 2002. 'Testing learner fluency: the role of "small-words"' in S. Granger, J. Hung, and S. Petch-Tyson (eds.).

Hatch, E. 1978. 'Discourse analysis and second language acquisition' in E. Hatch (ed.): *Second Language Acquisition*. Rowley, MA: Newbury House.

Hatch, E. and **A. Lazaraton.** 1991. *The Research Manual: Design Statistics for Applied Linguistics*. New York: Newbury House.

Hawkins, B. 1985. 'Is the appropriate response always so appropriate' in S. Gass and C. Madden (eds.): *Input in Second Language Acquisition*. Rowley, MA: Newbury House.

Hawkins, R. 2001. *Second Language Syntax: A Generative Introduction*. Oxford: Blackwell.

He, A. and **R. Young.** 1998. 'Language proficiency interviews: A discourse approach' in R. Young and A. He (eds.): *Talking and Testing*. Amsterdam: John Benjamins.

Heath, S. B. 1983. *Ways with Words: Language, Life, and Work in Communities and Classrooms*. Cambridge: Cambridge University Press.

Heaton, J. 1975. *Beginning Composition through Pictures*. London: Longman.

Hedge, T. 2000. *Teaching and Learning in the Language Classroom*. Oxford: Oxford University Press.

Henning, G. 1986. 'Quantitative methods in language acquisition research.' *TESOL Quarterly* 20: 701–8.

Heritage, J. 1987. 'Ethnomethodology' in A. Giddens and J. Turner (eds.): *Social Theory Today*. Cambridge: Polity Press: 224–72.

Heritage, J. 1997. 'Conversation analysis and institutional talk: analysing data' in D. Silverman (ed.): *Qualitative Research: Theory, Method and Practice* (pp. 161–82). London: Sage.

Heritage, J. 2001. 'Conversation analysis: sociological' in N. J. Smelser and P. B. Baltes (eds.): *International Encyclopedia of the Social and Behavioral Sciences* (2741–4). Oxford: Elsevier Science.

Heritage, J. and **J. M. Atkinson.** 1984. 'Introduction' in J. M. Atkinson and J. Heritage (eds.): *Structures of Social Action: Studies in Conversation Analysis* (pp. 1–15). Cambridge: Cambridge University Press.

Hinkel, E. 2002. *Second Language Writers' Text: Linguistic and Rhetorical Features (ESL and Applied Linguistics Professional Series)*. Mahwah, NJ: Lawrence Erlbaum.

Hoffman, E. 1989. *Lost in Translation: A Life in a New Language*. New York: Penguin.

Hoffman, R. and **S. Kemper.** 1987. 'What could reaction-time studies be telling us about metaphor comprehension?' *Metaphor and Symbolic Activity* 2: 149–86.

Holmes, J. 1988. 'Doubt and certainty in ESL textbooks.' *Applied Linguistics* 9: 21–44.

Horwitz, K. 1987. 'Surveying student beliefs about language learning' in A. Wenden and J. Rubin (eds.): *Learner Strategies in Language Learning*. London: Prentice Hall.

Housen, A. 1995. 'It's about time—the acquisition of temporality in English as a second language in a multilingual educational context.' Unpublished PhD Dissertation. Free University of Brussels.

Housen, A. 1998. 'An analysis of grammatical form-function mapping in L2 data using the CHILDES system' in S. Granger and J. Hung (eds.): *Proceedings of First International Symposium on Computer Learner Corpora, Second Language Acquisition and Foreign Language Teaching*.

Housen, A. 2002. 'A corpus-based study of the L2-acquisition of the English verb system' in S. Granger, J. Hung, and S. Petch-Tyson (eds.).

Howard, G. 1994. *The Good English Guide*. London: Macmillan.

Huebner, T. 1979. 'Order-of-acquisition vs dynamic paradigm: a comparison of method in interlanguage research.' *TESOL Quarterly* 13: 21–8.

Huebner, T. 1985. 'System and variability in interlanguage syntax.' *Language Learning* 35: 141–63.

Hughes, A. and **C. Lascaratou.** 1982. 'Competing criteria for error gravity.' *ELT Journal* 36: 175–82.

Hunt, K. 1965. *Grammatical Structures Written at Three Grade Levels*. Champaign, IL: National Council of Teachers of English.

Hutchby, I. and **R. Wooffitt.** 1998. *Conversation Analysis: Principles, Practices and Applications.* Cambridge: Polity Press.

Hyland, K. and **J. Milton.** 1997. 'Qualification and certainty in L1 and L2 students' writing.' *Journal of Second Language Writing.* 6: 183–205.

Hyltenstam, K. 1984. 'The use of typological markedness conditions as predictors in second language acquisition: the case of pronominal copies in relative clauses' in R. Andersen (ed.): *Second Language: A Crosslinguistic Perspective.* Rowley, MA: Newbury House.

Hymes, D. 1974. *Foundations in Sociolinguistics: An Ethnographic Approach.* Philadelphia: University of Pennsylvania Press.

Ibrahim, A. 1999. 'Becoming black: Rap and hip-hop, race, gender, identity, and the politics of ESL learning.' *TESOL Quarterly* 33: 349–69.

Ide, N., R. Reppen, and **K. Suderman.** 2002. 'The American National Corpus: More than the web can provide' in Proceedings of the Third Language Resources and Evaluation Conference, Las Palmas, Canary Islands.

Ioup, G. 1996. 'Grammatical knowledge and memorized chunks: A response to Ellis.' *Studies in Second Language Acquisition* 18: 355–60.

Iwashita, N., C. Elder, and **T. McNamara.** 2001. 'Can we predict task difficulty in an oral proficiency test? Exploring the potential of an information-processing approach to task design.' *Language Learning* 51: 401–36.

Jain, M. 1974. 'Error analysis: Source, cause and significance' in J. Richards (ed.).

James, C. 1998. *Errors in Language Learning and Use: Exploring Error Analysis.* London: Longman.

Janks, H. and **R. Ivanič.** 1992. 'Critical language awareness and emancipatory discourse' in N. Fairclough (ed.): *Critical Language Awareness.* London: Longman.

Jefferson, G. 1989. 'Preliminary notes on a possible metric which provides for a "standard maximum" silence of approximately one second in conversation' in D. Roger and P. Bull (eds.) *Conversation: An Interdisciplinary Perspective* (pp. 166–96). Clevedon: Multilingual Matters.

Johnson, D. M. 1992. *Approaches to Research in Second Language Learning.* New York: Longman.

Kapp, R. L. 2001. 'The politics of English: a study of classroom discourses in a township school.' Unpublished doctoral dissertation, University of Cape Town, South Africa.

Kasper, G. 1985. 'Repair in foreign language teaching.' *Studies in Second Language Acquisition* 7: 200–15.

Kasper, G. 1992. 'Pragmatic transfer.' *Second Language Research* 8: 203–31.

Kasper, G. 1996. 'Introduction: interlanguage pragmatics in SLA.' *Studies in Second Language Acquisition* 18: 145–8.

Kasper, G. and **M. Dahl.** 1991. 'Research methods in interlanguage pragmatics.' *Studies in Second Language Acquisition* 13: 215–47.

Kasper, G. and **E. Kellerman.** 1997. 'Introduction' in G. Kasper and E. Kellerman (eds.).

Kasper, G. and **E. Kellerman** (eds.). 1997. *Communication Strategies.* Harlow: Longman.

Kellerman, E. 1979. 'Transfer and non-transfer: where are we now?' *Studies in Second Language Acquisition* 2: 37–57.

Kellerman, E. 1983. 'Now you see it, now you don't' in S. Gass and L. Selinker (eds.): *Language Transfer in Language Learning.* Rowley, MA: Newbury House.

Kellerman, E. 1991. 'Compensatory strategies in second language research: a critique, a revision, and some (non-) implications for the classroom' in R. Phillipson, E. Kellerman, L. Selinker, M. Sharwood Smith, and M. Swain (eds.): *Foreign/Second Language Pedagogy Research.* Clevedon, Avon: Multilingual Matters.

Kellerman, E., T. Bongaerts, and **N. Poulisse.** 1987. 'Strategy and system in L2 referential communication' in R. Ellis (ed.): *Second Language Acquisition in Context.* London: Prentice Hall International.

Kemmer, S. and **M. Barlow.** 2000. 'Introduction: A usage-based conception of language' in M. Barlow and S. Kemmer (eds.): *Usage-Based Models of Language.* CSLI: Stanford.

Kinginger, C. 2002. 'Defining the zone of proximal development in US foreign language education.' *Applied Linguistics* 23: 240–61.
Klein, W. and **C. Perdue.** 1992. *Utterance Structure: Developing Grammars Again.* Amsterdam: John Benjamins.
Klein, W. and **C. Perdue.** 1997. 'The basic variety (or: Couldn't natural languages be much simpler?).' *Second Language Research* 13: 301–48.
Koch, S. and **S. Deetz.** 1981. 'Metaphor analysis of social reality in organizations.' *Journal of Applied Communication Research* 9: 1–15.
Kowal, M. and **M. Swain.** 1997. 'From semantic to syntactic processing: How can we promote metalinguistic awareness in the French immersion classroom?' in R. Johnson and M. Swain (eds.): *Immersion Education: International Perspectives.* Cambridge: Cambridge University Press.
Kramsch, C. 1995. 'The applied linguist and the foreign language teacher: Can they talk to each other?' *Australian Review of Applied Linguistics* 18: 1–16.
Krashen, S. 1977a. 'The Monitor Model for adult second language performance' in M. Burt, H. Dulay, and M. Finocchiaro (eds.): *Viewpoints on English as a Second Language.* New York: Regents Publishing.
Krashen, S. 1977b. 'Some issues relating to the Monitor Model' in H. Brown, C. Yorio, and R. Crymes (eds.): *On TESOL '77.* Washington DC: TESOL.
Krashen, S. 1985. *The Input Hypothesis: Issues and Implications.* London: Longman.
Krashen, S. 1994. 'The input hypothesis and its rivals' in N. Ellis (ed.): *Implicit and Explicit Learning of Languages.* London: Academic Press.
Krashen, S., J. Butler, R. Birnbaum, and **J. Robertson.** 1978. 'Two studies in language acquisition and language learning.' *ITL: Review of Applied Linguistics* 39: 73–92.
Kress, G. 1991. 'Critical discourse analysis.' *Annual Review of Applied Linguistics* 11: 84–99.
Kumaravadivelu, B. 1991. 'Language-learning tasks: Teacher intention and learner interpretation.' *English Language Teaching Journal,* 45: 98–107.
Kumaravadivelu, B. 1999. 'Critical classroom discourse analysis.' *TESOL Quarterly* 33(3): 453–84.
Labov, W. 1970. 'The study of language in its social context.' *Studium Generale* 23: 30–87.
Lakoff, G. 1986. 'A figure of thought.' *Metaphor and Symbolic Activity* 1: 215–25.
Lakoff, G. 1987. *Women, Fire and Dangerous Things.* Chicago: University of Chicago Press.
Lakoff, G. and **M. Johnson.** 1980. *Metaphors We Live by.* Chicago: University of Chicago Press.
Lakoff, G. and **M. Turner.** 1989. *More than Cool Reason: A Field Guide to Poetic Metaphor.* Chicago: University of Chicago Press.
Lam, W. S. A. 2000. 'L2 literacy and the design of the self: A case study of a teenager writing on the internet.' *TESOL Quarterly* 34: 457–82.
Lantolf, J. P. 1994. 'Sociocultural theory and second language learning: Introduction to the special issue.' *The Modern Language Journal* 78: 418–20.
Lantolf, J. P. 1996. 'Second language theory building: Letting all the flowers bloom!' *Language Learning* 46: 713–49.
Lantolf, J. P. 2000a. 'Introducing sociocultural theory' in J. P. Lantolf (ed.): *Sociocultural Theory and Second Language Learning.* Oxford: Oxford University Press.
Lantolf, J. P. 2000b. (ed.). *Sociocultural Theory and Second Language Learning.* Oxford: Oxford University Press.
Lantolf, J. P. and **M. Ahmed.** 1989. 'Psycholinguistic perspectives on interlanguage variation: A Vygotskyan analysis' in S. Gass, C. Madden, D. Preston and L. Selinker (eds.): *Variation in Second Language Acquisition: Psycholinguistic Issues* (pp. 93–108). Clevedon: Multilingual Matters.
Lantolf, J. P. and **A. Aljaafreh.** 1995. 'Second language learning in the zone of proximal development: A revolutionary experience.' *International Journal of Educational Research* 23: 619–32.

Lantolf, J. P. and **G. Appel.** 1994. (eds.): *Vygotskian Approaches to Second Language Research.* Norwood, NJ: Ablex.

Lantolf, J. P. and **A. Pavlenko.** 1995. 'Sociocultural theory and second language acquisition.' *Annual Review of Applied Linguistics* 15: 108–24.

Lardiere, D. 2003. 'Revisiting the comparative fallacy: A reply to Lakshmanan and Selinker, 2001.' *Second Language Research* 19: 129–43.

Larsen-Freeman, D. 1976. 'An explanation for the morpheme acquisition order of second language learners.' *Language Learning* 26: 125–34.

Larsen-Freeman, D. 1978. 'An ESL index of development.' *TESOL Quarterly* 12: 439–48.

Larsen-Freeman, D. 2000. 'Second language acquisition and applied linguistics.' *Annual Review of Applied Linguistics*, 20: 165–81.

Larsen-Freeman, D. and **M. H. Long.** 1991. *An Introduction to Second Language Acquisition Research.* London: Longman.

Layder, D. 1993. *New Strategies in Social Research.* Cambridge: Polity Press.

Lazaraton, A. 1995. 'Qualitative research in applied linguistics: A progress report.' *TESOL Quarterly* 29: 455–72.

Lazaraton, A. 2002a. *A Qualitative Approach to the Validation of Oral Language Tests.* Cambridge: Cambridge University Press.

Lazaraton, A. 2002b. 'Quantitative and qualitative approaches to discourse analysis.' *Annual Review of Applied Linguistics* 22: 32–51.

Lazaraton, A. 2003. 'Evaluative criteria for qualitative research in applied linguistics: Whose criteria and whose research?'. *The Modern Language Journal* 87(1): 1–12.

LeCompte, M. and **J. Preissle.** 1993. *Ethnography and Qualitative Design in Educational Research* (2nd edn.). London: Academic Press.

LeCompte, M. and **J. J. Schensul.** 1999. *Analyzing and Interpreting Ethnographic Data.* Walnut Creek, CA: Altamira Press.

Leech, G. 1983. *Principles of Pragmatics.* London: Longman.

Leech, G. 1998. 'Learner corpora: what they are and what can be done with them' in S. Granger (ed.): *Learner English on Computer.* London and New York: Addison Wesley Longman.

Leki, I. and **J. Carson.** 1997. '"Completely different worlds": EAP and the writing experiences of ESL students in university courses.' *TESOL Quarterly* 31: 39–69.

Lennon, P. 1990. 'Investigating fluency in EFL: A quantitative approach.' *Language Learning* 40: 387–417.

Lennon, P. 1991. 'Error: Some problems of definition, identification and distinction.' *Applied Linguistics* 12: 180–96.

Levelt, W. 1989. *Speaking: From Intention to Articulation.* Cambridge, MA: The MIT Press.

Lightbown, P. 1983. 'Exploring relationships between developmental and instructional sequences in L2 acquisition' in H. Seliger and M. Long (eds.).

Lightbown, P. 1985. 'Great expectations: Second language acquisition research and classroom teaching.' *Applied Linguistics* 6: 263–73.

Lin, L. H. F. 2002. 'Overuse, underuse and misuse. Using concordancing to analyse the use of it in the writing of Chinese learners of English' in M. Tan (ed.): *Corpus Studies in Language Education.* Bangkok: IELE Press.

Lococo, V. 1976. 'A comparison of three methods for the collection of L2 data: Free composition, translation and picture description.' *Working Papers on Bilingualism* 8: 59–86.

Loewen, S. 2002. 'The occurrence and effectiveness of incidental focus on form in meaning-focused ESL Lessons.' Unpublished PhD dissertation, University of Auckland, Auckland, New Zealand.

Long, M. 1977. 'Teacher feedback on learner error: mapping cognitions' in H. D. Brown, C. Yorio, and R. Crymes (eds.).

Long, M. 1980. 'Input, interaction and second language acquisition.' Unpublished PhD dissertation: University of California at Los Angeles.

Long, M. 1981. 'Input, interaction and second language acquisition' in H. Winitz (ed.): *Native Language and Foreign Language Acquisition.* Annals of the New York Academy of Sciences 379.

Long, M. 1983. 'Native speaker/non-native speaker conversation and the negotiation of comprehensible input.' *Applied Linguistics* 4: 126–41.

Long, M. 1988. 'Instructed interlanguage development' in L. Beebe (ed.): *Issues in Second Language Acquisition: Multiple Perspectives.* New York: Newbury House.

Long, M. 1990a. 'Maturational constraints on language development.' *Studies in Second Language Acquisition* 12: 251–86.

Long, M. 1990b. 'The least a second language acquisition theory needs to explain.' *TESOL Quarterly* 24: 649–66.

Long, M. 1991. 'Focus on form: A design feature in language teaching methodology' in K. de Bot, R. Ginsberg, and C. Kramsch (eds.): *Foreign Language Research in Cross-Cultural Perspective.* Amsterdam: John Benjamin.

Long, M. 1996. 'The role of the linguistic environment in second language acquisition' in W. Ritchie and T. Bhatia (eds.): *Handbook of Second Language Acquisition.* San Diego: Academic Press.

Long, M. 1999. 'Recasts in SLA: The story so far.' in M. Long (ed.): *Problems in SLA.*

Long, M., S. Inagaki, and **L. Ortega.** 1998. 'The role of implicit negative feedback in SLA: Models and recasts in Japanese and Spanish.' *The Modern Language Journal* 82: 357–71.

Long, M. and **P. Robinson.** 1998. 'Focus on form: Theory, research and practice' in C. Doughty and J. Williams (eds.): *Focus on Form in Classroom Second Language Acquisition.* Cambridge: Cambridge University Press.

Long, M. and **C. Sato.** 1983. 'Methodological issues in interlanguage studies: An interactionist perspective' in A. Davies, C. Criper, and A. Howatt (eds.): *Interlanguage.* Edinburgh: Edinburgh University Press.

Lorenz, G. 1998. 'Overstatement in advanced learners' writing: Stylistic aspects of adjective intensification' in S. Granger (ed.).

Loschky, L. and **R. Bley-Vroman.** 1993. 'Grammar and task-based methodology' in G. Crookes and S. Gass (eds.): *Tasks in a Pedagogical Context: Integrating Theory and Practice.* Clevedon: Multilingual Matters.

Low, G. 1999. 'Validating metaphor research projects' in L. Cameron and G. Low (eds.).

Lu, Y. 2002. 'Linguistic characteristics in Chinese learner English' in M. Tan (ed.): *Corpus Studies in Language Education.* Bangkok: IELE Press.

Lyster, R. and **L. Ranta.** 1997. 'Corrective feedback and learner uptake: Negotiation of form in communicative classrooms.' *Studies in Second Language Acquisition* 19: 37–66.

Macdonald, C. 2002. 'On the possibility of a cultural psychology theory of pedagogy.' *Journal for Language Teaching* 36: 118–33.

McEnery, T. and **N. A. Kifle.** 2002. 'Epistemic modality in argumentative essays of second-language writers' in J. Flowerdew. (ed.): *Academic Discourse.* Pearson: Edinburgh.

McHoul, A. 1978. 'The organization of turns at formal talk in the classroom.' *Language in Society* 7: 183–213.

McHoul, A. 1990. 'The organization of repair in classroom talk.' *Language in Society* 19: 349–77.

McKay, S. L. and **S-L. C. Wong.** 1996. 'Multiple discourses, multiple identities: Investment and agency in second-language learning among Chinese adolescent immigrant students.' *Harvard Educational Review* 66(3): 577–608.

Mackey, A. 1999. 'Input, interaction and second language development: An empirical study of question formation in ESL.' *Studies in Second Language Acquisition* 21: 557–87.

Mackey, A. and **J. Philp.** 1998. 'Conversational interaction and second language development: Recasts, responses and red herrings.' *The Modern Language Journal* 82: 338–56.

Mackey, A., S. Gass, and **K. McDonough.** 2000. 'Do learners perceive interactional feedback.' *Studies in Second Language Acquisition* 22: 471–97 .

McLaughlin, B. 1990. 'Restructuring.' *Applied Linguistics* 11: 113–28.

McNamara, T. 1997. 'What do we mean by social identity? Competing frameworks, competing discourses.' *TESOL Quarterly* 31: 561–7.

Maguire, M. H. and **B. Graves.** 2001. 'Speaking personalities in primary school children's L2 writing.' *TESOL Quarterly* 35: 561–93.

Major, R. 1996. 'Chunking and phonological memory: A response to Ellis.' *Studies in Second Language Acquisition* 18: 351–54.

Makino, T. 1980. 'Acquisition order of English morphemes by Japanese secondary school students.' *Journal of Hokkaido University Education* 30: 101–48.

Malvern, D. and **B. Richards.** 2002. 'Investigating accommodation in language proficiency interviews using a new measure of lexical diversity.' *Language Testing* 19: 85–104.

Marcus, G. 1998. *Ethnography Through Thick and Thin.* Princeton: Princeton University Press.

Markee, N. 1994. 'Toward an ethnomethodological respecification of second-language acquisition studies' in E. Tarone, S. M. Gass, and A. Cohen (eds.) *Research Methodology in Second-Language Acquisition* (pp. 89–116). Hillsdale, NJ: Lawrence Erlbaum.

Markee, N. 2000. *Conversation Analysis.* Mahwah, NJ. Lawrence Erlbaum.

Martins, J. R. 2000. 'Close reading: Functional linguistics as a tool for critical discourse analysis' in L. Unsworth (ed.): *Researching Language in Schools and Communities: Functional Linguistic Perspectives.* London: Cassell.

Matthews, P. 1997. *The Concise Oxford Dictionary of Linguistics.* Oxford: Oxford University Press.

Maynard, D. W. and **S. E. Clayman.** 1991. The diversity of ethnomethodology. *Annual Review of Sociology* 17: 385–418.

Mehnert, U. 1998. 'The effects of different lengths of time for planning on second language performance.' *Studies in Second Language Acquisition* 20: 52–83.

Meisel, J., H. Clahsen, and **M. Pienemann.** 1981. 'On determining developmental stages in natural second language acquisition.' *Studies in Second Language Acquisition* 3: 109–35.

Mesthrie, R., J. Swann, A. Deumert, and **W. L. Leap.** 2000. *Introducing Sociolinguistics.* Edinburgh: Edinburgh University Press.

Meunier, F. 1998. 'Computer tools for interlanguage analysis: A critical approach' in S. Granger (ed.).

Meunier, F. and **I. de Mönnink.** 2001. 'Assessing the success rate of EFL learner corpus tagging' in S. de Cock, *et al.* (eds.): *ICAME 2001. Future Challenges for Corpus Linguistics,* 59–60.

Meyer, B. 1975. *The Organization of Prose and its Effect on Memory.* Amsterdam: North-Holland Publishing Co.

Miles, M. B. and **A. M. Huberman.** 1994. *Qualitative Data Analysis.* (2nd edn.). Thousand Oaks, CA: Sage Publications.

Milton, J. and **N. Chowdhury.** 1994. 'Tagging the interlanguage of Chinese learners of English' in L. Flowerdew and K. K. Tong (eds.) *Entering Text.* The Hong Kong University of Science and Technology, Hong Kong, pp. 127–43.

Milton, J. and **K. Hyland.** 1997. 'Qualification and certainty in L1 and L2 students' writing.' *Journal of Second Language Writing* 6: 183–205.

Mitchell, R. and **Myles, F.** 1998. *Second Language Learning Theories.* London: Arnold.

Moerman, M. 1988. *Talking Culture: Ethnography and Conversation Analysis.* Philadelphia: University of Pennsylvania Press.

Mohan, B. and **Lo, W.** 1985. 'Academic writing and Chinese students: Transfer and developmental factors.' *TESOL Quarterly* 19: 515–34.

Montrul, S. 2001. 'Agentive verbs of manner of motion in Spanish and English as second languages.' *Studies in Second Language Acquisition* 23: 171–206.

Morgan, B. 1997. 'Identity and intonation: Linking dynamic processes in an ESL classroom.' *TESOL Quarterly* 31: 431–50.

Moskowitz, G. 1967. 'The FLint system: an observational tool for the foreign language classroom' in A. Simon and E. Boyer (eds.): *Mirrors for Behavior: An Anthology of Classroom Observation Instruments*. Philadelphia: Center for the Study of Teaching at Temple University.

Myles, F., R. Mitchell, and **J. Hooper.** 1999. 'Interrogative chunks in French L2: A basis for creative construction?' *Studies in Second Language Acquisition* 21: 49–80.

Naiman, N. 1974. 'The use of elicited imitation in second language acquisition research.' *Working Papers on Bilingualism* 2: 1–37.

Naiman, N., M. Fröhlich, H. Stern, and **A. Todesco.** 1978. *The Good Language Learner*. Research in Education Series No 7. Toronto: The Ontario Institute for Studies in Education.

Nassaji, H. and **M. Swain.** 2000. 'A Vygotskian perspective on corrective feedback in L2: The effect of random versus negotiated help on the learning of English articles.' *Language Awareness*, 9: 34–51.

Nattinger, J. and **J. DeCarrico.** 1992. *Lexical Phrases and Language Teaching*. Oxford: Oxford University Press.

Nemeth. N. and **Kormos, J.** 2001. 'Pragmatic aspects of task-performance: The case of argumentation.' *Language Teaching Research* 5: 213–40.

Nesselhauf, N. 2004. 'Learner corpora and their potential for language teaching' in J. Sinclair (ed.): *How to Use Corpora in Language Teaching*. Amsterdam: Benjamins.

Neuman, W. L. 1994. *Social Research Methods: Qualitative and Quantitative Approaches*. Boston: Allyn and Bacon.

Norris, J. and **L. Ortega.** 2001. 'Does type of instruction make a difference? Substantive findings from a meta-analytic review' in R. Ellis (ed.): *Form-Focused Instruction and Second Language Learning*. Malden, MA: Blackwell.

Norton, B. (ed.). 1997a. *TESOL Quarterly* 31. (Special topic issue.)

Norton, B. (ed.). 1997b. 'Language, identity, and the ownership of English.' *TESOL Quarterly* 31: 409–29.

Norton, B. (ed.). 2000. *Identity and Language Learning: Gender, Ethnicity and Educational Change*. Harlow: Longman.

Nystrom, N. 1983. 'Teacher–student interaction in bilingual classrooms: Four approaches to error feedback' in H. Seliger and M. Long (eds.).

Ohta, A. S. 2000. 'Rethinking interaction in SLA: Developmentally appropriate assistance in the zone of proximal development and the acquisition of L2 grammar' in J. P. Lantolf (ed.).

Ohta, A. S. 2001. *Second Language Acquisition Processes in the Classroom: Learning Japanese*. Mahwah, NJ: Lawrence Erlbaum Associates.

Oliver, R. 1998. 'Negotiation of meaning in child interactions.' *Modern Language Journal* 82: 372–86.

Oliver, R. 2000. 'Age differences in negotiation and feedback in classroom and pairwork.' *Language Learning* 50: 119–51.

Olshtain, E. and **A. Cohen.** 1983. 'Apology: a speech act set' in N. Wolfson and E. Judd (eds.), 1983. *Sociolinguistic and Second Language Acquisition*. Rowley, MA: Newbury House.

Olshtain, E. and **S. Blum-Kulka.** 1985. 'Degree of approximation: non-native reactions to native speech act behavior' in S. Gass and C. Madden (eds.): *Input in Second Language Acquisition*. Rowley, MA: Newbury House.

Onwuegbuzie, A., P. Bailey, and **C. Daley.** 2000. 'The validation of three scales measuring anxiety at different stages of the foreign language learning process: The input anxiety scale, the processing anxiety scale, and the output anxiety scale.' *Language Learning* 50: 87–117.

Ortega, L. 1999. 'Planning and focus on form in L2 oral performance.' *Studies in Second Language Acquisition* 21: 109–48.

Oscarson, M. 1997. 'Self-assessment of foreign and second language proficiency' in C. Clapham and D. Corson (eds.): *Encyclopedia of Language and Education, Volume 7: Language Testing and Assessment*. Dordrecht: Kluwer Academic.

Oxford, R. 1990. *Language Learning Strategies: What Every Teacher Should Know*. Rowley, MA: Newbury House.

Oxford, R. 2001. 'The bleached bones of a story': Learners' constructions of language teachers' in M. Breen (ed.): *Learner Contributions to Language Learning*. London: Longman.

Paribakht, T. and **M. Wesche.** 1999. 'Reading and incidental L2 vocabulary acquisition: An introspective study of lexical inferencing.' *Studies in Second Language Acquisition* 21: 195–224.

Parker, K. and **C. Chaudron.** 1987. 'The effects of linguistic simplifications and elaborative modifications on L2 comprehension.' *University of Hawaii Working Papers in ESL* 6: 107–33.

Pavesi, M. 1986. 'Markedness, discoursal modes and relative clause formation in a formal and informal context.' *Studies in Second Language Acquisition* 8: 38–55.

Pease-Alvarez, L. and **A. Winsler.** 1994. 'Cuando el maestro no habla español: Children's bilingual language practices in the classroom.' *TESOL Quarterly* 28: 507–35.

Peirce, B. 1995. 'Social identity, investment and language learning.' *TESOL Quarterly* 29: 9–31.

Pennycook, A. 1994. 'Critical pedagogical approaches to research' in A. Cumming (ed.).

Pennycook, A. 1998. *English and the Discourses of Colonialism*. London: Routledge.

Pennycook, A. 1999. 'Introduction: Critical approaches to TESOL.' *TESOL Quarterly* 33: 329–48.

Pennycook, A. 2001. *Critical Applied Linguistics: A Critical Introduction*. Mahwah, NJ: Erlbaum.

Perdue, C. (ed.). 1993. *Adult Language Acquisition: Cross-linguistic Perspectives. Volume 2: The Results*. Cambridge: Cambridge University Press.

Perdue, C. (ed.). 2000. 'Introduction: Organizing principles of learner varieties.' *Studies in Second Language Acquisition* 22: 299–305.

Perkins, K. and **D. Larsen-Freeman.** 1975. 'The effects of formal language instruction on the order of morpheme acquisition.' *Language Learning* 25: 237–43.

Pica, T. 1983. 'Adult acquisition of English as a second language under different conditions of exposure.' *Language Learning* 33: 465–97.

Pica, T. 1984. 'Methods of morpheme quantification: their effect on the interpretation of second language data.' *Studies in Second Language Acquisition* 6: 69–78.

Pica, T. 1992. 'The textual outcomes of native speaker–non-native speaker negotiation: What do they reveal about second language learning?' in C. Kramsch and S. McConnell-Ginet (eds.): *Text and Context: Cross Disciplinary Perspectives on Language Study*. Lexington, MA: D. C. Heath and Company.

Pica, T. 1996. 'The essential role of negotiation in the communicative classroom.' *JALT Journal* 18: 241–68.

Pica, T., R. Young, and **C. Doughty.** 1987. 'The impact of interaction on comprehension.' *TESOL Quarterly* 21: 737–58.

Pica, T., L. Holliday, N. Lewis, and **L. Morgenthaler.** 1989. 'Comprehensible output as an outcome of linguistic demands on the learner.' *Studies in Second Language Acquisition* 11: 63–90.

Pica, T., R. Kanagy, and **J. Falodun.** 1993. 'Choosing and using communication tasks for second language research and instruction' in G. Crookes and S. Gass (eds.): *Task-based Learning in a Second Language*. Clevedon: Multilingual Matters.

Pienemann, M. 1984. 'Psychological constraints on the teachability of languages.' *Studies in Second Language Acquisition* 6: 186–214.

Pienemann, M. 1985. 'Learnability and syllabus construction' in K. Hyltenstam and M. Pienemann (eds.): *Modelling and Assessing Second Language Acquisition*. Clevedon, Avon: Multilingual Matters.

Pienemann, M. 1989. 'Is language teachable? Psycholinguistic experiments and hypotheses.' *Applied Linguistics* 10: 52–79.

Pienemann, M., M. Johnston, and **G. Brindley.** 1988. 'Constructing an acquisition-based procedure for assessing second language acquisition.' *Studies in Second Language Acquisition* 10: 217–43.

Polio, C. 1997. 'Measures of linguistic accuracy in second language writing research.' *Language Learning* 47: 101–43.

Pomerantz, A. 1984. 'Agreeing and disagreeing with assessments: Some features of preferred/dispreferred turn shapes' in J. M. Atkinson and J. Heritage (eds.) *Structures of Social Action: Studies in Conversation Analysis* (pp. 57–101). Cambridge: Cambridge University Press.

Pomerantz, A. and **B. J. Fehr.** 1997. 'Conversation analysis: An approach to the study of social action as sense making practices' in T.A. van Dijk (ed.) *Discourse as Social Interaction. Discourse Studies: A Multidisciplinary Introduction. Volume 2* (pp. 64–91). London: Sage.

Poulisse, N. 1990. *The Use of Compensatory Strategies by Dutch Learners of English*. Enschede: Sneldruk.

Poulisse, N. 1997. 'Compensatory strategies and the principles of clarity and economy' in G. Kasper and E. Kellerman (eds.).

Pravec, N. A. 2002. 'Survey of learner corpora.' *ICAME Journal* 26: 81–114.

Preston, D. 1996. 'Variationist perspectives on second language acquisition' in R. Bayley and D. Preston (eds.).

Price, S. 1999. 'Critical discourse analysis: Discourse acquisition and discourse practices.' *TESOL Quarterly* 33: 581–95.

Publication Manual of the American Psychological Association: Fifth Edition. 2001. American Psychological Association.

Quirk, R., S. Greenbaum, G. Leech, and **J. Svartvik.** 1985. *A Grammar of Contemporary English*. London: Longman.

Rahman, T. 2001. 'Language-learning and power: A theoretical approach.' *International Journal of the Sociology of Language* 152: 53–74.

Ramanathan, V. and **D. Atkinson.** 1999. 'Ethnographic approaches and methods in L2 writing research: A critical guide and review.' *Applied Linguistics* 20: 44–70.

Rampton, B. 1987. 'Stylistic variability and no speaking "normal" English: Some post-Labovian approaches and their implications for the study of interlanguage' in R. Ellis (ed.): *Second Language Acquisition in Context*. London Prentice Hall International.

Ravem, R. 1968. 'Language acquisition in a second language environment.' *International Review of Applied Linguistics* 6: 165–85.

Rayson, P. and **R. Garside.** 2000. 'Comparing corpora using frequency profiling' in *Proceedings of the Workshop on Comparing Corpora*, 38th Annual Meeting of the Association for Computational Linguistics, Hong Kong, 1–6.

Richards, D. 1980. 'Problems in eliciting unmonitored speech in a second language.' *Interlanguage Studies Bulletin* 5: 63–98.

Richards, J. (ed.). 1974. *Error Analysis: Perspectives on Second Language Acquisition*. London: Longman.

Richards, J., J. Platt, and **H. Platt.** 1992. *Longman Dictionary of Language Teaching and Applied Linguistics*. Harlow: Longman.

Riggenbach, H. 1999. *Discourse Analysis in the Language Classroom. Volume 1: The Spoken Language*. Ann Arbor, MI: University of Michigan Press.

Rivers, W. and **M. Temperley.** 1978. *A Practical Guide to the Teaching of English as a Second or Foreign Language*. New York: Oxford University Press.

Robinson, P. 1995. 'Attention, memory, and the "noticing" hypothesis.' *Language Learning* 45: 283–331.

Robinson, P. 2001. 'Task complexity, task difficulty, and task production: Exploring interactions in a componential framework.' *Applied Linguistics* 22: 27–57.

Robinson, P. 2002. 'Learning conditions, aptitude complexes and SLA: A framework for research and pedagogy' in P. Robinson (ed.): *Individual Differences and Instructed Language Learning*. Amsterdam: John Benjamins.

Robinson, P. and **J. Lim.** 1993. *Cognitive Load and the Route Marked Not-marked Map Task.* Unpublished data, University of Hawaii at Manoa, Department of ESL, Honolulu, USA.

Robinson, P., S. Ting, and **J. Unwin.** 1995. 'Investigating second language task complexity.' *RELC Journal* 25: 62–79.

Römer, U. 2004. 'A corpus-driven approach to modal auxiliaries and their didactics.' in J. Sinclair (ed.): *How to Use Corpora in Language Teaching*. Amsterdam: Benjamins.

Rosansky, E. 1976. 'Methods and morphemes in second language acquisition.' *Language Learning* 26: 409–25.

Rose, K. 2000. 'An exploratory cross-sectional study of interlanguage pragmatic development.' *Studies in Second Language Acquisition* 22: 27–67.

Rose, K. and **G. Kasper** (eds.). 2001. *Pragmatics in Language Teaching*. Cambridge: Cambridge University Press.

Rulon, K. and **J. McCreary.** 1986. 'Negotiation of content: Teacher-fronted and small group interaction' in R. Day (ed.).

Ryan, G. W. and **H. R. Bernard.** 2000. 'Data management and analysis methods' in N. K. Denzin and Y. S. Lincoln (eds.).

Sacks, H. 1984. 'Notes on methodology' in J. M. Atkinson and J. Heritage (eds.) *Structures of Social Action: Studies in Conversation Analysis* (pp. 21–7). Cambridge: Cambridge University Press.

Sacks, H. 1992. *Lectures on Conversation*. Edited by G. Jefferson, Volumes 1 and 2. Oxford: Blackwell.

Sacks, H., E. A. Schegloff, and **G. Jefferson.** 1974. 'A simplest systematics for the organization of turn-taking for conversation.' *Language* 50: 696–735.

Sajavaara, K. 1981. 'The nature of first language transfer: English as L2 in a foreign language setting'. Paper presented at the first European-North American Workshop in Second Language Acquisition Research. Lake Arrowhead, California.

Sampson, G. 1982. 'Converging evidence for a dialectal model of function and form in second language learning.' *Applied Linguistics* 3: 1–28.

Sato, C. 1986. 'Conversation and interlanguage development: Rethinking the connection' in R. Day (ed.).

Sato, C. 1988. 'Origins of complex syntax in interlanguage development.' *Studies in Second Language Acquisition* 10: 371–95.

Sato, C. 1990. *The Syntax of Conversation in Interlanguage Development*. Tübingen: Gunter Narr.

Saville-Troike, M. 1988. 'Private speech: evidence for second language learning strategies during the "silent period".' *Journal of Child Language* 15: 567–90.

Scarcella, R. and **C. Higa.** 1981. 'Input, negotiation and age differences in second language acquisition.' *Language Learning* 31: 409–37.

Schachter, J. 1974. 'An error in error analysis.' *Language Learning* 27: 205–14.

Schachter, J. 1986. 'In search of systematicity in interlanguage production.' *Studies in Second Language Acquisition* 8: 119–34.

Schachter, J. and **M. Celce-Murcia.** 1977. 'Some reservations concerning error analysis.' *TESOL Quarterly* 11: 441–51.

Schatzman, L. and **A. Strauss.** 1973. *Field Research: Strategies for a natural sociology.* Englewood Cliffs, NJ: Prentice Hall.

Schecter, S. R. and **R. Bayley.** 1997. 'Language socialization practices and cultural identity: Case studies of Mexican-descent families in California and Texas.' *TESOL Quarterly* 31: 513–41.

Schegloff, E. A. 1968. 'Sequencing in conversational openings.' *American Anthropologist* 70: 1075–95.
Schegloff, E. A. 1982. 'Discourse as an interactional achievement: Some uses of "uhhuh" and other things that come between sentences' in D. Tannen (ed.): *Georgetown University Roundtable on Languages and Linguistics* (pp. 71–93). Washington, DC: Georgetown University Press.
Schegloff, E. A. 1987. 'Between macro and micro: Contexts and other connections' in J. Alexander, B. Giesen, R. Munch, and N. Smelser (eds.) *The Micro-Macro link* (pp. 207–24). Berkeley: University of California Press.
Schegloff, E. A. 1992. 'Repair after next turn: The last structurally provided defense of intersubjectivity in conversation.' *American Journal of Sociology* 97(5): 1295–345.
Schegloff, E. A. 1997. 'Whose text? Whose context?' *Discourse and Society* 8: 165–87.
Schegloff, E. A. 2000. 'When "others" initiate repair.' *Applied Linguistics* 21(2): 205–43.
Schegloff, E. A., G. Jefferson, and **H. Sacks.** 1977. 'The preference for self-correction in the organization of repair in conversation.' *Language* 53: 361–82.
Schegloff, E. A., I. Koshik, S. Jacoby, and **D. Olsher.** 2002. 'Conversation analysis and applied linguistics.' *Annual Review of Applied Linguistics* 22: 3–31.
Schegloff, E. A. and **H. Sacks.** 1973. 'Opening up closings.' *Semiotica* 7: 289–327.
Schiffrin, D. 1994. *Approaches to Discourse.* Oxford: Blackwell.
Schmidt, R. 1990. 'The role of consciousness in second language learning.' *Applied Linguistics* 11: 129–58.
Schmidt, R. 1994. 'Deconstructing consciousness in search of useful definitions for applied linguistics.' *AILA Review* 11: 11–26.
Schmidt, R. 2001. 'Attention' in P. Robinson (ed.): *Cognition and Second Language Instruction.* Cambridge: Cambridge University Press.
Schon, D. 1979. 'Generative metaphor: A perspective on problem-setting in social policy' in A. Ortony (ed.): *Metaphor and Thought.* New York: Cambridge University Press.
Schumann, J. 1978. *The Pidginization Process: a Model for Second Language Acquisition.* Rowley, MA: Newbury House.
Schumann, J. 1986. 'Research on the acculturation model for second language acquisition.' *Journal of Multilingual and Multicultural Development* 7: 379–92.
Schumann, J. 1997. 'The neurobiology of affect in language.' *Language Learning Monograph Series.* Malden, MA: Blackwell.
Schwandt, T. A. 1998. 'Constructivist, interpretivist approaches to human inquiry' in N. K. Denzin and Y. S. Lincoln (eds.).
Scott, M. 1997. *Wordsmith Tools.* Oxford: Oxford University Press.
Searle, J. 1976. 'The classification of illocutionary acts.' *Language in Society* 5: 1–24.
Seedhouse, P. 1997. 'The case of the missing "no": The relationship between pedagogy and interaction.' *Language Learning* 47: 547–83.
Seliger, H. 1984. 'Processing universals in second language acquisition' in F. Eckman, L. Bell, and D. Nelson (eds.): *Universals of Second Language Acquisition.* Rowley, MA: Newbury House.
Seliger, H. and **M. Long** (eds.): 1983. *Classroom-oriented Research in Second Language Acquisition.* Rowley, MA: Newbury House.
Seliger, H. W. and **E. Shohamy.** 1989. *Second Language Research Methods.* Oxford: Oxford University Press.
Selinker, L. 1972. 'Interlanguage.' *International Review of Applied Linguistics* 10: 209–31.
Selinker, L. 1984. 'The current state of interlanguage studies: An attempted critical summary' in A. Davies, C. Criper, and A. Howatt (eds.). *Interlanguage.* Edinburgh: Edinburgh University Press.
Sfard, A. 1998. 'On two metaphors for learning and the dangers of choosing just one.' *Educational Researchers* 27: 4–13.
Shapira, R. 1978. 'The non-learning of English: Case Study of an adult' in E. Hatch (ed.): *Second Language Acquisition: A Book of Readings.* Rowley, MA: Newbury House.

Sharwood Smith M. 1986. 'Comprehension vs. acquisition: two ways of processing input.' *Applied Linguistics* 7: 239–56.

Shiffrin, D. 1994. *Approaches to Discourse*. Oxford: Blackwell.

Simon, R. and **Dippo, D.** 1986. 'On critical ethnographic work.' *Anthropology and Education Quarterly* 17(4): 195–202.

Sinclair, J. 1991. *Corpus, Concordance, Collocation*. Oxford: Oxford University Press.

Sinclair, J. and **M. Coulthard**. 1975. *Towards an Analysis of Discourse*. Oxford: Oxford University Press.

Skehan, P. 1989. *Individual Differences in Second-language Learning*. London: Edward Arnold.

Skehan, P. 1996a. 'A framework for the implementation of task-based instruction.' *Applied Linguistics* 17: 38–62.

Skehan, P. 1996b. 'Second language acquisition research and task-based instruction' in J. Willis and D. Willis (eds.): *The Challenge and Change in Language Teaching*. Oxford: Heinemann.

Skehan, P. 1998a. *A Cognitive Approach to Language Learning*. Oxford: Oxford University Press.

Skehan, P. 1998b. 'Task-based instruction.' *Annual Review of Applied Linguistics* 18: 268–86.

Skehan, P. 2001. 'Tasks and language performance assessment' in M. Bygate, P. Skehan, and M. Swain (eds.).

Skehan, P. and **P. Foster.** 1997. 'Task type and task processing conditions as influences on foreign language performance.' *Language Teaching Research* 1: 185–211.

Skehan, P. and **P. Foster.** 1999. 'The influence of task structure and processing conditions on narrative retellings.' *Language Learning* 49: 93–120.

Skehan, P. and **Foster, P.** 2001. 'Cognition and tasks' in P. Robinson (ed.): *Cognition and Second Language Instruction*. Cambridge: Cambridge University Press.

Smagorinsky, P. 1998. 'Thinking and speech and protocol analysis.' *Mind, Culture, and Activity: An International Journal* 5: 157–77.

Sorace, A. 1996. 'The use of acceptability judgments in second language acquisition research' in W. Ritchie and T. Bhatia (eds.): *Handbook of Second Language Acquisition Research*. San Diego: Academic Press.

Spada, N. and **Lightbown, P.** 1993. 'Instruction and the development of questions in L2 classrooms.' *Studies in Second Language Acquisition* 15: 205–24.

Spada, N. and **Lightbown, P.** 1999. 'Instruction, first language influence, and developmental readiness in second language acquisition.' *The Modern Language Journal* 83: 1–22.

Spradley, J. P. 1980. *Participant Observation*. New York: Holt Rinehart and Linston.

Steen, G. 1994. *Understanding Metaphor in Literature: an empirical approach*. London: Longman.

Stenson, B. 1974. 'Induced errors' in J. Schumann and N. Stenson (eds.): *New Frontiers in Second Language Learning*. Rowley, MA: Newbury House.

Stockwell, R., J. Bowen, and **J. Martin**. 1965. *The Grammatical Structures of English and Spanish*. Chicago: Chicago University Press.

Storch, N. 2002. 'Patterns of interaction in ESL pair work.' *Language Learning*, 52: 119–58.

Strauss, A. and **Corbin, J.** 1998. *Basics of Qualitative Research: Techniques and Procedures for Developing Grounded Theory*. Thousand Oaks, CA: Sage Publications.

Street, B. 1997. 'The implications of the "new literacy studies" for literacy education.' *English in Education* 13: 45–9.

Stubbs, M. 1983. *Discourse Analysis: The Sociolinguistic analysis of natural language*. Chicago: University of Chicago Press.

Swain, M. 1985. 'Communicative competence: some roles of comprehensible input and comprehensible output in its development' in S. Gass and C. Madden (eds.): *Input in Second Language Acquisition*. Rowley, MA: Newbury House.

Swain, M. 1995. 'Three functions of output in second language learning' in G. Cook and B. Seidlhofer (eds.): *For H. G. Widdowson: Principles and Practice in the Study of Language*. Oxford: Oxford University Press.

Swain, M. 2000. 'The output hypothesis and beyond: Mediating acquisition through collaborative dialogue' in J. P. Lantolf (ed.).

Swain, M. and **S. Lapkin.** 2000. 'Task-based second language learning: The uses of the first language.' *Language Teaching Research* 4: 251–74.

Swain, M. and **S. Lapkin.** 2002. 'Talking it through: Two French immersion learners' response to reformulation'. *International Journal of Educational Research* 37: 285–304.

Swain, M., N. Naiman, and **G. Dumas.** 1974. 'Alternatives to spontaneous speech: elicited translation and imitation as indicators of second language competence.' *Working Papers on Bilingualism* 3: 68–79.

Swan, M. and **B. Smith.** 2001. *Learner English: A Teacher's Guide to Interference and Other Problems.* (2nd edn.). Cambridge: Cambridge University Press.

Swann, J. 2001. 'Recording and transcribing talk in educational settings' in C. Candlin and N. Mercer (eds.): *English Language Teaching in its Social Context.* London: Routledge in association with the Open University and Macquarie University.

Tajfel, H. 1974. 'Social identity and intergroup behavior.' *Social Science Information* 13: 65–93.

Takahashi, S. 1995. 'Pragmatic transferability of L1 indirect request strategies perceived by Japanese learners of English.' Unpublished doctoral dissertation, University of Hawaii at Manoa.

Tarone, E. 1980. 'Communication strategies, foreigner talk, and repair in interlanguage.' *Language Learning* 30: 417–31.

Tarone, E. 1981. 'Some thoughts on the notion of communication strategy.' *TESOL Quarterly* 15: 285–95.

Tarone, E. 1983. 'On the variability of interlanguage systems.' *Applied Linguistics* 4: 143–63.

Tarone, E. 1988. *Variation in Interlanguage.* London: Edward Arnold.

Tarone, E. 2000. 'Still wrestling with "context" in interlanguage theory.' *Annual Review of Applied Linguistics* 20: 182–98.

Tarone, E. and **G. Liu.** 1995. 'Situational context, variation, and second language acquisition theory' in G. Cook and B. Seidlhofer (eds.): *Principle and Practice in Applied Linguistics* (pp. 107–24). Oxford: Oxford University Press.

Tarone, E. and **B. Parrish.** 1988. 'Task-related variation in interlanguage: the case of articles.' *Language Learning* 38: 21–44.

Taylor, D. 1988. 'The meaning and use of the term "competence" in linguistics and applied linguistics.' *Applied Linguistics* 9: 148–68.

Taylor, G. 1986. 'Errors and explanations.' *Applied Linguistics* 7: 144–66.

Ten Have, P. 1999. *Doing Conversation Analysis: A Practical Guide.* London: Sage Publications.

Tesch, R. 1990. *Qualitative Research: Analysis Types and Software Tools.* New York: Farmer.

Thesen, L. 1997. 'Voices, discourse, and transition: In search of new categories in EAP.' *TESOL Quarterly* 31: 487–511.

Tognini-Bonelli, E. 2001. *Corpus Linguistics at Work.* Amsterdam: John Benjamins.

Tono, Y. 2000. 'A computer learner corpus based analysis of the acquisition order of English grammatical morphemes' in L. Burnard and T. McEnery (eds.): *Rethinking Language Pedagogy from a Corpus Perspective.* Frankfurt-am-Main: Peter Lang.

Tono, Y., T. Kaneko, H. Isahara, T. Saiga, E. Izumi, M. Narita, and **E. Kaneko.** 2001. 'The Standard Speaking Test (SST) Corpus: A 1 million-word spoken corpus of Japanese learners of English and its implications for L2 lexicography' in S. Lee (ed.): *ASIALEX 2001 Proceedings: Asian Bilingualism and the Dictionary.* The Second Asialex International Congress, August 8–10, 2001, Yonsei University, Korea.

Toohey, K. 2000. *Learning English at School: Identity, Social Relations and Classroom Practice.* Clevedon: Multilingual Matters.

Toolan, M. 1997. 'What is critical discourse analysis and why are people saying such terrible things about it?' *Language and Literature* 6: 83–103.

Towell, R. 1987. 'Variability and progress in the language development of advanced learners of a foreign language' in R. Ellis (ed.): *Second Language Acquisition in Context.* London: Prentice Hall.

Towell, R. and **Hawkins, R.** 1994. *Approaches to Second Language Acquisition.* Clevedon: Multilingual Matters.

Travers, M. 2001. *Qualitative Research through Case Studies.* London: Sage.

Tsui, A. 1995. *Introducing Classroom Interaction.* London: Penguin.

Turner, D. 1979. 'The effect of instruction on second language learning and second language acquisition' in R. Andersen (ed.): *The Acquisition and Use of Spanish and English as First and Second Languages.* Washington, DC: TESOL.

Turton, J. and **N. Heaton** (eds.). 1996. *Longman Dictionary of Common Errors.* London: Longman.

Van den Branden, K. 1997. 'Effects of negotiation on language learners' output.' *Language Learning* 47: 589–636.

Van Leeuwen, T. 1993. 'Genre and field in critical discourse analysis: A synopsis.' *Discourse and Society* 4: 193–223.

van Lier, L. 1988. *The Classroom and the Language Learner.* London: Longman.

van Lier, L. 1989. 'Reeling, writing, drawling, stretching and fainting in coils: Oral proficiency interviews as conversation.' *TESOL Quarterly* 23: 489–508.

van Lier, L. 1996. *Interaction in the Language Curriculum: Awareness, Autonomy and Authenticity.* London: Longman.

Vander Brook, S., K. Schlue, and **C. Campbell.** 1980. 'Discourse and second language acquisition of Yes/No questions' in D. Larsen-Freeman (ed.): *Discourse Analysis and Second Language Acquisition.* Rowley, MA: Newbury House.

VanPatten, B. 1990. 'Attending to form and content in the input.' *Studies in Second Language Acquisition* 12: 287–301.

VanPatten, B. 1996. *Input Processing and Grammar Instruction in Second Language Acquisition.* Norwood, NJ: Ablex.

VanPatten, B. and **T. Cadierno.** 1993: 'Explicit instruction and input processing.' *Studies in Second Language Acquisition* 15: 225–43.

Varonis, E. and **S. Gass.** 1985. 'Non-native/non-native conversations: a model for negotiation of meaning.' *Applied Linguistics* 6: 71–90.

Vidich, A. J. and **S. M. Lyman.** 1998. 'Qualitative methods: Their history in sociology and anthropology' in N. K. Denzin and Y. S. Lincoln (eds.).

Virtanen, T. 1998. 'Direct questions in argumentative student writing' in S. Granger (ed.).

Vygotsky, L. S. 1978. *Mind in Society.* Cambridge, MA: MIT Press.

Vygotsky, L. S. 1981. 'The genesis of higher mental functions' in J. V. Wertsch (ed.) *The Concept of Activity in Soviet Psychology.* Armonk, NY: Sharpe.

Wajnryb, R. 1990. *Grammar Dictation.* Oxford: Oxford University Press.

Washburn, G. N. 1994. 'Working in the ZPD: Fossilized and nonfossilized nonnative speakers' in J. P. Lantolf and G. Appel (eds.).

Watson-Gegeo, K. 1988. 'Ethnography in ESL: Defining the essentials.' *TESOL Quarterly* 22: 575–92.

Watson-Gegeo, K. A. 1992. 'Thick explanation in the ethnographic study of child socialization: A longitudinal study of the problem of schooling for Kwara'ae (Solomon Islands) children.' *New Directions for Child Development* 58: 51–66.

Watson-Gegeo, K. A. and **D. W. Gegeo.** 1995. 'Understanding language and power in the Solomon Islands: Methodological lessons for educational intervention' in J. W. Tollefson (ed.): *Power and Inequality in Language Education.* Cambridge: Cambridge University Press.

Weinert, R. 1995. 'The role of formulaic language in second language acquisition: A review.' *Applied Linguistics* 16: 180–205.

Wendel. J. 1997. 'Planning and second language production.' Unpublished EdD Dissertation, Temple University Japan.

Wertsch, J. V. 1985. *Vygotsky and the Social Formation of Mind.* Cambridge, MA: Harvard University Press.

Wertsch, J. V. and **C. A. Stone.** 1985. 'The concept of internalization in Vygotsky's account of the genesis of higher mental functions' in J. V. Wertsch (ed.): *Culture, Communication and Cognition: Vygotskian Perspectives.* Cambridge: Cambridge University Press.

White, L. 1977. 'Error-analysis and error-correction in adult learners of English as a second language.' *Working Papers on Bilingualism* 13: 42–58.

White, L. 1989. *Universal Grammar and Second Language Acquisition.* Amsterdam: John Benjamins.

Widdowson, H. G. 1990. *Aspects of Language Teaching.* Oxford: Oxford University Press.

Widdowson, H. G. 1998. 'The theory and practice of critical discourse analysis.' *Applied Linguistics* 19: 136–51.

Widjaja, C. 1997. 'A study of date refusals: Taiwanese females vs American females.' University of Hawaii Working Papers in ESL 15: 1–43.

Wiese, R. 1984. 'Language production in foreign and native languages: Same or different?' in H. Dechert, D. Möhle, and M. Raupach (eds.).

Wigglesworth, G. 1997. 'An investigation of planning time and proficiency level on oral test discourse.' *Language Testing* 14: 85–106.

Willet, J. 1995. 'Becoming first graders in an L2: An ethnographic study of L2 socialization.' *TESOL Quarterly* 29: 473–503.

Wode, H. 1976. 'Developmental sequences in naturalistic L2 acquisition.' *Working Papers on Bilingualism* 11: 1–13.

Wode, H. 1978. 'The L1 vs L2 acquisition of English negation.' *Working Papers on Bilingualism* 15: 37–57.

Wode, H., J. Bahns, H. Bedey, and **W. Frank.** 1978. 'Developmental sequence: An alternative approach to morpheme order.' *Language Learning* 28: 175–85.

Wolcott, W. F. 1982. 'Differing styles of on-site research, or, "If it isn't ethnography, what is it?"' *The Review Journal of Philosophy and Social Science* 7: 154–69.

Wolfe-Quintero, K., S. Inagaki, and **H. Kim.** 1998. *Second Language Development in Writing: Measures of Fluency, Accuracy and Complexity.* Honolulu, Hawaii: Second Language Teaching and Curriculum Center, University of Hawaii at Manoa.

Wolfson, N. 1983. 'Rules of speaking' in J. Richards and D. Schmidt (eds.): *Language and Communication.* London: Longman.

Wolfson, N. 1989. *Perspectives: Sociolinguistics and TESOL.* Rowley, MA: Newbury House.

Wood, D., J. S. Bruner, and **G. Ross.** 1976. 'The role of tutoring in problem-solving.' *Journal of Child Psychology and Psychiatry* 17: 89–100.

Wong, J. 2000. 'Delayed next turn repair initiation in native/non-native speaker English conversation.' *Applied Linguistics* 21(2): 244–67.

Wray, A. 2000. 'Formulaic sequences in second language teaching: Principle and practice.' *Applied Linguistics* 21: 463–89.

Young, R. 1996. 'Form-function relations in articles in English interlanguage' in R. Bayley and D. Preston (eds.).

Young, R. and **R. Bayley.** 1996. 'VARBRUL analysis for second language acquisition research' in R. Bayley and D. Preston (eds.).

Yuan, F. 2000. 'The effects of planning on language production in task-based language teaching.' Unpublished PhD dissertation. Philadelphia. Temple University.

Yuan, F. and **R. Ellis.** 2003. 'The effects of pre-task planning and on-line planning on fluency, complexity and accuracy in L2 monologic oral production.' *Applied Linguistics* **24: 1–27.**

Yule, G. and **D. McDonald.** 1990. 'Resolving referential conflicts in L2 interaction: the effect of proficiency and interactive role.' *Language Learning* 40: 539–56.

Zaki, H. and **R. Elllis.** 'Learning vocabulary through interacting with a written text' in R. Ellis (ed.): *Learning a Second Language Through Interaction.* Amsterdam: John Benjamins.

Zobl, H. and **J. Liceras.** 1994. 'Functional categories and acquisition order.' *Language Learning* 44: 159–80.

Zoda, H. 1997. 'The effect of guided generative output on incidental vocabulary acquisition and retention and on text comprehension and recall.' Unpublished PhD dissertation, Philadelphia, Temple University.

Index